The _____

SELF-RESTRAINING STATE

The
SELF-RESTRAINING STATE

Power and Accountability in New Democracies

edited by
Andreas Schedler
Larry Diamond
Marc F. Plattner

LYNNE
RIENNER
PUBLISHERS

BOULDER
LONDON

Published in the United States of America in 1999 by
Lynne Rienner Publishers, Inc.
1800 30th Street, Boulder, Colorado 80301
www.rienner.com

and in the United Kingdom by
Lynne Rienner Publishers, Inc.
3 Henrietta Street, Covent Garden, London WC2E 8LU

Library of Congress Cataloging-in-Publication Data
The self-restraining state :   power and accountability in new
   democracies /   edited by Andreas Schedler, Larry Diamond, and Marc F.
   Plattner.
        p. cm.
   Includes bibliographical references and index.
   ISBN 978-1-55587-773-6 (hc : alk. paper)
   ISBN 978-1-55587-774-3 (pbk : alk. paper)
   1. Political corruption—Prevention.   2. Responsibility.
3. Separation of powers.   4. Democracy.   I. Schedler, Andreas,
1964– .   II. Diamond, Larry Jay.   III. Plattner, Marc F., 1945– .
JF229.S47   1999
352.3'5—DC21   98-44668
                                                                    CIP

British Cataloguing in Publication Data
A Cataloguing in Publication record for this book
is available from the British Library.

Printed and bound in the United States of America

⊗   The paper used in this publication meets the requirements
     of the American National Standard for Permanence of
     Paper for Printed Library Materials Z39.48-1992.

10 9 8 7

Contents

Acknowledgments

This book has its origins in the Third Vienna Dialogue on Democracy, a conference cosponsored by the Austrian Institute for Advanced Studies (Vienna) and the National Endowment for Democracy's International Forum for Democratic Studies (Washington, D.C.) on 26–29 June 1997. Entitled "Institutionalizing Horizontal Accountability: How Democracies Can Fight Corruption and the Abuse of Power," the conference addressed one of the most pressing concerns of new democracies—namely, how state agencies can prevent other parts of government from becoming unaccountable. The success of the conference owed a great deal to the organizational assistance provided by Gertrud Hafner of the Institute for Advanced Studies and Debra Liang-Fenton of the International Forum. A report summarizing the conference presentations and discussions is available on the website of the National Endowment for Democracy (www.ned.org). The majority of the contributions to this volume consist of revised and updated versions of papers that were first presented at the conference.

This project was supported by grants from the Carnegie Corporation of New York; the Austrian Ministry of Science, Technology, and Transportation; Austria's Renner Institute; the Austrian Ministry of Foreign Affairs; the Vienna Institute for Development Cooperation; and the City of Vienna. We wish to thank all these institutions for their generous support, though it goes without saying that none of them holds any responsibility for any statements or views expressed in this volume. In addition, Andreas Schedler wishes to express his gratitude to the Austrian Academy of Science for supporting his work on the book through the Austrian Program for Advanced Research and Technology (APART).

We also would like to offer special thanks to our publisher, Lynne

Rienner, who attended the conference in Vienna and gave this book an extraordinary degree of personal attention.

Larry Diamond
Marc F. Plattner
Andreas Schedler

I

Introduction

LARRY DIAMOND,
MARC F. PLATTNER, AND ANDREAS SCHEDLER

Democracy, like so many objects of desire, is a moving target. The contemporary wave of transitions from authoritarian rule has swept more countries than ever before to the promised land of democracy. But now that these polities have reached democratic shores, often after years of intense struggle, they are discovering that they cannot just lean back, relax, and enjoy the democratic sun. Instead, they find themselves haunted by old demons that they had hoped to exorcise with democratic rule: violations of human rights, corruption, clientelism, patrimonialism, and the arbitrary exercise of power. These lingering maladies point to the weakness of the rule of law (rulers stand above the law instead of being subject to it), and they reveal the weakness of public accountability (rulers are free to act as they please, instead of being embedded in and constrained by an institutional infrastructure of "checks and balances").

As a consequence, we are witnessing today a growing awareness that liberal democracy requires governments that are not only accountable to their citizens but also subject to restraint and oversight by other public agencies. In addition to being restrained from below, the state must subject itself to multiple forms of *self*-restraint. Modern democratic constitutionalism requires elected political leaders, the state, and even the sovereign citizenry to agree to a complex series of "self-binding" mechanisms.[1]

Moreover, to the extent that the long-term survival of democracy depends upon both elite and mass commitment to its norms and procedures, there is perhaps no more common and profound obstacle to the consolidation of new democracies than widespread corruption, human rights violations, illegality, and abuses of authority by the holders of state power at all levels. These patterns of arbitrary and particularistic behavior undermine public esteem for democracy and discourage democratic actors from committing or habituating themselves to the legal rules and constitutional procedures of democracy.[2]

The growing body of literature on the democratic defects of the third-wave democracies draws attention to the fact that the absence or weakness of institutional restraints on the state also greatly diminishes the quality of democracy. As the structural imperfections of the new democratic polities are increasingly undermining the initial euphoria over their felicitous birth,[3] scholars are giving more and more systematic attention to the serious harm that unrestrained public officials, from presidents to police officers, do to democratic quality. It is becoming increasingly clear that without working systems that can provide "credible restraints" on the overweening power of the executive, democratic regimes tend to remain shallow, corrupt, vulnerable to plebiscitarian styles of rule, and incapable of guaranteeing basic civil liberties. In short, they tend to remain "low-quality" democracies.[4]

Thus, scholars now tend to perceive public accountability as a key attribute of both democracy and democratic quality, as well as an essential ingredient in democracy's long-term viability. High hopes indeed rest on the shoulders of accountability. Contemporary advocates for extending and deepening public accountability assert that doing so will help make economic reform programs coherent as well as sustainable,[5] facilitate effective democratic governance,[6] and combat corruption.[7]

Deficiencies of accountability are often more visible, dramatic, and urgent in new than in long-established democracies. But as we know, problems of democratic quality are by no means confined to fledgling democracies. In this sense, our decision to limit this book's universe of cases to "new democracies" (including semidemocracies) is based on pragmatic rather than theoretical considerations. The current mood of political disenchantment and cynicism reigning in many established democracies may, at least in part, be traced back to serious failures in securing public accountability. Institutional solutions are often temporary, and institutional failures as well as changing social, cultural, political, economic, and technological contexts impose new imperatives for institutional adaptation and reform, even in polities with some history of effective public accountability.[8]

Whether in new or old democracies, contemporary demands for public accountability usually share (at least implicitly) one core assumption: elections—however competitive, free, and fair—are by themselves too weak to guarantee "decent" government. They are a necessary but by no means a sufficient condition for keeping state power under control; protecting civil liberties; making public officials follow established rules and procedures; keeping them responsive to citizen preferences; making them observe norms of fairness and efficiency in the appropriation and expense of public money; and deterring them from exploiting public office for private gain. As a consequence, from multiple perspectives and for multiple reasons,

current debates on democracy and accountability are recovering and rein-
corporating classic insights:

> If men were angels, no government would be necessary. If angels were to
> govern men, neither external nor internal controls on government would
> be necessary. In framing a government which is to be administered by
> men over men, the great difficulty lies in this: you must first enable the
> government to control the governed; and in the next place oblige it to con-
> trol itself. A dependence on the people is, no doubt, the primary control on
> the government: but experience has taught mankind the necessity of auxil-
> iary precautions.[9]

In this book we choose to call these "auxiliary precautions" institutions
of "horizontal" accountability. The concept, developed by scholars such as
Guillermo O'Donnell and Richard Sklar,[10] refers to the capacity of state
institutions to check abuses by other public agencies and branches of government. Its "locus classicus" is the interbranch relations among the judiciary, executive, and legislature. These separated powers are supposed to
constrain, check, and monitor one another. Today, however, the functional
differentiation of the state has gone well beyond this simple tripartite division of powers. The list of "agents of accountability" has expanded to
include institutions as variegated as election commissions, electoral tribunals, auditing agencies, anticorruption bodies, ombudsmen, administrative courts, constitutional courts, human rights commissions, and central
banks. Horizontal accountability complements, but is to be distinguished
from, "vertical" accountability, through which citizens, mass media, and
civil associations seek to enforce standards of good conduct on public officials.[11]

This book adopts an unconventional analytical perspective. It barely
touches upon the key issue in most other discussions of horizontal accountability: executive-legislative relations. Instead of analyzing the role of parliaments in overseeing the executive, it focuses on independent, nonelective, specialized bodies of oversight (which may form part of any of the
three branches). These autonomous institutions of accountability are typically insulated from state officials and from the people as well. Clearly,
such institutions may come to clash with the principles of vertical accountability. As long as they are unaccountable themselves, agencies of accountability are therefore vulnerable to charges that they are undemocratic or
that they overstep their boundaries. Thus, in studying autonomous agents of
accountability we must be especially attentive to the ancient question: who
shall guard the guardians?

Counteracting the natural tendency toward scholarly specialization,
this volume does not limit its focus to just one type of institution. Rather it
brings together areas of research normally foreign to one another—electoral administration and dispute adjudication, judicial systems and constitu-

tional courts, anticorruption bodies, and central banks—with the goal of finding significant commonalities and inducing fruitful cross-fertilization.

This book has multiple purposes and approaches the issue of horizontal accountability from various angles. Part 1 discusses conceptual and normative aspects of public accountability. Each subsequent part contains a general historical overview, and most parts conclude with a chapter on international factors. The empirical case studies provide descriptive accounts, evaluative judgments, and explanatory hypotheses about the institutionalization of horizontal accountability. And the concluding chapter formulates some general theoretical propositions on the conflicts and constituencies of institutional reform.

*   *   *

The book begins with an essay exploring the conceptual terrain. In his analysis of the term *accountability*, Andreas Schedler suggests that it represents a broad concept encompassing many neighboring terms, such as oversight, monitoring, auditing, control, exposure, and punishment. Schedler holds that, semantically, the concept of accountability stands on two distinct pillars: answerability and enforcement. It denotes the obligation of public officials and agencies to provide information about their actions and decisions and to justify them to the public and to specialized accounting bodies with the authority to monitor their conduct (the answerability dimension). It further describes the capacity of an accounting party to impose sanctions on the accountable party in cases of manifest misconduct in office (the enforcement dimension). Both aspects usually go together, but some exercises of accountability may involve just one of them. Ombudsmen, for instance, often have no more than a mandate to investigate and issue recommendations without a corresponding power of enforcement; conversely, most citizens cannot interrogate electoral candidates in person but reward or punish them only through their vote. After exploring the concept's semantic topography, Schedler outlines several ways of constructing subtypes of political accountability (by looking at the accountable agents, the accounting agents, and the criteria of accountability); he pays special attention to the conceptual ambiguities that beset the distinction between vertical and horizontal accountability.

Next, Guillermo O'Donnell explores the normative foundations of the concept, tracing its origins in the history of ideas. He contends that modern liberal democracies (or "polyarchies") have not grown out of a single dominant strand of political thought. They embody varying mixes of three different traditions, in part complementary, in part conflicting: republicanism, liberalism, and democracy. The first emphasizes virtue; the second, freedom; and the third, equality. Although all three traditions converge in valuing the rule of law, O'Donnell sees the "monistic" democratic tradition as essentially hostile to horizontal accountability, while republicanism and liberalism are supportive of two different types of accountability: resisting encroachment is primarily a liberal concern, and combating corruption is a republican one.

There follow three comments on O'Donnell's chapter: Richard L. Sklar relates it to the age-old discussion of constitutionalism versus democracy, expressing his satisfaction that political scientists are no longer leaving constitutional analysis solely to lawyers. He also introduces the notion of "celestial" accountability, the appeal to metaphysical entities that has been giving energy and purpose to so many "heroes of accountability" around the world. Philippe C. Schmitter pleads against restricting the notion of horizontal accountability to intrastate relations. It should be used in a wider sense, he argues, covering relations between state and civil society as well. Schmitter also draws attention to the potential trade-offs that may arise between accountability and other values, such as efficiency and governability. Marc F. Plattner goes back to the history of political thought and tries to disentangle the complex normative traditions that lie behind the idea of public accountability. The conclusions he reaches are somewhat different from O'Donnell's, emphasizing the liberal origins of horizontal accountability but also its compatibility with the democratic principle that the people are the source of all political authority. This animated round of discussion concludes with a brief response by O'Donnell to his commentators.

The subsequent parts of the book analyze the (more or less successful) enforcement of horizontal accountability in four empirical fields: electoral administration and dispute settlement (Part 2), judicial systems (Part 3), anticorruption bodies (Part 4), and central banks (Part 5). Each of these parts opens with a brief history of the institutional field in question. Robert A. Pastor reviews the scant literature on independent electoral commissions. Herman Schwartz recapitulates the history of the judicial review. Michael Johnston reconstructs the development of autonomous agencies set up to combat public corruption. And Sylvia Maxfield traces divergent paths to central bank independence in emerging market economies and evaluates some of its effects. We believe that these historical accounts, despite their brevity, are quite useful, as they explore fields that have been neglected by both historians and political scientists. The historical information they present is often tentative and incomplete, but it is more than has been available up to now. The agencies of accountability this book analyzes are relatively new ones. Even if their antecedents may be traced back to earlier periods, they have all made their careers after World War II. And at least in the realms of electoral administration and corruption control, most of them have been created in the so-called developing world, where the wish to see such organizations insulated from the rest of the state apparatus has apparently been most intense. Their full histories are still to be written, and the book's brief historical accounts are not only treasures of information but invitations for future research.

In the field of electoral administration (Part 2), the chapters by Todd A. Eisenstadt and E. Gyimah-Boadi both describe regime changes without government changes—the tortuous transition from an authoritarian system that enjoyed considerable popular support toward free, fair, and competitive elections.[12] Since the two countries they examine—Mexico and Ghana, respectively—are cases of "democratization through elections," the building of impartial and credible electoral institutions represented the key operation, the "Archimedian point," of regime change. In both cases, opposition parties were the driving force behind the process. And in both cases, having in place a trusted electoral commission (as well as, in the Mexican case, a reliable electoral tribunal) constitutes an extremely valuable asset for the future. The mere existence of these institutions is likely to impede a regression toward authoritarian rule.

Part 2 closes with a chapter on the international dimensions of electoral administration and dispute settlement. Pastor analyzes the role of international monitors and mediators in national elections, showing how the rise of external election monitoring in new democracies has undermined the traditional legal concept of national sovereignty and noninterference in internal affairs. He describes a plethora of new international actors and outlines some conditions of their successful intervention in transitional elections. Above all, he contends, international monitors must have an invitation, they must know the country, they must be sensitive to the prevailing structure of conflict, and they must deliver comprehensive, contextualized, and impartial judgments about the electoral process they have been observing. In his concluding section, Pastor provides an overview of recent efforts to collectively defend fledgling democracies and discusses the strategic alternative of "consolidating" versus "extending" democracy in the world.

Part 3 reviews efforts to enhance judicial independence on three continents. In her contribution, Pilar Domingo describes the myriad technical and organizational deficiencies that beset Latin American courts: the lack of human capital, inappropriate or inoperative appointment procedures and rules of promotion, administrative inefficiency, financial dependence, and low remuneration. Yet she stresses cultural and political obstacles to judicial reform in the region, such as the tradition of judicial subordination and executive encroachment and the corresponding resistance to change by judges and presidents. Nevertheless, Domingo identifies several potential constituencies for reform: entrepreneurs, the media, and civil associations. She concludes her chapter with an evaluation of Latin America's most recent wave of judicial reform in the 1990s.

Jennifer Widner responds to the scarcity of data about judicial independence in Anglophone Africa with methodological creativity. On the basis of in-depth interviews with leading judges and of surveys among lawyers in Botswana, Tanzania, and Uganda, she reconstructs the complex bundle of strategies judges in these countries use to foster judicial independence. In the end, she comes to reject theories that explain comparative variations in judicial independence with reference to environmental factors. These theories may work in the Western industrialized countries, she contends, but they do not look very plausible in Anglophone Africa. Instead, she proposes some hypotheses that grant greater explanatory weight to citizen attitudes as well as to factors internal to the courts—above all, judges themselves and their jurisprudential practice.

Schwartz turns his analytic attention to Eastern Europe and the former Soviet Union. After outlining the differences between the U.S. system of decentralized constitutional review and the continental European tradition of centralizing the judicial review of legislation in a specialized court, he sets out to describe and explain the "surprising success" of the new Eastern European constitutional courts. In the successful postcommunist experiences that he reviews (Poland, Hungary, Slovakia, and Bulgaria, but not Russia), self-assertive constitutional courts were able to defend and maintain their fledgling independence against hostile or at least recalcitrant executives. What, he asks, distinguished these success stories from the unqualified "failures" of other constitutional courts that were subdued by unaccountable, authoritarian presidents (as in Belarus or Kazakhstan)? Schwartz's answer is cautious but clear: it is democracy that makes the difference. Authoritarian rulers do not accept any separation of-powers. In nineteenth-century Western Europe, the historical sequence of political development allowed the rule of law to develop first and democracy to come later, but today it is only in democratic settings that governments can be forced to bow to the rule of law.[13]

In Part 4, two chapters report on specific national efforts to control corruption. John R. Heilbrunn focuses on Francophone Africa's showcase of political democratization, the Republic of Benin. A "culture of corruption" pervaded public administration in Benin under authoritarian rule, and the first two democratic governments (under presidents Nicéphore Soglo and Mathieu Kérékou, the former dictator who returned to power by defeating Soglo in an election) faced strong pressures to do something about it. While several Anglophone African countries have met demands for public probity by implementing (generally ineffective) anticorruption legislation, Benin's democratic governments adopted a more innovative two-track strategy. On the one hand, they organized a series of meetings between governmental and nongovernmental actors (somewhat grandiloquently called "États Généraux") that aired the prevalent discontent and formulated some possible solutions. On the other hand, Kérékou (whose long period of dictatorial rule had been ridden with corruption and scandals) founded a presidential commission "to improve the moral standards in public life." The commission is not independent from the president, and its initial performance has made it appear more an instrument of power than a check on power. Yet it does have some "positive attributes" and may eventually (though probably against the intentions of its creators) develop some genuine independence and effectiveness.

Jon S. T. Quah analyzes the not-so-brief history of anticorruption initiatives in South Korea and Thailand. Both countries have relied on what Michael Johnston describes as the "ICAC approach." That is, they have created (more or less) independent, Hong Kong–style commissions to battle against corruption. Both countries, however, were apparently unsuccessful in controlling corrupt behavior, even if South Korea seems to be well ahead of Thailand in the fight against this "endemic disease." Quah traces the differences between the two countries to differences in political leadership and political will: "The political leadership must be sincerely committed to the eradication of corruption," he writes. In Thailand, however, he finds the political elite "unconcerned" about corruption, adopting measures that range from "inadequate" to "hopeless."

The international anticorruption chapter, by Fredrik Galtung and Jeremy Pope, provides a comprehensive overview of the activities of Transparency International (TI), a Berlin-based transnational nongovernmental organization dedicated to combating corruption throughout the world. Galtung and Pope give an insider's account of TI's operation since its founding in 1993; they describe TI's evolving network of national chapters, analyze the organization's efforts to design and implement "national integrity systems," and review its main tool for raising public awareness about corruption—the Corruption Perception Index. TI's impressive success, the authors conclude, resides in a nonconfrontational approach that emphasizes broad coalition building among all people willing to join the protracted struggle against corruption. TI's most significant contribution, Galtung and Pope assert, has been "bringing civil society back in" to the struggle against corruption, thereby "challenging the monopoly previously claimed for governments and international agencies."

Part 5 deals with central banks. Juliet Johnson recounts the inglorious performance of the Central Bank of Russia after the fall of the Soviet Union. Until mid-1993 the bank enjoyed full legal and practical autonomy, she notes, and it made full use of it—in a way that inflicted considerable damage upon the Russian economy. The bank acted in an authoritarian and incompetent manner, deliberately counteracting the government's economic reforms. The bank's management, endowed with a heritage of weak human capital and socialist ideology, disdained the task that independent central banks are supposed to pursue with single-minded purity: the battle against inflation through restrictive monetary policies. Only when the bank was subject to presidential-cum-international authority in mid-1993 did it start acting in a more reasonable, responsible, and coherent fashion.

Johnson's analysis shows the folly of blindly embracing central bank autonomy for its own sake. It forcefully recalls that the value of central bank independence is not intrinsic but instrumental. The success of independent central banks is contingent on expertise, incentives, and economic worldviews that cannot be taken for granted.

In his international chapter, Paul Collier assesses the international financial institutions' record of imposing macroeconomic policy restraints on African governments in the absence of domestic "agencies of restraint" (such as autonomous central banks). His conclusion is devastating: external conditionality has been totally unsuccessful in establishing credible restraints on those governments, which are still handicapped by a strong collective reputation for unreliable behavior. In Africa, property rights are still perceived as insecure, and the perceived risks of investment continue to impede economic growth. In order to alleviate "the African credibility problem," Collier argues, international financial institutions must radically redesign their lending policies. Instead of imposing conditions based on future behavior, they should attach their credits to past performance; and instead of threatening negative sanctions, they should reward good behavior. As Collier passionately argues, externally imposed macroeconomic constraints are not credible; only self-restraints are. But to establish credible self-restraints, African governments need access to external conditionality on a different basis—one that is transparently voluntary.

Finally, in his concluding chapter, Schedler weaves together two recurring themes of the book: the conflicts and constituencies of accountability. He contends that the institutionalization of horizontal accountability is a conflictual enterprise that involves the strategic interaction between two antagonistic groups of actors: "conservatives" and "agents of change." He then identifies four different types of "heroes of accountability," who may trigger four correspondingly different modes of reform: members of the political elite may initiate reforms "from above"; civil society actors may trigger reforms "from below"; the personnel of existing institutions may carry out reforms "from within"; and international actors may promote reforms "from outside." The binary distinction between proponents and opponents of change and the fourfold classification of the sources of change are both of great simplicity, yet they offer a promising framework for analyzing processes of institutional change in other areas of politics as well.

Notes

1. See, e.g., Linz and Stepan, *Problems of Democratic Transition*, p. 248. For a succinct argument that democracy and constitutionalism constitute interdependent elements (rather than conflicting ones, as much conventional wisdom holds), see Holmes, "Constitutionalism." On the logical as well as empirical affinity between

liberalism and democracy (despite some historical instances of separation), see also Plattner, "Liberalism and Democracy."

2. See, e.g., Diamond, *Developing Democracy*. On the notion of democratic consolidation, see Schedler, "What Is Democratic Consolidation?"

3. See, above all, Collier and Levitsky, "Democracy with Adjectives," but also Cavarozzi, "La transición y el Estado"; Karl, "The Hybrid Regimes"; Kelley, "Democracy Redux"; and Stokes, "Democracy," pp. 59–60. On the concept of democratic quality, see Schedler, "Dimensionen der Demokratiequalität."

4. See, e.g., O'Donnell, "Delegative Democracy," and Diamond, "Democracy in Latin America."

5. See, e.g., Haggard and Kaufman, *The Political Economy*, and Stark and Bruszt, *Postsocialist Pathways*.

6. See, e.g., Lowenthal and Domínguez, "Introduction," p. 6.

7. See, e.g., Pope, *National Integrity Systems*, chapters 9–11 ("The Ombudsman," "The Judicial System," and "The Auditor-General") and chapter 15, "Independent Anti-Corruption Agencies."

8. See, e.g., Weir, "Primary Control."

9. *The Federalist Papers*, no. 51.

10. See, e.g., O'Donnell, "Delegative Democracy," and Sklar, "Developmental Democracy."

11. Readers may wonder why, despite its centrality, the term *horizontal accountability* does not appear in the title of this book. The reason is intelligibility. This technical term, when mentioned to people who are not familiar with the specialized literature, just earns blank stares, followed by the urgent request to translate it into commonsense language.

12. Schedler, "Hard to Observe," pp. 5–9, offers a sketchy working typology of democratic transitions according to the electoral fate that former authoritarian rulers suffer (or enjoy). In an era of free and fair elections, former authoritarian elites may disappear from the electoral arena, form a minor opposition party, establish themselves as the leading opposition force, or be maintained in office through the polls. Both Mexico and Ghana represent the last variant of maximum continuity between authoritarianism and democracy.

13. For another recent elaboration of this point, see Plattner, "Liberalism and Democracy."

Part I

Conceptual and Normative Issues

2

Conceptualizing Accountability

ANDREAS SCHEDLER

W hat is the essence of politics? What is the key variable of political
science? Common sense gives us a clear answer: it is power. But as
the earlier classical theorists knew: in politics, first comes power, then the
need to control it. "In framing a government . . . the great difficulty lies in
this: you must first enable the government to control the governed; and in
the next place oblige it to control itself."[1] Beginning with the ancient
philosophers, political thinkers have worried about how to keep power
under control, how to domesticate it, how to prevent its abuse, how to subject it to certain procedures and rules of conduct.[2] Today, it is the fashionable term *accountability* that expresses the continuing concern for checks
and oversight, for surveillance and institutional constraints on the exercise
of power. All over the world (wherever the term is halfway translatable),
international financial institutions, party leaders, grassroots activists, journalists, and political scientists have discovered the blessings and adhere to
the cause of "public accountability."[3]

Without doubt, the term sounds appealing. Its field of application is as
broad as its potential for consensus. And its semantic root, the notion of
accounting, is nicely ambivalent; it evokes narrative accounts as well as
bookkeeping. But do we know what it means? Are we clear about its
semantic boundaries and do we comprehend its internal structure? Not surprisingly, my answer is no: due to its relative novelty, accountability represents an underexplored concept whose meaning remains evasive, whose
boundaries are fuzzy, and whose internal structure is confusing.

This chapter does not set out to relate the concept of accountability to
the history of thought. Chapter 3 by Guillermo O'Donnell and the related
comments by Richard Sklar, Philippe Schmitter, and Marc Plattner accom-
plish a good deal of such philosophical reflection. The pretense of this

chapter is more limited. It aims at reconstructing the meaning of the concept as we currently use it. In essence, it claims that the notion of political accountability carries two basic connotations: answerability, the obligation of public officials to inform about and to explain what they are doing; and enforcement, the capacity of accounting agencies to impose sanctions on powerholders who have violated their public duties. This two-dimensional structure of meaning makes the concept a broad and inclusive one that, within its wide and loose boundaries, embraces (or at least overlaps with) lots of other terms—surveillance, monitoring, oversight, control, checks, restraint, public exposure, punishment—that we may employ to describe efforts to ensure that the exercise of power is a rule-guided enterprise.

A Two-Dimensional Concept

The attractiveness of accountability derives from its breadth. The concept is a comprehensive one. Rather than denoting one specific technique of domesticating power, it embraces three different ways of preventing and redressing the abuse of political power. It implies subjecting power to the threat of sanctions; obliging it to be exercised in transparent ways; and forcing it to justify its acts. I treat the first dimension under the heading "enforcement" and sum up the last two dimensions under "answerability." The three aspects together—enforcement, monitoring, and justification—turn political accountability into a multifaceted enterprise that copes with a considerable variety of actual and potential abuses of power.

Answerability

As with most terms we use in everyday language, we usually assume that we understand what we say when we talk about *accountability,* and that others do so as well. Related discussions therefore regularly proceed on the basis of implicit understandings, without recourse to any explicit definition of the concept. Yet whenever authors do define the term explicitly, they tend to associate it with *answerability* as its "closest synonym."[4] Accountability, one encyclopedic definition tells us, is "the ability to ensure that officials in government are answerable for their actions."[5] We think this provides a valid starting point. The notion of answerability indicates that being accountable to somebody implies the obligation to respond to nasty questions and, vice versa, that holding somebody accountable implies the opportunity to ask uncomfortable questions.

But what kind of answers to what kind of questions? In principle, accounting agencies may ask accountable actors for two kinds of things. They may either ask them to *inform* about their decisions or they may ask them to *explain* their decisions. They may ask either for reliable facts (the informational dimension of accountability) or for valid reasons (the argumentative dimension of accountability). Accountability thus involves the right to receive information and the corresponding obligation to release all necessary details. But it also implies the right to receive an explanation and the corresponding duty to justify one's conduct.[6]

On the one side, exercising accountability therefore involves elements of monitoring and oversight. Its mission includes finding facts and generating evidence. On the other side, the norm of accountability continues the Enlightment's project of subjecting power not only to the rule of law but also to the rule of reason. Power should be bound by legal constraints but also by the logic of public reasoning. Accountability is antithetical to monologic power. It establishes a dialogic relationship between accountable and accounting actors. It makes both parties speak and engages them both in public debate. It is therefore opposed not only to mute power but also to unilateral speechless controls of power.[7]

The etymological ambivalence of accountability, which stems from the double connotation of accounts, sustains both dimensions. Financial accounts contain detailed information prepared according to certain standards of classification and accuracy that make them both readable and reliable for outsiders. Narrative accounts are legitimating tales that present some relieving end as the compelling outcome of previous developments. Or more formally, they represent "definitional transformations of contested action," "explanations that excuse or justify questionable behavior by proposing a normative status for the behavior."[8] The informational dimension of accountability relates to the first connotation of accounts—bookkeeping; its discursive or explanatory dimension relates to the second one—storytelling.[9]

Enforcement

Up to now we have described the exercise of accountability essentially as a discursive activity, as a sort of benign inquiry, a friendly dialogue between accounting and accountable parties. Yet answerability, and the double quest for information and justification it implies, is not the whole story of accountability. Political accountability involves more than the generation of data and the interplay of arguments. In addition to its informational dimension (asking what has been done or will be done) and its explanatory aspects (giving reasons and forming judgments), it also contains elements of enforcement (rewarding good and punishing bad behavior). It implies the idea that accounting actors do not just "call into question" but also "eventually punish" improper behavior and, accordingly, that accountable persons not only tell what they have done and why, but bear the consequences for it, including eventual negative sanctions.[10] Exercises of accountability that expose misdeeds but do not impose material consequences will usually appear as weak, toothless, "diminished" forms of accountability. They will be regarded as acts of window dressing rather than real restraints on power.

The "tight coupling" of accountability and the availability of sanctions reflect neoinstitutionalist common sense about the conditions of effective institutions. According to much of the new institutionalist literature, for rules to be effective they must be accompanied by mechanisms of monitoring that prevent the eventual violation of rules from going unnoticed (the informational function of accountability). But they must also count with mechanisms of enforcement that "get the incentives right" by keeping acts of cheating from going unpunished (the enforcement dimension of accountability).[11]

Academic writers are often quite emphatic in stating that the capacity to punish forms an integral part of political accountability.[12] But political actors, too, usually have a very keen sense for the pivotal importance of effective enforcement mechanisms that will enable agencies of accountability to act forcefully. For example, in Taiwan, the Control Yuan (a branch of government that is charged with investigating the conduct of public officials) is able to "impeach" a public official—in effect, to indict and refer the official to the legal authorities for further investigation and possible prosecution. But because the ministry of justice is controlled by the ruling party, this means in practice that government officials (especially high-ranking ones) are rarely seriously punished. The one structural change that senior officials of the Control Yuan most want is the independent authority to prosecute and impose sanctions on offending officials.[13]

Similarly, during Nigeria's Second Republic (1979–1983) an elaborate code of conduct required public officials to report their assets. A Code of Conduct Bureau was set up to investigate the authenticity of these reports as well as charges of bribery and other wrongdoing. However, the Code of Conduct Bureau lacked the staffing to adequately investigate violations of the code by public officials, and the parallel Code of Conduct Tribunal never sat (because the national legislature never enacted the enabling legislation). Because politicians feared no consequences for corrupt behavior, gross abuses of public offices, such as bribery, embezzlement, extortion, and vote buying, quickly escalated out of control and generated the public disillusionment with democracy that helped bring about the military coup of December 1983.[14]

Concerning the nature of possible sanctions, in the world of politics, the destruction of reputation through public exposure represents one of the main tools of accountability. But the pool of sanctions is much wider. The severity of the sanction depends on the severity of the offense. In politics, removal from office often represents the most drastic consequence of misconduct. Both instruments, publicity and dismissal, appear as entirely appropriate punishments for a wide range of bad behavior. But as soon as actors violate legal dispositions, neither public criticism nor job loss appears sufficient. Illegal behavior, such as corruption or human rights violations, calls for appropriate legal sanctions. When presumptive agents of legal accountability, such as the Mexican National Human Rights Commission, for example, do not have prosecutory powers but can only issue nonbinding statements of an advisory nature, many observers will feel that the soft and quasi-voluntary version of "accountability light" they practice does not deserve its name and that, in essence, inconsequential accountability is no accountability at all. If a police officer kills someone in custody without due cause and still walks free, it does not satisfy the principle of accountability if a journalist documents this abuse of authority or if a human rights ombudsman recommends that the officer be arrested and stand trial. Unless there is some punishment for demonstrated abuses of authority, there is no rule of law and no accountability.

A Radial Concept

We may sum up the preceding reflections in the following one-sentence definition of accountability: A is accountable to B when A is obliged to inform B about A's (past or future) actions and decisions, to justify them, and to suffer punishment in the case of eventual misconduct. In experiences of political accountability, usually all three dimensions—information, justification, and punishment—are present. However, they do not form a core of binary "defining characteristics" that are either present or absent and that must be present in all instances we describe as exercises of accountability. They are continuous variables that show up to different degrees, with varying mixes and emphases. Furthermore, even if one or two of them are missing we may still legitimately speak of acts of accountability.

To begin with, sanctions form an aspect of accountability many consider to be indispensable. Yet some "agencies of restraint" come to equate accountability fundamentally with answerability. For instance, a good number of valuable agencies of accountability, such as the Chilean and the South African truth commissions set up to investigate human rights violations under predecessor regimes, have relied on only a "soft" form of punishment—namely, the public exposure of criminal action.

Furthermore, contemporary discussions on the autonomy versus accountability of central banks (e.g., with respect to the fledgling European Central Bank) reveal ideas of accountability that are entirely detached from notions of punishment. Central bankers, if they accept the idea of accountability at all, equate it to the mere need to publicly explain their decisions after the fact. In general, most expressions of "vertical" accountability where mass media and civil associations act as accounting agencies rely on purely discursive forms of contestation and constraint, with no possibility of applying "negative sanctions" other than public disapproval.[15]

The same way accountability may be divorced from sanctions, in some cases it may be an exclusive matter of sanctions. Accountability understood as enforcement may be cut off from questions of answerability. The Indonesian students who demanded the demise of General Suharto in early 1998 did not request further information, nor did they desire to hear any discourses defending the long-reigning president. Or, less dramatically, the idea of electoral accountability—of voters holding politicians accountable at periodic elections—is also primarily related to the possibility of punishing past behavior by "throwing the rascals out" (even if between elections incumbents may continually disclose their actions and justify them). Whereas in the first case, an outrageous as well as transparent violation of social norms makes any additional information superfluous and any additional justification useless, in the second case, the communicative asymmetries between elite actors and mass publics render any dialogic idea of accountability impractical.

The above examples illustrate that it is possible, in principle, to find instances where the idea of accountability is dissociated from one of its core dimensions—be it enforcement or answerability—without necessarily creating "diminished subtypes" of accountability as a result.[16] I conclude accordingly that accountability does not represent a "classical" concept displaying a hard core of invariable basic characteristics. Instead, it must be regarded as a "radial" concept whose "subtypes" or "secondary" expressions do not share a common core but lack one or more elements that characterize the prototypical "primary" category.[17]

A Modest Concept

Political accountability may be a broad and comprehensive concept. But it is also a modest concept. In part, its modesty stems from its potential one-dimensionality. As argued above, certain instances of accountability do not include aspects of answerability, while others go without elements of enforcement. But more fundamentally, political accountability is a modest enterprise insofar as it accepts the reality of power as well as the relative opacity of power.

The Uncertainties of Power

The guiding idea of political accountability is to control political power, not to eliminate it. In this sense, political accountability presupposes power. Far from harboring utopias of power disappearing, withering away, the notion of political accountability enters a world of power. Agencies of accountability strive to keep power from running wild; they strive to bound, to discipline, to restrain it. Their mission is to make power predictable by limiting its arbitrariness and to prevent or redress the abuse of power in order to keep its exercise in line with certain preestablished rules and procedures. The existence of power provides their very raison d'être. Without power, without the capacity to make decisions and the corresponding capacity to attribute decisions, it does not make any sense to talk about accountability. Nobody can hold anybody accountable for things beyond that person's control. I cannot hold you accountable for the bad weather (unless I subscribe to prescientific meteorological theories), nor can I hold you accountable for the wrong weather forecast (unless you are working in the meteorological office).

We might also say that accountability presupposes personal responsibility. The two terms look very similar and are often treated as close synonyms. Yet if one equates accountability with responsibility *to* someone, one has still to concede that there is no perfect overlap with responsibility *for* something. In fact, the latter presupposes the former, but the inverse is not true. Accordingly, responsibility for something may go entirely without responsibility to somebody. The premodern absolute ruler could be (and could admit to be) responsible for lots of things but still reject having to respond to anybody (but God and history). In modern times, the presumptive burden of responsibility has become an easy formula to legitimate political power (equivalent to the idea of risk taking in economic life). And it has also become a formula to shed off prospective accountability: I am the one responsible so I make decisions based on the way I feel I should; I need not tell anybody about those decisions before I make them; nor do I have to respond to anybody except to my personal conscience. In essence, while accountability forces power to enter into a dialogue, the notion of responsibility permits it to remain silent. While accountability builds on the modern idea that power and knowledge are separate goods, the notion of responsibility allows powerful actors to maintain the illusion that they know what they are doing and therefore to dismiss irritating questions that do nothing but disturb their solemn and responsible exercise of power.

If accountability indeed addresses agents who hold power and dispose of some margin of discretion, it follows that accountability should not be confused with narrow notions of regulation, control, or steering. Holding power accountable does not imply determining the way it is exercised; neither does it aim at eliminating discretion through stringent bureaucratic regulation. It is a more modest project that admits that politics is a human enterprise whose elements of agency, freedom, indeterminacy, and uncertainty are ineradicable; that power cannot be subject to full control in the strict, technical sense of the word; and that even in a hypothetical world of perfect accountability, political power would continue to produce harm, waste, and any other kind of irreversible "public bads" that even ideal agents of accountability could only ascertain, expose, and punish but neither repair nor undo.

Agents of accountability want to reach (partial) control over political decisionmakers. If they already were in (full) control, their mission would make no sense any more. If I control somebody, there is no point of making that person accountable to me. Accountable for what? For the things I induce him or her to do? Robots that assemble automobile parts in a Chrysler factory cannot be considered plausible addressees of accountability. The same applies to government officials who carry out decrees. They are supposed to do their work well (and may be held accountable for it), but they are not accountable for the rules they apply. Accountability concerns agents, not subjects. It concerns those who exercise power, not those who are subordinate to it. Or, more precisely, it concerns subjects only as far as we ascribe some degree of freedom to them. In an analogous way, it concerns public employees only as far as we envision administrative organizations not as mechanical conveyor belts of decisions from top to bottom, but rather as loci of decisionmaking at all hierarchical levels.

The Opacity of Power

Accountability as answerability aims at creating transparency. By demanding information as well as justification, it wants to shed light into the black box of politics. In this it is similar to notions such as oversight, supervision, and monitoring. But again its project is less ambitious. Agents of accountability do not pretend to supervise everything. In fact, they assume that nothing close to close oversight is taking place and accept that their genuine field of competence consists of unobserved and often unobservable actions.[18] In this sense, accountability (as answerability) presupposes imperfect information. If the exercise of power were transparent, there would be no need for holding anybody accountable. The demand for accountability (as answerability) originates from the opacity of power. In a world of perfect information, it would be pointless to ask political actors what they have been doing, or intend to do, and why. We would already know. In Jeremy Bentham's Panopticon, any pretense to exercise accountability is void. From its high center, we can see everything and intervene anytime. We do not have to ask anything. We just watch and punish. In the real political world, however, most things are not accessible to direct observation. And even if informational barriers to the political process did not exist, we could still not look into the future (which creates the need for retrospective accountability), nor could we look into decisionmakers' heads (which creates the need to ask for justifications).

When agents of accountability intrude into the opaque realms of power, they are concerned with the classical *arcanae imperii,* the dark playgrounds of power shut off from public scrutiny for no other reason than the self-contained arrogance of power. At the same time, however, legitimate realms of secrecy exist where decisionmakers deliberate and decide behind closed doors. We may think, for example, of central bankers setting exchange rates or court judges forming their judgments. Subjecting such zones of legitimate confidentiality to procedures of accountability should not open them to the eyes of the general public from beginning to end. But it should oblige the involved participants to give ex post explanations and reveal the grounds for their decisions to the public.

We should add that usually if it wants to be effective and perceived as such, democratic accountability must be public. As a rule, only public accountability can achieve its aim of curbing power, while confidential accountability, exercised behind closed doors, tends to be perceived as a farce, a caricature of accountability. For example, Soglo, former president of Benin, disclosing his personal assets secretly[19] hardly qualified him as a champion of accountability.

This "publicity principle" applies not only to accountable actors but also to accounting agencies. This makes accountability distinct from supervision, for instance. The supervisor may remain in the dark, the unseen eye. The agent of accountability must come to the forefront and open itself to second-order observation: the observer observed. In this sense, institutions of accountability are vampires in reverse. They can live only as long as they act in the daylight of the public sphere, and they crumble and die as soon as they enter the shadows of privacy and secrecy.[20]

The public nature of accountability serves all three aspects of accountability: information, reasoning, and punishment. It does more than bring the "forceless force of the better argument"[21] upon the conduct of the accountable party. It also involves an important form of sanction. It exposes cases of misconduct to public opinion, which often provokes highly damaging reputational consequences.[22]

Who Is Accountable for What?

In all walks of life we can hold people accountable for all kinds of things. In our private lives we wade in a constant stream of accountability initiatives. People hold their children, parents, partners, friends, neighbors, colleagues, and fellow citizens accountable for any kind of presumptive misbehavior—for political incorrectness, insubordination, disorderliness, bad memory, drinking and smoking, sexual misconduct, sinful behavior, lack of courtesy, strategic errors, factual ignorance, whatever. Because there are lots of rules that guide our private lives, there are lots of opportunities for private agents of accountability to step in to monitor and enforce compliance.

The vast realm of private accountability, of course, falls outside the jurisdiction of this book, which is concerned with *political* accountability in its wide sense—with acts of accountability addressed to public officials (the whole personnel employed by the modern state: politicians, civil servants, judges, police officers, military officers, diplomats, etc.). In its narrow sense, the term political accountability covers the activities of only the professional category listed first: politicians, such as cabinet members, legislators, and party leaders.

Parting from the broad concept of political accountability, which concerns the behavior of any public official, one might introduce a number of further subtypes according to the political subsystems that are subject to accountability. The referents and the labels of these subtypes will depend on the analytic distinctions one chooses to draw. A conventional way of slicing the modern political world would produce at least the following broad categories: governmental, legislative, bureaucratic, judicial, and military accountability.

Looking at the addressees of accountability (who is accountable?) is one way of ordering the wide field of political accountability. Inquiring into the criteria of accountability (accountable for what?) is another way. So, if we hold public officials accountable, what do we hold them accountable for? What yardsticks do we use? How do we define good and bad conduct in office? How do we accordingly define the abuse of office that the exercise of political accountability strives to prevent and punish?

It is obvious that we may hold public officials accountable for lots of things and that our acts of accountability may be inspired by many potentially conflicting principles. A quick search through different standards of accountability suggests that we should distinguish at least the following varieties of political accountability (in its broad sense): political accountability (in its narrow sense) assesses the appropriateness of both substantive policies and policymaking processes, but it also brings judgment on the personal qualities of political actors; administrative accountability reviews the expediency and procedural correctness of bureaucratic acts; professional accountability watches over ethical standards of professionalism, such as medical, academic, and judicial professionalism;[23] financial accountability subjects the use of public money by state officials to norms of austerity, efficiency, and propriety; moral accountability evaluates political acts on the basis of prevailing normative standards (independent of formal rules and regulations); legal accountability monitors the observance of legal rules;[24] and constitutional accountability evaluates whether legislative acts are in accordance with constitutional rules.[25]

Accountable to Whom?

Who are the agents of political accountability? Who are its social carriers and what are its institutional forms? It depends. Different forms of accountability rely on different enforcement mechanisms. The responsibility for exercising both political and moral accountability applies to citizens, civil associations, mass media, and opposition parties. Both administrative and financial accountability are often entrusted to specialized agencies, such as ombudsmen, administrative courts, accounting offices, and anticorruption organizations. Ethics commissions and disciplinary courts are common institutions of professional accountability. And judicial systems are in charge of guaranteeing legal as well as constitutional accountability. As this quick listing makes clear, distinguishing between different accounting parties constitutes a useful basis for constructing further subtypes of accountability. But we may easily drown in a sea of innumerable agents of accountability unless we drop some conceptual anchor that puts order into the potential proliferation of subtypes.[26] Guillermo O'Donnell's seminal distinction between vertical and horizontal accountability provides, I think, such a heuristic ordering device.[27]

The notion of vertical versus horizontal relations of accountability parts from the conventional spatial metaphor of power, the classic image of pyramidal hierarchies: height correlates with resources, "above" equals power, "below" equals powerlessness. In this sense, vertical accountability describes a relationship between unequals: it refers to some powerful "superior" actor holding some less powerful "inferior" actor accountable. Or vice versa! The concept is indeterminate in this crucial aspect of directionality. It leaves open whether accountability is meant to flow "top down" or "bottom up," whether it forms part of the normal exercise of power or whether it implies an inversion of usual power relations. The classic instance of the former is bureaucratic accountability, in which higher-ranking public officials ("principals") try to control their lower-ranking subordinates ("agents"). In representative democracies, the most important variant of the latter is electoral accountability, in which citizens hold judgment over their representatives through periodic elections.[28]

By contrast, horizontal accountability, taken literally, describes a relationship between equals: it refers to somebody holding someone else of roughly equal power accountable. In democratic theory, the division of power—the executive, legislative, and judiciary constraining each other through the classic "checks and balances"—represents its prototypical expression. Yet demanding a "rough equality" of power for horizontal relations of accountability establishes a tough criterion, an overly tough one. Power is a (relational) property that is hard to measure, and trying to identify instances of roughly equal political power in the real world of democratic politics is probably an impossible mission.

In addition, an accounting party, if it is to be serious, cannot stand on equal footing with the accountable party. At least in its sphere of competence, it must be even more powerful. And certainly within the boundaries of its jurisdiction, which may be very narrow, it must be, as O'Donnell puts it (in this book), "legally enabled and empowered" to impose sanctions on the accountable party, to punish improper behavior on its behalf. Relaxing the defining criterion of rough equality in order to replace it by some looser category, such as an approximate "equivalence" of power,[29] does not change this "paradox of horizontal accountability," of specialized agencies holding actors accountable who are immensely more powerful on all accounts except in the agency's specific sphere of competence. Besides, accountability as answerability does not even include the power to punish but only the right to get an answer. In terms of power, it may take place under extremely asymmetric conditions.

Some authors take these methodological and conceptual difficulties into account by complementing the binary spatial metaphor of verticality versus horizontality with some intermediate category, such as "diagonal" or "oblique" accountability.[30] This solution, however, does little to clarify the matter. How should one determine, in precise terms, intermediate angles of inclination between horizontal and vertical lines of accountability?

If indeed in relations of horizontal accountability the agent and the addressee of accountability need not possess comparable power resources but in fact may represent actors of grossly unequal powers, it does not seem helpful to comprehend horizontality in a literal way as a relationship between actors of equal or equivalent power. Rather, it seems more productive and of more general applicability to stipulate that the accounting party must be independent from the accountable party in all decisions that concern its field of competence. Ideally, both parties form "relatively autonomous powers"[31] that do not stand in a relation of formal subordination or superiority to each other. In other words, horizontal accountability presupposes a prior division of powers, a certain internal functional differentiation of the state.

Defining horizontality in terms of autonomy resolves one main conceptual problem that has accompanied the concept of horizontal accountability. Another problem concerns the concept's basic domain of application: where are the autonomous agents of horizontal accountability to be located? Just in the state? Or also in civil society? It is clear that vertical accountability may take place within the state as well as within civil society and across the boundaries of the two spheres. Tax officials who stage sit-ins in front of the finance minister's office are an example of vertical accountability within the state; union members who accuse their long-standing leaders of corrupt behavior are an example of vertical accountability within civil society; and citizens who vote incumbent parties out of office are an example of vertical accountability running from civil society to state. In principle, horizontal accountability too may take place both within and across state and civil society. A judge compelling a military officer to testify in court is an example of horizontal accountability within the state; a journalist denouncing nepotism within the bar association represents an example of horizontal accountability within civil society; and the chamber of commerce questioning the constitutionality of selective price subsidies may count as an example of horizontal accountability from civil society to state.[32]

The controversial question is, however, whether we should reserve the notion of horizontal accountability to intrastate relations, as O'Donnell proposes, or else also include in the category civil society actors that hold state agencies accountable, as authors such as Richard Sklar, Philippe Schmitter, David Stark, and László Bruszt suggest.[33] Both conceptualizations of horizontal accountability seem quite legitimate. The main objection against the second option of extending the notion of horizontal accountability to civil society–state relations resides in the structural asymmetry between state and nonstate actors. Civil associations may represent strong "factual powers" (*poderes fácticos*). But they can never match the state's monopoly of legitimate physical violence or its privileged position as the source of law—of uniform, centrally defined, collectively binding rules. Thus, speaking of horizontal relations between the two spheres always sounds like something of a euphemism. In addition, ascribing one clear meaning to the notion of horizontal accountability carries the benefit of avoiding conceptual ambivalence. Accordingly, most authors in this book follow O'Donnell, insofar as they assume that all cases where civil society actors (citizens, civil associations, or mass media) try to hold state agents accountable fall into the category of vertical accountability, reserving the notion of horizontal accountability to all acts of accountability that take place between independent state agencies.

As Robert Pastor (in this book) has forcefully reminded us, all the notions of accountability discussed so far share one basic presupposition: they take for granted that political accountability works within the confinements of national political systems. As a consequence, they overlook international actors (governmental as well as nongovernmental ones) as possible agents of accountability. Since these external actors do not fit easily into the vertical/horizontal dichotomy constructed along the distinction between state and civil society, they represent, as Pastor puts it, a "third dimension" of accountability.

Second-Order Accountability

When agents of accountability develop into powerful actors, when their criteria of judgment are controversial, and when it is difficult to monitor their performance, we face the problem of second-order accountability: how can we hold institutions of accountability accountable themselves? This problem seems particularly pressing with the kind of institutions discussed in this book: specialized, nonelective, autonomous state organizations that are supposed to pursue their narrow missions with professional single-minded-ness, while they are nevertheless vulnerable to inefficiency and abuse the same as any other locus of power.[34]

Of course, one may reformulate the challenge of second-order account-ability as a challenge of n-order accountability. Since any second layer of institutional accountability is susceptible to the same kind of failures as the first layer, we face the possibility of an infinite regress. There are two ways to avoid it. We may establish *reciprocal* accountability: two agents, A and B, "check and balance" each other. Or we may establish *recursive* account-ability: A is accountable to B, who is accountable to C, who is accountable to A again. It is hard to imagine that, at least in the long run, insulated and isolated institutions of accountability can survive unless they are embedded in such recursive cycles or systems of accountability. As O'Donnell puts it (in this book), "achieving a significant degree of . . . accountability requires the coordination of several agencies, each of them subject to *divide et impera* strategies."

Conclusion

Where did our surveying expedition into the structure of meaning of the concept of political accountability take us? Let us sum up the main coordi-nates of our conceptual journey. Political accountability, we stipulated, rep-resents a broad, two-dimensional concept that denotes both answerability—the obligation of public officials to inform about their activities and to justify them—and enforcement—the capacity to impose negative sanctions on officeholders who violate certain rules of conduct. In experiences of political accountability, both aspects are usually present. Yet instances exist where either the call for sanctions dominates (accountability as enforce-ment) or the quest for information and justification (accountability as answerability). Given that the notion of accountability is not built on the illusion that power is subject to full control and can be opened up to full transparency, but rather accepts and addresses the uncertainty and opacity of power, we characterized it as a modest concept. After clarifying the basic meaning of accountability, we stepped into the vast field of different sub-types of accountability. We sketched some ways of distinguishing different forms of accountability, according to its addressees, its criteria, and its agents. Given the thematic focus of the book, our discussion centered on the distinction between vertical and horizontal accountability. It defined the somewhat vague and metaphorical notion of "horizontality" as a relation-ship between state agencies that must possess a certain degree of mutual independence, rather than equivalent power resources.

This review of the concept's semantic field and internal structure should establish a reliable basis for the other chapters in the book, even if not all authors adhere to exactly the same interpretation of accountability and its subtypes. In more general terms, it should also provide useful analytical tools for understanding and advancing academic as well as political discussions on political accountability—this obscure object of political desire and institutional design.

Notes

In academic life, it represents a rare and precious event when an author receives several pages of detailed, sympathetic, and constructive feedback on a draft. I thank an anonymous reviewer and Larry Diamond for writing such comments. Without their insightful and often fundamental criticism, this chapter would be very different from what it is now. My sincere thanks to both of them.

    1. *The Federalist Papers,* no. 51.

    2. For a brief historical review of moral and institutional solutions to the problem of corrupt power, see Fontana, "The Roots of a Long Tradition."

    3. Richard Sklar even asserts that "the norm of accountability appears to be the most widely practiced of democratic principles" (Sklar, "Developmental Democracy," p. 714).

    4. Plattner, "Comments," p. 1.

    5. Hickok, "Accountability," p. 9. See also Sklar, this volume.

    6. See Plattner, "Comments," and Sklar, this volume. This twofold answerability refers to past as well as to future acts. Especially in political contexts, accountable agents have to stand up not only for what they have done (retrospective or ex post accountability) but also for what they plan to do (prospective or ex ante accountability). See also Maravall, "Accountability," and Schmitter, this volume.

    7. Stark and Bruszt, *Postsocialist Pathways,* define accountability as "monitoring" (p. 195), thus equating it with the "informational" dimension. Yet, at other places, they use the term *accountability* interchangeably with deliberation (p. 189), thus equating it with the "dialogic" dimension.

    8. Bennett, "The Paradox of Public Discourse," p. 794.

    9. Stark and Bruszt, *Postsocialist Pathways,* emphasize the connectedness of both aspects of accounts. They develop the metaphor of democratic politicians opening accounts, asking voters for credit, and giving accounts in order to maintain their creditworthiness in an original and insightful way (see pp. 192–196).

    10. See O'Donnell, "Delegative Democracy," p. 61.

    11. See, e.g., Ostrom, *Governing the Commons.*

    12. See, e.g., Collier, O'Donnell, Schmitter, and Sklar (this volume); Maravall, "Accountability."

    13. See Diamond, "How Well Is Taiwan's Democracy Doing?"

    14. See Diamond, "Political Corruption."

    15. On the distinction between horizontal and vertical accountability, see below.

    16. On "diminished subtypes," see Collier and Levitsky, "Democracy with Adjectives."

    17. On "classical" and "radial" concepts, see Collier and Mahon, "Conceptual 'Stretching' Revisited."

18. The preceding reflections do not apply for "accountability as enforcement." As we noted above, rule violations may already be in the open as public facts that are not opaque; neither does the punishment of those violations add to the transparency of politics.

19. As reported by Galtung, "Developing Agencies of Restraint," p. 11.

20. Of course, there are exceptions to the general rule of publicity. The "bureaucratic" accountability of subordinates to superiors usually remains an internal affair within the administrative organization concerned. And in some traditional realms of state secrecy, such as foreign intelligence services, accountability, if it takes place at all, does so in a confidential way, closed off to the eyes of the general public.

21. See, e.g., Habermas, *Theorie*, p. 47.

22. See, e.g., Pizzorno, "Representation," p. 8.

23. Much of "professional accountability" pertains to the sphere of civil society. At the same time, the category represents a weighty aspect of the accountability of public officials, and the more so, of course, the larger the public sector in a given country.

24. Note that the last three categories—moral, financial, and legal accountability—represent entirely crosscutting forms of political accountability that may strike any actor in the political system, be it a party leader, the head of government, a member of parliament, a judge, a simple state official, or whomever.

25. This volume basically covers the last two forms of accountability: legal and constitutional.

26. The picture would look even more complicated if we were to include forms of accountability not only to concrete actors but also to ideal, subjectless categories: to history (historical accountability), to our personal conscience (super-ego accountability), to God in heaven (celestial accountability), or to past generations (ancestral accountability). I owe the term "celestial" or "heavenly" accountability to Richard Sklar (this volume).

27. See O'Donnell, "Delegative Democracy." For a similar early conceptualization under the heading of "lateral" accountability, see Sklar, "Developmental Democracy."

28. Both types of relationship may be modeled along the lines of principal-agent theory (see, e.g., Maravall, "Accountability"; Moe, "Political Institutions," pp. 232–233; Roeder, *Real Sunset,* chapter 2, pp. 22–40).

29. See, e.g., Schmitter, this volume.

30. See also Schmitter, this volume, p. 62, note 4.

31. O'Donnell, "Delegative Democracy." See also Diamond, "The End," pp. 8–9.

32. For an insightful discussion of the many forms, sites, and protagonists of accountability, within the state as well as within civil society, see Sklar, "Developmental Democracy."

33. See the contributions of O'Donnell, Sklar, and Schmitter, this volume, as well as O'Donnell, "Delegative Democracy," Sklar, "Developmental Democracy," and Stark and Bruszt, *Postsocialist Pathways.*

34. For a refreshing recognition of the need for second-order accountability with relation to central banks, against the prevailing mainstream that favors maximizing unqualified central bank independence, see Johnson, this volume, Schürz, "Independence Versus Accountability," and Whitehead, "Models of Central Banking."

3

Horizontal Accountability in New Democracies

GUILLERMO O'DONNELL

For Gabriela,
my beloved agency of horizontal accountability

I

My interest in what I labeled "horizontal accountability"[1] stems from its absence. Many countries, in Latin America and elsewhere, have recently become political democracies, or polyarchies. By this I mean that they satisfy the conditions stipulated by Robert Dahl for defining this regime type.[2] Satisfying these conditions is no mean feat: some countries continue under authoritarian rule, and others, even though they hold elections, do not satisfy the conditions of fair and free competition stipulated by the definition of polyarchy.[3] In this chapter I do not deal with the latter cases; my focus is on those that are polyarchies, in the sense just defined, but have weak or intermittent horizontal accountability. This refers to almost all the Latin American countries, including some rather old polyarchies such as Colombia and Venezuela.[4] This category also pertains to some new Asian polyarchies, such as the Philippines, South Korea, and Taiwan, as well as, increasingly so, an old one, India, and some of the postcommunist countries that might qualify as polyarchies—Russia, Belorussia, Croatia, Slovakia, and Ukraine,[5] and perhaps also Hungary, Poland, and the Czech Republic.[6]

By definition, in these countries the electoral dimension of vertical accountability exists. Through the means of reasonably fair and free elections, citizens can punish or reward incumbents by voting for or against them, or the candidates they endorse, in the next election. Also by definition, the freedoms of opinion and of association, as well as access to reasonably varied sources of information, permit articulating demands to, and eventually denouncing wrongful acts of, public authorities. This is helped by the existence of reasonably free media, also demanded by the definition

29

of polyarchy. Elections, social demands that usually can be articulated without suffering state coercion, and regular coverage by the media of at least the more visible of these demands and of apparently wrongful acts of the public authorities are dimensions of what I call "vertical accountability." These are actions performed, individually or by means of some kind of organized and/or collective action, with reference to those who occupy positions in state institutions, elected or not.

Of course, what is arguably the main facet of vertical accountability—elections—occur only from time to time. Furthermore, it is not clear to what extent this facet of vertical accountability is effective. Even in formally institutionalized polyarchies[7] recent analyses[8] conclude on a skeptical note about the degree to which elections are truly an instrument with which voters can punish or reward incumbents. Whatever may be the case (something I will not try to elucidate here), it seems clear that under the conditions that prevail in many new polyarchies (inchoate party systems, high volatility of voters and parties, poorly defined public policy issues, and sudden policy reversals),[9] the effectiveness of electoral accountability tends to further diminish.

On the other hand, the impact of social demands and of the media, insofar as they denounce and/or demand restitution or punishment for allegedly wrongful actions by public authorities, depends to a large extent on the actions that properly authorized state agencies may undertake in order to investigate and eventually sanction the wrongdoings. Lacking these actions, social demands and media coverage, especially if they are abundant and refer to issues that are considered important by public opinion, tend to create a climate of public disaffection with the government (and sometimes with the regime itself) that may obstruct its policies and lead to its defeat in the next round of elections. But these events do not necessarily trigger appropriate public procedures, even if they may be required by existing legislation. When, as often happens in the new polyarchies, there is a generalized feeling that the government repeatedly engages in corrupt practices, the media tend to become surrogate courts. They expose alleged wrongdoings, name those supposedly responsible for them, and give whatever details they deem relevant. Lacking state action, some officials are thus spared the sanctions that would have probably resulted if the courts and/or other public agencies had intervened. Others, however, who may be innocent of any impropriety, and those whose eventual wrongdoings could not be proved, see themselves tainted, and often condemned by public opinion, without having had anything resembling due process for their defense.

II

The existence of vertical accountability presupposes that these polyarchies are *democratic,* that is, citizens can exercise their participatory right to choose who is going to rule them for some time, and they can freely express their opinions and demands. But the weakness of horizontal accountability means that the *liberal* and the *republican* components of many new polyarchies are feeble. This statement springs from my belief that polyarchies are the complex synthesis of three historical currents or traditions: democracy, liberalism, and republicanism. Here I depart from most present discussions in the current literature, which tend to see polyarchies as tensioned between just two poles: liberalism versus democracy, or liberalism versus republicanism. Furthermore, some of these discussions see these currents, or traditions, as mutually exclusive. I think, rather, that even though their boundaries tend to blur in some writings and political discourses, there are not just two but three traditions, and that they have converged into the institutions and to some extent the practice of modern polyarchies. I also believe that this convergence is partially contradictory, in the sense that some of the basic principles of each of these currents are inconsistent with the basic principles of at least another one. This inconsistency gives to polyarchies, jointly with some of their predicaments, their uniquely dynamic and open-ended characteristics.

By the liberal component that has been injected into modern polyarchies I mean, basically, the idea that there are some rights that should not be encroached upon by any power, including the state. By the republican component I mean, basically, the idea that the discharge of public duties is an ennobling activity that demands careful subjection to the law and devoted service to the public interest, even at the expense of sacrificing the private interests of the officials. Both the liberal and republican traditions posit a crucial distinction between a public and a private sphere, but the implications of this split are very different. For liberalism, the area of proper and eventually fuller development of human life is the private one. This is the reason for its inherent ambiguity toward the state and, more generally, the public sphere: on one hand, the state has to have enough power to guarantee the freedoms enjoyed in private life and, on the other hand, it has to be prevented from yielding to the ever-present temptation— lurking, as liberalism sagely knows, anywhere power accumulates—to encroach on those same freedoms.[10] In its turn, for republicanism, the area of proper and fuller human development is the public one. It is there that the exacting demands of dedication to the public good require, and nurture, the highest virtues. If liberalism is basically defensive, republicanism is basically elitist: whether democratically elected or not, those who claim that they have the right to govern because of their superior virtue are inclined to look down on those who devote themselves to the lesser undertakings of the private sphere. In its turn, the democratic tradition ignores these distinctions: factually there may be private activities, but, first, those who participate in the collective decisions are not a virtuous elite but the very same people who may undertake an active private life,[11] and, second and foremost, as Socrates and others discovered, the demos can rule over any matter—it has the full right to decide on whatever issue it deems appropriate.[12]

These traditions and the principles that define them are different and have different origins: democracy in Athens; republicanism in Rome, sometimes in Sparta, and later in some medieval Italian cities; liberalism in feudal society and, later and more pointedly, in the England of Locke and the France of Montesquieu. In some important aspects these traditions are conflictive. At the very least, the values attached to the public and to the private spheres by liberalism and republicanism lead to diverging, if not opposing, conclusions about political rights and obligations, political participation, the character of citizenship and of civil society, and other issues that are the very stuff of political debate.[13] On its side, democracy is not dualistic but monistic; it knows of no valid limits or distinctions between a private and a public sphere. Furthermore, in democracy the exercise of public duties does not require, as in republicanism, that those who discharge them be particularly virtuous and fully dedicated; rather, the ultimate democratic procedures, rotation or selection by lot,[14] presuppose that all are roughly equally qualified for those roles. Finally, when it comes to voting, the democratic principle is strongly majoritarian, in a double sense.

First, short of unanimity the collective will of the demos has to be identified, and some kind of majority is the commonsense criterion for such identification when all members are considered equal. Second, as already noted, whatever is decided does not recognize barriers—other than those established for the workings of the demos itself[15]—for being valid and effective. In contrast, even though liberalism and republicanism trace and value it differently, the dualistic split postulated by liberalism and republicanism entails the idea of limits, or boundaries, that should be strictly acknowledged. This dualism of liberalism and republicanism led to the adoption of the mechanism of political representation while, on the other hand, the monism of democracy—as practiced in Athens and as Rousseau, consistent with this premise, concluded—makes it alien, if not hostile, to the very idea of representation.

The directionality of rights and obligations is also different: liberalism basically attaches defensive rights to individuals placed in the private sphere; republicanism basically attaches obligations to individuals placed in the public sphere; and democracy basically asserts the positive right of participation in the decisions of the demos. But there is an important convergence. Democracy (in its equalizing impulses), liberalism (in its commitment to protect freedoms in society), and republicanism (in its severe view of the obligations of those who govern) each in its way supports another fundamental aspect of polyarchy and of the constitutional state that is supposed to coexist with it: the rule of law. All citizens are equally entitled to participate in the formation of collective decisions under the existing institutional framework, a democratic statement to which it is added the republican injunction that no one, including those who govern, should be above the law, and the liberal caution that certain freedoms and guarantees should not be infringed. We shall see, however, that the actual effectiveness of the rule of law registers important variations across different kinds of polyarchies.

III

Let us now look at these currents from another angle. In part, democracy and republicanism embody two commonsense views of political authority. In relation to democracy: why should those who are in charge of the common good accept restraints on what they decide? In relation to republicanism: why should those who are better, or more virtuous than the rest, be prevented from governing for the sake of the common good? Instead, liberalism is profoundly counterintuitive: only in a small part of the world, influenced by the traditions of feudalism, conciliarism, and natural rights and shocked by the horrors of religious wars, was it persuasively argued that there were sets of rights that should not be infringed upon by any public or private agent.

On the other hand, liberalism cannot justify the eventually coercive exercise of political authority over a territory except by recurring to the artificiality of a foundational social contract. In its turn, republicanism does not go beyond an assertion that is typical of all kinds of authority: that it is for the good of the subjects of its rule. But this stream contributed another historically counterintuitive idea: that part of the required virtue of the rulers is that they should subject their actions to the law, no less and even more than ordinary citizens. Democracy, for its part, introduced long before liberalism and republicanism another radical and counterintuitive novelty: that it is not only a type of rule that is *for,* but also *from* and, albeit in actual practice more disputably, *by* those who in some sense[16] are members of a given society.

These three currents have combined in complex and changing ways throughout the history of the formally institutionalized polyarchies that exist in most of the highly developed countries. Consequently, it is mistaken, albeit often tried, to postulate a certain dimension as the "basic" or more fundamental foundation of polyarchy. The exaggerated assertion of liberalism becomes liberism,[17] the discourse of economic laissez-faire and oligarchic rule of those entrenched in their privileges. The risks of majoritarian democratic rule have been too exhaustively discussed elsewhere to merit discussion here. Republicanism, if it becomes the dominant principle, tends to become the paternalistic rule of a self-righteous elite. Polyarchy is a complicated and at times exasperating mix; but it is vastly preferable to types of rule based on only one of its main component traditions.

At this moment I wish to posit three considerations: (1) the need to distinguish the different ways in which liberalism and republicanism predicate a boundary between a public and a private sphere, as well as to contrast such a split with the monism of the democratic tradition; (2) the three currents of thought—liberalism postulating a sphere of protected rights, republicanism subjecting rulers to the law, and democracy asserting that those subject to rule are the very sources of such rule—led to some radical, counterintuitive, and historically original discoveries; and (3) the complex and changing mix of these three elements as important elements for characterizing polyarchies, the really existing democracies of the modern world.

IV

One might ask what the preceding discussion has to do with horizontal accountability. The answer is that polyarchy is the condensation of various historical processes, many of them concomitant with a phenomenon, capitalism, which was born in the same part of the world as liberalism. Even though at a very high (and often not terribly useful) level of abstraction one may speak of capitalism as a single entity, many valuable efforts have been devoted to the comparative study of various kinds of capitalism. These studies spring from the recognition that a series of historical and structural factors has determined the emergence of specific configurations that, even though they share the generic characteristic of being capitalist, exhibit important variations, and that these variations must be taken into account when aiming to describe and/or assess the tendencies of change in given cases. The same happens with polyarchy. All cases in this genus belong here because they share the attributes specified at the beginning of this chapter.

Using this definition we can perform two basic operations. One is similar to the one we perform when, armed according to our preferences with a neo-Marxian or a neo-Weberian definition of capitalism, we distinguish between societies that are capitalist and those that are not (or were not) capitalist; the discussion may differentiate the set of cases that are polyarchies from the whole set of all other cases that are not. Another operation, and for the purposes of this essay a more interesting one, is to look within the set of polyarchies and ask what differences exist among these cases and what accounts for such differences. This is the route I am taking here.

I do not presume to undertake the Weberian task of discussing the factors (including capitalism) that contributed to the emergence and expansion of polyarchy.[18] I just want to be certain that the three currents I sketched above are included among those factors. These currents and their basic principles are not just ideas floating abstractly in space: they have been memorably stated by some authors and discussed and revised by many others; they have inspired innumerable discussions and tracts, have been evoked in the most varying circumstances and rituals, have imbued constitutions and innumerable pieces of legislation, and through all this have profoundly influenced, although with varying intensity from country to country and period to period, the repertoire of political thought, debate, and policy.[19]

In particular, these currents converged in the constitutions and in much of the legislation of a peculiar entity that came into full existence more or less simultaneously with liberalism and capitalism but after democracy and republicanism were initially formulated: the territorially based state. If each of these currents has its own logic, in the sense that it articulates reasonably consistent basic principles and corollaries, the state also has its own logic, and one that also is partially inconsistent with these three currents. This is a complicated issue that need not be explored here. Two points will suffice. One is that most of whatever law exists is law issued and/or backed by the state—or, more precisely (as continental theorists have long recognized and Anglo-Saxon ones have too often forgotten), the legal system is one of the constitutive dimensions of the state.[20] The second point is that state bureaucracies are crucial seats of the power resources that come into play when matters of horizontal accountability are at stake. Like capitalism, states exhibit great variation across time and space. Although not much can be added to the sweeping generalities I have proposed here, it seems obvious that the kind of capitalism as well as the kind of state we find in a given country will significantly influence the kind of polyarchy the country is likely to have as well as the ways it is likely to change. The problem is that, in contrast to the various useful comparative typologies of capitalisms and states we have, there are few that compare polyarchies—and most of these focus mainly, if not exclusively, on the formally institutionalized cases.[21] This problem is even more acute if we take into account that, in addition to but not independent of the factors noted above, in polyarchies the relative weight of the liberal, the republican, and the democratic currents exhibits important variations across time and space.

To illustrate the latter point, one may say that in the history of the United States, the democratic component has been relatively weak, while the republican and (especially) liberal ones have been strong;[22] in France, the democratic and republican components have been relatively strong and the liberal weak;[23] in contemporary Germany, probably as a reaction to the democratic emphasis of the Weimar period, the liberal and the republican ones predominate; while in many new polyarchies, both the liberal and the republican components are weak (the democratic one is not terribly strong, either, but its relative effectiveness stands in stark contrast to the weakness of the other two).

V

Even though the differences I have noted are highly simplified, they suggest that there are important historically textured variations in the kinds of existing polyarchies, just as there are in the types of capitalism and states. Polyarchies are complex and unstable mixes of the four elements—the three traditions and the state—I have sketched. Many political struggles can be read as arguments about which mix should be a more proper one at any given time in a certain country. Each of these streams stresses diverging values and, ultimately, different views of human nature. After Britain began to develop practices and institutions that nowadays we recognize as forerunners of polyarchy, it drew the often admiring attention of intellectuals and political leaders of other countries.

Diffusion, first from Britain, and later from the United States and France, has been a major factor in shaping the polyarchies that emerged later—after the originating countries, polyarchy has never been a truly homegrown product.[24] The main actors in these originating countries looked to Greece and Rome for the concepts, edifying examples, and cautionary disgraces stemming from their respective democratic and republican traditions. Some of these actors—in Britain, the United States, and later in France itself—obsessed with the horrors that the claims to the democratic principle and to republican virtue had produced during the French Revolution, reinforced or reformulated their belief in some sort of liberal formula for averting these risks. Even today, when other actors in other countries aim at establishing polyarchy, they have in mind those original polyarchies, their founding myths, their "classic" thinkers, and the power and prestige of the originating countries.

The latecomers,[25] as shown by some of the oldest (and least effective) constitutions in the world, those of Latin America in the nineteenth century, found themselves with what they felt were almost ready-made institutional packages, which in most cases were chosen depending on which of the formal or informal empires each of the latecomers belonged to. Both East and South, the transplantation of constitutions and legislation and the initial hopes that these institutions would be the great propellers toward political and economic modernity have created what perhaps is the more persistent, and often heated, cultural and political debate in these countries: the ways to evaluate and eventually close the visible gap between the *pays légal* and the *pays réel*[26] that resulted from those transplants. Irrespective of the position taken on this issue, it has a strong factual grounding that legions of politicians, historians, novelists, and social scientists have commented on: the big difference that often exists between formally prescribed rules and norms and what most people actually do most of the time. As a consequence, whether one might want to firmly establish the *pays légal* or to organize political life around the traditions of the *pays réel,* successful navigation of the existing social and political world requires keen awareness of both codes and their interlacings. This is true everywhere; but in general it is more true the farther we get in time and in space from the geographical core where the three currents of polyarchy originated.

The fact is that, for a long time and with only few exceptions, outside this core none of the counterintuitive principles of democracy, liberalism, and republicanism fared well. Many kinds of rule continued or emerged East and South, but few of them were polyarchies, even though (interestingly enough, witnessing the particularly strong influence of the democratic tradition) some of them appealed to elections to provide a mantle of legitimacy for the rulers. These various kinds of authoritarian rule denied the protective frontiers of liberalism, although out of expediency or impotence they tolerated a varying range of autonomous activities in society. Also, even though, as I have suggested, republicanism can be conceived in an authoritarian way, most authoritarian rulers were not at all republican. Rather, they behaved in ways that, following Max Weber and Juan Linz,[27] may be labeled neopatrimonialist, if not in some cases sultanistic: they claimed (as do all kinds of authority) that they were for the common good of the population but considered themselves *de legibus solutus* (that is, not obligated to obey the law) and often ignored (to their personal advantage) the ethical injunctions of republicanism. However, as already noted, in some of these cases, elections (albeit not competitive) were held, and even in countries (such as under the typical military junta of Latin America) where elections were suppressed, the population could look back to periods when elections had been reasonably fair (that is to say, in their memory, "democratic" times), but when not much liberalism or republicanism had been effective.[28]

Even though rotation and lot, not elections, are the truly democratic procedures, it is elections that have become identified with "democracy," both in many theories and what I take is an almost universally widespread common sense. This view is reinforced when—in what I gather is a mix of simplism and cynicism—many governments certify as democratic countries where this kind of election is more or less plausibly considered to be held, even though, as in the cases of Yeltsin and Fujimori, the executive runs roughshod over congress and the judiciary. One way or the other, in the historical memory of many populations and in the expectations of many actors, the idea of democracy (i.e., polyarchy) has become closely identified with the process of elections—into which the democratic principle has been interpreted in modern times. The consequence is to blur the perception of the no less constitutive role that liberalism and republicanism play in polyarchy. We shall see that this creates problems when, among other things, we want to discuss horizontal accountability.

VI

I have gone swiftly through several important and complicated issues, each of which calls for a huge bibliography. But I needed this *tour d'horizon* to put the theme of this chapter into some context. Now I define what I mean by horizontal accountability: it is the existence of state agencies that are legally enabled and empowered, and factually willing and able, to take actions that span from routine oversight to criminal sanctions or impeachment in relation to actions or omissions by other agents or agencies of the state that may be qualified as unlawful.[29] Such actions can affect three main spheres. One, democracy, is impinged, for example, by decisions that cancel freedom of association or introduce fraud in elections. These are important and worrisome actions, but I do not consider them here because they entail the abolition of polyarchy.[30]

Another sphere is the liberal, which is infringed when, say, state agents violate or allow private actors to violate liberal freedoms and guarantees, such as the inviolability of the domicile, the prohibition of domestic violence and of torture, the right of everyone to a reasonably fair trial, and the like. In polyarchies (not necessarily in authoritarian regimes), most of these actions are perpetrated at the frontiers between the state apparatus and the weaker and poorer segments of society, usually by officials of low rank who are not directly accountable to the electoral process (even though when these phenomena become widespread and systematic they usually include the participation or connivance of higher-placed officials).[31]

The third sphere affected is republicanism. It refers to actions by officials, elected or not, most of whom are highly placed in the state or the regime. These actions entail serious disregard for the demands placed on these officials by the republican tradition—that is, to subject themselves to the law and/or to give determinate priority to public interests, not their private ones.

For certain conceptions of political authority, which I call "delegative," not to mention those that are directly authoritarian, it is this republican dimension of restraint that is the more counterintuitive. Why recognize powers other than one's own when one is presumably trying to achieve goals that are conducive to some aspect of the public good? And why not benefit personally and bestow favors on one's family, friends, and business associates while in public office if at the same time one is (at least supposedly) aiming at some aspect of the public good? This is a topic that has interested me for a long time. In countless conversations spanning many years and several countries, I have been impressed by how little problem my interlocutors have with these questions. These were not crooks, nor did they respond as if they were: they were trying to contribute to some kind of common good while at the same time crossing the republican boundaries. They were not alone; families, party and clique members, and/or business associates assumed that the officials would behave in this way and would have strongly condemned them had they not—there are strong normative expectations for such behavior. For all these actors, informal rules prevailed over formal ones, with no detectable bad conscience. But formal rules were not entirely immaterial; they had to be taken into account in order to find ways to prevent their violation or circumvention from causing damaging consequences for the officials and their affiliates.

I cite this admittedly undisciplined ethnography because it tells us something important: plain crooks who do not have the slightest intention of serving some aspect of the public good are indeed a serious and often pervasive problem in many countries, polyarchical or not. But they are the tip of the iceberg; I am persuaded that many of the deficiencies of horizontal accountability are the product of manifold actions that take, by those who commit them and by those who somehow are related to these actions, as a given that republican injunctions are something to which one should at most pay lip service[32] and that one should eventually take into account to prevent damaging consequences.

The main issue here is about boundaries, or limits, in two related senses. One is the liberal and republican split between a public and a private sphere. The other boundary—closely related to (or, more precisely, derived from) these two currents—is implicit in the definition of horizontal accountability I have proposed: for this kind of accountability to be effective there must exist state agencies that are authorized and willing to oversee, control, redress, and/or sanction unlawful actions of other state agencies. The former agencies must have not only legal authority for proceeding in this way but also, de facto, sufficient autonomy with respect to the latter. This is, of course, the old theme of the division of powers and the system of checks and balances. It includes the classic institutions of the executive, the legislative, and the judiciary; but in contemporary polyarchies it also extends to various overseeing agencies, ombudsmen, accounting offices, *fiscalías,* and the like.

An important but seldom noticed point is that if these agencies are to be effective, they very rarely can operate in isolation. They can shake public opinion with their proceedings, but normally their ultimate effectiveness depends on decisions by courts (or eventually by legislatures willing to consider impeachment), especially in cases that are salient and/or involve highly placed officials. Effective horizontal accountability is not the product of isolated agencies but of networks of agencies that include at their top—because that is where a constitutional legal system "closes" by means of ultimate decisions—courts (including the highest ones) committed to such accountability.[33] We shall return to this topic, because it gives us a glimpse of some of the peculiar difficulties, and some of the possibilities, implied by the purpose of enhancing horizontal accountability.

The basic idea is the prevention, and eventual sanctioning, of the actions to which the officials I characterized above are commonsensically prone—that is, their extralimitation, their transgressing of the limits of their formally defined authority. To be autonomous, institutions must have boundaries; these boundaries must be acknowledged and respected by other relevant actors; and still other actors must be available to defend and eventually restore the boundaries if they are transgressed.[34] At the level of the three[35] major institutions of polyarchy, as Bernard Manin has shown,[36] the wisdom of the Federalists provided not for the rather mechanical division of powers proposed by their opponents but for institutions that partially overlap in their authority. This produced an arrangement that, by building several strong powers that partially intruded on each other, enhanced the autonomy of each of them with respect to what would have resulted from a simple separation of such powers.

VII

I have noted problems that stem from what I suspect are widespread and deep-seated views about the exercise of political authority in many countries, polyarchical or not. An additional problem results from the monistic bent of democracy, particularly as interpreted in many new polyarchies. Plebiscitarianism, caesarism, populism, and other cognate terms have deep historical roots in many of these countries. Nowadays, when they have become polyarchies, these terms can be read in a delegative code: democracy is about electing in reasonably fair elections who is to govern the country for a certain time; governing is what is done by the executive; whoever is elected has the right and the duty to look after the good of the country as he[37] and his direct collaborators see fit; and if the electorate are unhappy with the performance of the government, they can vote it out in the next elections—no less and not much more.[38] In this view, evidently shared by many political leaders and an indeterminate but surely not insignificant part of public opinion in many new polyarchies,[39] the existence of powers that are sufficiently autonomous with respect to the executive, especially when or if they are supposed to exercise controls over the latter, is an utter, unalloyed nuisance. In the short term, the common sense of the delegative executive wanting to discharge the broad responsibilities with which it feels it has been exclusively charged, is to ignore those other agencies and, in the longer run, to exert itself in eliminating, coopting, or neutralizing them. Starting from a delegative conception of its own authority, the executive has strong incentives to proceed in this way: as long as it is successful, it has more freedom for making decisions. For this purpose, the executive can rely on similar conceptions of authority held by other officials[40] and, presumably, on the agreement with this view by no small part of public opinion. With the good conscience resulting from its felt obligation to attend the public good, a scarcely liberal and republican executive will attempt to maximize its power by eliminating or denying the validity of other, potentially controlling state and social powers—the monistic logic of the demos, transplanted to the logic of delegation, reverberates here.

At this point I should add that what I have said does not mean that the executive is all-powerful. As some authors have noted,[41] this kind of executive finds limits, even among its political allies, in various kinds of power plays during which legal rules may be invoked. But the crucial difference is that these rules are instruments of such plays, not ones that, by being acknowledged in their independent validity, set the legal parameters of stabilized institutional interactions. Another limitation springs from the sheer size of some countries and/or their federalism,[42] both of which tend to allow for the existence of local powers, often no less delegative and unaccountable than the central one, among which intricate power relations exist that often partake of a rather unabashedly instrumental utilization of legal rules.

It may be that in the long run the executive would maximize its power by subjecting itself to horizontal controls, but in these cases, except for some economic issues where these advantages may be quite immediate and visible,[43] in each round of decisions the path of nonaccountability seems to be the dominant strategy. In contrast, it is not obvious what may be the incentives of other state agencies to resist or sanction unlawful actions by the executive (or another institution, such as the congress). The problem is further complicated if we remember that to a large extent the effectiveness of horizontal accountability depends not just on single agencies dealing with specific issues but on a network of such agencies that includes courts committed to supporting this kind of accountability. Proper incentives for building sufficient institutional autonomy must, consequently, be spread and coordinated through several state agencies. But if in addition we note that Menem, Fujimori, Yeltsin, and other delegative leaders are very good at dividing and conquering those agencies, clearly it is no easy task to build adequate autonomy and incentives in them.

There are two main directions in which horizontal accountability can be violated. Even though in some cases these directions may in fact coincide, they are distinct. One consists of the unlawful encroachment by one state agency upon the proper authority of another; the second consists of unlawful advantages that public officials obtain for themselves and/or their associates. Let me call the first kind "encroachment" and the second, even though it covers some behaviors that do not truly fit the term, "corruption." Liberalism fears the direct and indirect consequences of encroachments by rulers and thus coincides with republicanism in expecting that they are subject not only to the existing law, as the latter would demand, but also to a kind of law that protects the freedoms and guarantees that liberalism cherishes, as both Locke and Montesquieu argued. But liberalism in itself does not have much to say about corruption. Republicanism, in its turn, prohibits encroachment and very broadly and strongly condemns corruption (*corruptio optimi est pessima*), even understanding by it, in its more classical versions, the same neglect of public affairs on which liberalism looks so benevolently. Finally, the monistic view of democracy ignores the very idea of encroachment.

There is another aspect of democracy that makes an important contribution to horizontal accountability. This contribution derives from democracy's notion that political authority comes from each and every member of the demos: if this is the case, those citizens who temporarily—by rotation, lot, or election—happen to be in charge of public affairs must make their decisions having in view the good of all. Furthermore, if power is from all and if every citizen is at least potentially a participant in the making of collective decisions, then—as it was in Athens—all decisions must be public, in the double sense that the process that leads to them is open to broad participation and that the content of the decisions is made available to everyone. Even though these democratic expectations do not bear directly on horizontal accountability, they have the consequence of demanding a high degree of transparency in political decisionmaking, which has at least a potential anticorruption implication. By contrast, in itself, liberalism is indifferent to the requirement of transparency, and in some cases it may gladly waive it if this seems conducive to better protection, while presumably virtuous republican rulers tend to find excellent reasons for the nontransparency of their decisions. Somewhat curiously, on the one hand, the monistic democratic principle does not interpose obstacles to encroaching, but, on the other hand, it fosters a jealous attention to corruption. If we take into account that in new polyarchies it is the democratic current that is the stronger, there may be a reverberation of this predominance in the attitude of (apparently) many who are relatively indifferent toward encroachments by a delegative executive but much less tolerant of its suspected corrupt acts.

However, I suspect that in the long run, encroachment is more dangerous than corruption for the survival of polyarchy: a systematic utilization of the former simply liquidates polyarchy, while a systematic spread of the latter will surely deteriorate polyarchy but not necessarily eliminate it. Furthermore, encroachment places a stronger obstacle than corruption to the emergence of the relatively autonomous state agencies acting according to properly defined authority that characterizes formally institutionalized polyarchies. In these latter cases, it is probably no accident that there is more corruption than encroachment. In contrast, the democratic current provides little help against encroachment in cases, such as those of many new polyarchies, where the liberal and the republican components are weak.

VIII

But in relation to these problems there is some good news. Even if it mixes in complex and often ambivalent ways with the above-noted views about how public duties should be discharged, in many new polyarchies there is, more than in any preceding period, a generalized mood of condemnation of at least one aspect of unlawful behavior by public officials. I refer to corruption, the spread of which, survey after survey show, is a major concern in these countries. We know that what counts as corruption in country A may be perfectly legal and morally permissible in country B; but there does seem to be a basic core—directly embezzling public funds or taking bribes—that seems to be considered condemnable in most if not all countries.[44] This chapter is not specifically about corruption, even though this plague is in part expression and in part consequence of feeble horizontal accountability. The point is that, insofar as some forms of corruption become highly visible and are generally condemned by public opinion, they can provide a handle for thinking more positively than I have done so far about how to enhance horizontal accountability.

Another piece of good news is that, largely as a consequence of the manifold abuses perpetrated during the preceding periods of authoritarian rule, in many new polyarchies various organizations have emerged (some of them human rights organizations that have broadened the initial definition of their mission) that vigorously demand that state officials respect the basic liberal freedoms and guarantees of (mostly) the weak and the poor. Other organizations supervise elections and undertake other democratic tasks, such as trying to educate the population in the knowledge and exercise of their political rights. Still others act as republican watchdogs of the lawfulness of state actions in terms both of their possible encroachment over other state agencies and of appropriate ethical conduct by public officials.[45] As already mentioned, these actions have limited effects if properly authorized state agencies do not take them up. But, jointly with journalistic reports, these actions highlight wrongful doings that otherwise would go unnoticed and provide potential allies for state agencies that, even against strong odds, might decide to undertake appropriate action.

IX

What can be done to enhance horizontal accountability? This is a matter about which, at least in the short term and in most cases, it is difficult to be very optimistic. All I can offer at this point are some modest and scarcely original suggestions. First, give opposition parties that have reached some reasonable level of electoral support an important, if not the main, role in directing agencies (*fiscalías,* as they are usually called in Latin America) that are in charge of investigating alleged cases of corruption. However, nothing guarantees that in these matters the opposition is any better than the government[46] or that the latter, as has happened in several new polyarchies, will not ignore, deprive of necessary resources, and/or coopt such agencies.

Second, it is no less important that agencies that perform an essentially preemptive role, such as general accounting offices or *contralorías,* are highly professionalized, endowed with resources that are both sufficient and independent of the whim of the executive, and insulated as much as possible from the latter. In its turn, this does not prevent corruption from penetrating these agencies or the executive from coopting them; nor does the legislative faculty to determine agencies' budgets prevent congress from being as anxious as its executive counterpart to eliminate or neutralize such agencies.

Third, it would help a lot to have a judiciary that is highly professionalized, well endowed with a budget that is as independent as possible from the executive and congress, and highly autonomous in its decisions with respect to both. But such "autonomy" is tricky: it may facilitate the control of the judiciary by a political party or faction or coalition of not very commendable interests or may promote a privileged and archaic self-definition of the judicial corporation and its mission, without any accountability of its own to other powers in the state and in society.[47]

Fourth, as we have seen, these and similar or concurrent institutional devices have serious and not too unlikely drawbacks. But implementing these devices in a Madisonian spirit of sober mistrust of the republican inclinations of everyone is preferable to the situation in many new polyarchies, where such institutions do not exist or have been rendered ineffective by delegative presidents and acquiescent legislatures.

Fifth, referring now to the liberal side of horizontal accountability, especially the one that deals with the manifold encounters of the weak and the poor with state agents, it is abundantly obvious that there is a world to be done there, as works already cited show. This is perhaps the hardest problem of all: in societies marked not only by pervasive poverty but also, and even more decisively for our theme, by deep inequalities, how to ensure that the weak and the poor are at least decently treated by those agents?[48] This theme is just too complicated to be dealt with in an essay mainly concerned with the republican dimension of horizontal accountability.[49]

Sixth, reliable and timely information is essential. Reasonably independent media and various research and dissemination institutes should play an important role, but this does not fully substitute for agencies that should be publicly supported but independent from the government that gather and make widely available data on a broad set of indicators, including (but not exclusively) economic ones.[50] What those indicators should be, the methodology of their collection, and the periodicity with which they are gathered and diffused should be decided by a pluralist, not purely governmental, authority.

Seventh, in all these matters we can hope for very little without the lively and persistent participation of the domestic actors—the media and various social organizations of vertical accountability—I have already mentioned. Transnational organizations and networks are helpful, too. But their injunctions and recommendations risk being dismissed as undue or insensitive "external interference" if they are not adopted and, so to speak, "nationalized" by domestic agents. The impact on public opinion all these actors can produce on at least issues of high corruption and egregious encroachments provides crucial, if not indispensable, support for state officials willing to pursue horizontal accountability. This is tantamount to saying—and I would like to stress this conclusion—that the effectiveness of horizontal accountability is to a significant extent contingent on the kinds of vertical accountability (including, but by no means exclusively, elections) that only polyarchy provides.

Finally, I evoke a factor that is not easy to pin down but that I do believe is important: individuals, especially political and other institutional leaders, do matter. Even in countries with a tradition of widespread corruption and repeated encroachments, the good example of highly placed individuals who act, and persuade that they act, according to the liberal and republican injunctions, can generate perhaps diffuse but still valuable public opinion support. No less important, these attitudes may encourage other strategically located individuals or agencies to risk taking similar positions. Why and how such leaders emerge is a mystery to me. The melancholy fact is that they do not seem too abundant, or successful, in most new polyarchies and that, when they reach the highest positions, they do not always live up to the expectations they raise while aiming at these positions.

These reflections and their not very optimistic mood reflect a problem to which I alluded above: the incentives for many powerfully positioned individuals and their affiliates to continue with their scarcely liberal and republican practices are extremely strong, and the prevailing democratic component of the overall situation, especially when read in a delegative code, does little to ameliorate this situation. In contrast, except for particularly altruistic individuals, the incentives for pursuing horizontal accountability are weak, especially if, as I have insisted, achieving a significant degree of such accountability requires the coordination of several agencies, each of them subject to *divide et impera* strategies.[51] The issue, finally, is the one that Madison and his allies tried to resolve: how to build powers that in a liberal and a republican mood check the trespassing temptations of other powers and that still satisfy the democratic demand of having effective governments that do not forget that they owe themselves to those who are the source of their claim to rule.

Notes

I would like to express my appreciation for the comments of Larry Diamond, Gabriela Ippolito-O'Donnell, Marcelo Leiras, Juan J. Linz, Scott Mainwaring, Sebastián Mazzuca, Gerardo Munck, Andreas Schedler, and Philippe C. Schmitter.

    1. O'Donnell, "Delegative Democracy."

    2. See, especially, Dahl, *Democracy and Its Critics,* p. 221. The attributes stated by Dahl are: (1) elected officials; (2) free and fair elections; (3) inclusive suffrage; (4) the right to run for office; (5) freedom of expression; (6) alternative information; and (7) associational autonomy. In O'Donnell, "Illusions About Consolidation," following several authors cited there, I have proposed adding: (8) elected officials (and some appointed ones, such as high court judges) should not be arbitrarily terminated before the end of their constitutionally mandated terms; (9) elected officials should not be subject to severe constraints, vetoes, or exclusion from certain policy domains by other, nonelected actors, especially the armed forces; and (10) there should be an uncontested territory that clearly defines the voting population. These ten attributes I take as jointly defining polyarchy.

    3. These cases, following Karl, "Imposing Consent?" I call "electoral regimes."

    4. The exceptions are Costa Rica, Uruguay, and, with the important caveat resulting from the constitutional privileges retained by the armed forces, Chile.

    5. As argued by Merkel, "Institutions." On South Korea and Russia, see Ziegler, "Transitional Paths"; on Russia, see also Merritt, "Review Essay."

    6. In view of sharply conflicting opinions about this matter and my own lack of direct knowledge, I prefer to suspend judgment as to the degree to which these countries may or may not have achieved reasonable degrees of horizontal accountability, comparable to those of Uruguay and Costa Rica.

    7. I use this not-self-evident term for consistency with the arguments I develop in O'Donnell, "Illusions About Consolidation." For present purposes this term can be understood as including most of the old polyarchies, those that the current literature considers to be highly institutionalized.

    8. Przeworski and Stokes, "Citizen Information," argue that, on the one hand, "democratic institutions contain no mechanisms for enforcing prospective representation," but, on the other hand, "retrospective voting, which takes as information only the past performance of the incumbent, is not sufficient to induce governments to act responsively." The authors list some institutional innovations that might ameliorate this problem, but, as we shall see, the effectiveness and even the very creation of these institutions is what should not be taken for granted under the conditions in which many new polyarchies function. In turn, looking at the functioning of governing parties in Spain but drawing more general conclusions, Maravall, "Accountability and Manipulation," argues that the control of politicians by voters faces extremely difficult, if not insurmountable, "problems of information, monitoring, and commitment" (p. 5). But see also Klingemann et al., *Parties,* and Keeler, "Opening the Window," who show that, by and large, in formally institutionalized polyarchies the policy positions presented in the electoral platforms of parties are quite good predictors of their policy orientations when in government. In contrast,

in Latin America, at least in the last two decades and in the context of the implementation of neoliberal economic policies, Przeworski and Stokes, "Citizen Information," make clear that this predictability has been almost entirely lacking.

9. See, for Latin America, Shugart and Carey, *Presidents and Assemblies;* Mainwaring and Scully, *Building Democratic Institutions;* and Mainwaring and Shugart, *Presidentialism.*

10. I believe that this inherent ambiguity is an important reason for the primarily defensive character of liberalism, in spite of recent efforts to cast it in a more positive, close to republican, light (see, e.g., Macedo, *Liberal Virtues*). I hasten to add that this does not deny that some of the "negative liberties" and constitutional constraints typical of liberalism can have empowering consequences for their individual or institutional carriers, as argued especially by Holmes, "Precommitment" and Holmes, *Passions and Constraint.*

11. In the words of Pericles, as rendered by Thucydides: "Our public men have, besides politics, their private affairs to attend to, and our ordinary citizens, though occupied with the pursuits of industry, are still fair judges of public matters" (Thucydides, *Peloponnesian War*). Before Pericles, Athens had adopted the radical innovation of paying the equivalent of a day's work for taking part in its various decisionmaking institutions, thus making possible the participation of its poor citizens (see Hansen, *Athenian Democracy*).

12. On this matter, see Finley, *Democracy,* Finley, *Politics,* and Jaeger, *Paideia;* although somewhat reluctantly, Hansen, *Athenian Democracy,* agrees with this view.

13. In this respect, although they present the issue as between two terms, not three as I am doing here, I have found Sartori, *Theory of Democracy Revisited,* Walzer, "Citizenship," Taylor, "Modes of Civil Society," and Offe and Preuss, "Democratic Institutions," extremely useful.

14. See Hansen, *Athenian Democracy,* and Manin, *Metamorphoses.*

15. By this I mean that the decisions of the Athenian assembly were subject to revision by the Dikasterion (People's Court) in terms of their conformity with written laws; but these controls were by and from the public sphere, without any purpose or idea of protecting or recognizing private rights against the demos. On this and related matters, see Hansen's masterful *Athenian Democracy.*

16. I say "in some sense" because in itself the democratic principle is mute about who should be members, or citizens, of its demos. But this need not concern us at this moment.

17. As Sartori, *Theory of Democracy Revisited* (vol. 1), recalling a term coined by Benedetto Croce, has expressed. In Latin America, this has been the main, secular guise of liberalism, which helped to create a fertile terrain for the caesaristic and delegative views I discuss below.

18. Among contemporary works in this vein, I should mention the excellent study by Rueschemeyer, Stephens, and Stephens, *Capitalist Development.* For Latin America, the most important and comprehensive reference is Collier and Collier, *Shaping the Political Arena.*

19. Or, as Rawls, "Justice as Fairness," p. 225, says in a similar context, these are "basic intuitive ideas that are embedded in the political institutions of the culturally plural societies of the modern West . . . and in the public traditions of their interpretation." Of course, it is difficult to identify authors that argue from only one of these streams, especially among the more creative—and hence less simplistic—ones. But some names stand out: Thucydides/Pericles, Rousseau, and, in his own way, Marx in the democratic stream; Hobbes, Locke, Montesquieu, and Constant in the liberal one; and Cicero, Sallust, Livy, and the Machiavelli of the *Discourses* in

the republican stream. But notice that I am arguing that the degree to which these currents became "embedded" in the actual practices, not only the formal institutions, of various polyarchies has varied quite widely.

20. I develop this argument in O'Donnell, "On the State."

21. Prominently the work of Lijphart, beginning with his seminal *Democracies.*

22. Rereading *The Federalist Papers* I was once again struck by the immense wisdom with which Madison stated and combined liberalism and republicanism. Just to insert one citation that condenses the former: "The diversity in the faculties of men, from which the rights of property originate, is not less an insuperable obstacle to a uniformity of interests. The protection of these faculties is the first object of government" (*The Federalist Papers,* no. 10). In relation to what I call below the encroachment dimension of republicanism, let us again hear Madison when he is discussing the various "departments" (i.e., main institutions) projected for the Constitution: "[N]one of them ought to posses, directly or indirectly, an overruling influence over the others in the administration of their respective powers. It will not be denied that power is of an encroaching nature and that it ought to be effectually restrained from passing the limits assigned to it" (*The Federalist Papers,* no. 48); and "Ambition must be made to counteract ambition. The interest of the man must be connected with the constitutional rights of the place . . . the private interest of every individual may be a sentinel over the public rights" (*The Federalist Papers,* no. 51). As is well known, the Federalists were avowedly antidemocratic; only later on, in a long process that arguably was completed only with the civil rights struggles of the 1950s and 1960s, were more democratic elements introduced into the U.S. Constitution, legislation, and jurisprudence; see Wood, *Radicalism,* Wood, "Democracy," and Fishkin, *Democracy and Deliberation.*

23. Among the many sources that could be cited in support of this statement, see the fascinating account Rosanvallon, "The Republic," gives of the meaning of elections in nineteenth-century France as contrasted with the Anglo-Saxon cases.

24. I do not ignore the fact that several small European countries established very early and original polyarchies. But within the scope of this chapter, I do not deal with these countries because, with the partial exception of Belgium and the Netherlands, they did not have the imperial influence that Britain, France, and the United States did.

25. Some European latecomers, not only as polyarchies but also as territorial states (Italy and Germany), were devoured by fascism and until World War II inspired reactionary, not polyarchical, alternatives. Nowadays, by contrast, the great influence of Germany in east-central Europe is evinced by the high rate of adoption of its main constitutional and electoral rules by many of these countries.

26. That I am using the French terms of this dichotomy shows that even in this very early polyarchy, the issue was a major one—one of which only Britain and the United States were spared.

27. Weber, *Economy and Society,* vol. 1, pp. 226–237, and vol. 2, pp. 1006–1069; and Linz, "Totalitarian and Authoritarian Regimes." For an interesting reelaboration and application to Latin America of these concepts, see Hartlyn, *The Struggle.*

28. In various works (see, especially, *La parole et le sang*) Touraine has insisted on a similar view, which I also elaborate in some detail in O'Donnell, *Bureaucratic Authoritarianism,* chapter 1.

29. In this definition I exclude from consideration what Collier, "Africa's External Relations," calls "agencies of restraint." I concentrate here on actions or omissions that are presumably unlawful, not on the constraints that may result from,

say, granting autonomy to a central bank or accepting various forms of economic conditionality in agreements with international agencies. These decisions are "regime neutral," in the sense that they may be adopted either by polyarchical or by authoritarian regimes. Admittedly, an argument might be made to the effect that the credibility of these agreements is enhanced if they are made by proper polyarchical procedures, but the example, among others, of Pinochet's Chile recommends adding a *ceteris paribus* caveat to such an assertion. Furthermore, not every new polyarchy has proceeded in a lawful way when making such decisions.

30. This, of course, does not mean that I consider the role of electoral courts and watchdogs unimportant. Rather, I consider this role so important that, when these institutions and their domestic and international allies cannot guarantee fair elections, the given countries cannot be considered polyarchies.

31. Paulo Sérgio Pinheiro and his collaborators in Brazil have been producing valuable work about these matters (see Pinheiro, "The Legacy," "Democracies Without Citizenship," and "Popular Responses"). In Méndez et al., *Rule of Law*, we and our collaborators look at the situation that now prevails in Latin America in relation to various ethnic minorities, women, behavior of the police, conditions of imprisonment, and the like. The best that can be said about these matters is that the liberal guarantees are partial and intermittent.

32. There is a dictum of the colonial times of Hispanic America referring to the king's legislation that tersely synthesizes this: *La ley se obedece pero no se cumple,* which rather freely translated means: the law is acknowledged but not implemented.

33. As is the case with other assertions I make here, this one implies a much larger and complicated topic. Briefly, it means that the legal systems of polyarchies are supposed to "close," in the sense that all decisions by state officials must be made according to law and are ultimately controlled by constitutional rules, including the making of new laws or regulations. Authoritarian rulers, instead, arc *de legibus solutus:* there is always the possibility that the absolutist king, the vanguard party, the military junta, or the caudillo may act with discretion, without backing of or reference to existing law.

34. Arthur Stinchcombe, *Constructing Social Theories,* usefully remarks— although he puts this issue in terms (of legitimacy) I would not use here—that the authority of state agents does not depend so much on their individual power but on their ability to mobilize other centers of power in support of their claims; the ability will be limited, "for this backing will be available only on terms accepted in other centers of power" (pp. 159–163).

35. I say "three" following the conventional usage. However, in most polyarchies, in good measure for the purpose of enhancing horizontal accountability, these institutions are actually four, as results from the division of the legislative into a senate and a chamber of deputies, or equivalents.

36. See Manin, "Checks."

37. I use the masculine because, with the exception of Indira Gandhi and Isabel Perón, and the more doubtful one of Corazón Aquino, it is almost always a "he."

38. For further discussion, see O'Donnell, "Delegative Democracy."

39. Even though this might be an extreme case, in a survey I applied in 1991 in the metropolitan area of São Paulo (n = 800), 57 percent of respondents "agreed completely" and 16 percent "agreed in part" to the statement "Instead of political parties, what is needed is that the people follow a capable and decisive man who achieves national union," and 45 percent "agreed completely" and 16 percent agreed in part with "It is preferable to have a government that imposes its will, if it

makes fast decisions" (*Em vez de partidos políticos, o que é preciso é o povo seguir um homem competente e decidido que faça a unidade nacional,* and *É melhor um governo que imponha a sua vontade, desde que tome medidas logo;* my translation). /

40. An Argentine anecdote: when criticized for the rather blatant subservience of the supreme court to President Menem, a judge of this court argued that, since Menem had been elected by a majority of Argentines and consequently embodies (*encarna*) the popular will, it would be improper for the court to interfere with his policies.

41. See, for example, Palermo and Novaro, *Política.* Scott Mainwaring insisted on the same point in a personal communication.

42. For recent analyses of federalist patterns and some implications relevant to the present discussion, see Gibson, "The Populist Road," and Mainwaring and Samuels, "Robust Federalism."

43. This is another reason for differentiating this kind of issue from the unlawful ones I discuss here.

44. The use of the word *directly* points to the larger latitude that exists in some countries for actions that in others would still be considered the unlawful, albeit indirectly derived, enrichment of a public official, such as "consultancies" provided by associates of officials to business dealings with their agencies, or various kinds of *pantouflage.* Another caveat: in the text I mean by "bribes" those that in a given culture are considered large or for some reason morally outrageous; giving some money to a petty official for accelerating a bureaucratic process or to a policeman for avoiding a speeding ticket is hardly considered condemnable in many countries.

45. In terms of the argument I am presenting here, it may be of some interest to note that in all countries with which I am familiar, the division of labor among these organizations follows quite closely this tripartite—democratic, liberal, and republican—pattern.

46. In which case, for example, it may use these positions for blackmailing the government.

47. Brazil is an example of this. The Brazilian judiciary has obtained a very high degree of autonomy in relation to the executive and congress, but no visible improvement in its (in most cases extremely poor) performance has occurred. But the judiciary has used this autonomy for assigning to judges and other personnel extremely high salaries and, especially in the case of high courts and some state courts, enormous privileges.

48. I allude here to Avishai Margalit's interesting idea that a decent society is one that has institutions that do not humiliate its members (see Margalit, *The Decent Society*). For commentaries and doubts about this notion, see the special issue of *Social Research* (Spring 1997).

49. I discuss some aspects of this theme in my chapter in Méndez et al., *The Rule of Law.*

50. It is surely no accident that in one of the two more fully democratic countries in Latin America, Costa Rica, an independent group, jointly sponsored by the Office of the Ombudsman, the Council of National Universities, and various social organizations, issues every year a valuable and widely discussed report (*Estado de la Nación*) of the kind I suggest above. This same group, led by Miguel Gutiérrez Saxe and Jorge Vargas Cullell, is exploring the publication of another report, specifically aimed at assessing changes in the "quality of democracy" in this country.

51. Further research on this emerging theme of horizontal accountability in new polyarchies will have to take into account the interesting literature about the controls that, especially, the United States Congress attempts to exercise over the executive, including the semiautonomous agencies of the latter. Insofar as it mainly

focuses on Congress, this literature touches on only one—and not the most decisive one in new polyarchies—of the institutions of horizontal accountability. But, in particular, the distinction that some of these authors make between controls in the form of "police patrols" and of "fire alarms" seems to me very suggestive; see, especially, McCubbins and Schwartz, "Congressional Oversight Overlooked," McCubbins et al., "Administrative Procedures," Weingast and Marshall, "The Industrial Organization," Kiewiet and McCubbins, *The Logic of Delegation,* and Tsebelis, "Monitoring." Even though this matter requires more detailed analysis, I suspect that the effectiveness of the permanent preventive mechanisms characterized as "police patrols" and, even more, of the presumably more effective mechanism of "fire alarms" (by which various actors, private and public, occasionally find reason to trigger mechanisms of horizontal accountability), presupposes the existence, authorization, and empowerment of the very public agencies whose absence, weakness, or cooptation defines the problems I discuss in this chapter.

4

Comments on O'Donnell

■ Democracy and Constitutionalism
RICHARD L. SKLAR

Accountability is an elusive conception. To my mind, it implies the right of persons who are affected by an action or decision to receive an explanation of what has been done and to render judgments on the conduct of those who were responsible for doing it. Guillermo O'Donnell has classified the forms of political accountability thus. Horizontal accountability connotes the obligation of officeholders to answer for their actions to one another; vertical accountability signifies the right of persons who are affected by the actions or decisions of officeholders or leaders to renew, rescind, or revise the mandates of those who exercise authority.

Conceptions of horizontal and vertical accountability correspond to the ideas of constitutionalism and democracy, respectively. In practice, the processes associated with the latter set of ideas are closely related. Often those processes are conflictual and mutually reinforcing at one and the same time. For example, constitutional checks and balances are designed to repel threats to democracy by demagogic politicians. Conversely, popular power can often prevent the degeneration of constitutional government into an oligarchy of officeholders and their influential supporters. Clarity about the difference between these two forms of accountability, and the functional qualities of each, is needed to avert both intellectual confusion and the ensuing dangers of political disillusionment.

The relationship between constitutionalism and democracy has always been a vital issue for political scientists who work in the field of public law. During the past half century, however, professional political scientists have largely abandoned the study of constitutionalism to legal scholars, for whom questions of political theory are relatively incidental. I do not mean to imply that legal scholarship is any less theoretical than disciplinary political theory, or to underestimate the significance of contributions by contemporary political scientists to the theory of constitutional government. Yet, as anyone who is familiar with the discipline of political science would know, behavioral, quantitative, and, more recently, ahistorical methodologies have crowded constitutionalism to the margins of disciplinary discourse. However, the concept of accountability, as it is understood by O'Donnell, may foreshadow the revival of constitutionalist thought as a branch of comparative politics. If so, it would be useful for comparativists to revisit the debates of an earlier generation of constitutional scholars.

For discerning guidance into the issues of constitutionalist political theory in the twentieth century, one may turn to an illuminating essay by Harvey Wheeler, published in the 1975 *Handbook of Political Science*.[1] The central issue, as seen by Wheeler,[2] is defined with reference to the rival theories of Charles Howard McIlwain and Francis Dunham Wormuth, authors of books that may well be the two most significant works on this subject in the English language.[3]

McIlwain believed that constitutional freedom is a product of the rule of law, which, he declared, has been present in the words of jurists and philosophers since ancient times. In his opinion, which presupposed the relatively independent progress of ideas in history, no particular structure of government would ever be absolutely necessary for the rule of law to prevail. Indeed, he was specifically opposed to the structural separation of powers, entailing separate and distinct legislative, executive, and judicial branches of government, as practiced in the United States. Instead, he favored a British-style emphasis on popular democracy manifest, in modern times, through effective, issue-oriented, political parties. Hence, McIlwain thought that constitutional government rested on a dualistic historical foundation comprising "the higher-law and vox-populi traditions"[4]—one being an intellectual heritage of the Western world, the other embodied in the democratic institutions of every free people.

In the metaphorical idiom adopted for this book, McIlwain's perspective was entirely vertical: it encompassed the idea of democratic accountability (of rulers to the people) as well as that of celestial or heavenly accountability. The latter idea, however, cannot be incorporated into a strictly empirical theory of government. Yet an "appeal to heaven" (Locke), or to "the laws of nature and of nature's God" (the Declaration of Independence of the United States of America), will signify an affirmation of the proverbial rule of law, which is widely and correctly considered to be the very essence of constitutionalism.

In opposition to McIlwain, Wormuth insisted on the primacy of structure. He conceived of constitutionalism as a form of government designed to protect certain principles of liberty whether or not they are supported by popular currents of opinion. The first principle of constitutional government is that law must be general and prospective in its application: general in that it should apply to all citizens equally; prospective in that it should not impose penalties on past actions that were not illegal when they were carried out. Wormuth discovered the origin of this fundamental principle in the thought of the seventeenth-century Levellers, who were stalwart democrats, and other persons who, like the Levellers, espoused republicanism and proposed innovative constitutional ideas during the era of the English civil wars. Although the separation of powers as an institutional device expired in Britain, when the monarchy and House of Lords were resurrected, the idea migrated to republican America, where it became the cornerstone of American constitutional theory more than a century later.

Comparative constitutional theorists who adopt a Wormuthian-structuralist perspective will be heartened and stimulated by O'Donnell's elucidation of the forms of horizontal accountability. His basic distinction between the liberal and republican components of horizontal accountability appears to be as fruitful in this context as it has been in recent and current analyses of citizenship.[5] Formulated as a structural conception, it can be advanced as an approach to constitutionalism that is not derived exclusively or primarily from Western precedents or political theories. Although O'Donnell has traced the origin of republicanism to ancient Rome, and that of liberalism to the feudal societies of medieval Europe as well as seventeenth-century England and eighteenth-century France, non-European historical origins of limited (or liberal) and responsible (or republican) government can be identified in every part of the world with reference to the political histories of the peoples concerned.

In O'Donnell's essay, "the republican dimension of horizontal accountability" has been highlighted for special attention. Just as the liberal dimension is often compromised by the "unlawful encroachment" of officeholders into jurisdictions beyond the scope of their legitimate authority, so too is the republican dimension imperiled by the blight of corrupt conduct. In recent years, the problem of corruption in fledgling democracies, or polyarchies (the term favored by O'Donnell for "really existing democracies"), has engaged the attention of analysts who have described its debilitating effects but have not yet explained why corruption necessarily subverts the democratic (or polyarchic) form of government. O'Donnell does so by demonstrating the utility of the republican idea as an intellectual tool for coping with the problem of corrupt conduct by persons in authority. Such conduct erodes the republican foundation of public service by leaders and officeholders whose duty it is to place the common good ahead of their private interests. This portion of O'Donnell's essay imparts cohesion to the book as a whole by establishing a relationship, born of republican virtue, between electoral and judicial topics, on the one hand, and ethical as well as fiscal issues, on the other. Furthermore, with respect to abuses of authority by public officials, O'Donnell has drawn attention to the need for empirical research and thinking on the all-too-commonplace maltreatment of relatively defenseless and underprivileged people by governmental agents. Although O'Donnell conceives of horizontal accountability as being a relationship between agencies of the state, the idea could be broadened to encompass remedies for abuses of authority by the officials of nongovernmental public institutions—for instance, health maintenance organizations and universities. In modern societies, it is not at all uncommon for the principles of constitutional government to regulate the conduct of voluntary membership organizations as well as the agencies of sovereign states.

While the horizontal dimension of accountability can be enlarged to incorporate relationships that lie beyond the jurisdiction of the state, it still cannot embrace the entire field of constitutional thought and practice. There is yet the realm of metaphysical thought, and beliefs in justice, based on philosophical principles and customary rights. The juristic theory of constitutions, espoused by McIlwain, is manifest in the moral dedication of individuals who have the courage to declare, with celestial fervor, that the abuse of governmental power is intolerable, that tyrannicide is just, and that no one should have to endure duplicity on the part of rulers in silence.

In every age, martyrs and prisoners of conscience remind us that constitutionalism is a value of universal importance. Although their sacrifices may often appear to be in vain, they can, and sometimes do, make an indelible impression on thought and change. Consider these contemporary examples: Nelson Mandela, president of South Africa (after twenty-seven years in prison) and a staunch constitutionalist; Moshood Abiola, elected president of Nigeria in 1993, who languished until his suspicious death in 1998 in a military prison after his refusal to relinquish his rightful claim to office in 1994; Daw Aung San Suu Kyi, under house arrest for six years and subject subsequently to restrictions on her movement in Myanmar, for refusing to countenance military usurpation following her political party's electoral victory in 1990; Wei Jingsheng, imprisoned and maltreated for eighteen years in China for his constitutional and democratic beliefs.

Why do such persons emerge as political leaders? O'Donnell calls it "a mystery," which it is. The appeal to heaven—celestial accountability—is neither horizontal nor structurally vertical. It is properly termed juristic and metaphysical; hence it defies systematization.

In U.S. jurisprudence, both traditions of constitutional thought have been maintained with vigor by justices of the Supreme Court. In structuralist thought, the separation of powers is often cited as a bulwark of liberty. For example, in 1965, the Court invalidated a law that prohibited service in an official capacity by, or employment of, a member of the Communist

Party in a labor union, holding that the act in question violated the bill of attainder clause in Article I, Section 9 of the Constitution. Chief Justice Earl Warren cited the intent of the framers of the Constitution in support of his contention that this clause was meant to implement the overall separation of powers, itself "a general safeguard against legislative exercise of the judicial function, or more simply—trial by legislature."[6]

Concurrently, the juristic tradition, consisting mainly of ideas derived from philosophical or spiritual beliefs, has been manifest in landmark judgments involving personal rights, including privacy and childbearing. Thus, in 1961, Justice John Harlan introduced the idea of "a rational continuum" to represent the traditions of freedom that bind the American people.[7] This formulation has appealed to jurists of diverse ideological persuasions. It has been interpreted broadly to embrace the abstract, Roman and Christian, traditions of natural law as well as specifically Anglo-American principles of individual liberty. In 1992, the moral authority of Harlan's theory was invoked by Justice Sandra Day O'Connor to uphold the right of a woman to decide whether or not to terminate her pregnancy.[8] Justice O'Connor's opinion for the Court displayed the vitality of both jurisprudential traditions in American legal thought.

Between the sixteenth and twentieth centuries, agents of Western imperial expansion propagated Western political ideas, including the concepts of natural law and right, throughout the world. In our time, the intellectuals of non-Western countries increasingly rely on their own philosophical traditions for constitutional and political guidance. Although the "grand tradition" of Western political ideas is universally respected, it is no longer the supreme source of moral authority for most of the world. By contrast with juristic conceptions of constitutionalism, structuralist conceptions are imbued with little spiritual content. For that reason, they are likely to appeal to proponents of liberty in many different cultures who wish to establish the principles of free government on philosophical principles derived from indigenous sources.[9] For that reason too, scholars in the field of comparative government will be attracted strongly to the transcultural qualities of structuralist thought.

Still, structuralist constitutionalism without the appeal to heaven would be a mechanical and somewhat soulless artifact. By itself, structuralism is not enough. We need both traditions—that of McIlwain, or his counterparts in other cultures, and that of Wormuth. We need the juristic rule of law as well as the rule of law derived from principles of structural analysis, each in due and sufficient measure.

Notes

I am indebted to Scott R. Bowman for his wise counsel.
    1. Wheeler, "Constitutionalism."

2. Ibid., pp. 33–37.

3. See McIlwain, *Constitutionalism,* and Wormuth, *The Origins.*

4. Wheeler, "Constitutionalism," p. 33.

5. See Peled, "Ethnic Democracy," Halisi, "From Liberation to Citizenship," Ndegwa, "Citizenship and Ethnicity."

6. *United States v. Brown,* 381 U.S. 437, 442 (1965); see also Wormuth, "Legislative Disqualifications."

7. *Poe v. Ullman,* 367 U.S. 497, 523 (1961). Harlan, J., dissenting.

8. *Planned Parenthood of Southeastern Pennsylvania v. Casey,* 505 U.S. 833 (1992).

9. The principles of procedural due process, as they have been developed in the United States, are frequently cited by courts throughout the world. For an African example, see Sklar, "Reds and Rights."

*   *   *

■ The Limits of Horizontal Accountability
PHILIPPE C. SCHMITTER

Guillermo O'Donnell has (as usual) given us something important to reflect upon. His concept of "horizontal accountability" should be of considerable utility for those who are seeking to understand the type and quality of democracy that may be emerging in the aftermath of recent regime changes—provided it is used circumspectly and sparingly. I suspect that it will be much less useful to those who are merely trying to discern whether any kind of democracy will be consolidated in these countries.[1]

My basic sympathy with his approach should be apparent to anyone reading the article I wrote with Terry Karl entitled "What Democracy Is . . . And Is Not" in which we define modern political democracy (note the qualifying adjectives) as "a regime or system of governance in which rulers are held *accountable* for their actions in the public realm by citizens, acting indirectly through the competition and cooperation of their representatives."[2] Accountability is central to virtually all "procedural"—as opposed to substantive—definitions of democracy. But note that Terry Karl and I stressed exclusively the classical *vertical* relationship between citizens and rulers. We quite explicitly argued that this link between those in positions of authority and those subjected to their actions was manifold and not confined to the periodic process of choosing between electoral candidates proposed by political parties, but we deliberately left out any mention of the "format" of executive-legislative-judicial power. O'Donnell's conceptualization of horizontal accountability forcefully invites us to include it.

Horizontal accountability belongs to a widely populated genus of arguments that assert the necessity for democracy to protect itself from its own potential for self-destruction. Beginning with Aristotle, theorists have argued in favor of "mixed regimes"—modes of political decisionmaking that tempered the extremes of any one "pure" form of rule with elements coming from other forms. So, government by the many (democracy) had to be offset by other institutions that incorporated the few (aristocracy) and the one (monarchy) if it were to avoid rule by the undifferentiated and easily incited masses (mob-archy?). This line of reasoning was recast in a more modern mold by Montesquieu in his disquisition on the separation of executive-legislative-judicial powers and the establishment of a stable system of checks and balances among them. Virtually any contemporary text in constitutional law—especially if it is written by an Anglo-American or German author—takes such a position for granted.

If we take a look at O'Donnell's definition of horizontal accountability, we shall see that it conforms very closely (too closely in my opinion) to this classical genus: "the existence of *state* agencies that are legally enabled and empowered, and factually willing and able, to take actions that span from routine oversight to criminal sanctions or impeachment in relation to actions or omissions by other agents or agencies of the state that may be qualified as unlawful" (p. 38, this volume, emphasis added).

The most glaring limitation is to restrict the notion to "state" agencies and thereby exclude the possibility that horizontal accountability might also be exercised by nonstate actors—media organizations, party secretariats, trade union confederations, business peak associations, lawyers' guilds, mass social movements, even large capitalist firms—that could not only denounce the infractions of officials but even bring appropriate sanctions to bear on them. At least in countries with a strong state tradition, I believe that there is every reason to suspect that state agencies, no matter how formally independent from each other, will tend to collude—all in the name of "the national interest," *Staatsraison*, or, simply, the corporate interests of the state bureaucracy. Horizontal accountability might be better served if it were rooted in permanent organizations that were well informed and powerful enough to face up to state agencies/agents without sharing the same public legal status or the same collective mentality.

The second questionable assumption is that the "triggering mechanism" for horizontal accountability should be unlawfulness. Not only does this presume that the law itself is "democratic" and neutral with respect to conflicting conceptions of interest or passion, but it also implies that actions that are legal must also be legitimate in the eyes of the citizenry. One has only to glance at the recent headlines of U.S. newspapers to discover that minor legal infractions can be used by partisan opponents to thwart the clearly expressed preference of the public-at-large and that rulers can be held accountable to cultural standards of behavior that are not necessarily unlawful. I submit that one of the proper democratic functions of horizontal accountability should be to hold rulers accountable for the political and not just legal consequences of their behavior in office.

The definition itself does not specify which state agencies should be empowered to act "horizontally" in defense of lawfulness. In the body of O'Donnell's chapter, it becomes clear that he has in mind the usual three suspects—the legislature, the judiciary, and the public administration—and that their primary responsibility (in Latin America) is to keep the executive in check. Elsewhere, in less presidential settings, O'Donnell would presumably agree that the source of illegal, arbitrary, or undemocratic action could originate in any one of these three powers and that it would then be the function of the executive to countermand or override its actions. But what about such perfectly legitimate state agencies/agents as the general staff of the armed forces, the central bank, the governor of a particular subnational unit, the chief executive of the national airline, or the head of the national board of film censorship? Should all of these be formally entitled to exercise "horizontal powers"? Just those who have themselves been popularly elected or approved by some elected body? And what might be the consequences if too many state agencies/agents were accorded such powers? Would it not be likely that so many potential "veto players" interacting with so many different interpretations of the law would simply produce a stalemate? Whatever the polity would have gained in terms of the quality of its democracy, it might risk losing even more in terms of the quality of its capacity to act.

Finally, O'Donnell's definition leaves out one very critical dimension of accountability—whether vertical or horizontal—which is time. It makes a great deal of difference whether rulers can be prevented ex ante from taking measures that are either unlawful or impolitic or whether these sanctions are only applied ex post, that is, once the actions have been implemented and had their impact on citizens who are then entitled to complain or sue for redress. With his emphasis on lawfulness, I presume that O'Donnell is referring only to the ex post variety since most legal actions require evidence of injurious actions previously taken. If, however, one were to free the concept from its legalistic and statist constraints, then horizontal accountability could be invoked by a wide range of organizations that would be responsible for signaling their dissent before a given measure was even enacted, much less implemented. In other words, just as vertical accountability is not restricted to "throwing the bastards out" after they have disappointed the voters, the horizontal variety should also have the capacity to set and restrict agendas and not just react to whatever authorities have already done.

To conclude, I agree that horizontal accountability is a potentially important concept, but I would define it generically as follows: the existence of permanently constituted, mutually recognized collective actors at multiple levels of aggregation within a polity that have equivalent capacities to monitor each other's behavior and to react to each other's initiatives.[3] These countervailing powers can be constituted of different mixes of public and private organizations, and they may act out of purely political as well as legal motives. Ideally—that is, in the highest-quality democracies—their power resources would be as close to equal as their different numbers and intensities would merit, and their internal composition would be based on the principle of citizenship, that is, on the equality of rights and obligations of their respective members. Following this argument, the most democratic form of horizontal accountability would be rooted in a constitutional design that maximizes the probability that independent constituencies of citizens based on overlapping territorial and functional criteria compete with each other in setting the policy agenda, making the policy choices, and monitoring the policy consequences. For the most concise statement of this "democratic-liberal-republican-pluralist" position, see James Madison's *Federalist Papers,* no. 10.

Of course, in the world of "really existing" democracies, many of these horizontally countervailing organizations will not be constituted only by citizens, and some may even be found within the state apparatus. This, however, is decidedly suboptimal from the perspective of democratic practice, and it is certainly suboptimal from the perspective of democratic theory.[4]

Notes

1. For lack of assigned space, I will (reluctantly) pass up the chance to comment on the second major theme that is present in the aforementioned article and other of his recent writings—namely, the confident assertion that all of Latin America's neodemocracies (and some of its archeodemocracies) have been unusually "poor" or even "perverse" in their respective performances. It is, of course, of the very nature of the concept of democracy that it is never perfectly embodied in "really existing" institutions; hence, democratic theorists unfailingly point to the defects in any system they are studying. Just to make things worse, the criteria for evaluation are constantly becoming more demanding. No one criticizes today's democracies for not living up to the much lower standards set by their nineteenth-century forerunners. But even if one banishes from one's theoretical memory the rotten boroughs, the restricted franchises, the machine politics, the "class justice" of so many courts, the financial scandals, the pervasive vote buying and vote stealing—not to mention the outright racial intimidation and social coercion that deprived so many citizens of their rights—I wonder whether today's so-called delegative democracies are really that bad. I am even more skeptical about assuming that this is the outcome for the foreseeable future and that such "mis-founded" or "mis-guided" democracies have no intrinsic capacity to use their mechanisms of competition and cooperation to correct whatever initial perversions they may have suffered. This blanket judgment—presumably based on a normative comparison with neodemocracies in other parts of the world—forms the backdrop for the narrower reflections raised in this essay, since it is the alleged absence of horizontal accountability that is in large part responsible for the alleged poor performance.

2. See Schmitter and Karl, "What Democracy Is," p. 76 (emphasis added).

3. Note that I did not say "equal"—just equivalent in the sense that they have some capacity to deter or extract compensation from each other, but not necessarily enough to prevent action from being taken. Note also that this is a putative property of any and all levels of a given polity, not just something one might expect to find at the national level.

4. I may have a solution that will please both O'Donnell and me. What if we restricted the notion of "horizontal accountability" to purely state institutions that enforce legal norms on each other and adopt the notion of "oblique accountability" to cover efforts by nonstate or semistate institutions that seek to wield countervailing powers in order to hold rulers accountable, not just for their legal transgressions but also for their political misdeeds, but depend on their oblique capacity to enhance citizen awareness and collective action in order to back up their actions?

*   *   *

■ Traditions of Accountability
MARC F. PLATTNER

Guillermo O'Donnell's essay on horizontal accountability is characteristically original, insightful, and thought provoking. Beginning from the practical problems confronting new democracies in Latin America and elsewhere, he quickly finds his way back to fundamental questions of political institutions and political theory. In the process he rediscovers not only the continuing importance of the doctrine of the separation of powers but the wisdom of that doctrine's leading eighteenth-century exponents, especially James Madison. The terrain that O'Donnell explores is extremely fertile for understanding the character and the dilemmas of contemporary democracies.

The most novel of his suggestions is that "polyarchies" (the term he borrows from Robert Dahl to describe "really existing democracies") are an uneasy synthesis of what he calls the "liberal," "republican," and "democratic" traditions. As he himself notes, by separating out three distinct components of our modern democratic heritage, he is departing from the more common analyses that point to a tension between only two traditions: either liberal versus republican, or liberal versus democratic. Yet the very fact that this two-sided opposition is presented in these two different versions provides prima facie evidence that O'Donnell is on to something.

Liberalism, with its emphasis on the protection of the private sphere and of the rights of individuals and minorities, may be opposed to republicanism, with its emphasis on civic unity, public-spiritedness, and active citizenship. But liberalism may also be opposed to democracy, with its emphasis on egalitarianism and the rule of the majority. While republicanism and democracy are often found in combination, they are not intrinsically linked; there can be, and have been, aristocratic republics. Liberalism too may be combined with democracy (understood in terms of universal suffrage), as it almost invariably is in the contemporary world, but it has also been compatible with such nonegalitarian regimes as constitutional monarchy.

In arguing for the existence of a separate "democratic" tradition that cannot simply be subsumed under the liberal or the republican, one may also point to the common egalitarian strand that links modern liberal democracies with premodern and nonliberal ones. That is why both the rosy depiction of Athenian democracy in Thucydides' account of Pericles' funeral oration and Socrates' critical depiction of Athenian-style democracy in Book VIII of Plato's *Republic* strike us as portraying a regime resembling those of the present day.[1]

In characterizing the differences among the three traditions, O'Donnell is generally on target in his description of the liberal tradition. The same cannot always be said about the way in which he characterizes the republican and democratic traditions. Correctly noting that republicanism, contrary to liberalism, exalts the public above the private sphere, he puzzlingly concludes from this that republicanism emphasizes the crucial distinction between these two spheres, while democracy is "monistic," admitting no valid distinction between them. Yet Sparta, which he cites along with Rome as the source of the republican tradition, was immensely more restrictive of the private lives of its citizens than was Athens, which he identifies as the source of the democratic tradition. O'Donnell also dubiously contends that the republican tradition embraces the idea of political representation, which he correctly notes was rejected by Athens and by Jean-Jacques Rousseau, whom he identifies as a champion of democracy. Yet Sparta and Rome, like Athens, were essentially "direct" rather than representative democracies; as for Rousseau, he was a much greater admirer of Sparta and Rome than of Athens. O'Donnell also claims that republicanism is "elitist," in that it stresses the importance of virtue, understood as dedication to the public good. But Rousseau argues that virtue so understood—the "sublime science of simple souls"[2]—is within the reach of all, and hence that a society that honors virtue is more democratic than one that honors talents.

When he comes to his more concrete discussion of the issue of horizontal accountability, O'Donnell seems to view the republican tradition as calling primarily for political leaders to be subordinated to the law and prevented from pursuing their private interests at the expense of the public interest. Given republicanism's emphasis on probity and its exaltation of the public good above all private interest, this is not unreasonable, but it is perhaps somewhat misleading. Virtually all political regimes—and not just polyarchies or other popular governments—endorse law-abidingness and oppose corruption. Every government must be concerned with holding its subordinate officials accountable so that they obey that government's rules and serve its interests, rather than using their office to procure illicit private benefits to its detriment. The most despotic governments have laws against corruption and sometimes punish government officials for violating them. Even a mafia chieftain must be concerned lest his subordinates are stealing from him.

The characteristically republican solution to the problem of corruption, however, was not the separation of powers, which, after all, is a modern innovation. Premodern republics were all small polities where the citizens were directly engaged in governing themselves and were typically themselves involved in "examining the accounts, the acts, the stewardship of the magistrates; in calling them to appear in front of the assembled people, in accusing, condemning or absolving them."[3] Rather than resorting to elaborate institutional mechanisms, they relied primarily on the public-spiritedness of their citizens and accordingly put great emphasis on morals and education.

Reliance on horizontal accountability (fostered by the separation of powers) to control government officials, I would argue, stems primarily from the liberal tradition. While the thinkers in this tradition did not altogether neglect the importance of educating citizens, they were more skeptical about its effectiveness. As James Madison put it in *The Federalist Papers,* no. 10, "If the impulse and the opportunity be suffered to coincide, we well know that neither moral nor religious motives can be relied on as an adequate control." And in *The Federalist Papers,* no. 51, where he explains the principle of constitutional checks and balances, he speaks of the "policy of supplying, by opposite and rival interests, the defect of better motives."

This was not merely a matter of the liberal tradition taking a less optimistic view of human nature than the republican. Many of the goods the liberal tradition sought to foster were incompatible with the austere virtue and selflessness demanded by republicanism. The liberal tradition encouraged individuals to occupy themselves with the pursuit of wealth and favored commerce over war. It valued the protection of private rights, especially the right of property. Republicanism, because it sought to promote civic unity and involvement, was at home in the small city-state. Liberalism, by contrast, favored "extend[ing] the sphere" in order to embrace a multiplicity of different interests among the citizens. For these reasons, liberalism adopted the principle of representative government.

In a larger country, government must necessarily be more remote from the people. Moreover, in a society where people are primarily concerned with their private affairs and with preventing government from encroaching on their private rights and liberties, limiting the reach and scope of government becomes essential. Under such conditions, the issue of accountability takes on particular urgency. One might say that for republicanism the overarching concern is that government be able to fulfill its proper ends, while for liberalism the most important consideration is that government not overstep its proper boundaries. The latter view obviously heightens the imperative for seeking to hold government accountable.

Where does the democratic tradition fit in all this? The classic formulation of the separation of powers argument by Montesquieu does not have a specifically democratic character. Taking England as his model, he calls for the executive branch to be occupied by a monarch and for one house in the legislative branch to be composed of a hereditary nobility. Only the lower house of the legislature represents and derives its power from the people (a term Montesquieu still uses in opposition to, and not as inclusive of, the nobility).[4] By contrast, the authors of *The Federalist Papers* make it clear that all the branches of the government derive from the people (in the inclusive sense of the term).[5]

In *The Federalist Papers,* no. 49, in the midst of five papers explicitly devoted to the issue of the separation of powers (nos. 47–51), Madison considers the suggestion made by Thomas Jefferson for establishing a mechanism that would allow disputes between the branches of government to be settled by recourse to a convention of the people. Madison finally rejects this idea on a variety of practical grounds, including "the danger of disturbing the public tranquility by interesting too strongly the public passions."

This no doubt is the kind of thing O'Donnell has in mind when he speaks of "the Federalists" as being "antidemocratic." Yet Madison fully endorses the theoretical premise underlying Jefferson's proposal—namely, that "the people are the only legitimate fountain of power, and it is from them that the constitutional charter, under which the several branches of government hold their power, is derived."[6] In a liberal democracy, the fundamental law to which governmental officials are held accountable is the constitution, which in turn draws its authority from the explicit consent of the people. Despite their reluctance to have the people in their collective capacity directly engage in political affairs on a continuing basis, the authors of *The Federalist Papers* consistently reaffirm the view that "all legitimate authority"[7] derives from the people, and that governments are merely their "agents and trustees."[8]

It is this democratic dimension, the notion that governments are simply agents and trustees for the people, that gives the concept of accountability its centrality in contemporary discussions of democracy. Thus, as Philippe Schmitter notes in his own contribution to this book, he and Terry Karl have defined modern political democracy as "a system of governance in which rulers are held accountable for their actions in the public realm by citizens, acting indirectly through the competition and cooperation of their representatives."[9] It is hard to imagine monarchy, aristocracy, or indeed any other type of regime being defined in terms of accountability. It is precisely because the people do not rule directly but are the source of all political authority that accountability—ultimately meaning accountability *to the people*—can be seen as a defining feature of modern liberal democracy.

Notes

1. Thucydides, *History of the Peloponnesian War,* vol. 2, pp. xxxv–xlvi; Plato, *The Republic,* pp. 557a–562a.

2. Jean-Jacques Rousseau, "Discourse on the Arts and Sciences," in Rousseau, *The First and Second Discourses,* p. 64. On virtue versus talents, see ibid., p. 58; on Rousseau's praise of Sparta over Athens, see ibid., p. 43.

3. Benjamin Constant, "The Liberty of the Ancients Compared with That of the Moderns," in Constant, *Political Writings,* p. 311. This splendid essay is an excellent guide to the contrast between the ancient republican and the modern liberal spirit.

4. Montesquieu, *The Spirit of the Laws,* Book 11, p. 6.

5. This point is overlooked in Philippe Schmitter's contribution to this volume when he presents the separation of powers as a version of a "mixed regime."

6. Ibid., pp. 313–314.

7. *The Federalist Papers,* no. 22.

8. *The Federalist Papers,* no. 46.

9. Schmitter and Karl, "What Democracy Is," p. 76.

*   *   *

■ A Response to My Commentators
GUILLERMO O'DONNELL

I begin by thanking the editors of this book for the privilege of having invited three distinguished scholars to comment on my chapter. It goes without saying that I am no less thankful to Philippe Schmitter, Marc Plattner, and Richard Sklar for their interesting and incisive commentaries. Together, even though my responses range from almost complete disagreement to almost complete agreement, I hope we have jointly advanced in a discussion that is as classic as it is timely.

I

Philippe Schmitter has (as usual) written an interesting and incisive commentary. I am glad that he considers the concept of horizontal accountability of "considerable utility," and I strongly agree that its utility is contingent on using this concept "circumspectly and sparingly." Precisely because I agree with this caveat, I disagree with most of what Schmitter proposes in the rest of his piece.

Schmitter presents a list of "nonstate" agents that, in a way that defeats his well-taken caveat, he suggests might be conceived as exercising still another kind of accountability, an "oblique" one. I prefer to see these agents (which in my chapter I subsume more succinctly under the rubric of various social agents and demands) as exercising vertical accountability in addition to elections. The basic image here is, of course, of society through its organizations and movements and of individuals through elections addressing, and eventually calling into account, the incumbents of positions in the state and the regime.

The opposite image, of horizontality, points to relations among these incumbents. There is nothing particularly "legalistic and statistic" in this view. It happens that, when horizontal accountability is reasonably effective, the respective actors are individuals and institutions that occupy positions in the regime and the state and that these positions are legally defined and regulated. As a consequence, the "triggering mechanism" of horizontal accountability (but not of many other conflictive interactions into which these actors may enter too, and which Schmitter seems to confuse with the former) is, indeed, the presumed unlawfulness of a given action.

Such action may not be necessarily already undertaken, but Schmitter argues that the concept I have proposed leaves out "time." Rather, I would have thought obvious that my view does not preclude actions that, under appropriately (that is, legally) defined circumstances, certain state agents may undertake to prevent the implementation of decisions by other such agents. Furthermore, Schmitter wonders if some nonelected but "perfectly legitimate state agencies/agents" such as a central bank and others may exercise horizontal accountability. The answer, again, seems to me quite obvious. First, this kind of question is better answered by a specific study of the particular country and institution in question. Second, in general, it is conceivable that—again, according to appropriately defined criteria—some of these institutions may be endowed with the authority of exercising, or promoting, horizontal accountability within the scope of their respective jurisdictions.

Perhaps the context of these criticisms is the concern that Schmitter expresses about excesses and stalemates that horizontal accountability may provoke. I concur with this (classic) preoccupation. But I hasten to add that this risk seems to me vastly preferable, and probably easier to remedy, than the problems that result from the situations of at best tenuous and intermittent horizontal accountability that have motivated my text.

Finally, Schmitter's ruminations about our disagreements concerning "today's so-called delegative democracies" are too complex and important to be confined to a footnote and to the couple of paragraphs I could devote to this matter here.

II

As for Marc Plattner's interesting and learned commentary, we are basically in agreement. At least, our disagreements exist in the context of a shared overall view of the relatively distinct, partially overlapping, and in some important senses conflictive contributions of three currents—democracy, liberalism, and republicanism—to contemporary polyarchies. Given this shared perspective, I can comment rather briefly on our disagreements.

First, I realize I should have been more explicit when I referred to Sparta as, "according to some authors," an important antecedent of republicanism. With that expression I wanted to indicate that such a view was not shared by all republican authors. The author I did have in mind as having such a view was indeed Rousseau, as Plattner properly perceived. In this sense our disagreement turns around our respective readings of an author so particularly complex and in various senses profoundly ambivalent as Rousseau was—a topic we cannot hope to elucidate here.

Second, I wonder if Plattner's statement that "[e]very government must be concerned with holding its subordinate officials accountable" is a normative or an empirical one. If it is the first, there is no dispute here. If it is the second, I must disagree with the additional assertion that "[v]irtually all regimes . . . endorse law-abidingness and oppose corruption." Some authoritarian regimes are arbitrary to the extent that they have little or no notion of lawfulness, while others may impose their own laws on the subject population, but all of them share the (antirepublican) view that rulers are *de legibus solutus,* above the law.[1] Furthermore, as an abundant literature attests,[2] some regimes not only are systematically predatory but they also ignore the very meaning of the term *corruption.* Finally, even though as Plattner asserts, and I concur in my chapter, that the republican tradition "put[s] great emphasis on morals and education," one should not forget that the arguably purer example of republicanism, the Italian republics, resorted to extremely "elaborate institutional mechanisms" of horizontal control of the *podestás* and other high officials.[3]

Third, in relation to the Federalists, as was the case with Rousseau, Plattner's disagreement with my opinion that they were much more liberal and republican than (in the sense specified in my chapter) democratic, entails from both of us reference to a huge and highly disputed literature. Although, again, this is not the occasion—nor, in the present theme, the author—appropriate for settling this issue, I am persuaded that, on balance, a reading of the Federalists and of this literature[4] supports my view on this matter.

Finally, Plattner cites approvingly a text by Terry L. Karl and Philippe C. Schmitter, in which they define "modern political democracy" as "a system of governance in which rulers are held accountable for their actions in the public realm by citizens, *acting indirectly* through the competition and cooperation of their representatives" (italics added). I find extremely vague the meaning of "acting indirectly," especially if those who, according to this definition, are held accountable are the same through whom the citizens "act." Actually, what is at issue here is no less than the problem of political representation. As recent studies have cogently shown, this problem requires analyses that are much more careful and, indeed, skeptical than the view Plattner endorses.[5] This, of course, does not mean that we disagree that the (democratic) idea of the people, or demos, as the true source of political authority is one of the fundamental legacies of the traditions we are discussing. However, I cannot join Plattner in his conclusion that "[i]t is hard to imagine monarchy, aristocracy, or indeed any other type of regime being defined in terms of accountability." To begin with, we saw that the definition that supports this assertion is not satisfactory. Second, kings, communist secretaries-general, religious leaders, and even mafia chieftains have been accountable to various kinds of councils and constituencies. The difference, which takes us back to the various combinations of democracy with liberalism and republicanism, is accountable to whom and by means of what mechanisms.

III

In its turn, the wise and learned comment by Richard Sklar begins most usefully to bridge the gap that he notes exists between political scientists and legal scholars. As Sklar argues, the reasons for this are quite powerful but, as his own text shows, not invincible. This gap, as Sklar argues and I strongly concur, is a serious hindrance for advancing in the knowledge of the various kinds of democracies that presently exist—the undertaking in which my commentators and myself coincide.

Notes

1. I discuss this topic in more detail in O'Donnell "The (Un)Rule of Law."

2. For a thoughtful discussion and data, see Evans, "Predatory, Developmental, and Other Apparatuses," and Evans, *Embedded Autonomy.*

3. See, on this matter, Waley, *The Italian City-Republics.*

4. See, among others, Appleby, *Liberalism,* Horowitz, "Republicanism and Liberalism," Kramnick, "The 'Great National Discussion,'" Kramnick, *Republicanism,* and Wood, *The Creation.*

5. See Manin et al., *Democracy.*

Part 2

Electoral Administration

5

A Brief History of Electoral Commissions

ROBERT A. PASTOR

At one and the same time, elections are both the supreme political act and a complicated administrative exercise. Elections determine who leads by a set of routine tasks. Because the stakes are so high, violence could be the consequence of a failure to conduct the exercise efficiently and impartially. The boundary line between politics and electoral administration is one that requires constant surveillance and policing in all democracies.[1]

In developing countries with weak states and bureaucratic incapacity, democracies sometimes falter because one political party interprets electoral irregularities as politically biased. The character, competence, and composition of electoral management bodies (EMBs) can determine whether an election is a source of peaceful change or a cause of serious instability. Independent election commissions (ECs), which emerged after World War II and often have been strengthened with help from international election mediators, have become important vehicles for ensuring both horizontal and vertical accountability.

Even in advanced countries, democracy is a work in progress; it is nowhere perfect. After the general election of 1996, the two major U.S. political parties challenged each other for perpetrating voter fraud by the misuse of absentee ballots in Louisiana or voting by noncitizens in California. The credible and effective conduct of elections requires monitoring in all countries by political parties, the press, and nongovernmental organizations, and people need to search for new formulas to prevent social and economic inequalities from distorting democracy's promise of political equality. As an electorate becomes better informed and a country's norms change, the rules of elections need to be adjusted to reduce the influence of monetary interests.

Free and fair elections are the moment when people exercise their sovereign power simply by marking a ballot in private. If the leaders fail to demonstrate their responsiveness, then the people replace them. One can best appreciate the significance of this act of changing leaders peacefully by comparing it to the more prevalent alternative: violent coups d'état.

Electoral Administration in Advanced Countries

Particularly in advanced countries, most people take for granted the administrative dimension of elections. There has been so little attention given to the conduct of elections that I was unable to locate a book or even an article on election commissions or their history. Comparative studies of elections or democracies omit references to ECs or even to the administration or conduct of elections.[2] A handbook, *Electoral System Design*, was developed by eighteen scholars of democracy from throughout the world under contract to the Swedish-based International Institute for Democracy and Electoral Assistance. "Aimed in particular at political negotiators and constitutional designers in new, fledgling, and transitional democracies," the handbook acknowledges that the administrative aspects of elections are of "critical importance," but it does not address them. Instead, it concentrates most of its attention on constitutional issues.[3]

Why? For too long, political scientists have defined "electoral systems" in terms of what one could call the 4 Ps: politics, parties, polling, and proportionality. The last category is the most complex and incorporates three families of systems: the plurality-majority, the semiproportional, and the proportional.[4] In a comparative study of twenty-seven democracies, Arend Lijphart discusses the issue from a similar direction, but in the book, he fails to mention ECs or electoral administration.[5]

When people think of electoral systems, they do not think of the conduct of elections but rather of constitutional questions—for example, a presidential or a parliamentary system—or of election procedures or practices—for example, campaign finance.[6] When scholars write on democracy and administration, as Göran Hydén does in an excellent essay on the subject, their purpose is to explore whether democracies, using oversight techniques, exhibit more honest and efficient administration. Hydén does not examine the question of how the administrative capacity of a country permits or impedes the effective conduct of elections.[7]

One of the characteristics of advanced countries is the relatively high level of administrative competence, and that is the reason that political scientists who study comparative democracies have given so little attention to the conduct of elections. Most of the services that advanced countries provide their citizens are much more complicated than registering voters or conducting elections. Indeed, in most industrialized and a few developing countries, people learn the results of elections from television projections, not from vote counts. Few citizens even know the rules and procedures for counting, announcing, and certifying the results because they take for granted that the process will be honest and impartial. And they take that for granted because they believe the press and the judiciary would prevent or overturn any serious election fraud.

In Great Britain and the United States, the major election-related issues of the nineteenth and early twentieth centuries concerned the extension of the suffrage beyond a small group of male white landowners. The secret ballot was not even introduced in Great Britain until 1872. In the United States, elections have long been conducted at the county level and supervised by each state. Only after Watergate in 1974 did the United States establish the Federal Election Commission, which was not to conduct elections but only to administer and enforce campaign finance laws.[8]

In neither the United States nor Great Britain does there exist a central office for conducting national elections, and the local institutions responsible for administering elections are not independent: they reside in government offices. This is not exceptional. Of twenty advanced industrialized democracies, the governments—not independent commissions—are responsible for conducting the elections in fifteen, or 75 percent.[9]

Conducting Elections in Developing Countries

It is a constant effort even in advanced countries to keep the electoral machinery updated and insulated from the incumbent government and the political process; in developing countries, the problem is compounded by the lack of administrative capacity. To understand the seriousness of this technical problem, contemplate the range of activities that need to be undertaken in a short time and often in a very tense, politicized environment. The conduct of elections includes the following: appointing and training registration and election officials; delineating the boundaries of voting areas; designing a voter registration system and establishing voting sites; registering voters on-site or at home and aggregating and publishing a registration list at national and local levels; publishing and distributing the list widely enough to provide voters and parties an opportunity to review and correct the list; establishing and enforcing rules on campaigning, access to the media, and financing; ensuring security of the voters, the candidates, and the polling stations; registering and qualifying political parties and candidates; collecting information on all voters and processing the data onto voter identification cards; distributing voter identification cards and ensuring that they are received by the right people; producing election materials; printing and securing the ballot; delivering the election materials to the appropriate sites; certifying that voters are on the registration list and that they vote privately and in accordance with the procedures (often including dipping one's finger in ink); counting the ballots; ensuring that the results are delivered to the election offices; adding the count and announcing the results; investigating and adjudicating complaints; and certifying the final results.

If there are problems in registering voters, training election officials, or shipping election materials to the right polling sites in transitional countries, most people assume these problems are politically inspired. But in most developing countries with little or no experience in democracy, the officials charged with administering and conducting elections are generally unskilled, and technical irregularities are the rule. There are good explanations for the correlation between the level of economic, administrative, and political development, but the connection has not been adequately explored. It is not impossible for a poor, illiterate country to be democratic, but it is also not easy, because every technical problem is interpreted by one party or another as politically motivated.

States have tried a number of different strategies to prevent incumbents from manipulating electoral procedures to ensure their reelection. After its revolution, sparked by electoral fraud by a long-standing dictator, Mexico wrote a constitution preventing presidential succession. But the new rules were soon manipulated by the governing Institutional Revolutionary Party (PRI). After World War II, two states—Costa Rica and India—of very different size, population, and ethnic composition at different ends of the world established election commissions to try to insulate politics from elections. These ECs are not important in advanced democracies where people have confidence in the conduct of elections, but they are of central importance in countries where many people assume that the conduct of elections is manipulated to serve one party's interests.

Electoral fraud in the 1948 Costa Rican election provoked a revolution by José Figueres, a young social democratic leader. After his army overthrew the government, Figueres dismantled the armed forces, allowed elections for a constituent assembly, and handed power back to the legitimately elected president. The new constitution gave responsibility to conducting the entire election to a new institution, the Supreme Electoral Tribunal (TSE), a fourth branch of government.

The TSE is composed of three magistrates and three alternates, all elected by a two-thirds vote of the Supreme Court of Justice to six-year staggered terms. Two alternates are chosen by the Supreme Court to sit with the three to form a tribunal of five members. In addition to appointing all the election officials at each level, the TSE supervises the Civil Registry, which issues identification cards and sets requirements for legal recognition of political parties and candidates.[10]

India needs to train more election officials each year—2.3 million— than there are voters in Costa Rica. But it too has an EC that was authorized by its constitution of 1950. Article 324 is very precise and complete, giving the EC "the superintendence, direction, and control of the electoral rolls for, and the conduct of all elections to parliament and to the legislature of every state and of elections to the offices of President and Vice President."[11]

The framers of India's constitution wanted to consolidate control over electoral matters in a single chief election officer, who would be "placed beyond the reach of 'party government' and have responsibility both for national and all state elections."[12] Because of the high rate of illiteracy and the diversity of ethnic groups and castes, the authors of the Indian constitution wanted to make sure that no state government could exclude a group of voters. The EC chair is appointed by the president but is supposed to be separated from both legislative and executive influence. Most chairs have been career civil servants, but apparently they have been quite different in terms of their competence and impartiality. The first chair, Sukumar Sen, succeeded in establishing the institution's reputation for fairness and effectiveness in the 1950s and 1960s. B. L. Fadia believes that subsequent chairs did not maintain the integrity or the leadership of the first and that the EC is less independent today than it was at the beginning.[13] Fadia recommends that the EC expand to include new members, who would be appointed by a committee of the Supreme Court.

Most other electoral management bodies in developing countries are not nearly as independent, impartial, or competent as these two ECs. There are four different places to locate EMBs:

1. *Within the government.* This approach works well in advanced countries where the civil service is respected as independent and politically neutral.
2. *Within a government ministry but supervised by a judicial body.* The independent election commission is composed of selected judges, who oversee the government ministry responsible for conducting the elections.
3. An *independent election commission* manned by experts and directly accountable to the parliament. When the parliament is not one-sided, such a commission can be very credible.
4. A *multiparty election commission* composed of representatives of the political parties. If there are too many parties in a parliament, these ECs become unworkable.[14]

The struggles for free elections in most new democracies have often pivoted around ECs. In Guyana, the opposition insisted on a new formula for choosing an EC chair before participating in the 1992 elections. Later, in Haiti and Cameroon, opposition political parties decided to boycott elections when the government refused to alter the composition of the election commissions.

Mexico's EMB was traditionally viewed as partial, and whether true or not, the perception was widespread and responsible for the popular distrust with the process. When I raised the issue of the location of the EMB with the Mexican president in 1988, the president insisted on a "French model" where the EMB was run by the government. This approach did not work, and within two years, reforms were approved that permitted the EMB to become more autonomous. The establishment of the Federal Electoral Institute and its growing independence improved the credibility of the electoral process in Mexico to the point that most viewed the 1997 congressional elections as honest. At the same time, the Mexican government also established the independent Federal Electoral Tribunal in order to adjudicate complaints about the elections. Continuous improvements in both institutions enhanced the credibility of the process.[15]

Virtually all the Eastern European governments that made the transition to democracy when the Berlin Wall fell established election commissions. In Africa, there is also a trend in the same direction, although the ECs have much less autonomy. In Latin America, there is considerable diversity. In Argentina, Brazil, Chile, and Uruguay, the EMB is independent, but it operates within the judicial branch.[16] In brief, ECs play an increasingly important role in democratic transitions. International mediators can help them establish their credibility by distinguishing between technical irregularities and political fraud.[17]

Given the continued fragility of democracy, researchers need to delve more deeply into the subject of electoral management bodies. Is it true that independent commissions are much more needed in the early stages of democratization than in latter periods? Is the relationship between successful democratic elections and levels of administrative development more important than the relationship between democracy and economic development? Which procedures have proven most effective in ensuring the independence of ECs? Is it useful or necessary for the adjudicatory dimension to be separate from the ECs?

A new focus on the administrative side of elections could prove of lasting importance to the enterprise of democratization. It is the one dimension that seems to have been overlooked consistently, but given the wide but thin character of contemporary democratic experiments, perhaps the best way to prevent backsliding or democratic failure is by strengthening the institutions that ensure that the allocation of power reflects popular preferences.

Notes

I wish to thank Larry Diamond and Andreas Schedler for comments on an earlier draft and David Berger and James Ruhlman for research assistance.

1. "Lack of confidence in the verdict of the ballot box not only destroys the faith of the public in the democratic process, but also discredits the public services. The electoral administration, which is the foundation of representative government, should, therefore, be placed beyond the reach of the party government" (Bhalla, "Election Commission of India," p. 12).

2. For one of the best volumes on comparative democratic practices, which does not address the more specific subject of election administration, see LeDuc et al., *Comparing Democracies.*

3. Reynolds and Reilly et al., *The International IDEA Handbook,* pp. 2, 7.

4. Ibid., pp. 17–39. The *Handbook* does a superb job of identifying the three broad families and the nine subfamilies—the ways in which individual votes are translated into different numbers and kinds of representation.

5. Lijphart, *Electoral Systems,* examines the consequences of three properties of the electoral system: the electoral formula (PR or plurality); the number of representatives per district; and the minimum needed for a party to participate.

6. Lijphart and Waisman, "Institutional Design and Democratization," and Nohlen, "Electoral Systems."

7. Hyden, "Democracy and Administration," pp. 242–262.

8. Previous to the Federal Election Commission of the 1970s, Congress had created an electoral commission a century before—in 1876—but for a very specific purpose: to resolve the disputed presidential election of that year.

9. DeBusk, *1996 International Directory.* I am grateful to David Berger for helping to organize the data presented in this directory.

10. Institute for the Comparative Study of Political Systems, *Costa Rican Election Factbook,* pp. 33–34.

11. Fadia, "Reforming the Election Commission," p. 78.

12. Ibid.

13. Ibid., pp. 85–86.

14. Harris, "An Electoral Administration."

15. Carter Center, "The Carter Center Delegation," and Eisenstadt, "Electoral Justice in Mexico." Also see Chapter 6, this volume.

16. Harris, "An Electoral Administration," pp. 11–13.

17. Pastor, "Mediating Elections."

6

Off the Streets and into the Courtrooms: Resolving Postelectoral Conflicts in Mexico

TODD A. EISENSTADT

M exico's 1997 congressional elections have been widely regarded as "watershed elections in the quest for democracy,"[1] featuring a "playing field of Mexican politics [which] had become far more level,"[2] created by reforms yielding "one of the most complete, well-regulated and convenient" electoral laws in Latin America.[3] Yet the institutions of horizontal accountability that set the stage for this electoral success arose in a regime that was only dubiously democratic. Unlike several of the "new democracies" studied in this book (such as the Eastern European cases and some of the East Asian cases), Mexico was at best a "semidemocracy,"[4] making the construction of institutions sufficiently autonomous from a single-party state all the more unlikely. Indeed, Mexico was the longest-reigning hegemonic-party state in the world. The successful implementation of institutions of horizontal accountability was quite unlikely in this context, making it a "hard case" for analysis, from which much can be gleaned for the study of institutional development and democratization.

Is Mexico's regime of election-administering institutions (the Federal Electoral Tribunal) sufficiently autonomous from the executive branch to ensure that democratization continues through the electoral route? How were these institutions created, and what forces perpetuate their continuous reforms, over the last decade, toward greater independence from Mexico's formerly all-powerful executive? I argue in this chapter that Mexico's electoral institutions are indeed independent, fostering continued competitiveness of opposition parties, which by the end of 1997 had won an unprecedented seven governorships,[5] mayorships in nine of the country's ten largest cities, and control of the lower house of Congress for the first time since the Institutional Revolutionary Party (PRI) was founded.

However, the electoral institutions were allowed to guarantee horizontal accountability only as a result of several factors: a weakening of the authoritarian regime's seventy-year monopoly on power, long-standing pressures for democratization by both leftist and rightist opposition parties, and an increasing pursuit by Mexico of an international profile requiring more enlightened domestic governance.

In this chapter I outline the dramatic advances in federal electoral administration resulting from enhanced electoral competition, especially since 1988. I briefly describe the fifty-year struggle of the rightist National Action Party (PAN) for a rule of law in the electoral realm joined on the left by the nascent Democratic Revolutionary Party (PRD) in the late 1980s. I then document the electoral decline of the PRI and the rise of autonomous electoral institutions by the mid-1990s, which reinforced and accelerated electoral opening. After elaborating on the political context of the electoral reforms and their content, I briefly contrast successes at the federal level with failures at the local level. But before discussing the increasing success of federal electoral administration in Mexico, it is worth noting the most notorious case of the failure of electoral administration: the 1988 presidential election.

In 1988, the electoral college (the congressional members who ratified their own elections) certified the PRI's candidate, Carlos Salinas de Gortari, as winner, even though he won through an unfair campaign and election-day fraud that culminated in a mysterious "blackout" of the vote-tallying computers, which yielded a surge of pro-PRI votes when the lights went back on.[6] The embittered loser, the PRD's Cuauhtémoc Cárdenas, did not recognize the legitimacy of the Salinas government and for a few weeks held Mexico's governability in the balance, as the PAN briefly joined Cárdenas's PRD in discrediting Salinas's election. However, the savvy Salinas cut a deal with the PAN, promising recognition of PAN electoral victories in exchange for votes on PRI legislative initiatives. The resulting six-year de facto alliance between the PAN and the PRI gave Salinas the support his initiatives required[7] and allowed Salinas to punish Cárdenas and the PRD his whole term by summarily disregarding PRD local electoral victories and acquiescing to local hard-liners' repression against party activists. The 1988 postelectoral fiasco had been the most egregious violation of norms for free and fair elections in modern Mexico, as it was the most competitive election ever, and the margin of electoral tampering required to deliver PRI victory seems to have been greater than at any other historical moment.[8] But this example was far from the only failure of the PRI state to recognize opposition electoral victories, particularly at the local level. Indeed, until quite recently, the electoral history of modern Mexico was a history of improprieties, both real and alleged, by the PRI state.

The History of Postelectoral Negotiations

Postelectoral "negotiation," that is, denial of opposition victories (particularly to the PAN) in exchange for crumbs from the table of power (dubbed *concertacesión,* a Mexican colloquialism combining the Spanish words for concession plus concertation), became routine in the transitional 1980s and early 1990s as the PRI state sought to ally with the PAN against the leftist (and at moments regime-threatening) PRD, and the PAN sought footholds of authority from which it could build bureaucratic expertise and a visible record in public office. These postelectoral conflicts carried a theatrical air in their staging after close defeats in dozens of major urban PAN strongholds. They represented opening gambits by the long-standing opposition PAN in its postelectoral negotiations with the regime.

Ranking PAN leaders acknowledged that a "special relationship" between the PAN and the PRI existed during Salinas's term and that the PAN privileged itself as the regime's loyal opposition. National PAN officials also admitted conducting direct communications with national PRI leaders, the interior secretary, and in some cases with Salinas himself in the pursuit of national solutions to local problems.[9] In all of its most notorious *concertacesiones,* such as the governorships of Guanajuato and San Luis Potosí in 1991 and mayoral races in Mazatlán in 1991, Mérida in 1993, Monterrey in 1994, and Huejotzingo in 1996, the national PAN negotiated with the national PRI leadership, finding "gentleman's agreement" solutions that "washed" PRI victories through political (rather than judicial) institutions—such as state legislatures or bipartisan bargaining tables—to find compromises acceptable to the PAN.[10]

The PRD has experienced nothing close to the good fortune of the PAN in negotiating postelectoral conflicts. The PAN managed to persuade the national PRI to pressure local PRI chapters to resign electoral victories so the PAN could claim the wins (and maintain the PAN-PRI national policy alliance intact). Contrarily, the PRD until recently had nothing valuable to offer the PRI at the national level. The PRD consistently opposed PAN-PRI economic and social policies and for the first several years of Salinas's term did not even recognize the PRI's candidate as the proper winner of the 1988 balloting. So where the PAN received backdoor access to the regime's power elites, the PRD had to play threats of ingovernability from the grassroots as attention-grabbing, postelectoral cards. The PRD did manage, after systematically fraudulent elections such as local races in Michoacán in 1992 and Chiapas in 1995, to receive concessions of "plural" local governments, involving regents from the PRD as well as the PRI. But they have never managed to overturn PRI victories outright like the PAN has, and they have never received such concessions in gubernatorial races or important urban-area mayoral contests. A near exception, the PRD's successful negotiation of the departure of the official PRI victor in the 1994 Tabasco governor's race, fell apart at the last minute as local PRI leaders reneged on their deal to sacrifice their governor in exchange for a national-level truce between the PRI and the PRD.[11]

The small inroads that have been made by the PRD have been quite costly, as the *segunda vuelta* (or second round) could be a deadly affair. Scores of PRD activists were slain in fisticuffs with authorities and activists from the PRI and government authorities in the late 1980s and early 1990s, as groups spontaneously rebelled against PRI-imposed electoral results, occupying town halls for weeks or months at a time before giving up, being conceded the de facto victory, or being forcedly removed, sometimes by the military. While PANista postelectoral conflicts in the 1980s resulted in a few deaths and some injuries, the only non-PRD postelectoral conflict yielding more fatalities than Michoacán in 1992, for example, was the slaying of dozens of rightist (but not PANista) regime opponents in León, Guanajuato, in the 1940s.

During much of the 1990s, until the 1996 electoral reforms fully "vested" the opposition parties and gave federal authorities jurisdiction to overturn local elections, the staging of such conflicts, both PAN-style and PRD-style, was the ultimate referendum on the credibility of individual elections. Only very recently have such conflicts been removed from the streets to the courtrooms, offering definitive evidence that opposition parties have finally accepted the electoral institutions offered by Mexico's one-party regime.

If political parties are the ultimate arbiters of electoral justice, their participation in or abstention from this system should be the final measure of whether it works. The best means of assessing party opinion about Mexico's regime of electoral institutions is to consider the position of opposition parties—chiefly the PAN and the PRD—both of which have harshly criticized Mexico's long tradition of election fraud. But even for all their severe recriminations, both major opposition parties have sometimes succumbed to offers by the PRI to accept consolation prize pacts, in which they were given administrative posts in a contested city council or even an interim governorship. President Salinas alone (1988–1994) named seven interim governors as a direct result of postelectoral negotiations and created some sixty plural municipal councils to manage conflictive localities where opposition mobilizations prevented PRI mayors from taking office. These deals were made with the interior secretariat, the arm of the president charged with keeping the peace between political parties as part of its broader charge of maintaining domestic security. They always entailed the replacement of "hard-line PRIsta" governors or mayors with more moderate partisans of the PRI, compromise opposition candidates, or "plural" governments (the solution usually adopted in mayoral races), in which regents from the PRI and the electoral runner-up governed a plural council.

Postelectoral bargaining (rather than strict obedience to the verdicts of electoral courts and commissions) is nothing new. Since the promulgation of the 1917 constitution, there have been more than sixty documented federal executive initiatives to supersede state's rights, and intervene, through the cutting of deals with opposing forces to resolve postelectoral conflicts and other localized political crises.[12] Political interventions in federal elections are also notorious, albeit less transparent than in 1988. But as we will now see, by the late 1990s, the gradual tightening of electoral laws had made such postelectoral conflicts the exception rather than the rule by the mid-1990s.

Successive Rounds of Regime-Tolerated Electoral Reforms

Mexico's elite settlement after the convulsive Mexican Revolution consolidated the PRI party state by the late 1930s. That was a tumultuous decade, however, as populist general-turned-president Lázaro Cárdenas (the father of Cuauhtémoc Cárdenas) decisively squelched political opposition and won great popular support for his agenda of social programs, including extensive agrarian reform. In rebellion against Cárdenas's policies, a group of conservative lawyers and business leaders created the PAN, in 1939, which was originally intended as a principled debating forum of symbolic opposition but soon evolved into the feisty and rebellious group that would bear the brunt of political liberalization efforts (from within the regime) for fifty years. The PAN won its first mayorship in 1940 in a tiny town in the central state of Michoacán and its first federal congressional representation in 1946. But mostly the PAN was denied any access to all but the most symbolic of positions until the 1960s, when it won the state capitals of Mérida and Hermosillo (and was denied several other victories that were annulled due to "irregularities" and resolved through appointment of PRI interim mayors) after protracted and grave postelectoral conflicts.

General assemblies during the first several decades of the PAN's existence were punctuated by frequent debates about whether to participate in elections (and accept losing even if the election was unfair) or abstain and "punish" the PRI by unmasking the regime's elections as uncompetitive shams. The 1976 presidential election was preceded by a particularly fierce internal debate, and the divided party failed to nominate a candidate. Not surprisingly, the PRI won (although with only 82 percent of the vote in a one-candidate field), but the regime felt discredited. In 1977, the PRI state conducted a nonthreatening electoral reform, designed to increase the presence of the fledgling oppositions, at least to the point of making the authoritarian regime appear more democratic. The outlawed Communist Party was legalized, as were other small leftist parties, and additional proportional representation seats were created in the lower chamber of the Congress in an effort to encourage greater participation and to counterbalance the PAN's growth with a leftist presence. The PRI commenced a liberalization process "snowball" it would later prove unable to stop.

Although the reforms of 1977 are credited as the first in Mexico's electoral opening, the real overhaul of Mexico's electoral institutions commenced in 1990. The most critical autonomous institution for mediating the "levelness" of the electoral playing field, the Federal Electoral Institute (IFE), was created at that time. The previous institution for monitoring elections, the highly controversial Federal Electoral Commission, was run directly by the interior secretary as a dependence of the executive branch. Largely unchanged since its creation in 1946, this institution was notorious for directing elections toward outcomes dictated by the president and his party, rather than for its accountability to the voting public. The Federal Electoral Tribunal (TFE) was also created in 1989 as an autonomous body capable of challenging IFE decisions.[13]

The IFE was still dependent on the interior ministry, but less directly. Like its director, the policy-setting body of the IFE was selected via executive nomination. The powers of the IFE were limited, as there was no regime of rules setting limits on party finance (in which the PRI grossly outspent its rivals), on the traditionally stilted media coverage favoring the PRI, or on the PRI's deployment of bloated state bureaucracies for the partisan cause. Still, the legislation did limit PRI overrepresentation in the lower house of the Mexican Congress, provide for a new electoral registry to minimize ballot stuffing and other overt fraud, and create a lottery system of randomly selecting and training poll workers off the electoral registry (rather than allowing government-named electoral officials to select poll workers sympathetic to the governing party). Allegations of fraud by the PAN and the PRD were still commonplace, centered mostly on continuing irregularities in the electoral registry, but the 1991 midterm elections generated nothing close to the conflict of 1988. The PRI recovered its absolute congressional majority, and by a landslide, without any serious threats to the legitimacy of the process.[14]

The 1993 and 1994 electoral reforms, implemented for the 1994 presidential race (during the regime of PAN-PRI cooperation), extended the autonomy and jurisdiction of the IFE, further scaled back PRI overrepresentation—this time in both houses of the national Congress—and codified a role for electoral observers. No longer nominated by the president, the IFE's policymaking body was now composed of representatives from the political parties, the legislative branch, and nonpartisan citizen "ombudsmen" nominated and approved by the Congress. Exorbitant albeit concrete limits were placed on party campaign spending and election-related media coverage, both to be regulated by the IFE; and the electoral registry was tightened with the introduction of a voter photo ID card. The Federal Electoral Tribunal was also fortified, and the use of the electoral college to certify federal elections was eliminated in all but the presidential race. The electoral process was deemed to be fairly transparent by most observers despite persistent complaints, largely by the PRD, about subtle forms of manipulation by electoral authorities of the electoral registry and gerrymandering of congressional districts.

Unlike in 1988, Cuauhtémoc Cárdenas's second presidential candidacy created little stir in 1994, as he placed a distant third to the PRI and the PAN after running a poor campaign. Moreover, the federal electoral institutions seemed to function autonomously for the first time, as several conflictive PRI congressional victories were stripped from that party by the electoral court and handed to the PAN and PRD.[15] Problems remained in the equity of electoral administration, but they had much more to do with the need for tighter regulation of campaign spending than with the active perpetration of election-day fraud.

The 1996 reforms (in anticipation of the 1997 midterm elections) resulted from a different interparty bargaining dynamic than the pre-1991 and pre-1994 reforms. Having been elected by the smallest margin ever and without much of his party's support, Ernesto Zedillo found himself needing to forge consensus on both the right and left, so his administration sponsored dialogues for reforming government in which PRD and PAN demands were taken seriously. The result was a hard-hitting set of electoral reforms[16] that further distanced the IFE from the executive and legislative branches by finally allowing the collegial body of citizen counselors to select their own director (rather than relying on executive nomination) and by giving these citizen counselors (who now set policy without counting the votes of political parties or legislators) the ability to make personnel changes and monitor their own affairs. In the most significant reform to the electoral court, it was placed in 1996 directly under the jurisdiction of the Supreme Court, with magistrates nominated by the judicature rather than by the executive (with legislative confirmation). Perhaps the most important aspect of the 1996 reform was granting the electoral court jurisdiction to resolve election-related constitutional conflicts arising at the local level, where great disparities still exist between the ideal of electoral justice and its practice. The other significant changes prior to the 1997 midterm elections included the first congressional redistricting in twenty years and the tightening of IFE control over public funds used by political parties. While the opposition parties continued to express qualms about electoral administration, the 1997 election results were hard to refute, with the opposition winning 52 percent of the Chamber of Deputies seats to the PRI's 48 percent.

The electoral reforms of the past decade in Mexico have been dramatic, bringing an electoral system designed to provide legal "cover" of authoritarianism to the doorstep of democracy, and with sufficient legal safeguards to carry Mexico's democratic consolidation as far as the new electoral competition leads. Refinements are still needed in federal electoral laws, but the focal point of democratization has shifted in Mexico to redefining executive-legislative relations and placing new limits on Mexico's excessive presidentialism. The impetus for yet another round of reforms may now come from the opposition-dominated Chamber of Deputies but risks excess if it attempts further major overhauls.

Negotiating the PRI Out of Absolute Power

The successful implementation of horizontal accountability at Mexico's federal level is largely the result of opposition party compliance with the electoral rules, after decades (in the case of the PAN) of contesting electoral institutions and their results through postelectoral conflicts. The regime has been forced to concede a series of electoral reforms leading to this point for a combination of reasons: the weakening of the electoral power of the PRI and internal divisions within the party, the rise of the opposition, and the influence of the international community. After examining each of these, I turn the discussion from the critical successes of horizontal accountability in the electoral realm at the federal level to some of its critical failures, at the local level.

Despite isolated cases of PAN postelectoral mobilizing success in the 1960s, with the regime's recognition of PAN victories in Mérida and Hermosillo, such cases were quite exceptional and due more to PRI selection of corrupt and/or inept candidates rather than to any real electoral inroads by the opposition. This started to change by the mid-1980s, however, after the 1982 debt crisis induced negative economic growth and shrinkage of federal budgets several years in a row. The PRI's traditional means of culling support—pork barrel politics—was no longer effective, as funds were scarce and the bloated state apparatus could no longer serve the populace. The disenchanted electorate turned to the PAN as the only electoral alternative, as the Communist Party had been outlawed in the 1960s, and other leftist parties had largely opted to wage their battles outside the legal system (that is, through several guerrilla movements that had sprung up in the 1970s). As the state shrank, the traditional statist politicians were subordinated to a new class, the economistic "technocrats" (exemplified by Salinas), who extolled the virtues of neoliberal market efficiency over traditional patronage politics.[17] In 1987, a great number of the remaining left-leaning "traditionalist" PRI leaders, including Cuauhtémoc Cárdenas, abandoned the party in order to found the PRD, which they promised would remain more loyal to Mexico's legacy of state activism in the economy. The PRI's electoral decline had begun and was exacerbated by each electoral reform that further removed electoral administration from the PRI state's hands.

But why would the PRI state accede to reforms that would prompt its own demise as Mexico's hegemonic party? The growth of the PAN on the right provided the initial answer, as Salinas found himself without a qualified majority in the legislature and thus had to negotiate electoral reforms with the PAN in 1989–1990. The PAN, however, took advantage of the PRI's disposition to negotiate, making postelectoral *concertacesiones* the rule rather than the exception during Salinas's administration. To the cry of "no more *concertacesiones!*" the PRI agreed to one more "definitive" reform in 1993–1994, which the PAN utilized to further extricate the PRI from electoral administration. In 1996, another reform was needed because the PRD acceded to engaging in official dialogues with Mexico's new PRIsta president, Ernesto Zedillo—but only on the condition that electoral reforms be included in the reform agenda. Zedillo had even less of a public mandate than Salinas, as he became the PRI's candidate only at the last minute, after the pregroomed candidate was assassinated, and he wanted cordial relations with the rapidly growing PRD. Many think the moderate Zedillo also favored reformers as a way of restraining hard-liners within his party.[18] So the PRI was gradually negotiated out of its hegemonic position, even though it remains the largest party in a three-party system.

The other oft-cited but less directly important reason the PRI would allow the Mexican party state to at least partially reform itself out of a monopoly on government is that Mexico's full-scale opening to the international economy, culminating in its four-year negotiation of the North American Free Trade Agreement (NAFTA), implemented in 1994, and its reliance on the United States for a short-term economic bailout in 1995, forced Mexican elites to accept international norms of democracy as a matter of course. While Mexican and U.S. government officials deny overtly pressing Mexico to conduct cleaner elections as part of the NAFTA negotiations, Mexican diplomats in Washington acknowledge that the appearance of clean domestic elections grew in importance to the Mexican government, following the NAFTA negotiations, as a subject "on everyone's mind."[19] Indeed, interactions between Mexican and international nongovernmental organizations in the realms of human rights and election monitoring seemed to provoke greater domestic pressures within Mexico than government-to-government pressure tactics.[20] The international effect was diffuse, and certainly insufficient without the much more tangible increases in electoral competition and divisions within the PRI. But international pressure certainly played a role, especially as opposition parties and human rights groups started leveraging international pressure to promote domestic changes, such as the PAN's successful Interamerican Human Rights Commission complaint against the government of the state of Nuevo León for its stilted electoral law that was resolved in 1991 in favor of the PAN, to the great embarrassment of the Mexican government.

The single most important event in establishing the imperative for electoral reforms was clearly the 1988 federal election and Salinas's subsequent credibility gap. The 1994 election of Zedillo clearly transpired under much fairer conditions, although Zedillo's election was still ratified by an electoral college, the incoming congressional members-elect of the lower house. In 2000, there will be no political certification by an electoral college, only judicial reconsideration of any fraudulent votes by the fortified Federal Electoral Tribunal. It is uncertain that the politically inexperienced Zedillo has the authority within the increasingly belligerent PRI to pick his successor, as have all his predecessors, without implementing consensual mechanisms within the party. Furthermore, with the debilitation of the PRI and the increasing public presence of protagonists from the PRD and PAN, it is uncertain whether the PRI's designee will even be able to win the presidency in 2000. In short, the minimum conditions of democratization have been met in Mexico—the credible possibility of voter-determined alternation in power—at least at the federal level. However, the administration of local elections in some states is still another matter.

The Battle Between Federalism and Electoral Justice

Having established that the key to horizontal accountability is actor compliance, let us now consider cases where opposition leaders have not tended to cooperate with the regime's dictates—in conflictive local races. If real institutional changes were in place at the federal level by 1991, they were several years slower in Mexico's states (and have not yet arrived in some of the country's poor southern states). The "definitive" reforms of 1996 effectively forced the states to tighten their electoral laws in line with those at the federal level, by granting the federal electoral court the ultimate jurisdiction over state and local electoral complaints, as well as over those raised at the federal level. Furthermore, the incorporation of the fortified Federal Electoral Tribunal into the Supreme Court ensured the judicial branch jurisdiction over overtly political matters for the first time since the 1870s. The principal advances of this reform for the electoral court's jurisdiction were twofold: the ability to interpret the constitution directly, and the ability to offer the final say in all electoral disputes as an appellate court for local and state conflicts.

This authority will be especially important in socially conflictive states, such as Chiapas and Tabasco, governed by old-style PRI machine governors. None of the eighty-nine locally filed postelectoral complaints in conflictive local races in these PRD stronghold states was ruled as even partially founded. In Tabasco (1994), all twenty complaints were summarily rejected before even reaching magistrate consideration, whereas in Chiapas (1995), none of the sixty-nine electoral court complaints filed resulted in the annulment of even one vote.[21] Even if the electoral courts' rejection of so many complaints was based on solid judicial reasoning, and the complaints were too poorly formulated to be accepted for consideration, this horrible "founded" rate would seem to say more about the accessibility of electoral justice in these states than about the quality of the complaints filed—namely, that the institutions created to serve as a forum to avert postelectoral conflicts are functioning poorly. While the PAN *concertacesiones* allegedly "washed" through the state electoral courts (such as Guaymas in 1991, Huejotzingo in 1996, and possibly Monterrey in 1994), ruling more on the basis of political pressures than on the weight of judicial arguments, it may at least be said that the electoral courts are being used as a forum for dispute adjudication (even if they distorted justice and accustomed the PAN to using the courts as a bargaining table). When electoral courts will not accept *any* complaints (and some of them were well formulated even by federal standards), it is hardly surprising that the PRD opted for the mobilization route, launching postelectoral conflicts in 18 percent of Tabasco's seventeen municipalities and in 34 percent of Chiapas's 109 municipalities.[22]

Contrary to these state-level failures in the administration of electoral justice, the thrice-reformed federal electoral court acted independently in the July 1997 congressional elections,[23] and in its capacity as appellate to local elections, the electoral court excelled, overturning several PRI-regime victories. The federal court has intervened in municipalities to revoke PRI victories in heartland towns and cities from Tepetlaoxtoc, Mexico State (population 16,000), to Uriangato, Guanajuato (population 47,000), to Aconchi, Sonora (population 2,500). These verdicts have been advertised as a warning to local electoral *caciques* (machine bosses) by local and federal electoral officials. To Mexico State Electoral Tribunal president Francisco Olascoaga Valdés, for example, the federal electoral court's second-guessing of his local verdict served notice to all state and local electoral officials that they are being monitored. Prompted by "the ghosts of Huejotzingo [Puebla] and Tabasco,"[24] the reform creating this powerful challenge, approaching the judicial authority of a de facto electoral *amparo*[25] (constitutional appeal right, but granted to individuals and not covering political "rights") was the opposition parties' crowning achievement in the 1996 reforms.[26] The landmark application of federal electoral law to the Tepetlaoxtoc local case[27] may retain long-term significance, as electoral judges promise and opposition leaders hope that it may be used to clamp down on remaining perpetrators of electoral fraud—the local *cacique* "bosses" in traditional PRI bastions like Puebla, Tabasco, and Yucatán.

Recall that prior to the mid-1990s, differing postelectoral strategies characterized PRD and PAN behavior at the local and national levels. The PAN conducted postelectoral negotiations from the top down, the PRD from the bottom up. The PAN negotiated freely with the PRI; the PRD only hesitantly dealt with the PRI. The PAN, composed of middle-class, professional (including many lawyers), business, and urban constituents, concentrated electoral and postelectoral efforts on *concertacesiones* (concession agreements) over electoral outcomes in major cities. The PRD, an almost lawyerless party of peasants, urban poor, and intellectuals, tended to focus its grassroots postelectoral mobilizing—known as *la segunda vuelta* (the second round)—in smaller, rural areas. Since the 1996 reforms, this has all changed. There have been no major postelectoral mobilizations since 1996,[28] and with their new power in the federal Chamber of Deputies, both major opposition parties have been able to leverage support for legislation against the conduct of fair local elections. Furthermore, the federal electoral courts are perceived by all parties as being fair overall, even if they can all cite transgressions of electoral justice.

The Need for National Opposition Party Compliance

Opposition parties, and particularly the PRD, insisted prior to 1997, when Cárdenas won the Mexico City governorship and the party made notable advances in central states like Veracruz and Morelos, that the entire system of electoral justice was flawed and that it was incumbent upon the federal electoral courts to adopt improvements to set precedents for the states, where the pillars of electoral justice are indeed much less steady. Both opposition parties conveyed misgivings about the extreme formalities of case filing procedures, which were only partially reformed in 1996. As of 1997, both parties still wish to loosen filing requirements,[29] but they would both seem to agree that any remaining shortcomings of electoral justice at the federal level are largely "a problem not of institutions but of the people who staff them."[30]

The PRD's position represents a more radical departure with that party's past. In 1994, the PRD responded to the extreme demands posed by rigid electoral laws by filing generic, "blanket" writings of protest on the day of the election with hopes of "saving their place to fill in complaints later" during the three-day complaint filing period.[31] The party also filed a mimeographed generic complaint 320 times challenging the construction of the electoral registration list, an issue resolved well before the election and no longer a legitimate source of challenge on election day.[32] TFE magistrates responded unfavorably to having to repeatedly reanswer hundreds of pages of allegations that had already been addressed in a special complaint to appeal IFE General Council decisions, but the PRD strategists insisted that they were not trying to sabotage the judicial process by filing the bulky pre-elaborated format. Rather, they argued that the "list-shaving" complaint had been sent by the national party to local chapters merely as a didactic guide on how to file complaints.[33] Some 72 percent of the PRD's 906 post-electoral complaints filed in that process were based on pre-elaborated formats, with well over half of these filing the "registration list" generic format without any unique supplemental material.[34] The strategy was controversial even within the party, but particularly among the electoral court magistrates, who felt, justifiably, that the party was wasting their time.

By 1997, the new PRD officials responsible for the judicial defense of the vote were themselves openly critical of the party's 1994 position. As a result of the overall moderation of the party's philosophy, as well as the loss of some PRD local victories in the conflictive state of Guerrero in 1996, officials realized that the party would not gain any new benefits from the pre-elaborated defenses; they understood that unless PRD lawyers defended the party's victories via the judicial route, the party risked "losing" electoral victories in the courtrooms. This sobering prospect, plus the "new reality of political competition" in which the PRD has more to gain (and lose) by participating in the electoral institutions rather than undermining them, has caused the PRD, admittedly deficient in training pollwatchers and complaint filers, to seek to improve in these areas.[35]

Indeed, both major opposition parties now fully consider electoral courts in their postelectoral calculations. While wily activists admitted prior to 1997 that their objective was to win (via the ballot box or via negotiations to diffuse situations of "ingovernability"), they still saw an increasingly useful role for electoral courts in the postelectoral process. As of 1997, however, the opposition parties seemed no longer to opt for the extralegal route. Channeling postelectoral conflicts into courts does reduce postelectoral violence, which has cost the lives of dozens of PRD activists, at least until partisans receive verdicts, by which time they often have desisted from mobilizing. As of late 1997, the judicial "route" was increasingly the only course of postelectoral action, rather than merely one of several means deployed by parties to win or wrangle public offices. During the transitional early 1990s, parties frequently negotiated with local and/or national authorities even while conducting judicial proceedings, hoping to use the electoral court more as a sort of "showing of the first card" in a lucky poker hand, rather than revealing the entire hand before bidding ceased. Given the long-standing tradition of electoral fraud, particularly in certain regions of the country, postelectoral complainants realized that "you have to cover all the bases—the judicial, negotiations with the state [and sometimes national] executive, and the street."[36] As of the late-1990s however, this dual strategy was relegated to only the most conflictive cases and was not a generalized practice.

The Unfinished Agenda: Democratizing State Institutions

If electoral competition is at least partially responsible for Mexico's political opening, then one would predict alternation of power in traditional opposition electoral strongholds. This scenario, dubbed "centripetal" democratization,[37] is driven by an assault on national governance by local forces as they acquire administrative experience and public credibility. Until very recently, the PAN carried the banner for this "outward in" reform. The party in 1997 governed six of Mexico's thirty-one states and seven of Mexico's ten largest municipalities (including Guadalajara and Monterrey). However, as of July 1997, the PRD no longer held decisive power in rural enclaves alone. The party's growing urban draw was acknowledged with the recognition, finally, of Cárdenas's victory as governor of Mexico City's 20 million residents.[38]

In full democracies, the ascent of opposition party mayors in regions where they hold electoral majorities is a rather obvious given. However, in liberalizing but semidemocratic Mexico, it could not be assumed until 1997 that superior electoral performance automatically translated directly into the transfer of power. Some of Mexico's most informed analysts have devoted entire treatises to the country's long history of electoral fraud.[39] Even high-ranking PRI and government officials acknowledged that systemic fraud and "horse trading" of victories was standard practice in Mexican elections until the mid-1990s.[40] Even as democratization and Mexico's self-proclaimed "new federalism" are implemented, strong reserve domains exist, where local *cacique* electoral bosses, including several Salinas-era governors, known as "the union of governors" or simply as "the dinosaurs," actively repress dissent.[41] High-ranking government officials, striving to depoliticize federal government funding allocations to the states—which used to flow almost entirely through the governors—have acknowledged the system's pre-1997 bias against "transparent" and patronage-free funding allocations.[42] In short, democratization in Mexico is far from finished, even if the focus has shifted from overt "leveling" of the electoral playing field to the more subtle task of reforming funding allocations and equilibrating the balance of power between the executive, legislative, and judicial branches.

The democratic consolidation literature's moderation of initially optimistic predictions, by accounting for democratization's blind spots with concepts like "tutelary powers" and "delegative" democracies, are also applicable to Mexico, even though the line between initial democratization and subsequent consolidation is much more blurred. Subnational social and political movements find resonance or repression at the national level depending on the authoritarian incumbent's exercise of a strong veto.[43] The regime's willingness to reform has always been based less on the imperative to liberalize politically and more on the imperative of appearing to liberalize politically. Given these stark limits on authoritarian willingness to recognize legally existent rights (such as that of free and fair elections), the opposition has extricated regime compliance with formal rules via repeated episodes of postelectoral negotiations, reform by reform, election by election. Negotiations tested not the autonomy or independence of institutions at the state level, but rather opposition parties' strength vis-à-vis the regime at a given contextual moment to force the regime to "make good" on enforcing laws, however enlightened they appeared on paper.

As long as the PRI-led government institutions remained gatekeepers of opposition party electoral victories, the PRI decided which opposition victories to allow and which to deny, either through outright fraud or, when opposition mobilizations persisted, by diffusing opposition mobilizations through the granting of selective concessions (always smaller than outright victory and usually offered to the PAN rather than the PRD). However, as the authoritarian incumbents faced an increasing need to liberalize, they found themselves ceding in these postelectoral "adjustments." Indeed, the establishment of an autonomous federal regime of election administration and dispute adjudication was also the single most important stimulus to the gradual approximation of electoral justice at the local level, where the most heinous violations occurred.

Political reformers first focused on representation, opening up opposition congressional representation in the late 1970s through the mid-1980s. In the late 1980s and early 1990s, reforms honed in on leveling the pre-electoral playing field (methods for constructing voter registration lists, overseeing ballot box placement, monitoring campaign finance, etc.). It was not until 1996, in the last major electoral reform, that the system of electoral justice was finalized. It became obvious that even with substantial reforms in other areas, as long as postelectoral conflicts continued, they cast a shadow on the future of "free and fair" elections, drawing attention to the unfinished business of electoral reforms.

It is important to note that despite all these changes, there have been some fundamental continuities. It has been argued that the creation of a regime of electoral courts required a rare historical opportunity—namely, the regime's embarrassment by a *lack* of electoral competition in 1976, followed by its embarrassment by an *excess* of frustrated electoral competitors in 1988. To create electoral courts that served as more than window dressing also required another unique condition: the imperative for international "democratic" credibility in NAFTA negotiations. And the final fortification of these institutions required that such reforms be in the interests (at least in the short term) of a significant portion of the PRI—the reformist moderates led by Zedillo, who needed to check party hard-liners to deliver on efforts to establish the "rule of law" throughout Mexico.

Conclusion

As I have demonstrated in this chapter, particularistic bargaining has largely been absent from federal electoral administration since the reforms of 1993–1994. The federal electoral institutions have acquired sufficient autonomy to fairly regulate postelectoral disputes at the national level, where such disputes are nearly always less severe than in the localities. However, with the Mexican Congress's October 1996 granting of the Supreme Court jurisdiction over local and state election outcomes, the era of extralegal bargaining over local electoral outcomes may also finally be over. Technically, this landmark jurisdiction extends only to constitutional controversies relating to electoral outcomes, but it is quite significant because it removed the resolution of local postelectoral conflicts from the exclusive purview of often biased local authorities (that is, state electoral courts) for the first time ever.

The federal reform came too late to bring some of the most recent alleged electoral law violators to justice, such as Tabasco's governor, Roberto Madrazo.[44] However, reformers within the opposition and the incumbent regime hoped that even if the Supreme Court's authority was quite limited, the mere threat of exposing local electoral corruption might improve compliance with the laws. The 1996 reform formally subordinated electoral courts within the constitution as a special circuit of the Mexican Supreme Court rather than continuing their existence as independent ombudsman-type agencies outside the standard jurisdictional hierarchy. Furthermore, these reforms ended the transitional role of local electoral courts, anchoring them within the emerging system of federal accountability. With the electoral law's passage, the linkage of local and federal electoral justice regimes commenced. Between the 1989 establishment of the first state electoral court and the 1996 federal reform, state electoral courts were reformed in waves that loosely followed the federal electoral court reforms of 1985 and 1991, but with varying lags. Now state legislators throughout Mexico have to scramble to reform their electoral laws into compliance with the federal standard, now the final arbiter of electoral justice, before their antiquated laws are exposed in high-profile federal electoral court rulings that overturn them.

The preceding analysis suggests the overall difficulty of analyzing horizontal accountability of autonomous institutions, because autonomy surely means that judicial institutions must be independent of the executive. It may also imply independence from public accountability. If such institutions are independent of both of these principals, incentive-driven analysis becomes difficult; actors' behavior may confirm the hypotheses of legal theorists, based on pure legal theory, but confound political theorists looking for interests and interest-based actions. Luckily for seekers of interest-based interpretations, institutional origins offer lenses through which we can understand the dependent evolution of even the most autonomous institutions, before they become insulated from politics. Such is the case of Mexico's electoral institutions, which are only now rising above the partisan fray to embody the broader interests of electoral transparency that all political party actors seem to now recognize, however reluctantly, as an essential prerequisite to democratic consolidation in Mexico.

Notes

I acknowledge the helpful comments of the editors and, especially, Andreas Schedler's extensive suggestions.

1. See Peschard-Sverdrup, *Mexican Midterm Elections,* p. 19.

2. See International Foundation for Electoral Systems, *Mexico's Mid-Term Elections,* p. 13.

3. See United Nations Development Programme, *Análisis del sistema,* p. 7.

4. Mexico is still only a "semidemocracy" because while alternation in power has occurred in the legislative branch and in gubernatorial and mayoral races, it is still not certain that the conditions exist for this to be a credible possibility in presidential elections. Following Przeworski, *Democracy and the Market,* pp. 88–92, I argue that democracy requires uncertainty about electoral outcomes. If the 2000 elections are won by the PRI, if they are seriously contested and the opposition is given a real chance of winning (and having an opposition victory accepted by what remains of the PRI state), then Mexico will have attained "full" democracy status. However, the completion of political opening prompts entry into a consolidation stage.

5. As of November 1997, all but one of these governorships were held by the PAN and included some of the country's most important states: Baja California, Chihuahua, Guanajuato, Jalisco, Nuevo Leon, and Querétaro. The single most important, the newly created Mexico City governorship, was won for the first time ever by the PRD.

6. It was revealed in 1994 by a former director of Mexico's Federal Electoral Institute that the computer had been "forced to fail" based on high-level orders. See Domínguez and McCann, *Democratizing Mexico,* p. 152.

7. While this arrangement was never formally signed, its existence is well known. For example, see Lujambio, *Federalismo,* pp. 38–39, or Molinar, "Changing the Balance," pp. 153–154. These initiatives were: the extensive trade and financial liberalization that accelerated between 1989 and the signing of NAFTA in 1993, the 1992 reform of church-state relations, and the 1992 privatization of state agricultural lands, called *ejidos.*

8. The percentage of votes fell from 98 percent in 1934 to 49 percent in 1994, with the PAN's vote share increasing from 8 percent in 1952 to 26 percent in 1994, and the left's share increasing from zero through the 1970s to 31 percent in 1988 and 17 percent in 1994.

9. Juan Miguel Alcántara and Carlos Castillo Peraza, interviews.

10. A partial exception may be Monterrey 1994, where PAN officials admitted to electoral negotiations with the national PRI but would not acknowledge "whitewashing" the results. In fact, the PRI victory was overturned in favor of the PAN through the appeals court of the state electoral tribunal. I could not independently verify press allegations of pressures on electoral court magistrates to "rule" in favor of the PAN, but they would be consistent with the other cases mentioned, where independent confirmation was obtained from at least one of the firsthand participants.

11. Indeed, the negotiator of this pact was the savvy former Tabasco PRI leader, Andrés Manuel López Obrador. López Obrador had been the only known

PRD leader to open channels with the interior secretary in Tabasco's 1991 local elections, taking three (out of seventeen) "plural" governments from the clutches of a PRI landslide. López Obrador, the PRD's current national president, has a post-electoral bargaining style much more akin to that of the PAN than to that of other PRD leaders (namely Cárdenas).

12. See González Oropeza, *La intervención federal,* pp. 155–232. There have also been dozens of unofficial (and unconstitutional) federal interventions. Some of these, with regard to mayoral and gubernatorial postelectoral conflicts, are discussed in Eisenstadt, "Courting Democracy." It is notable that since the 1930s, when Lázaro Cárdenas deposed some nineteen governors, and his successors Manuel Avila Camacho and Miguel Alemán together removed twenty-four in their bids to consolidate central authority once and for all, there was no other president who removed anywhere near that number until Salinas, who removed seventeen in his effort to placate the PAN, repress the PRD, and triumph over the "hard-liners" in his own party.

13. An antecedent institution, the Tribunal of Electoral Contention (or TRI-COEL), had been inaugurated for the 1988 federal elections, but its decisions were widely ignored and largely irrelevant.

14. One election, District V in Coahuila, was annulled by the Federal Electoral Tribunal, due to technical flaws in the counting of ballots. There were demonstrations by opposition parties, but these had much more to do with challenges to concurrent local elections, where fraud was much more widespread and its effects more concentrated, than with the federal races.

15. Concretely, PRI victories were annulled in Puebla District IV (with the special election won by the PAN) and Veracruz District XXII (with the special election won by the PRD); PRI victories in Michoacán District III and Veracruz District XXIII were reverted to the PRD; and in Jalisco District VII, a PRI victory was reverted to the PAN.

16. These reforms proved so potent that many PRI congressional members, in an unprecedented lack of discipline, voted against the reforms, which had been previously agreed upon by the party's leadership.

17. For extensive discussions of the 1980s economic crisis, the rise of the PAN, and the partial disintegration of the PRI, see Alvarado, *Electoral Patterns,* Centeno, *Democracy Within Reason,* and Mizrahi "Democracia."

18. Indeed, the hard-liners rebelled in the Seventeenth National Assembly (September 1996), managing to have internal party statutes rewritten to ensure that any future presidential candidate had served previously in a significant elected capacity (as congressional member or governor), thus giving the political "hands" an advantage over the technocrats who had dominated the PRI's candidate slates for a decade (neither Zedillo nor Salinas had ever held elected office before being nominated as the PRI's presidential candidates).

19. Federico Salasy, interview.

20. See Dezalay and Garth, "Building the Law."

21. On Tabasco, see Eisenstadt, "Confrontation." On Chiapas, see Chiapas Electoral Tribunal, *Memoria,* pp. 32–89, passim.

22. These statistics were compiled from a database of postelectoral conflicts, which I coded from the local and national press throughout Mexico for the years 1989–1996. See Eisenstadt, "Courting Democracy."

23. Indeed, the current president of the electoral court, José de la Peza Muñoz, is the first electoral court president to have been nominated by the opposition. He was a PAN nominee in 1987, when the parties were responsible for nomination.

24. The citation, from an interview with Ojesto Martínez Porcayo, refers to the

1995 mayoral race in Huejotzingo, Puebla (population 42,000), and the 1994 governor's race in Tabasco (population 1.5 million). The crucial Tabasco governor's race is referred to in note 44. The Huejotzingo contest was somewhat less transcendent—the election was important in symbolic terms, however, because it was there where the PAN drew its line in the sand regarding corruption of electoral courts. The PAN had been declared victorious in November balloting, but the win was reversed by the state electoral court on dubious grounds (through the inconsistent application of causes of annulment not similarly applied to cases of PAN challenges to PRI victories). The PAN blackmailed the PRI by abandoning the national electoral reform bargaining table, which President Zedillo had vowed would result from a consensus among the country's electoral forces. After six months of national demonstrations and local city hall occupation by PAN activists, the PRI mayor "mysteriously" resigned and a municipal council was formed by the state legislature, headed by a PANista. For more on Huejotzingo, see Eisenstadt, "Courting Democracy."

25. There is no perfect common law analogy to the writ of *amparo* in the civil law tradition, but loosely stated, it is "a general constitutional guarantee protecting one's civil rights against violation by public authorities, a writ issued against final judgment in certain cases where no other recourse is available" (Díaz and Lenhart, *Diccionario,* p. 37). An essential difference between an *amparo* and a common law appeal on constitutional grounds is that while common law cases carry the power to set precedent, *amparo* cases may apply only to the individual case at hand without setting precedent for future cases.

26. The exception being the subjection of the presidential election to electoral court jurisdiction and the elimination of the electoral college once and for all. However, this reform will not acquire relevance until the next presidential race, in 2000.

27. In this case, the PRD successfully filed a federal appeal of the results in six voting stations, turning a PRI win into a PRD victory, after the state electoral court had ruled in favor of the PRI. The PRD argued that vote counts were performed in unauthorized areas, that PRD party representatives were expelled from polling stations, that "error or malice" existed in computing votes, that pressure was exerted on poll workers, and that citizens were allowed to vote without appearing on voter rolls (Tribunal Electoral del Poder Judicial de la Federación, complaint 1/96, pp. 4–8). The federal electoral court ruled that all these complaints were invalid, except one, that the votes from the decisive polling station were counted at an unauthorized site, casting sufficient suspicion on the results to discount these votes and to overturn the results (Tribunal Electoral del Poder Judicial de la Federación, complaint 1/96 resolution, pp. 30–37).

28. The two partial exceptions are Campeche, where the the PRD runner-up in the close gubernatorial race won by the PRI launched several mobilizations and filed electoral court complaints. The Federal Electoral Tribunal ruled that PRD complaints of electoral fraud were valid but not decisive in the election's outcome (see the resolution to TEPJF complaint 68/1997). The Tabasco 1997 local elections were also contested through the mobilizational route, but not with great success. In fact, PRD national president López Obrador ordered the state's PRD legislators-elect not to take office, and they all broke ranks with the national PRD leadership and took their seats when the Tabasco legislature was convened.

29. Party positions derived from position papers submitted during the Seminario del Castillo de Chapultepec, a dialogue between the parties and federal government, sponsored during most of 1995 by IFE citizen counselors Santiago Creel, Jaime González Graf, and José Augustín Ortiz Pinchetti.

30. This is a paraphrase of a statement by Congressman Fernando Pérez Noriega, who said that with the 1996 reforms, the PAN was satisfied that the electoral playing field was level. Pérez Noriega, an important member of the judicial support team that traveled from Mexico City to the sites of particularly contested local races to prepare electoral court challenges, said that problems still exist in electoral courts in places like Puebla (citing the Huejotzingo case), but that such problems transcend institutional solutions (Pérez Noriega interview).

31. Juan Romero interview.

32. More specifically, the complaint charged the IFE with "shaving" the names of PRD supporters off the electoral list and finding means to allow PRI supporters to vote multiple times (by granting them multiple voter IDs, creating several names for the same person, etc.). The complaint charged that the creation of this list was biased and that its external audit was also compromised. TFE judges ruled the mimeographed presentations to be "unfounded" in cases where they were not complemented by concrete allegations of election-day fraud. Magistrates argued in their resolutions that the PRD's "list shaving" charge had been fully considered and answered in the appropriate venue, an appeal complaint from the IFE (Tribunal Federal Electoral, appeal complaint 400/94, passim).

33. José Luis Tuñon interview.

34. These figures are based on author calculations that are in turn based on a review of an unbiased 25 percent sample of all the cases filed in 1994. For a full report of the findings from this review compared to study of the 1988, 1991, and 1997 complaints, see Eisenstadt, "Courting Democracy."

35. Interviews with Fernando Villavicencio, Vargas, and Hector Romero.

36. Interview with Germán Martínez.

37. See, for example, Cornelius et al., *Subnational Politics,* Mizrahi, "Democracia," and Rodríguez and Ward, *Opposition Government.*

38. In 1996, the PRD also won the municipal election in Nezahualcóyotl (population 1.3 million), Mexico City's largest slum suburb; and in 1997, it won the mayoral race in Xalapa, the capital of Veracruz (population 500,000). Previously, the only important mayoral victory recognized by the regime had been Michoacán's capital, Morelia (population 500,000), which it governed from 1989 to 1992. In late 1996 and early 1997, the PRD also won some medium-sized municipalities in Guerrero, Mexico State, Morelos, and Veracruz.

39. See, for example, Crespo, *Urnas de Pandora,* Gómez Tagle, *Alquimia al fraude,* and Molinar, *Tiempo de la legitimidad.*

40. This was revealed during interviews with Lamadrid, Moreno Uriegas, and Nuñez. See also Bruhn, *Taking on Goliath,* pp. 140–150.

41. While the existence of such reserve domains in the electoral realm in Chiapas and Tabasco have been noted, these local bastions of authoritarian rule are often sites of more heinous human rights abuses. The most blatant recent evidence of what amounts to state government impunity (or at least a lack of accountability) was the execution-style massacre of some forty-five peasants in Acteal, Chiapas, in December 1997, with apparent complicity by mayors and other local officials.

42. These comments were made in a 27 January 1997 talk by treasury subsecretary Santiago Levy at the University of California, San Diego's Center for U.S.-Mexican Studies.

43. These terms come from Smith, "Crisis and Democracy," Valenzuela, "Democratic Consolidation," and O'Donnell, "Delegative Democracy," respectively. For case studies of federal government decisionmaking in the face of regional and local defiance, see Cornelius et al., *Subnational Politics.* The Mexican case is harder to classify between democratization (or liberalization) and consolidation, as

political opening has been a twenty-year process, rather than an abrupt regime change such as in the 1980s democratization literature's prototypical cases in Eastern Europe and South America.

44. Evidence was found by a federal attorney general that PRI candidate Madrazo spent fifty times the legal limit on his 1994 gubernatorial campaign. After a debate about whether the federal government was empowered to conduct such a probe of Tabasco state matters, the federal Supreme Court ruled that the Tabasco state attorney general was the proper authority to investigate the matter. The investigation was turned over to that rather powerless agency, which ruled that Madrazo indeed violated spending laws, but that "electoral crime" punishments were not specified in the state penal code. The opposition-led Chamber of Deputies tried to reopen a federal probe in 1997 but was stalled by a states' rights lawsuit filed by Tabasco against the federal government.

7

Institutionalizing Credible Elections in Ghana

E. GYIMAH-BOADI

K ey among the issues confronting new democracies such as Ghana is electoral credibility. Against a background of manifest credibility problems in the first transition elections of 1992, Ghana was faced with a formidable challenge of institutionalizing electoral credibility. The electoral playing field was widely perceived as *not* level, and fraud was allegedly rampant. Most important, the results of the 1992 elections were bitterly disputed and the entire process of return to constitutional rule was nearly derailed. And yet the elections in December 1996 were relatively successful, and their outcomes appear to have won broad public acceptance. In this chapter I review the steps taken to restore a measure of fairness and cleanliness to elections and to institutionalize electoral credibility before the elections of 1996. I also evaluate the degree to which the deficit in electoral credibility has been reduced and identify the gaps and problems that lie in the way to the institutionalization of that process in Ghana.

The Heritage of Mistrust

The presidential election of 1992 had left in its trail widespread mistrust of the electoral process among opposition groups in the country. It appeared to confirm the suspicions of the opposition parties and their supporters that the Interim National Electoral Commission (INEC) lacked independence and neutrality in discharging its responsibilities for the electoral aspects of the transitional program. This suspicion arose at least in part from the fact that the members of the election body were appointed unilaterally by the incumbent government—the Provisional National Defense Council

(PNDC)—without consulting opposition forces. It became particularly heightened when Flight Lieutenant J. J. Rawlings, the head of government, decided to contest the presidential election as a civilian. It is not surprising then that the results of the presidential elections that brought Rawlings to power as the first president of the Fourth Republic were bitterly disputed.

While a number of international observer groups, notably the Commonwealth Observer Group, gave an overall positive rating to the actual conduct of the election, it was vehemently rejected by the opposition. Tagging onto the defective register, the losing candidates and parties made a host of allegations covering every conceivable irregularity and fraud in the election code.[1] They included intimidation and interference by security personnel and "revolutionary" organs; multiple voting, impersonation of voters, and ineligible voters; prestuffed ballot boxes; ballot dumping; bribery and other corrupt practices; and collaboration and collusion of the electoral authority.

Indeed, the declaration of Rawlings as the winner of the presidential polls triggered a spate of postelection violence, including the detonation of four bombs in different parts of Accra by a shadowy group called the Alliance of Democratic Forces (ADF); the politically motivated burning to death of the chair of the western region branch of the ruling National Democratic Congress (NDC); and rioting by supporters of the main opposition party, the New Patriotic Party (NPP), in many large cities, notably in Ghana's second largest city and opposition stronghold, Kumasi.

Most significant, disputes over the outcome of the November 1992 presidential elections led to a boycott of the parliamentary elections scheduled for the following December by the main opposition parties: NPP, National Independence Party (NIP), People's National Convention (PNC), and Heritage Party. This singular action turned the first parliament of Ghana's Fourth Republic into a de facto single-party body and posed a grave danger to the consolidation of the nascent democracy.[2]

Many factors account for the credibility problems faced by Ghana's electoral process in 1992. The elections were called in a rather snap manner after eleven years of quasi-military rule during which competitive elections had been virtually ruled out on the grounds that they were inappropriate for the country. The election authority found itself having to administer a crowded program of electoral events, with a high probability for otherwise avoidable shortcomings and imperfections on election day. At the same time, the newly formed political parties had little time to get off the ground, and the candidates had even less time to mount credible campaigns.

As transitional elections held to end a decade of military rule and to usher the country into civilian and constitutional governance, the 1992 elections presented peculiar administrative problems. The transitional arrangements offered too short a period to permit the election authority,

INEC, to prepare adequately for the elections. The management of election logistics proved exceedingly challenging in the face of acute time constraints, and electoral events could not be carefully planned and details worked out. For instance, INEC conducted a referendum on a new draft constitution for Ghana's Fourth Republic on 28 April 1992. In the referendum, the people were asked not only to approve or reject the new constitution, but also to agree on 7 January 1993 as the date for a return to constitutional rule. In addition, the ban on political party activity, in force since 1982, was lifted on 15 May of that year. Thus, although the way was paved for the formation of political parties and their registration by INEC, the amount of time the parties had to organize before the elections was very short. The first political party received certification in mid-July upon satisfying the requirements laid down in law. Meanwhile, the presidential election had been scheduled for 3 November and legislative elections for 8 December 1992. The first party to receive certification had barely four months to prepare for the elections.

Second, the electoral mechanism had gone unused for a decade, except for staggered local-level elections in 1988–1989, and was therefore rusty. Key among the problems associated with a nonperforming electoral mechanism was the flawed nature of the existing voters' register (electoral roll), which had been originally compiled (by the National Commission on Democracy, which used paid volunteers instructed to register as many people as they could) in 1987 and not updated since. The absence of reliable population figures and information on where people lived, and the absence of a firm demographic basis for determining the distribution of voters for purposes of siting polling stations, were additional problems. Consequently, some duly registered voters were disenfranchised because they could not find their polling stations on election day, creating suspicions that INEC and the incumbent regime had connived to disenfranchise opposition voters.

Third, severe logistical problems were experienced on election day, largely because of the short time available for the procurement of all the supplies needed for the election. And delays in resource mobilization affected the ability of INEC to distribute election materials according to planned schedules.

Fourth, time and resource constraints seriously impaired the capacity of the election authority to carry out effectively the important tasks of educating the electorate on voting procedures and the need to exercise their franchise, and of educating thousands of election personnel on the laws and regulations governing the elections and training them in the technical aspects of the administration of the elections. Noticeably, election officials made mistakes or failed to follow proper procedures on election day, casting doubt on the credibility of the election process.

The Legal Framework[3]

Against the background of disputed elections of 1992 and with key political actors and their supporters deeply mistrustful of the electoral process, Ghanaian democracy and, in particular, its election authorities were faced with formidable challenges of building both confidence and credibility. The Electoral Commission, with the assistance of international donors, embarked on a relatively comprehensive program of reforming the electoral process and enhancing credibility.

The provisions of the 1992 Constitution[4] were crucial to the process of establishing electoral credibility in Ghana's Fourth Republic. Article 43 of the Constitution provided for the establishment of an Electoral Commission of Ghana consisting of seven members—a chair, two deputy chairs, and four other members—appointed by the president on the advice of the Council of State (a constitutional body of eminent citizens whose duty is to advise the president and other state actors in the discharge of their functions). The major responsibilities and powers of the commission, set out in considerable detail in the constitution and amplified by statute, included the following: (1) the conduct of all referenda and national and local government elections; (2) the delimitation of electoral constituencies; (3) the compilation and updating of the voters' register; (4) voter education; and (5) the registration of political parties.

The Constitution also gave the Electoral Commission the power to make regulations (by constitutional instrument) for the effective performance of its functions. The existence of a body of laws and explicit rules and regulations relating to its functions provided the Electoral Commission with a measure of insulation and put the body in a stronger position lawfully to resist undue external pressures and interference in its work. It also provided the commission with both a guide for and a defense of its actions. And above all, the laws formed the framework for the resolution of electoral conflict within the limits of the laws of Ghana. In an attempt to make the Electoral Commission autonomous, the 1992 Constitution provided that in performing its functions, the commission "shall not be subject to the direction or control of any person or authority"; that once appointed, the three chairpersons (chair and two deputy chairs) have permanent tenure until retirement and are removable only by impeachment; and that the commission's expenses are charged directly to the country's Consolidated Fund.

The Challenges of 1996

With the inauguration of the Fourth Republic, the life of the Interim National Electoral Commission officially came to an end. A new Electoral

Commission was inaugurated in August 1993. The new commission decided to reform the electoral system against the backdrop of events surrounding the 1992 elections. It recognized that the row over the results and the compendium of allegations of fraud (many of them unsubstantiated) had left in their trail lingering suspicion and mistrust of the election authority as an independent and impartial arbiter of democratic elections and a battered faith in the ballot box. Above all, it saw a clear need for electoral reforms with a view to achieving greater transparency in all aspects of the election process. In addition, it sought to create popular faith in the ballot box as the arbiter of a democratic electoral contest; to eliminate, or at least minimize, dispute over election outcomes; and, as a by-product, to build confidence in the commission. In practice, it meant the new commission had to undertake the following tasks: (1) address the legitimate concerns of the political parties about the shortcomings of the 1992 elections, especially the demands made by the opposition parties in the aftermath of the elections as a condition for their participation in any future elections, such as the compilation of a new voters' register (copies of which must be given to them well ahead of elections), the issuing of identity cards to all registered voters, the holding of presidential and parliamentary elections on the same day, and the use of transparent ballot boxes; (2) develop a more comprehensive program of voter education; (3) provide better training for election officials; and (4) plan electoral events in more detail well ahead of election time and in a more organized fashion.

Registering Voters Anew

In September 1995, an entirely new voters' register was compiled to replace the flawed one used for the 1992 elections. This time, the political parties were actively involved in the planning and implementation of the registration exercise, in a collective effort to create a comprehensive, accurate, and reliable register. After thorough discussions with the political parties, a consensus was reached on the design of the registration form, the structure and contents of the register, the methods for compiling it, and other related matters. The parties were allowed four agents or monitors (two for the parties in government and two for the nongovernment parties) at each registration center during the entire fifteen-day registration period. The agents were trained by the Electoral Commission alongside its own registration officials to ensure that both officials and agents understood the process.

Registration took place at 20,000 centers nationwide. At each center, daily records of the number of persons registered were kept, signed by the registration officer and countersigned by the party agents. The agents, as indeed every citizen, could challenge a person applying for registration on the ground that he or she was not qualified according to the laid-down requirements. Such challenges were decided by district-based registration review committees on which political party representatives sat, with a right of appeal to the High Court for a person aggrieved by the committee's decision. Altogether, 9.2 million people registered as voters, of whom 49.7 percent were women. Each elector was given a numbered ID card. To make it easy for people to identify their polling stations, the place where a person registered was designated as his or her polling station on election day, and the station number was endorsed on the ID card.

After the field collection of the registration data, scanning technology was used to compile the register as a means of cutting down on time and errors in computer data entry. A two-week period of exhibition (public scrutiny) of the register in May 1996 at the 20,000 registration centers/polling stations followed the compilation of the provisional register. Objections against the presence in the register of names deemed to be unqualified were entertained during the exhibition period. Such objections were resolved by district judicial officers, with a right of appeal to the High Court. At the exhibition, 6.5 million or 73 percent of all the registered voters checked their particulars. Copies of the final register of voters were given to the political parties in both paper and computer-readable (CD-ROM) form.

Training Election Officials and Party Agents

To ensure that election officials clearly understood the rules and regulations governing the elections and followed proper procedures, the Electoral Commission wrote down detailed, step-by-step procedures to be followed by each category of election officials. This was buttressed by a practical, hands-on training designed to give the various categories of officials prior experience in what they were required to do in connection with the elections. After their training, the officials were sworn by a judicial officer to faithfully execute the election law.

Additionally, since every candidate contesting an election was entitled by law to appoint an agent to represent him or her at each polling station in the constituency, the training program was expanded to include candidate or party agents. Like the election officials, the party agents were required to take an oath to uphold the election laws and regulations and to sign the polling station results form (or otherwise give reasons in writing for failing to do so) and to receive a certified copy for their candidates. In this way, any challenges to the results could be easily verified and resolved. Knowledgeable party agents who witnessed the relevant activities before, during, and after polling were particularly well placed to testify to the credibility of the election.

Educating the Public

To reduce widespread misunderstandings and suspicions about the election process, which made people easily prone to believe allegations of impropriety and wrongdoing in the administration of elections, the commission embarked on a public education program that went beyond familiarizing the voting public with the mechanics of voting to providing basic information about the election process. The aim was to foster an electorate sufficiently knowledgeable about the dos and don'ts of elections and therefore better able to evaluate allegations of impropriety and wrongdoing.

The voter education program was extensive and multifaceted. It was carried out through the electronic and print media, pamphlets, posters, stickers, and discussions with organized groups. Women and young voters were targeted as groups needing extra attention. As an innovation, a drama presentation woven around unacceptable election practices was shown several times on national television in English and many of the local languages and was performed live for the public in some of the principal towns. For persons living in the remote parts of the country who were unlikely to benefit from the pamphlets or the print and electronic media programs because of illiteracy or lack of access, the Electoral Commission mounted a special awareness campaign whereby trained personnel went to their locations, took them through the voting procedure at meetings specifically organized for the purpose, and held discussions with them on the election process in general.

Recognizing that it could not reach everybody effectively by itself, the Electoral Commission solicited the assistance of religious groups and various nongovernmental and public interest organizations in expanding its public education effort. They were supplied with carefully prepared materials to ensure accuracy of content. The enthusiasm with which the groups and organizations responded indicated widespread public interest and willingness to participate in the democratization effort.

Redesigning Electoral Instruments

On the assumption that people's perceptions and suspicions form part of the electoral landscape and need to be confronted as reality, the Electoral Commission introduced other innovations into the election process. Among them were transparent ballot boxes and cardboard voting screens. These were intended to forestall allegations of stuffing ballot boxes before voting and ballot dumping during voting made in connection with the 1992 elections by losing candidates and widely believed by the general public. A transparent ballot box that was not empty on arrival at the polling station would be self-evident. On the other hand, a cardboard screen placed on top of a table in full public view of the voter preserved the secrecy of the ballot while enhancing the detection of the introduction of any extra ballot papers concealed on the voter's person.

The Inter-Party Advisory Committee

Perhaps the most important mechanism for managing distrust of the Electoral Commission by the opposition parties and among the various political parties was the innovative Inter-Party Advisory Committee (IPAC). Initiated in late 1993 by the Electoral Commission with the encouragement of donors, and convening its inaugural meeting in March 1993, IPAC brought representatives of the political parties and the election authority together in regular meetings to discuss preparations for the elections. It opened a line of communication and dialogue between the political parties and the election authority and among the parties themselves. IPAC operated under the following clear guidelines: (1) a meeting would be held at least once a month; (2) every registered political party was free to send representatives; (3) meetings would be closed to the public and the press to facilitate the frank exchange of views; (4) the parties would bring their concerns to the Electoral Commission for discussion; (5) the commission would bring its election plans and programs to the IPAC for comment and input; and (6) as a nonstatutory, purely advisory body, IPAC's decisions would not be binding on the commission, which, in accordance with the country's constitution, would have the final word on how elections are to be administered.

In spite of being purely advisory, IPAC played a crucial role in building considerable consensus on the election process and reforms toward the 1996 elections. While twenty-five of the total fifty-two suggestions for change made by the parties were deemed to lie outside of the authority of the Electoral Commission (and hence of IPAC), twenty-one were adopted in their entirety and another three were adopted partially. In all, the open channel for dialogue and active collaboration provided by the IPAC proved mutually beneficial to the Electoral Commission and the political parties and helped to clear misunderstandings and diffuse tensions about the election process. Indeed, IPAC became so successful as a forum for resolving electoral conflict that it was replicated in the regions and districts—with the regional IPAC getting off the ground in early 1996, followed midyear by the district committees.

Independent Election Observers

The active involvement of civic bodies and key elements of civil society in the polling process was also a key factor in reducing electoral conflict and enhancing credibility. As noted above, key elements of civil society (prominent national organizations—such as the Christian Council of Churches/Catholic Secretariat—and civic groups—such as the Ghana Legal Literacy Resource Foundation) had collaborated closely with the political parties, statutory bodies such as the National Commission on Civic Education, and the Electoral Commission to embark on political/voter education campaigns. But the epitome of societal involvement in the electoral process was the formation of two domestic poll-watching groups: Ghana Alert and the Network of Domestic Election Observers (NEDEO).

The NEDEO comprised twenty-three national organizations, including the Christian Council/Catholic Secretariat, Federation of Muslim Councils, Ahmadiyya Muslim Mission, Trades Union Congress, Ghana Bar Association, Ghana Union Traders' Association, Ghana Association of Women Entrepreneurs, Ghana Journalists Association, Ghana National Association of Teachers, Ghana Registered Nurses Association, and others. The groups helped to mobilize most of the available domestic resources for nongovernmental election monitoring. They selected suitable personnel from their organizations for training and deployment as monitors; they placed communication, transport, and other equipment at the disposal of the network; and they established a machinery for monitoring the pre-election environment. Between NEDEO and Ghana Alert, the domestic poll-watching groups trained more than 4,200 personnel nationwide and deployed them to all 200 constituencies of the country and some 3,100 polling stations—representing more than 21 percent of all polling stations and covering most of the conflict-prone parts of the country, such as the Kokomba-Nanumba areas of northern Ghana (which had been the scene of communal violence in 1994).

Preparations to monitor the elections by the domestic bodies began in July 1996, four months before the elections. Thus, they were well placed to observe and report on developments before, during, and after voting. The involvement of local monitors, with a better knowledge of the local scene than most external observers and, especially, the ability to set up mechanisms for at least a crude parallel vote count and to assist in efforts to check claims of fraud, enhanced the transparency of the election process and boosted public confidence in the outcomes of those elections. Indeed, placing the domestic poll-watching bodies in a position to vouch for the integrity of the Electoral Commission proved very useful in enhancing the credibility of the election authority. The presence of such domestic election observer organizations provided an opportunity for the Electoral Commission to demonstrate its independence from the ruling party, as the latter and its agents expressed strong opposition to the domestic groups and put pressure on the Electoral Commission to deny accreditation.

The Achievements of the Electoral Reforms

The benefits of the reforms in the electoral system after 1992 were very much in evidence in the elections of December 1996 and the events leading up to them.[5] The reforms were helpful in creating the conditions for relatively competitive elections in which the ruling party was compelled to campaign with a little more seriousness and opposition parties rated their chances of success as generally fair. It created the minimum conditions for the opposition to return to the electoral process and to stay in it, in spite of lingering misgivings. In addition to an impressively high voter turnout of 78 percent on 7 December 1996, voting was generally smooth, and voting day and the immediate aftermath passed peacefully. Not only did widespread fears of pre- and postelection violence fail to materialize, but Ghana's history of electoral conflicts (especially in 1956 and 1978)[6] was not repeated.

In a marked contrast to 1992, international and independent domestic observers were unanimous in evaluating the election as free and transparent. The report of the National Democratic Institute stating that "the manner in which the elections were conducted represents a positive step forward in strengthening Ghana's democracy and its electoral process,"[7] and the conclusion of the Commonwealth Observer Group that "overall conditions allowed a free expression of the will of the electors,"[8] were generally consistent with the reports of the independent domestic observers.[9] Most significant, the losing opposition parties conceded defeat and graciously congratulated the winner, while the winning party congratulated the losers for a competitive campaign. In the days immediately after the polls, the opposition parties began to develop strategies for performing better in the next elections scheduled for 2000.

Indeed, the Electoral Commission had demonstrated its independence in a number of important ways in the course of preparing for the 1996 elections. It acted firmly and decisively and stood its ground on a number of "test cases" where it was convinced that its position was reasonable and lawful. For instance, in connection with the registration of voters, the commission refused to yield to two demands of the ruling party. One was related to the issuance of voter identification (ID) cards. The ruling party took the position that either every registered voter was given a photo ID card or everybody should be given a thumbprint ID card. The commission disagreed on grounds that there were not enough resources to cover the issuing of photo identification cards to every registered voter. It stuck to its position and issued photo ID cards only to registered voters residing in the country's major towns (where voter impersonation was more likely to occur because of heavy population concentrations and relative anonymity); thumb-print IDs were issued to those in the rural areas.

The second demand was to extend the registration period from fifteen to thirty days. Again, the commission refused, arguing that the period afforded persons who really wanted to register ample opportunity to do so. Also, the Electoral Commission ignored the vehement objections to the presence of domestic election observers and resisted pressures to deny accreditation to NEDEO and Ghana Alert by elements within the ruling party.

The Electoral Commission was able to resolve some conflicts simply by explaining the reasons for its actions or indicating the sources of its authority. For example, when it became apparent that there was agitation for the government to set the date for the presidential election, the Electoral Commission pointed to the constitutional provision empowering it, and not the government, to do so. Again, the commission explained its refusal to allow an alliance formed by two parties to use one symbol to contest the elections by reference to the law requiring a candidate to use the symbol of his or her political party. Similarly, the commission refused to permit party executives to withdraw duly nominated candidates of their party on the ground that the right of withdrawal is given in the law only to the candidate himself or herself.

Reform Failures and Shortcomings

Notwithstanding the above achievements, a number of disturbing elements emerged in the electoral process. The expenditure of more than U.S.$13 million (with donors providing as much as U.S.$10 million of this)[10] on the elections may be modest by comparison with other transition elections on the continent, such as the so-called gold-plated elections of Mozambique in 1994. However, it appears to be rather high for a second transition election and in a country that was not emerging out of a civil war. Moreover, in spite of all the money spent, extensive preparations, and heavy involvement of the political parties and civil society, the 1996 elections were marred by serious lapses. The voter registration figures alone were disturbing: 9.2 million voters were enrolled in a country with only about 18 million people, many of whom are under age fifteen. Add to this the episodes that domestic and international monitors witnessed of registration and voting by children, especially in remote areas, and the integrity of voter registration comes gravely into question.

In addition, there were genuine doubts about a level playing field. In 1996 as in 1992, the ruling party and its presidential candidate, Jerry Rawlings, enjoyed clear advantages of incumbency and visibility over their rivals, but the Electoral Commission was powerless to do anything about that. The ruling party cornered state resources, including the print and electronic media, while the opposition parties had only the very weak private sector to rely on for resources. The state-controlled media, especially the press and radio, displayed a pronounced bias in favor of the ruling party in contravention of Article 55, Sections 11 and 12 of the Constitution[11] and contrary to the guidelines on "fair and equitable" election coverage laid down by the National Media Commission.[12] The Electoral Commission could do nothing to stop the ruling party from converting major state functions into political rallies or President Rawlings from making a radio and television broadcast to the nation two days after the period of election campaigning had officially ended and eight hours before the start of polling. Indeed, the NDC campaign had been a lavish affair. Its billboards were splashed around the country; its fleet of campaign vehicles vastly outnumbered the opposition. It sustained months of advertising blitzes and reportedly threw a lot of money around. Where the money came from is largely a mystery, but the Electoral Commission has only limited powers and capabilities to enforce postelection accountability among the political parties.

Of course, the electoral reforms and extensive preparations reflected the deep political polarization in Ghanaian society. The "charm offensive" of the commission was largely an attempt to respond to the trenchant criticisms and claims of electoral fraud in 1992 and to mollify the opposition parties that had insisted they would not return to the electoral process without significant reforms. However, deep and widespread suspicion persisted among the articulate public (in the urban areas), and especially the opposition parties, that the electoral body was inherently biased in favor of the Rawlings government—in spite of all the efforts put into addressing opposition demands for greater transparency, and after putting so much international assistance into reforms. This became apparent on the day of the election and in the immediate aftermath, when technically defensible developments such as a delay in announcing the final results of the elections within seventy-two hours (as casually promised by an official of the commission) caused considerable public anxiety, agitation, and suspicion that the results were being "cooked" in favor of the government.

To be sure, suspicions reflect, at least in part, paranoia on the part of the Ghanaian opposition. But they also underscore the persistence of wide gaps in electoral credibility and limitations in the efforts to institutionalize electoral fairness. Lingering suspicions over the impartiality of the Electoral Commission derive largely from the origins of the election authority. The commission is basically a holdover from the preconstitutional-rule Interim National Electoral Commission. Its chair (Kwadwo Afari Gyan) had been INEC's deputy chair, and its deputy chair (David Kanga) was a commissioner of INEC. In addition, and as noted above, INEC was widely perceived (rightly or wrongly) to have been complicit in the "rigging" of the November 1992 transition election in favor of the NDC.

INEC had been hastily established to administer a "snap" election, and its commissioners had been appointed by the quasi-military Rawlings government unilaterally and without consulting the opposition. INEC itself was grafted unto the National Commission on Democracy (NCD), the body that had been created by a decree of the Provisional National Defense Council as part of the Rawlings populist revolution to replace the existing Electoral Commission.[13] It is instructive to note also that Justice D. F. Annan, who headed the NCD from 1984 until 1993 when he was appointed by the elected Rawlings government as speaker of parliament, was also a ranking member of the ruling National Defense Council. The commission's efforts had gone mainly into canvasing the government's position against liberal democracy in general and multiparty and competitive elections in particular,[14] and in the mid- to late 1980s it had provided employment to cadres of the revolution returning home from training in East-bloc countries. With such antecedents, the composition of the top and middle levels of the commission continue to be dogged by credibility problems, notwithstanding the constitutional guarantees of autonomy and insulation from political influence and the institution of IPAC.

The appointment of the members of the Electoral Commission by the president on the advice of the Council of State was intended to inject bipartisanship and consultation into the composition of the electoral body. But the Council of State itself is composed in roughly equal parts of individuals handpicked by the president and elected ones. And besides, the president is not compelled to take the advice of the council on any action he takes, including the appointment of electoral commissioners. He is widely perceived to exercise his appointive powers in a highly partisan manner and without consulting the opposition.

Charging expenditures to the Consolidated Fund as provided for in the Constitution should have helped foster the financial independence of the Electoral Commission. But Ghana's Consolidated Fund is notoriously thin. Thus, the electoral body and the reforms it initiated were heavily dependent on the generous financial and technical support received from international donors. For example, the U.S. government provided $6.9 million for the purchase of election materials and equipment, technical assistance for the registration of voters, and the payment of some other expenses for electoral administration. Denmark provided U.S.$3 million to purchase transparent ballot boxes; to train registration staff, exhibition staff, polling staff, and political party agents; and to conduct voter education. Britain gave U.S.$0.8 million for voter registration forms and equipment for scanning data on registration forms.[15] External funding enabled the commission to build a substantial material and manpower capacity toward the delivery of fair elections, but it remains to be seen whether such funding can be sustained, especially at such high levels.

Individuals and parties aggrieved by the actions of the Electoral Commission can go to the courts to seek relief. Ghana's election law permits not only political parties and election candidates but also practically any elector to bring a court action against the commission. So far, court cases instituted against the commission fall into the following categories: individual citizens questioning the adequacy of preparations for elections; political parties questioning the commission's authority for taking certain measures; and losing candidates disputing election results. With the singular exception of a Constituency Boundaries Tribunal, proposed in the Constitution to be set up by the chief justice from time to time to deal with delimitation grievances, the country's general court system constitutes the framework for the resolution conflicts that arise over the performance of the commission's functions.

However, this generalized conflict resolution mechanism has not lent itself to the speedy resolution of electoral conflict usually associated with specialized electoral tribunals. Election cases tend to drag on seemingly interminably, partly because of the appellate system and partly because there is no codified election case law and correlatively no clear legal principles readily available to guide judges in the resolution of electoral conflict. For instance, a case in an Accra constituency in which one of the contestants was seeking to overturn the declaration of the results of the 7 December 1996 polls in his favor dragged on for about one year—despite admission of the Electoral Commission that it made a mistake in tallying the results and that a ballot box for one polling station in that constituency had been left uncounted. It is beginning to appear that once declared, reversal of election results is most unlikely, especially where such a reversal is adverse for the ruling party. That would seem to create an incentive to rig the initial declaration of election results in one's favor in the hope that results already declared are difficult to reverse.

The idea of election observation by nonpartisan external and domestic bodies appears to have been firmly established in the 1996 polls. However, its sustained practice cannot be taken for granted. Domestic civil society is certainly high on enthusiasm and desire to play an active role in electoral processes. The existing human resource base for civic work is quite adequate. But it is woefully lacking in organizational capacity and financial resources. While the 1996 experience generated considerable capacity building, the domestic poll-watching groups had depended heavily on external agencies for resources to implement their programs and to resist governmental efforts to scuttle their initiatives. Financial and moral support from external donors, especially the National Democratic Institute and the USAID Mission in Ghana, had been crucial to the work and eventual success of NEDEO. But for all its potential as a "permanent" nonpartisan domestic poll-watcher and a facilitator of mediation between the Electoral Commission and political parties and among the parties, NEDEO has gone defunct after the 1996 elections—for want of funding.

The Way Ahead

In preparing for the 1996 elections, the Electoral Commission of Ghana undertook several electoral reforms that contributed to the delivery of fair elections and the general acceptance of the results. In its reform program, the Electoral Commission sought to do well the things for which it was responsible as an election authority. In most cases, it responded effectively to concerns about the electoral system and created a transparent and verifiable election process that facilitated the resolution of electoral conflict. It sought to achieve transparency and accountability not only through electoral arrangements but also through dialogue and partnership with the political parties. It recognized that as the primary stakeholders in democratic elections, political parties have a role to play in the administration of elections, and that in the case of newly emerging democracies, their input and involvement in the implementation of electoral programs were crucial. Constant dialogue between an election authority and the political parties helped to lessen unnecessary tensions and apprehensions and to keep complaints to a minimum.

However, Ghana is far from institutionalizing electoral fairness. The Electoral Commission continues to be dogged by doubts over its integrity and impartiality among politically important elements of Ghanaian society. It will take time and more effort to remove such perceptions. Certainly the IPACs should be maintained and strengthened—if possible by making them independent of the Electoral Commission and rooting them firmly in civil society. At the very least, the committees at the national, regional, and district levels should be broadened to include key elements of Ghanaian civil society.

A general reform to enhance the independence of the Ghanaian judiciary, improve its operational efficiency, and increase its overall efficiency would facilitate the institutionalization of electoral fairness. But that is a tall order. What may be feasible is to establish a court or tribunal dedicated to the adjudication of election disputes or to create a "rocket docket"[16] facility in the implementing legislation of existing electoral law that would enable election cases to be jumped ahead of the queue and processed with maximum dispatch. And insofar as adjudication is concerned, a body of case law and clear principles for the resolution of electoral conflict will emerge out of the several election-related cases coming before the courts.

The possibility of recomposing the Electoral Commission on the basis of bipartisan consultation and agreement or the inclusion of representatives of identifiable political and social forces (along the lines of Benin's election authority) must be considered. However, the latter arrangement may render the Electoral Commission overtly partisan and heighten rather than reduce the credibility problems of the body.

At any rate, elections form only a part of a democratic framework. The democratization of the general environment to create a democratic culture supportive of democratic elections remains imperative. But relatively successful elections in December 1996 suggest that an electoral system and an election authority with suspect origins can be rendered credible enough to produce outcomes that meet with broad public acceptance. However, reforming the electoral system to achieve a more congenial election environment should be a continuing, and not a one-shot, activity. In that sense, the quality of the electoral process and the ability of the election body to serve as an effective agency of horizontal accountability must be judged by the extent to which the present accomplishments are sustained and improved upon in future elections. This would require that the possibility of funding political parties to achieve a more level playing field, equal access to the media by all political parties, and real or perceived excessive exploitation of incumbency be seriously addressed. Similarly, the legal and technocratic capacity of the Electoral Commission to effectively audit the expenditures of the various parties, foster postelection accountability, and reduce the incentive on the part of the political parties to resort to illicit and unfair means of financing their election campaigns must be significantly enhanced.

Notes

This chapter was researched and written under a grant from the United States Institute of Peace (1996–1997). The analysis benefited greatly from the critical insights and suggestions of Sean Hall of USAID and Steven Snook of the International Foundation for Electoral Systems in Accra.

1. These allegations are covered in detail in a document of the New Patriotic Party, *The Stolen Verdict.*

2. For details of the 1992 elections and their negative implications for democratic consolidation, see Gyimah-Boadi, "Ghana's Uncertain Political Opening," and Gyimah-Boadi, "Notes on Ghana's Current Transition."

3. The following sections rely extensively on the narrative of Kwadwo Afari-Gyan, chair of the Electoral Commission of Ghana, "Towards the Delivery of Fair Elections."

4. The provisions establishing the Electoral Commission of Ghana and assigning its functions and powers are found in Chapter 7, Articles 43–54 of the Constitution of Ghana, 1992. Other statutes governing the electoral system in Ghana are Political Parties Law (PNDC Law 284), 1992, and Representation of the People (Parliamentary Constituencies) Instrument (LI 1538), 1992.

5. For a fuller discussion of the December 1996 elections, see Lyons, "Ghana's Encouraging Elections," and Gyimah-Boadi, "Ghana's Encouraging Elections."

6. For a recent account of Ghanaian political history highlighting elections and other conflicts, see Boahen, "Conflict Reoriented," and Chazan, "The Anomalies of Continuity"; for a vivid account of the conflicts in the pre-independence elections in 1954 and 1956, see Austin, *Politics in Ghana.*

7. See National Democratic Institute, "Preliminary Statement."

8. *Report of the Commonwealth Observer Group on Ghana's Elections*, p. 29.

9. See, for example, the statement on the elections issued by NEDEO at the Ghana International Press Center on 12 December 1996.

10. Only partial information on external funding of the elections is available. My own estimates suggest external funding of U.S.$12–U.S.$15 million for Electoral Commission activities. Some of this funding is reported in Afriyie Badu and Larvie, *Elections in Ghana*, pp. 75–76.

11. Article 55, Section 11 stipulates that "[t]he State shall provide fair opportunity to all political parties to present their programmes to the public by ensuring equal access to the state-owned media." Section 12 of the same article provides that "[a]ll presidential candidates shall be given the same amount of time and space on state-owned media to present their programmes to the people."

12. The Media Commission has the constitutional mandate to promote and ensure the freedom and independence of the media and to insulate the state-owned media from government control. As part of its efforts to give meaning to the constitutional provision of "equal access," the commission issued detailed guidelines on political reporting, including coverage of party political activities, campaigns and politics, candidates for public office, party manifestos, political advertising, party political broadcasts, etc.

13. Polling in Ghana has been administered by an independent electoral commission since 1968.

14. The NCD, established under Section 6 of the PNDC (Establishment) Proclamation, 1981, was charged with the exercise of the functions of the Electoral Commission established under the suspended 1979 Constitution. Under Section 32 of the PNDC Law 42, the NCD was assigned additional functions as follows: (1) disseminate within society the objectives of the revolutionary transformation being embarked upon by the council in the interest of real democracy; (2) identify regularly from contacts with the population the real needs of people, especially in the remote areas of the country and the deprived sections of the community and notify the government regularly of these needs; (3) assess for the government's information the limitations to the achievements of true democracy arising from the existing inequalities between different strata of the population and make recommendations for redressing these inequalities; (4) monitor the implementation of government policies designed to meet the urgent needs of the population, and report to the government regularly its observations concerning such implementation; (5) formulate for the consideration of the government a program for a more effective realization of democracy in Ghana; and (6) terminate political parties that were in operation before 31 December 1981 and recover all assets of such parties for disposal or use (see Information Services Department, *The Search*).

15. For details, see Afriyie Badu and Larvie, *Elections in Ghana*, pp. 75–76.

16. The idea of a "rocket docket" was suggested to me by H. Kwasi Prempeh, a Washington-based Ghanaian lawyer (personal communication).

8

The Third Dimension of Accountability: The International Community in National Elections

ROBERT A. PASTOR

D emocracy is a right of *all* people, but it is exercised in a defined area—a village, a province, or a nation-state.[1] The legitimate role of the international community with regard to national democracy has never been clearly defined. The presumption is that a people should exercise their democratic rights without outside interference; but what if a people are denied their rights by a dictator? What then should the international community do? The charters of the United Nations and other international organizations offer contradictory guidance, and most governments have used the calculus of their national interest to decide whether to help or harm the prospects of democracy in other countries. Only as the Cold War began to wane in the late 1980s did the international community begin to find its voice on behalf of democracy. Since then, foreign governments, nongovernmental organizations (NGOs), and intergovernmental organizations (IGOs) have become increasingly important in facilitating democratic transitions and sustaining constitutional government—so much so that they sometimes function as surrogates for domestic institutions that have not yet established their competence or autonomy.

The essence of democratic government is accountability, and it has two dimensions: (1) people must have the unfettered right to elect their leaders (vertical accountability), and (2) institutions of government must not encroach on the legitimate areas of responsibility of other institutions (horizontal accountability). Each axis poses a different democratic challenge. The vertical, transition challenge is to hold elections that are viewed as free, fair, and acceptable by the major political parties. The horizontal, consolidation challenge is to construct barriers or deterrents to encroachment between the key institutions of governance.

The impartial and credible conduct of elections is the point that connects the two axes. Viewed from this perspective, democracy requires establishing an autonomous and competent electoral authority and securing the participation of all the political parties in both the electoral process and the results. The thesis of this chapter is that the international community has begun, without fully realizing it, to reinforce the point at which the two axes of accountability intersect: political elections.

With greater awareness and a deliberate strategy, the international community could do much more to facilitate and solidify democratic transitions, prevent the destabilization of democracy, and restore democracy when one institution in a country intrudes on another. This would constitute a third dimension of accountability: enhancing vertical accountability by making sure elections are successful and strengthening the horizontal axis by calling encroaching institutions to account for their actions.

I begin the chapter with a discussion of the political and juridical question of the proper role of the international community in national democracy. An answer proved elusive until the end of the Cold War permitted a redefinition of sovereignty and a recognition of a third dimension of accountability. In the second part, I outline the different roles and activities the various international actors have come to play in national elections. Third, I examine a number of cases in order to understand how the international community gains access to the electoral process of a country and to identify the conditions for successful elections. Finally, I offer some thoughts on how the international community can enhance its ability to reinforce democracy.

Redefining Sovereignty to Enhance Accountability

The issue of how to relate to democracy has bedeviled the United Nations (UN), the Organization of American States (OAS), and other IGOs since their creation. IGOs are torn between the preamble of the UN Charter that begins, "We the peoples of the United Nations," and its membership, which consists of states, not people. More significant is the UN Charter's seemingly air-tight prohibition against any interference "in matters which are essentially within the domestic jurisdiction of any state" (Article 2[7]). Because national elections are judged a domestic matter, the combination of the two norms—the right of a people to have a democratic government, and the right of a state to be free of outside intervention—made the democratic promise collectively unenforceable.

The rigid boundary line separating domestic from international affairs has become less compelling as a result of two sets of changes in the world. From the one side, traditional conceptions of economic sovereignty have been eroded by advances in technology, communications, and transportation and by increasing trade and investment. At the same time, during the last decade, the line has been blurred by the following political trends: the growth and power of the human rights movement, the demise of the Cold War, and the spread of democracy. Together, these trends have made governments more permeable to outside influence.

One of the consequences of the global spread of democratic governments was that the issue of elections—an acutely sensitive internal issue—was placed on the international agenda. After General Manuel Noriega annulled the election in Panama in May 1989, the OAS held an emergency meeting of foreign ministers. The OAS condemned Noriega and sent a mediation team to negotiate a peaceful transfer of power to the democratically elected government. The mediation failed but established an important precedent—that IGOs have a right to address internal political issues.

The next important precedent occurred in August 1989 when the Sandinista government in Nicaragua invited the international community—the UN, the OAS, the Council of Freely Elected Heads of Government (a nongovernmental group of current and former presidents coordinated by the Carter Center at Emory University in Atlanta), the Center for Democracy, and many others—to observe their electoral process in 1989 and 1990. International monitoring and mediating of elections sits at the intersection of the twin rights of states and people. Some believe that international mediators trespass sovereign rights to act on behalf of democracy, but technically they do not if they are invited by the sovereign government.[2]

The decision by Nicaragua to open itself politically preceded the end of the Cold War, but the implosion of the Soviet Union and the cessation of superpower competition accelerated the erosion of traditional definitions of sovereignty. The end of the Cold War meant that the United States and the Soviet Union stopped looking at every civil war as a place to lose or score points over the other. This extracted some of the poison from conflicts like those in El Salvador, Kampuchea, and Angola. Solutions, however, were not automatic. Active mediation by international actors was essential to help the parties to a conflict reach a solution.

The end of the Cold War also made possible the emergence or expansion of many NGOs in the international community that were able to play critical transnational roles in the sensitive area of democratization. As a result of the Nicaraguan precedent, the international community expanded its role in monitoring elections. In June 1990, the OAS decided to establish a Unit for Democratic Development to respond promptly to requests from member states to observe elections and provide advice on conducting elections. In December 1991, in a vote of 134 to 4, the UN General Assembly approved a resolution calling on the UN Secretary General to create an Electoral Assistance Unit "to ensure consistency in the handling of requests of member states in organizing elections." The next large step for the UN was the administration of the elections in Cambodia in April 1993, with 20,000 personnel.

By trial and error, IGOs, often prodded by NGOs, developed procedures and techniques for observing elections that assisted democrats and deprived authoritarian leaders of legitimacy if they rigged elections. The number of international missions to monitor and mediate elections has grown very quickly, and the impact on the process has grown proportionately.[3]

In considering the factors responsible for gaining international support for democracy, one should not underestimate the power of a universal norm when a critical mass of countries is committed to it. The norm of democracy was written into the charters of the UN and the OAS, but it was taken seriously by each of these institutions only when a healthy proportion of its members became democratic. As an example, in the mid-1970s, Latin Americans were still arguing about the desirability and the meaning of democracy. Some believed that true democracy should be judged by mass participation rather than by the choices people face in the privacy of a voting booth. The spread of Latin American governments based on popular consent settled the debate on the definition of democracy and vanquished the idea that elections are an ethnocentric North American invention alien to the Latin cultural tradition. A further example occurred in Cartagena in December 1991, when thirteen Latin American presidents agreed that Cuba could be fully integrated into the Latin American community only if it moved toward democracy.[4] The end of the Cold War not only eliminated the ideological threat of communism, but it also neutralized its more powerful siamese twin, anticommunism, thus permitting more space for democracy.

International Support for Elections: Monitors and Mediators

Democracy was not the reason U.S. presidents Theodore Roosevelt and William Howard Taft intervened so often in the Caribbean Basin in the first decade of the twentieth century. But after the intervention, democracy became part of their strategy for withdrawing. The goal was to use free elections to locate the leader with the most popular support, thereby restoring some modicum of stability. However, U.S. policymakers discovered then, and many times afterwards, that democracy could take root only if the native soil was fertile.[5] Among the European imperialists, Great Britain tried hardest and was relatively most successful in instilling democratic values and institutions in its colonies, although a recent study by Axel

Hadenius suggests that the nationality of the colonizer was less important than the duration of the colonization in explaining the durability of democracy. "The longer they [developing nations] were colonized, the higher, and distinctly so, the level of democracy," wrote Hadenius. "Interestingly enough, the same holds true for the former French territories."[6]

Since then, the role of governments—even democratic ones—in supporting democracy has been mixed, as that interest had to be weighed against others. The United Nations and the OAS defined a modest role in the area of democracy, undertaking missions to observe elections. Until the case of Nicaragua, the UN's responsibility extended only to dependent territories or those areas making the transition to independence. The OAS sent observers to more than fifteen countries between 1962 and 1989, but their teams were small and stayed for a short time. Their purpose was less to monitor the electoral process than to show moral support for the elections and the incumbent.

NGOs, like the International Human Rights Law Group and, by the late 1980s, the National Democratic and the International Republican Institutes for International Affairs, also observed elections or plebiscites, including important ones in the Philippines in 1986, Chile in 1988, and Panama in 1989. A technique used by domestic monitors—with help from these organizations—in each of these elections was the parallel vote tabulation or "quick count," a random sample of results collected and counted within hours of the closing of the polls and long before the official count was ready. The quick count served to either keep the electoral authorities honest or denounce them if they tried to manipulate the count. The first systematic effort of "election monitoring" of an independent country occurred in Nicaragua in 1989–1990.

The transition from an authoritarian regime to free and fair elections is difficult and uncertain. To establish fair rules for elections requires a certain level of trust among the key political actors, negotiation skills, and a willingness to compromise. These qualities are almost always lacking in countries with little or no experience in free elections. In Nicaragua until 1990, elections were always manipulated by the incumbent regime; the opposition could choose to legitimate a fraud by participating, or it could boycott. If it wanted to take power, the only option was by violent "revolution."

When the incumbent Sandinistas announced elections for 25 February 1990, the opposition united under a coalition referred to as "UNO," but none of its members believed that the Sandinistas would ever permit a free election. For their part, the Sandinistas believed that the opposition would boycott the election as they had in 1984 rather than risk losing. Left to themselves, the Nicaraguans would have been condemned to repeat their tragic past—believing the worst of their opponents and not being disappointed.[7]

Fortunately, the Sandinistas were so confident of their popularity and so fearful that the United States would not recognize their victory that they decided to invite international groups that they trusted and that were credible internationally. The invited leaders mediated the rules of the electoral game and acted as surrogates for an inchoate political system and an election commission that was perceived as biased by the opposition.

The International Monitors

The following are among the many actors who monitor elections: IGOs, including the UN, the OAS, the Commonwealth, the Organization of African Unity, the European Union, and the Organization of Security and Cooperation in Europe; governments; and NGOs, including the Inter-Parliamentary Union, party institutes, international labor and business organizations, the International Institute for Democracy and Electoral Assistance (IDEA) in Stockholm, and groups, like the Council of Freely Elected Heads of Government and the International Human Rights Law Group, that have expertise on constitutions and electoral procedures. Among the international party institutes that have played the most important roles are the Christian Democratic International, the Socialist International, the Liberal International, and the National Democratic and International Republic Institutes for International Affairs. These organizations play different roles in accord with their comparative advantages. The IGOs can mobilize vast resources, field large observation teams, and generate publicity so that it would be very costly for a government to try to rig an election. IGOs, however, have two liabilities. First, one of the parties to the election—the government—is a member of the IGO, and the opposition often believes that the IGO is biased in favor of the incumbent. Mediation is difficult under those circumstances. Second, precisely because its members are states, IGOs tend to be very cautious about criticizing one of them. IGOs rarely declare an election a fraud, although some have become more assertive.

Some NGOs, like the National Democratic Institute for International Affairs (NDI), the International Republican Institute for International Affairs, and the Center for Democracy, also monitor the electoral process. Depending on the specific case, some of these play a more active role than others. While they try to be impartial, in a few cases, notably Nicaragua in 1990, these NGOs supported or were identified with the opposition. Party institutes are particularly good at training political parties and civic groups in poll-watching and civic education. Other organizations, like the International Foundation for Election Systems (IFES), provide election equipment and technical advice. Prestigious NGOs like Carter's council can and have mediated electoral reforms in many countries.

Roles and Activities

By their presence, international observers give confidence to voters that their vote will count and voting will be safe because the world is watching through their eyes. Since an opposition boycott can delegitimize the electoral process, international groups can increase the prospects for a genuine election if they mediate electoral reforms and level the electoral playing field. Monitors can deter fraud by credibly threatening to denounce it if it is detected, and they can encourage all sides to accept the results if they are internationally respectable and judge the election to be fair.[8]

There is considerable confusion about the roles and activities of international groups observing elections. Even two knowledgeable scholars of elections mistakenly referred to the UN's role in monitoring the 1990 Nicaraguan elections as "supervising" the elections.[9] The UN did supervise and conduct elections in Namibia in 1989 and in Cambodia in 1993, and the Economic Community of West African States (ECOWAS) did play a leading role conducting and securing elections in Liberia in 1997; but these are rare cases. As a general rule, national election authorities conduct and supervise elections.

To understand the comparative advantage of each international group, it is essential to distinguish the roles in each aspect of the electoral process: (1) administering or supervising an election (this is done by national authorities, although international groups, particularly IFES, are often asked for technical or material assistance); (2) providing advice and material assistance to political parties or civic groups (party institutes have been helpful in this regard); (3) observing, monitoring, and mediating the electoral process. This is the subject of this chapter, and the activities that are covered by these three concepts range from passive observation to verifying results to actively mediating electoral or political reforms. Monitors can be nationals—civic groups and party poll-watchers—or foreigners.

"Observation" missions tend to arrive a day or so before the election and leave the day after the election. They rarely assess the election in a systematic way. The "election amateurs" that concern Thomas Carothers fall within this category.[10] Most organizations with expertise in elections made a natural evolution in the 1990s from simply observing to "monitoring," even though some continue to use the terms interchangeably. Monitoring teams adopt a more comprehensive, deliberate, and systematic approach. They follow a checklist of potential problems through each stage of the electoral process, from pre-election through inauguration. On election day, the group divides into teams, and each visits polling sites throughout the country. Monitors fill out survey forms to help them determine whether there is a systematic pattern to the technical irregularities that are to be expected. After the election, the group meets to compile their separate snapshots into a broader picture of what happened. A brief preliminary statement assessing the election is presented. Some of the group remain to monitor the electoral challenges and to develop a fuller report, which is published later.

A "mediation" effort envelops the monitoring mission but adds a more assertive posture aimed at helping the political leaders of a country negotiate the rules of the electoral game. "Election mediation" was first developed in Nicaragua in 1989–1990 by the members of Carter's Council of Freely Elected Heads of Government, a group composed today of thirty leaders from the Americas. Over time, and learning from mistakes, the council and other groups have mediated among conflicting parties or actors. Elliott Richardson, the special representative of the UN Secretary General, did so in Nicaragua, despite the initial aversion of the UN to such activities. Stephen Solarz, a former U.S. congressman, led an NDI delegation to the Dominican Republic in 1994 and worked with the Canadian director of the OAS Electoral Unit to mediate an agreement between the contending leaders. The former chancellor of Austria, on behalf of the Organization for Security and Cooperation in Europe (OSCE), also helped mediate the rules of the electoral game, in Albania in 1997. Richardson explained why he modified the UN's approach: "The very fact that the future of Nicaragua literally depended on the fairness and freedom of the elections would have made a purely passive role for ONUVEN [the UN group] morally unacceptable."[11]

Mediation has long been used to resolve conflicts. As a way to ensure clean and binding elections, however, mediation is a relatively novel but increasingly important instrument. Two elections in Haiti—in 1990 and 1995—illustrate what mediation can do. Both elections were marred by many technical problems. This is not surprising since elections are difficult to administer in a country with few roads, a small middle class, high illiteracy, and little or no experience with democracy. The 1990 election was a success because the major political parties accepted the results, and that was because the incumbent did not run, and invited international mediators made sure that the parties' concerns with the electoral process were addressed. Because of the mediators' expertise, they were able to establish that the technical irregularities were not biased in favor of or against any party; and because of their stature and relationship with the political leaders, they were able to persuade the parties that the process was impartial. In 1995, in contrast, the incumbent kept mediators away, hinted he would retain power, and only at the last moment designated a successor. Most political parties boycotted, and only 28 percent of those who registered voted.

The distinctions between observing, monitoring, and mediating are quite significant, with the first two meaning that the outside group stands back from the process and hopes that, by its presence and its questions, it will induce the local actors to play by the rules. This sometimes works. The presence of a prestigious group can deter electoral fraud and give local people a sense that their election has a larger importance. This can increase turnout and encourage people to believe their vote is secret and will count. To increase the prospects that such hopes are realized, mediators use quick counts to gather critical and timely information they can use to privately negotiate a smooth transition. That was used effectively in Nicaragua, Haiti, the Dominican Republic, Guyana, and other countries.

Most nongovernmental organizations cannot mediate because their members do not have the stature or credibility or the access to the country's leadership necessary to persuade all parties to accept the rules of the electoral game. International civil servants feel constrained by their institution's mission from interfering so directly in a country's internal affairs, and so, with some exceptions, they tend to avoid this role as well. The successful mediators, like Carter's council, the OSCE, and some UN envoys, need an expert team and the time to develop close personal relationships with the political actors of a country. Their success often depends on their ability to separate the technical from the political side of problems. The political problem diminishes to the extent that the technical problem is solved. Foreign mediators are very helpful in "transitional elections" where the entire process is seriously questioned, but their effectiveness often depends on the number and professionalism of local party poll-watchers, because the foreign monitors are usually too few in number to be able to cover all the polling stations. Indeed, the role a foreign monitor usually plays is as an interpreter or judge of complaints by local party poll-watchers. When the complaints have substance, the foreign monitor has the credibility and access to bring them to the attention of the authorities in a way that increases the prospects that the problem can be corrected rather than used as a reason for a boycott.

The most difficult question for monitors to answer is whether the election has been free and fair. To answer that effectively, monitors need to evaluate the entire electoral process.[12] Irregularities of some kind occur, and the problem is to try to determine a pattern to the irregularities that could have biased the election in favor of a particular party or candidate. Some NGOs and IGOs shy away from the difficult conclusion of condemning an election, saying that the ultimate judge of the election is the local people, but if parties reject the results, as the opposition did in Haiti in June 1995 or in Albania in May 1996, most IGOs are still reluctant to call the election a failure. Still, honesty requires that a successful election be defined as one in which the major parties accept and respect the results. That only occurs when they are convinced that the process is fair, and where there are transitional elections that often require a mediator.

The Conditions of Access and Success

The international community can be helpful in mediating the rules of an election, provided it (1) is welcome, (2) understands the problems associated with each stage, and (3) is sensitive to the principal cleavages that divide a country.

Those delegations that are not welcome by all parties are generally viewed as partial to one of the parties. For example, the U.S. government sent a delegation to the election in Panama in 1989 without seeking permission or visas, and the Panamanian government simply barred the group. In the Nicaraguan elections of 1990, many NGOs were openly partial to either the Sandinistas or UNO. Their role was to be international megaphones on behalf of the Nicaraguan party. Obviously, none of these groups could mediate disputes and, indeed, in a country as polarized as Nicaragua and as connected to a global competition, there were very few groups who could mediate.

The patterns in countries just beginning to make the transition to democracy are quite similar even when the cultural or political landscape differs. The most evident similarity is that all the political parties are deeply suspicious of each other. The first step for a potential mediator is to be invited by the appropriate electoral body and be welcomed by the major political parties. The next step is to gain and secure the trust of all the parties. The opposition party or parties are most likely to invite international observers because of fears that the election machinery favors the incumbent government. In the case of Guyana, Cheddi Jagan, the leader of the opposition, visited the Carter Center several times in 1989 and 1990 to request its involvement in the elections. The Carter Center/council's routine response is that it will consider observing elections only if invited by all parties, and so Jagan demanded the government to join him in issuing an invitation. The government resisted until the donor community encouraged it to change its position in September 1990.

In the cases of Panama in 1989 and Nicaragua in 1990, the opposition parties' eagerness for international observers also was not shared by the governments. As executive secretary of the Carter Center's council, I played a more active role of trying to persuade the incumbent governments to invite international observers. In his memoirs, Panamanian general Manuel Antonio Noriega blames me for pressuring him to accept observers: "We had been reluctant to do so. . . . I had argued with Pastor that given the United States' attitude, this would just be another infringement on our rights."[13] He accepted observers, largely because it was awkward for a Panamanian leader to deny entry into the country by Jimmy Carter, the president who negotiated the Panama Canal treaties.

In the case of Nicaragua, I met with the president and vice-president and told them that their defense of Panama in the OAS in June 1989 was being interpreted as meaning that they intended to manipulate the election as Noriega did. The best way to disprove that assertion was to invite the person who had denounced Noriega's fraud. Moreover, they knew and trusted Carter as a president who had invited them to the White House for frank discussions in November 1979 and subsequently visited Nicaragua in 1986.

In other controversial cases, the incumbent accepted international observers because of a desire for legitimacy or because of the pressure of national and international public opinion, which becomes more important in a post–Cold War democratic world. In some cases, like in Guyana, a coalition of donors can use the leverage of foreign aid to secure the acceptance of observers. The invitation is important for two reasons. First, it communicates mutual respect; the government respects the observer group enough to invite it into its house, and the group acknowledges that it would not come without an invitation. Second, and more important, it is a source of future leverage. It is, at best, awkward for a party that invites observers to denounce their comments on the process.

In the case of Guyana, before accepting the invitation, Carter visited the country and concluded that he could not observe the elections unless there was a new registration list (the existing one was so flawed that it contained the name of the deceased dictator) and a new procedure for counting ballots. Prior to announcing these conclusions, he met and discussed these issues with President Desmond Hoyte, who recognized that he had no option but to accept the reforms.

The definition of a successful election as one that has to enjoy the support of all parties infuriates ruling parties, who fear it gives too much power to the opposition to blackmail the electoral process. This was the argument that senior government officials in Haiti and the United States made about the opposition boycott in Haiti in 1995: "They have no popular support; they boycott because they know they will lose." Election mediators encounter this argument all the time. The answer is equally simple: by and large, the opposition boycotts not out of fear of losing but because they believe no one is listening. That was the case in Haiti in 1995.

The mediator should aim to develop a relationship of trust with leaders from the parties, listen closely to their concerns, and, when appropriate, try to elicit a response from the electoral authorities. In most predemocratic countries, the system rarely responds. The most remarkable transformations I have witnessed in transitional elections are what happens to hard-core opponents of a regime when the rules are changed because of opponents' complaints. The individuals gradually begin to adapt, compromise, and participate. Those who do not adapt lose credibility. Thus, the incumbent party has good reason to invite mediators; they can minimize petty objections and isolate the intransigent opposition. Complaints that are resolved can no longer be grounds for boycott. A frequently heard question in first elections is whether the other party is serious about competing. Electoral rules and procedures can test the parties' seriousness, but only if mediators hold the parties to their promises. As each party complies, the process can move forward.[14]

Instead of evaluating the elements of what constitutes an adequate or ideal election, mediators concentrate on persuading the parties to participate in the process from registration through the transfer of power. In effect, the mediators encourage parties to use the electoral process to begin playing the democratic game of give-and-take. As the parties begin to approach these issues in the right frame of mind, mediators can borrow ideas from a deep well of democratic theory and practice.[15] By going back and forth, and concentrating on technical problems rather than on political complaints, the mediators solve problems and facilitate the political evolution of parties, which lack experience in democratic compromise.

In a systematic analysis of twenty-three elections in Latin America and the Caribbean from 1988 to 1995, Jennifer McCoy tried to determine the causes of successful elections, defined as those in which all parties accept and respect the results. Seven of the eight "pivotal" elections that were "successful" involved international monitors and mediators, a commitment by international donors, and an incumbent seeking legitimacy. The second group of "incomplete electoral processes" saw a higher number of flawed elections and a "less extensive international role in mediation and in providing explicit incentives or sanctions."[16] Still, the most successful elections were those where all four factors—monitoring, mediation, donor commitment, and an incumbent seeking legitimacy—were present. In the third class of elections, "shaken democracies," international monitors did not play an important role, and the result was four of five flawed or failed elections. The analysis suggests that international mediators are critically important not only in first or pivotal elections, but perhaps even more so in subsequent elections.

The real contribution of international monitors of elections is most apparent either where they are not invited because the regime fears a free vote or where they are not needed because the democracy is consolidated. In solid democracies, the role of international monitors is played by independent election commissions, nonpartisan poll-watchers (like the League of Women Voters), an aggressive and independent press, and independent courts—in brief, the horizontal institutions of democracy.

The Collective Defense of Democracy

A distinguished lineage of scholars and statesmen from Immanuel Kant through Woodrow Wilson have sought to solidify democracy by devising systems of "perpetual peace" or "liberty pacts." Carlos Tobar, an Ecuadoran diplomat, recommended that governments deny recognition to a regime that comes to power by violent means until it holds a free and popular election. The Tobar Doctrine was embedded in the Central American Peace Treaties of 1907 but was pretty much ignored.[17]

There were several subsequent attempts, but none gathered sufficient support until the OAS passed the Santiago Commitment in June 1991. The resolution deplored unconstitutional changes in government and called for an emergency meeting of the OAS foreign ministers to discuss appropriate action if such an event were to occur. Three months later, the Haitian military overthrew President Jean-Bertrand Aristide, and the Santiago Commitment was put to the test. During the next three years, the OAS and the UN gradually ratcheted up sanctions against the military regime, culminating finally in UN Security Council Resolution 940 in July 1994, authorizing member states to use whatever means necessary to implement UN resolutions calling for Aristide's return.

President Clinton's leadership produced this watershed event: the first time that the United Nations defined the interruption of democracy as a threat to international peace and authorized force to respond to that threat. Armed with this resolution, and President Clinton's decision to use force, former president Jimmy Carter, Senator Sam Nunn, and General Colin Powell negotiated an agreement that returned Aristide to power without a violent invasion.[18]

Haiti was the most forceful example of collective intervention on behalf of democracy, but there were many other important cases where the international community called those leaders to account for their actions in disrupting or destroying a democratic transition. Shortly after President Alberto Fujimori closed the Congress in Peru in early 1992, the OAS General Assembly met. Fearful of being condemned by his colleagues, President Fujimori journeyed to the meeting in the Bahamas and explained his reasons in full to the assembled foreign ministers. This was an unprecedented session—the first time that a sitting president had felt the need to explain and defend his actions before a committee of his neighbors. Fujimori promised the group that he would conduct elections for a constituent assembly soon. He fulfilled that promise, but many of the governments were still worried about the precedent.

Therefore, the next year, when the Guatemalan president closed his government's Congress, the international community was much more forceful and worked closely with an alliance of business leaders and military that led to the president's being replaced with a human rights lawyer. In Paraguay, in May 1996, General Lino Oviedo rejected an order by the newly elected civilian president. The next day, Oviedo changed his mind after being warned by generals in Brazil and Argentina, who were ordered to do so by their civilian presidents. Much had changed from the time fifteen years before when generals in Brazil and Argentina gave orders to civilians and rejected any interference in their countries' internal affairs.

In December 1992, in Managua, the OAS met again and passed an amendment to the OAS charter that would expel any regime installed by an unconstitutional seizure of power. At the same time, new civilian leaders explored innovative ways to collectively strengthen their new democracies. Brazil, Argentina, Uruguay, and Paraguay attached a "democracy clause" to their common market agreement, Mercosur. The agreement establishes an automatic expulsion of any member country in which the democratic system is interrupted.[19] The European Union (EU) used the attractiveness of its market as an incentive for southern European nations to democratize. Europe made clear that the prerequisite for entry by Greece, Spain, and Portugal to the EU was democracy. Since 1991, the EU has insisted on a "democracy clause" in each trade agreement with a Third World government.

During the 1990s, Africa has experienced the widest swings between elections and military coups. The presence of international observers, according to Michael Bratton, was "crucial in helping to extend or withhold political legitimacy to elected governments."[20] Despite the swing back to authoritarian governments in some countries, there are also some encouraging developments—for example, the strong reaction by the Organization of African Unity in June 1997 after the military overthrew the elected government in Sierra Leone, and the support by Nigeria and other West African states to facilitate a free election in Liberia in July 1997. Nigeria's readiness to use force to restore the democratic government in Sierra Leone in February 1998 was an unprecedented act in Africa—comparable to what the United States and the UN did in Haiti—but it was also ironic. The Nigerian military government used force to bring democracy to its neighbors while preventing its own people from exercising their democratic rights. Also positive is the emerging leadership of South Africa in trying to mediate political transitions in the Democratic Republic of Congo and condemning human rights violations in Nigeria.[21]

Perhaps the most effective international mechanisms for helping institutionalize democracies are the transnational support mechanisms, like the Inter-Parliamentary Union and informal contacts among legislators. There are also increasing exchanges between developed and developing democracies among election commissions, courts, and the armed forces. These institutional relationships are part of the third dimension of accountability.

A Global Strategy for Democracy

The world has a moral and security stake in promoting democracy. No system of government is better at protecting human rights than democracy.

Democracies, we have learned, rarely fight each other, although new democracies sometimes do. So many of the conflicts in the Third World in the last forty years were initially civil wars: Greece, Korea, Cuba, Vietnam, Nigeria, Nicaragua, El Salvador. Democracy would not have precluded these divisions, but it has a formula for allocating power peacefully and an incentive for groups to compromise with each other.

Systematic analyses of more than 100 developing countries over a decade demonstrate that democracies also perform better economically than dictatorships. According to Mark Lindenberg, who did the analysis, "Democratic regimes grew seven-tenths of one percent faster than their nondemocratic counterparts." More established democracies in the developing world outperformed both new democracies and authoritarian governments.[22] On the margin, and in the long term, democracies do better economically.

Some believe that democracy exacerbates ethnic divisions, such as occurred in the former Yugoslavia, but there are only three ways to deal with such divisions: first, to divide the state according to ethnic groups, but this is increasingly impractical in most countries; second, to allow one ethnic group to dominate, but this is a recipe for chronic instability; or third, to try to fashion a democratic formula that would ensure the rights of minorities and encourage coalitions across ethnic boundaries. In considering what the international community can do to help local actors succeed, the place to start is with the Hippocratic Oath: do no harm. During the Cold War, communist governments or movements often undermined or sabotaged "democracy as practiced in the West." But even democratic governments like the United States and France sometimes took actions that harmed democracies, largely because the more powerful governments did not like the particular face of democracy—because it was leftist, Islamic, or anti-American or anti-French. Democracy is a "process," but powerful governments have not always respected the process or accepted the results.

The United States undermined democratic governments in Guatemala in 1954 and Chile in 1970–1973 because both governments were leftist and anti-American. This strategy, however, was shortsighted and wrongheaded. These actions made U.S. claims of support for democracy ring hollow; they strengthened groups that resisted change at a time when the region demanded it; and they told young idealists that peaceful change was not possible—revolution was the only way. In the long term, the United States is better off in a world where some democracies are unfriendly than in a world where all dictators are "friendly."

A first rule for a democratic strategy should be: *do not undermine the democratic process or acquiesce if others do, regardless of the outcome,* even if the democratic credentials of the victors are questionable—such as in Algeria in 1992, in Albania in 1996, and in Turkey in 1997—or when stability seems so important, such as in Mexico in 1988 or in Haiti in 1995.

The Algerian case is a particularly important one. After an election in

December 1991 showed the power of the Islamic fundamentalists and the bankruptcy of the old elite, the military aborted a runoff election and seized power. They feared that if the runoff were permitted and the Islamists won, it might be the country's last free election. But the coup unleashed a war so horrific that it is hard not to conclude that the medicine—a coup—was worse than the disease could ever have been.

One of the worst aspects of the Algerian crisis was the silence in the international community, born evidently of shared fears of Islamism. There are some who argue that Islam and democracy are incompatible. But Islam—like the other great religions and cultures—has both authoritarian and democratic strains, and so the political experience in Islamic countries is hardly uniform or wholly negative. Turkey has a long, if interrupted, experience with democracy; Jordan is moving toward competitive elections; Pakistan and Bangladesh have had mixed experiences; the elections in the West Bank and Gaza in January 1996 went quite smoothly; and Malaysia has built a solid democratic tradition. The issue in the Middle East is similar to that in many predemocratic countries: how to incorporate those who are alienated but well organized. One can try to suppress these groups, as Algeria and Egypt have tried, but they return, often more violent and destructive than before. The only alternative is to bring them into the system.

In many ways, this was the heart of the issue in war-torn Central America. During the wars, it was very difficult for the governments of El Salvador, Honduras, and Guatemala to allow political space for left-wing parties, any more than it was possible for Nicaragua to permit political space for the right-wing parties. The genius of the Arias Plan of 1987 and the election mediations that followed was in cutting the Gordian knot that connected internal strife with external intervention. By giving guarantees of rights to participate and win elections to those who wanted to change the government by force, the Arias Plan brought the guerrillas in from the cold and permitted a framework of peaceful change to take hold.

Remarkable and previously unthinkable transformations occurred. As a twenty-two-year-old Sandinista, Dora María Téllez was one of the leaders of the daring seizure of the Nicaraguan National Palace in 1978. Years later, as a member of Congress, she employed equally impressive political skills to forge compromises on property disputes with former conservative landowners.

With the rapid spread of democracy, scholars have asked whether to give priority to consolidating these democracies or to extending democracy to new countries. Samuel Huntington recommends the first, concentrating on those Western countries—primarily in Latin America—that have conducted competitive elections, and deepening these regimes into more genuine democracies.[23] History suggests the limitations of cultural arguments.

For many years, Max Weber's thesis that democracy has been the result of Protestantism and capitalism held sway. But during the past two decades, the largest increase in democracies has been in Catholic countries.

It is not clear why one has to choose between a "containment and consolidation" strategy and "an extension and enlargement" approach, since not many external resources are needed to pursue both strategies at the same time. But even if one needed to choose, I would suggest the extension strategy. Until a country crosses the threshold to a "founding election," that government is likely to exhibit classic authoritarian symptoms. Once a government accepts the idea of a free election and invites international observers, an electoral logic takes hold. It becomes very costly to manipulate the process, and as General Noriega learned, the cost of nullifying an election is worse than not having any election.

In other words, the international community should aim to get as many countries on the election treadmill as possible. The process of deepening "electoral democracies" is more complicated and takes more time. This approach should be pursued but not at the expense of facilitating transitions toward electoral democracy. A variant on the extension approach would be for the international community to forge strategies to address the transition problems of pivotal countries—that is, large countries that have a more profound influence on their neighbors. From a global standpoint, the transitions in Russia and China are of the greatest strategic significance. From a regional perspective, the eventual transition in Indonesia will undoubtedly affect the rest of Southeast Asia. The same is true of Nigeria and West Africa, Algeria and northern Africa, Egypt and the Middle East, and Iran and the Gulf. If their eventual transitions succeed, they will have a positive effect on their neighbors and the world; if they fail, it might be difficult to preclude some form of regional or global conflict.

President Clinton declared the "enlargement of democracy" as a core element of his foreign policy, and he is right to give it that emphasis. But the formula for relating governments to NGOs and IGOs in a way that will significantly increase the prospects for democracy's success has proven elusive. If the U.S. government were to try to manage a democratic process in the strategic or pivotal countries, it would probably evoke a negative, nationalistic response. If it tried to mediate between contending parties, it would not be likely to succeed because of nationalism and because the United States has too wide a set of interests to negotiate the rules of an electoral game. The failed mediation in Haiti in August 1995 confirmed this point. Such a mediation is better left to nongovernmental organizations.

There are moments when a single foreign government can play the role of *enforcer*, but in the era of democracy, it would be far better if the international community collectively played the role of *reinforcer*. The premise of this approach is that there is an active debate in each transitional country between those who are willing to risk the democratic process and those who want the certainty of an election victory. Influencing that debate is not easy, particularly by a single government.

What foreign governments can do is finance and backstop both transnational and local NGO efforts, providing leverage at critical moments. As we have seen, the challenge in each stage of democratization is different, requiring a mix of strategies. In the early stages, NGOs and IGOs should help develop civil societies, by advising new democrats as they establish political parties, legislatures, and the judicial system. The appropriate international mediators should be found, and local governments should be encouraged to invite them.

A critical step to help governments make the transition to consolidated democracies is to develop competent and independent election commissions. In Cameroon, after the government refused to allow the creation of an independent election commission, the three major opposition parties boycotted the presidential election on 12 October 1997. Without real opposition, the incumbent president, Paul Biya, won, and a Cameroonian intellectual told the *New York Times:* "All of the ingredients are now in place for a civil war. You have a President who has built a power base around his own ethnic group, an economy that has been horribly mismanaged, and a political system that forecloses any possibility of peaceful change."[24]

From the other direction, the confidence of the Mexican people in the electoral process has grown in the 1990s as the Federal Electoral Institute has become more autonomous and more professional.[25] The decision by the Guyanese president to reform the electoral commission in the spring of 1991 had a similar effect. The formula was a simple one: the opposition proposed a list of five independent people, and the president selected one as chair.[26] A similar formula was proposed to Haitian president Jean-Bertrand Aristide in June 1995 after the flawed legislative elections. Aristide agreed but never implemented the proposal, and the result was that the opposition boycotted the subsequent elections.[27]

Election monitors and mediators often work with officials from election commissions (ECs) to help them deal with technical problems. International organizations need to undertake long-term efforts to help ECs obtain the necessary equipment and administrative competence. A first and necessary step was to develop regional networks of ECs. In 1990, an Inter-American Conference on Electoral Systems was held in Caracas; the next year, one was held among Central and Eastern European ECs; in 1994, a colloquium was held among African ECs; and additional ones are planned for Caribbean and Asian ECs. The International Foundation for Election Systems has played an important catalytic role in organizing these meetings.

Even as ECs become more competent and impartial, opposition parties often continue to perceive them as biased. International mediators can help on that problem. Foreign governments should forge "democracy caucuses" with democratic governments in each region to improve collective defenses of democracy and develop strategies to facilitate transitions and prevent reversals. The OAS, as we have seen, has taken a number of decisions to strengthen the collective message to potential coup plotters. Each success sends an important message.

Vaclav Havel, president of the Czech Republic, argued that NATO expansion should aim to secure democracies in Central Europe.[28] This is a logical and powerful argument. Security in Europe today depends on democracy surviving in East Central Europe. The problem is that, rhetoric notwithstanding, NATO is a conventional military alliance that has given little thought to the problem of securing democracy. If NATO took such a mandate seriously, its members would develop guidelines for monitoring threats to democracy and forge collective rules to defend against those threats.

There is no simple formula that could be applied mechanically to all cases, but there is a powerful idea that can be extracted from previous cases. The essence of the democratic challenge is to find a way to give all groups a stake in a process of peaceful change. Every state has deep divisions based on religion, race, ethnic group, geography, language, or wealth. These differences are suppressed in authoritarian regimes, offering the illusion of stability. Democracy offers a peaceful, albeit sometimes disorderly, way to sort out these differences. The recipe is to help reduce the fears of minorities by guaranteeing their rights. A democratic strategy should aim at the universal goal of persuading groups to accept an impartial electoral process.

Notes

1. "The basis of the authority of government . . . [should be] the will of the people . . . [and] this will shall be expressed in periodic and genuine elections which shall be by universal and equal suffrage and shall be held by secret vote or by equivalent free voting procedures" (Universal Declaration of Human Rights, 1948, Art. 21).

2. For an extended discussion of the redefinition of economic and political sovereignty, see Pastor, *Whirlpool,* pp. 13–15.

3. For a review of these activities, see Chand, "Democratization from the Outside-In," pp. 543–561.

4. See the press reports and final communiqué from the Fifth Summit of the Group of Rio at Cartagena.

5. See Pastor, *Whirlpool,* chapter 10, Drake, "From Good Men," and Smith, *America's Mission.* Drake describes "a painful learning process . . . [as] neither the instruments employed by the United States nor the conditions within most of Latin America proved conducive to deep and durable democratization" (Drake, "From Good Men," pp. 3–7).

6. Hadenius, *Democracy and Development*, p. 132.

7. Pastor, *Condemned to Repetition*.

8. See McCoy et al., "Pollwatching," Carroll and Pastor, "Moderating Ethnic Tensions," and McCoy, "Mediating Democracy."

9. Elkit and Svenson, "What Makes Elections Free and Fair?"

10. Carothers, "The Observers Observed," pp. 17–31.

11. Letter to the UN Secretary General from Elliott Richardson, 22 March 1990, cited in Pastor, *Whirlpool*, p. 247.

12. For a broad discussion of the problems in answering the question, see Elkit and Svenson, "What Makes Elections Free and Fair?" and Pastor, "Mediating Elections."

13. Noriega and Eisner, *Memoirs*, p. 145.

14. I am indebted to Shelley McConnell for this point.

15. Virtually every group has a checklist. For two concise published versions, see Goodwin-Gill, *Free and Fair Elections*, and Gould and Jackson, *A Guide for Election Observers*.

16. McCoy, "Monitoring and Mediating Elections," p. 23.

17. For an interesting essay on the Tobar Doctrine and why it failed in Central America in the first two decades of the twentieth century, see Stansifer, "Application of the Tobar Doctrine." For other ideas, see Pastor, *Whirlpool*, chapter 10, Pastor, "How to Reinforce Democracy," Smith, *America's Mission*, and Fossedal, *The Democratic Imperative*.

18. For a description of those negotiations, see Pastor, "With Carter in Haiti."

19. See "Inter-American Affairs."

20. Bratton, "Deciphering," p. 81.

21. See "Sierra Leone Military Arrests Five Cabinet Officers."

22. Lindberg, *The Human Development Race*, pp. 51–62.

23. Huntington, "After Twenty Years."

24. French, "Outcomes of Cameroon Vote."

25. Carter Center, "The Carter Center Delegation."

26. Carroll and Pastor, "Moderating Ethnic Tensions."

27. Pastor, "Mission to Haiti," pp. 15–16, 19–23.

28. Havel, "NATO's Quality of Life."

Part 3

Judicial Systems

9

A Brief History of Judicial Review

Herman Schwartz

Although constitutional courts are novel, they did not spring out of nothing. They have long, if often obscure, antecedents. Moreover, right from the beginning, no matter how ambiguous or uncertain their functioning, these courts saw their role as enforcing some kind of horizontal accountability.

The *fons et origo* of today's Eastern European constitutional courts was the U.S. Supreme Court decision in *Marbury v. Madison* in 1803. In 1801, a Maryland politician named William Marbury was appointed to a relatively minor judicial post by the defeated Federalist president John Adams as part of an effort to raise a conservative obstacle against the Jeffersonians. Unhappily for Marbury, Jefferson's secretary of state, James Madison, refused to complete the appointment of Marbury, setting up the great confrontation.

Chief Justice John Marshall treated the case as a test of the rule of law, despite its heavily political aspects. In the Court's first great decision and opinion, Marshall established the basic principle that the executive is accountable to a court of law for an alleged failure to obey "particular acts of Congress and the general principles of *law*" (emphasis added) to the detriment of a person's individual rights. The Court went further, however, and applied this same principle to the legislature. Insisting that the Constitution is "a fundamental and paramount law, established by the people to limit the powers of the diverse branches of government including most particularly the legislature," the Court declared that a legislative act "repugnant" to the "fundamental paramount law" is "void" and does not bind the courts. It was the function of "the judicial department, to say what the law is," declared Marshall.

This insistence on the Constitution as establishing a set of "fundamental and paramount" laws that are distinct from politics and enforceable by courts like any other laws, lies at the heart of the claim to judicial review of the constitutional validity of both legislative and executive action. It similarly underlies this claim by the European constitutional courts, regardless of any differences, except that unlike the United States, in Europe (and almost everywhere else), the claim is almost always explicitly supported in the text of the constitution.

The U.S. Supreme Court's assertion of judicial power, though not shocking to Americans—there were a number of precedents for that as well as the authority of *The Federalist Papers*—was anathema to many Europeans. It ran directly counter to the insistence on parliamentary supremacy fostered by the French Revolution. In response to the reactionary ancien régime magistrates who had used their authority to stifle any threat to aristocratic privileges, the French revolutionaries reduced the judiciary to little more than clerks performing the relatively mechanical function of applying a detailed legal text to a factual situation. Rousseauian notions that only its legislature embodies a society's general will also contributed to downgrading the judicial function. And though the antecedents of judicial review of legislative acts could be traced to seventeenth-century English doctrine in *Dr. Bonham's Case* (1610), by the late eighteenth century, Great Britain too had long since abandoned that doctrine in favor of parliamentary supremacy.

For the next century and a half, parliamentary supremacy was the reigning doctrine in Europe, at least nominally. Judges were supposed to limit themselves to applying detailed legal codes designed to leave the judges with no or little discretion. The effort inevitably failed, for it was, of course, soon realized that the judges needed to interpret the laws in order to apply them, and this gave the judges a good deal of control over the content of law. This power of interpretation did not go unchallenged. Efforts were made to limit it, but these were, inevitably, unsuccessful.[1] Moreover, as knowledge of the American experience filtered into Europe, some of the more adventurous legal circles began to think of emulating it. As early as 1848–1949, the Frankfurt Assembly proposed a special tribunal to resolve constitutional questions, including alleged violations of individual rights. Austrian theorists came up with a similar idea.[2] The collapse of the 1848 revolutions effectively ended this, though many German legal experts continued to support the idea in both Germany and Austria.[3]

Despite the French and German reluctance, which was certainly very influential in Europe, there were modest stirrings in some countries. Following the lead of the United States, most Latin American nations authorized judicial review of legislation during the nineteenth century, but this did not amount to meaningful judicial oversight. These unstable regimes, frequently subject to violent coups and takeovers, were hardly an ideal setting for so delicate a function.

On the Continent, as early as 1847, Greece authorized judicial review of legislation by its Supreme Court. Initially, this was limited to the review of formal defects in legislation, but in 1871 and 1897, it was expanded to include substantive matters.[4] In Norway and Denmark, review by the regular courts also existed, but it was rarely invoked. And in Romania, in 1912, a lower court struck down a statute as unconstitutional, despite the absence of any constitutional or statutory authority. The 1923 and 1938 Romanian constitutions granted a limited version of this power to the Court of Cassation, but there is no evidence that it was ever invoked.

Despite all this obvious judicial lawmaking, the official ideology insisting on judicial passivity persisted. Nevertheless, in the 1920s, the movement toward judicial review began. Despite the continuing rejection of judicial review in most of Europe, Hans Kelsen designed a specialized constitutional tribunal to decide constitutional questions, which Austria and Czechoslovakia established. It became the model for almost everything that came after.

Kelsen, one of the most influential legal theorists of the twentieth century, had been asked to draft a constitution for the new Austrian republic that emerged from the ruins of the Austro-Hungarian Empire in 1919. Believing with Marshall that constitutions should be considered as a set of legal norms superior to ordinary legislation and should be enforced as law, he also recognized (and probably shared) the prevalent distrust of the established judiciary as a vehicle for such a function. He therefore hit on the same kind of mechanism that the Frankfurt Liberals had come up with in 1849 and Jellinek in 1885—a specialized tribunal separate and apart from the regular judiciary that would monitor legislation, with the power to nullify a law if the tribunal found that it ran afoul of the constitution.[5] To counter arguments that this tribunal would be doing the kind of policymaking that should be done only by a legislature, Kelsen deliberately omitted a bill of rights from his constitution, restricting the tribunal to what he called "negative" lawmaking. "Standing," the right to invoke the tribunal's jurisdiction, was thus given only to specific high public officials and to the ordinary courts, which would be required to refer to the court any issues relating to the constitutionality of a law.

Although Kelsen designed this model for Austria, the first constitutional court to be established on his model was actually not in Austria but in Czechoslovakia, in February 1920. In its entire eighteen-year history, however, the Czech court never got to deal with the constitutionality of a single statute.[6]

The Austrian court, which came into being a few months later, in October 1920, and was modified by constitutional amendments in 1925 and 1929, was very similar to the Czechoslovak court, except that its jurisdiction was wider: it decided not only constitutional questions, but also disputes growing out of Austria's federal structure, accusations against high state officials, and questions concerning elections and referenda.

Although standing was originally limited to high state officials in both the Austrian and Czechoslovak systems, in 1929 Austria extended standing to the *Länder* (the regional units in Austria's federal structure), to challenge certain federal actions. Private parties could get to the court only if a constitutional question about the applicable statute or ordinance arose in an administrative or judicial proceeding and the Supreme or other high court wanted the issue decided by the constitutional court.[7]

Germany also experimented with judicial review during the Weimar regime. The 1919 Constitution provided for a special constitutional tribunal to decide constitutional controversies involving the German *Länder,* and for the impeachment of high state officials. Although the tribunal decided a few cases, it did not become an important institution. In 1921, the Federal Supreme Court also asserted the power of judicial review, charging that it had always had this power, a dubious claim according to almost everyone.[8] The court used this power sparingly, and primarily to protect property interests, arousing the ire of the left.[9]

Even in France, there was an increasing interest in judicial review that spread among major figures in French public law, such as Duguit and Geny. Fears that it would result in the same hostility to social reform then dominant on the U.S. Supreme Court stalled any effort to formally introduce judicial review into France until well into the post–World War II period.

The end of World War II saw the true rise and spread of these courts, not only in Europe but in much of the world. Germany and Italy led the way, because according to Louis Favoreu and others,

> the fiction of legislative self-limitation fell apart in the face of the experiences of the German Weimar and Italian Fascist parliaments. . . . And it seems today that it is not possible to have a truly democratic Constitution without having a constitutional justice to assure the rule of law.[10]

Kelsen's continental model—a special tribunal outside the regular judiciary to provide a "constitutional defense" against unconstitutional legislative action—was the preferred form. Partly this was out of concern that the narrow bureaucratic mentality of the average civil law judge could not be trusted to handle this kind of jurisdiction. Partly also, this was because of the existence in many countries of a diverse set of separate court systems, such as tax courts, labor courts, administrative courts, and the like, but no single overarching and superior Supreme Court, whose decisions on constitutional questions could be binding on all courts.

Professor and former German constitutional court judge Helmut Steinberger has called the establishment of such special constitutional courts "the only truly novel institution within the parliamentary systems of

Western Europe," and the same holds true for the emerging nations in Central and Eastern Europe. Although Austria led the way in 1945, reestablishing its prewar constitutional court, followed by Italy in 1948, the German court was the most influential, adopting express provisions in the 1949 Basic Law for constitutional review and a Kelsen-style constitutional court. Unlike Kelsen's model, however, and probably because of the bitter interwar experience, the protection of human rights was intended from the first to be an essential element of the tribunal's jurisdiction, and so it has turned out.

Greece, Spain, Portugal, Belgium, France, and other countries soon followed suit, and in almost all of them, the court has become a significant political and judicial force. Human rights issues have accounted for a significant proportion of these courts' jurisdiction almost everywhere, as has federalism in federal states like Germany, Spain, and Belgium. Some of the communist countries also experimented with judicial review: Yugoslavia established a constitutional court in 1963,[11] and Poland authorized a relatively weak tribunal in 1982, which went into operation in 1986. And under Mikhail Gorbachev, even the Soviet Union adopted a constitutional committee in 1988 that had a not insignificant impact on the Soviet legal system.

By 1989, almost every Western European country had some provision for judicial review of the constitutionality of legislative and administrative acts, as did Japan, the Latin American countries, and the newly emerging nations in Africa. It is thus hardly surprising that all the nations emerging from communism and seeking to become members of the Western community should almost automatically adopt some kind of constitutional tribunal.

Notes

1. Kelley, *Historians and the Law*, pp. 43–45.
2. Eisenmann, *La justice constitutionelle*, pp. 110–111.
3. In 1885, the Austrian Georg Jellinek proposed a high constitutional court for Austria to prevent parliamentary abuse to which legislative minorities and the government could appeal (see ibid., pp. 157–160).
4. Brewer-Carías, *Judicial Review*, pp. 168–171.
5. Kelsen's own explanation for a separate tribunal was set out in a 1942 article in the *Journal of Politics* (Kelsen, "Judicial Review," pp. 185–186) as follows:

It was not considered desirable to grant to every court the unlimited power of passing on the constitutionality of statutes. The above mentioned danger of non-uniformity in constitutional questions was too great; for in Austria as well as in other countries of the European continent the administrative authorities had no power to test the constitutionality of statutes and were therefore obliged to apply a statute even if a court, e.g. the Supreme Court (*Oberster Gerichtshof*), had declared the statute unconstitutional. It must be added that in Austria, as well as in many other countries of the European continent there were other courts besides the ordinary courts, especially administrative courts which occasionally had to apply the same statutes as the ordinary courts. Hence a contradiction between administrative courts and ordinary courts was not at all precluded. The most important fact, however, is that in Austria the decisions of the highest ordinary court, the so-called *Oberster Gerichtshof,* concerning the constitutionality of a statute or an ordinance had no binding force upon the lower courts. The latter were not forbidden to apply a statute which the *Oberster Gerichtshof* had previously declared unconstitutional and which it had, therefore, refused to apply in a given case. The *Oberster Gerichtshof* itself was not bound by the rule of *stare decisis.* Accordingly, the same statute which the court had declared in a given case unconstitutional could be declared by the same court as constitutional and be applied in another case. For these reasons a centralization of the judicial review of legislation was highly desirable in the interest of the authority of the constitution.

6. In the aftermath of Prague Spring in 1968, the victorious communists enacted a major constitutional amendment that included a restored constitutional court, but it was never established. The country had to wait until 1991 before a constitutional court became a reality.

7. Kelsen, "Judicial Review," pp. 194–196.

8. The Bavarian and Prussian Constitutions did, however, explicitly confer this power upon their courts (see Eisenmann, *La justice constitutionelle,* p. 374).

9. Ibid. Efforts to establish judicial review in Poland were made during this period but failed. Many Polish jurists supported the effort, but because French influence dominated the constitutional process, that support was not enough (see Brzezinski, "The Emergence of Judicial Review," pp. 153, 161, 164).

10. Favoreu, "La modernité des vues," p. 374.

11. For a discussion of this unique early Socialist experience in Yugoslavia, see Brewer-Carías, *Judicial Review,* pp. 236–242.

10

Judicial Independence and Judicial Reform in Latin America

PILAR DOMINGO

In the current context of democratization and economic liberalization, the issue of rule of law and judicial politics has come to the forefront of the political and economic debate. At the heart of the problem of rule of law lies the pressing concern with mechanisms of legal accountability, effective limited government, and rights protection. In the political sphere, democratization has inevitably drawn attention to the need for effective implementation of mechanisms that control and limit political power. In social terms, rule of law brings to mind the need for the social penetration and embeddedness of rights and obligations of the newly enfranchised citizens living under democratic rule. And regarding economic aspects, the current predominant paradigm of liberalization, privatization, and free-market policies has brought new emphasis on the need for a predictable and reliable legal framework.

Clearly, one of the major challenges for the new democracies is to establish credible mechanisms of accountability. Accountability is one aspect of rule of law, by which public officers are made answerable for their actions within a pre-established legal and constitutional framework that sets the limits and powers of state agencies and government organs. What we find instead in Latin America is a legacy of weak, personalist—although extensive and overbureaucratized—states with a decreasing redistributive capacity and alarmingly lacking in transparency or operative mechanisms of accountability. It is in this context that the role of the judiciary gains relevance in contemporary endeavors to acquire regime legitimacy and a meaningful form of democratic practices.

The judiciary is a key institution in the tasks of legal accountability and constitutional control. The issue of legal accountability should be addressed not only in terms of how effectively the judiciary fulfills its function of rendering public office legally responsible and accountable; we should also address the internal accountability of the courts. How are these to be monitored and controlled? The general impression is that Latin America's new democracies (as well as some of its old ones) fail dismally in complying with minimum standards of accountable government, as is clear from corruption scandals and the low esteem in which democratic institutions are held in the public opinion. But this is by no means less true for the justice institutions that are seen as corrupt, inefficient, costly, and unreliable (notwithstanding the differences between countries).

This chapter reviews the role of the judiciary in the recent democratic experiences of Latin America. The first section briefly examines the place of the judiciary in democracy and the relevance of judicial independence for rule of law. The second section addresses the main obstacles that have hindered the development of credible legal institutions in Latin America. The third section identifies those agents of change that are acting specifically to promote changes within the judiciary, and more generally to enhance the importance of rights protection and rule of law. The nature of the agents of change is relevant, among other reasons, because the relative strength of these groups will have a bearing on the direction of reform and on which areas of the justice system are most likely to be addressed effectively. The fourth section summarizes the reform efforts in Latin America and offers tentative observations on their success.

Democracy and the Rule of Law

The liberal democratic tradition appeals to the necessary linkage between rule of law and political democracy. Essentially, rule of law refers to those established rules of a general and impersonal nature that order the relationship between state and society, between individuals in society, and within the state itself. Clearly, rule of law is a contested term and one that defies clear-cut definition. For our purposes, rule of law is taken as government by law, and with adherence to a predictable and working legal order. Rule of law is in place when government is constrained or bound by the law— through effective limits or checks and balances on political power and public office, usually prescribed in a constitutional format.

Traditionally, the institutional design of legal accountability takes the form of various arrangements of separation of powers, on the one hand, and electoral control on the holders of public office through regular elections, on the other hand. Rule of law refers to those control mechanisms by which the state and the powerholders are limited and can be brought to account according to established normative criteria (usually embodied in a written constitution), with the objective of consolidating responsible and limited government. For this, the rules must be substantively binding and overriding (although susceptible to change with the times).

Rule of law also refers to the meaningful protection of certain rights, however these may be defined, that mediate the relationship between state and society and between individuals in society. The variations on the constitutional definition of these are innumerable, as is the extent to which they remain purely enunciatory formats and correspond or not to the reality of a national context. To a large extent, how rights are perceived and filtered into society will determine the nature of citizenship and ultimately affect a regime's legitimation capital. The universalism of rights protection that underpins liberal democratic notions of rule of law by no means corresponds to the reality in much of Latin America.[1] Access to justice and rights protection is a key element of democratic consolidation, as it is through this that citizenship can be made effective. The development of citizenship and the adequate protection and respect for the rights this involves are integral to the notion of accountability of public office to civil society. The effective realization of rights acts as a further constraint on the abuse of public authority and it is a necessary one for the advancement of regime legitimacy.

Thus, the role of the courts is key to democratic consolidation, as it is the judiciary that underpins the establishment of rule of law and legal accountability to constitutional norms. The judiciary fulfills the following functions: it guards the law and constitutional principles; it provides the forum for the settlement of disputes between individuals in society and between individuals and the state; and, finally, it is part of the system for administering criminal justice.[2] The judiciary is crucial in the process of building regime legitimacy, which increasingly in Latin America is dependent on the capacity of these regimes to create credible mechanisms of accountability, public responsibility, and the effective advancement of citizen rights.

Optimizing Judicial Independence

Judicial independence is critical for courts to have the capacity to fulfill their functions of constitutional control, legal accountability, and justice administration. Autonomy of the courts and judicial independence are necessary to achieve impartiality in the task of adjudication and to ensure the advancement of rule of law and effective legal accountability. But independence from whom? And how much independence? First, political autonomy from other government branches is essential, especially in the quest for horizontal accountability. This is crucial to ensure that judges' decisions are not influenced by short-term political considerations in matters concerning the constitutionality of legislation and acts of authority and in checking the legality of acts of public power. Second, insularity from the conflicting parties is necessary to achieve neutrality in the judges' decisions. Bribery is an outright form of influence on judges, but more subtle forms, such as cultural or social bonds, can also impair the detachment of the judge from the parties. Third, a more subtle form of insularity is independence from particular ideologies. This is much harder to identify or check.[3] Finally, it is also desirable that judges be isolated from populist or plebiscitary pressures, especially in a time of mass media and increasing public scrutiny of judicial practices. While bottom-up scrutiny is positive, it may imperil the neutrality of judges in the task of adjudication as they become visible public figures, especially in cases that are of public interest. The impact of public pressure through the mass media can be a threat to the principle of judicial independence, all the more so in the absence of strong and consolidated judicial institutions.

In the task of legal and constitutional control, and in the function of justice administration, clearly judicial independence is valued—but not unqualified independence. There is a tension between democratic rule and judicial independence. As Owen Fiss points out, democracy is a matter of principle and preference, where the role of judges is to guard the principle of constitutional rule, not to be left to the whims of short-term majority preferences.[4] However, in the same way that the judiciary ideally acts as a check on other government branches, it is desirable also that the judges be subjected to some degree of political control to ensure a level of democratic accountability within the judicial branch. This is all the more important when judicial decisions have a political impact, because through their decisions judges are also participating in the lawmaking and social control functions of the state. Thus, the objective of the separation of powers principle is to achieve an optimum rather than a maximum degree of institutional independence.

The mechanisms by which judicial independence is achieved are above all institutional. First, the appointments procedure determines the degree of political (or clientelist) influence on who gets elected to judicial office. Second, the tenure system affects how independence is achieved from the appointing institution. For instance, life tenure, in principle, means that judges need not respond to the political body that elected them. Finally, financial autonomy and decent salaries will help isolate the judiciary from pressures, from both political sources and the litigating parties.

However, the political role of the judiciary is determined by other additional factors. The scope of judicial review and legal control powers attributed to the judiciary will determine the impact of judicial decisions. And, finally, the political environment in which a legal system is embedded will determine the extent to which the judiciary in a specific country makes full use or not (for whatever reasons) of its powers in its relation with the other branches of state.[5]

These factors are intimately interlinked. In the measure to which a judicial system lacks autonomy, it is unexpected that it will exercise constitutional control with an adequate degree of impartiality. On the other hand, even if independence is adequate, if the scope of action is constitutionally limited, the impact of the control mechanism on the political system will be reduced. And, finally, a constitutional text may well prescribe an optimal balance of independence and judicial review powers, but these might not be effectively put into practice for reasons that range from lack of resources, to regime instability, to the powerful presence of undemocratic practices and forces.

There is no clear format for the best balance between the institutional factors, nor indeed universal consensus on their design. There are significant variations on how the judicial function of control of legality and constitutionality has developed, according to legal families (custom law or Roman law), and whether constitutional principles are fundamentally founded on the notion of separation of powers or not. Continental European countries, founded on code law, exhibit a different notion of constitutional review (on the whole more limited) from the one that has developed in U.S. constitutionalism, or Anglo-Saxon law. Interestingly, Latin American constitutionalism, while inheriting the tradition of European code law, rapidly incorporated the U.S. model of separation of powers, in tune with presidential forms of government. Latin American constitutions provide unequivocal statements on the principle of the independence of the judiciary and its sole responsibility to the supremacy of the law and constitution, although judicial review powers are generally more limited. But the prevailing reality seems to have been the inability of the supreme courts to assert their political function effectively.

Independence is only one of the problems of the court systems in Latin America that undermines the impartiality and credibility of the courts. Equally damaging to the problem of legal accountability and rule of law are the questions of judicial efficiency and the predictability of legal proceedings. Adjudication requires not only independent judges, but also a framework of reliability and predictability in court rulings, as well as minimum degrees of efficiency in the protection of rights and general transparency in the functioning of the courts. It is the combination of these interrelated problems that undermines the court systems in the region. The following section examines some of the obstacles to a proper functioning of the judiciary in Latin America. It is important to stress that the nature of the problems varies from country to country. In some cases it may well be that the problem of deficient legal structures lies not in the lack of political independence at the level of the supreme court's relation with the executive, but rather in the infrastructural and organizational weaknesses of the courts.

Obstacles to Judicial Independence and Effectiveness in Latin America

Surveys throughout the region place the judicial apparatus in a dismal light. In Argentina, only 13 percent of the public have anything good to say about the judiciary; in Peru, 92 percent distrust the judges; in Brazil, 70 percent distrust the justice system.[6] Judicial systems reproduce an image of corruption, clientelism, and inefficiency and are not viewed as impartial administrators of justice or autonomous agents of constitutional and legal control. Judicial structures by all accounts do not fulfill the function of rendering public office legally accountable. Nor, does it appear, is the judiciary itself subjected to satisfactory mechanisms of internal transparency and accountability. Thus, it is not only a problem of strengthening the judiciary vis-à-vis other powers of state, but also of improving the internal workings of the court systems.

The judiciary in Latin America is traditionally viewed as an inefficient administrator of justice and as subordinated to executive interests. The supreme courts of the region are held to be politically dependent on and dominated by the political environment in which they operate.[7] The problems of judicial dependence in Latin America are rooted in a number of factors, both external to and inherent in the formal constitutional provisions with regard to the judicial function. Judicial weakness in Latin America stems from political causes, from constitutional and organizational arrangements, and from the limited scope of judicial review powers. It is important to stress that the history of the courts varies considerably from country to country.

Political Obstacles

To a large extent, the fate of judiciaries in Latin America has been the product of political environments that have not been conducive to the development of strong judicial institutions. The degree of judicial independence courts can attain will be greatly determined by the role that a political class and society wish it to have. Judges will seldom lead political processes, but as democracy is deepened it appears to be the case that courts now, more so than in the past, are called upon to undertake a more active role in the political systems throughout the region.

A first obstacle to the independence of the courts has been the relationship between the judiciary and the executive in strongly presidentialist systems. The executive throughout the region has been characteristically, both formally and in practice, overwhelmingly powerful with respect to the other branches of government (again, with considerable variations). This has inhibited judicial independence vis-à-vis political pressures and executive orders, particularly regarding politically delicate matters. With the transition to democracy, judiciaries have increasingly played a more prominent political role in confronting executive interests. Countries that exhibit greater prominence of the judiciary are Brazil, Bolivia, and even Mexico. In Argentina, despite a greater prominence of the judiciary, the Supreme Court remains in reality highly subservient to the executive—a situation that has in fact deteriorated under Menem.[8] Some countries, however, do exhibit judicial politics that have traditionally been more independent but not necessarily confrontational in their relationship with the executive. The Colombian Supreme Court has on several marked occasions confronted the executive on important questions of unconstitutionality.[9] The Colombian case not only reflects a tradition of constitutional independence of the judiciary, but is also the result of relative regime stability, if not political stability. The Chilean Supreme Court is also traditionally independent, and has remained so with the 1980 Constitution, but its conservatism led to its apparent complicity with the Pinochet regime and accounts for its leniency toward human rights violations under military rule.[10]

A second factor that has affected the role of the judiciary is the problem of political and institutional instability combined, in many countries, with the absence of a tradition of democratic practices. This has severely undermined the institutional continuity that arguably is required in constitutional rule for different branches to develop and accommodate over time to their functions. Abrupt regime changes have frequently led to arbitrary changes in judicial posts and at times have led to the outright public restriction of the judicial function.[11] To this is added, even in times of democratic rule, the constant reforms of constitutional texts that undermine institutional continuity and thus stability; and processes of accommodation to new rules take time to become consolidated. Constitutional changes that affect the judiciary have at times led to the replacement of the sitting magistrate. Institutional and regime continuity is key in the development of judicial institutions.

The experience of military authoritarianism goes a long way toward explaining the institutional instability that has undermined the capacity of judiciaries to develop as politically independent organs. However, democratic rule is in itself not sufficient to advance the cause of improving judicial independence. Democratically elected executive bodies may be even more concerned with ensuring compliant judicial bodies, precisely because court rulings more so than under authoritarian rule cannot be disregarded. Executives may be reluctant to relinquish control over the judiciary, all the more so in times of difficult policy decisions that may be contested at the level of their constitutionality. The Menem administration in Argentina has made considerable effort to ensure judicial loyalty toward the executive. Over time, it appears that the pressure is for the political subordination of the judiciary to be diminished, both through reforms and through the development of a political environment more conducive to independent judicial politics. But this is not an immediate or inevitable process under democratic rule.

An additional obstacle to strengthening judicial independence is the problem of corruption and the vested interests this creates, which further inhibits impartial adjudication. Recently, the overwhelming strength of drug mafias has dramatically undermined the states' capacity to combat drug-related corruption at all levels of state bureaucracy. This is rapidly eroding the credibility of the new democracies, as corruption is found in high public office and corruption scandals abound. The courts are seen as incapable of bringing to account corruption within the state. The general perception is that judges are easy prey to bribery, all the more so at lower court levels where judicial salaries are low. Corruption has a highly detrimental effect on the credibility of legal institutions that are viewed as accomplices to and beneficiaries of corrupt practices. In some instances, it may be the case that political influence is not as much the issue at the level of supreme courts, but rather that lower courts are susceptible to corruption from private parties or local and regional political strongmen.[12]

In some cases, as in Brazil under Collor de Mello or Venezuela under Carlos Andrés Pérez, public pressure against corruption gathers momentum, to the point that legal scrutiny becomes highly demanded and eventually is addressed. But it is still not the case in Latin America that combating corruption in high office is systematically undertaken by the legal institutions, or that transparency and accountability exists. In addition, corruption in public office appears to reflect a deep-rooted lack of rule observance and law-abidingness, and long-established habits of impunity and disrespect for the law.

Institutional, Infrastructural, and Organizational Obstacles

The above factors imply forceful obstacles for the establishment of independent judicial bodies. Judicial independence and impartiality are also to a large extent defined by constitutional formulas regarding appointment mechanisms, tenure, and budgetary provisions for the judiciary. In addition, there are numerous infrastructural and organizational factors that affect the quality of court services.

If we briefly examine the institutional aspects of appointment procedures and tenure of judges at the level of supreme courts (although these vary significantly), they are not necessarily more politicized than, say, the U.S. method of Supreme Court appointments. There is normally a combination of selection from lists of candidates drawn up either by the congress, the executive, or the supreme court, to be made by another branch, and sometimes with the approval of the third branch. More damaging has been, as mentioned above, the disrespect of appointment provisions under authoritarian rule than the provisions themselves. In addition, what is also lacking in Latin America are broader mechanisms of public scrutiny with regard to the reliability of appointments to high court positions. Unlike in the United States, where Supreme Court appointments are normally the object of great public debate and scrutiny through the media, and also through the opinion of the American Bar Association, in Latin America, appointments to the high courts have in the past generally appeared as affairs that have not been widely acknowledged by the public. Bar associations do not play a prominent role in overseeing the qualifications or reliability of appointments to the high tribunals.

Equally varied is the duration of judges' mandates in the supreme courts. Only four Latin American countries have life appointments (Argentina, Brazil, Chile, and Paraguay); the rest range from four to fifteen years. While the lack of life tenure arguably mars the principle of judicial independence, in that supreme court members will be more prone to want to please political interests for their renewal, as long as renewal does not coincide with government elections, there is scope for some independence; this is perhaps best exemplified by the Costa Rican case.

Time-tested repetition of these procedures will give them a greater degree of institutional stability and continuity, which will foster judicial independence and strengthen the principle of separation of powers. Again, the historical burden of regime rupture and its consequences on judicial tenure is still present in the politics of judge selection and in the behavior of judges. For instance, recent constitutional change has resulted in opportunities for executive branches to "pack" the higher courts, as exemplified in Argentina under Menem in 1991 when the number of Supreme Court members was increased, and in Mexico under Zedillo in 1995 when the constitutional reforms were followed by a complete renewal of the Supreme Court. Over time, however, as institutional reaccommodation settles down, the political links between supreme court appointments and executives will fade as tenure is respected. Also, as pluralism in congress increases and alternation in power is routinized, the political biases within the high courts will be tempered.[13] Furthermore, it is the case that some recent reforms have reduced the political influence of the executive on supreme court appointments by increasing the role of congress in appointments procedures, raising the percentage of the vote required for appointment approval or, in some instances, introducing judicial councils that participate in the election of supreme court members.

Of great consequence is the general lack or inadequacy of institutionalized professional assessment mechanisms of the judicial staff (or *escalofón judicial*), especially if we contrast Latin American countries with their continental European counterparts, where professional competence is based on competitive examinations. Requirements for appointment to judicial positions, and notably to the supreme courts, rarely go beyond the form of constitutional statements of a very general nature (age, years in the legal profession, years in the judicial system). Before the creation of *consejos de judicatura,* or judicial councils (discussed below), lower appointments were normally carried out within the judicial system and at the level of the supreme courts. If supreme court appointments were vitiated from the top for the reasons suggested above, the likelihood that lower appointments would be subject to clientelism and patronage rather than merit-based criteria was greater.[14] A culture of clientelism within the judicial apparatus breeds corruption and impedes the possibility of impartial and independent judicial rulings.

This combines with serious structural problems of court administration, resulting in high levels of inefficiency. In many countries, administrative tasks were or are concentrated in the high courts. At every level, judges are burdened with administrative tasks.[15] Recent reforms that establish judicial councils aim, among other things, to reduce the administrative burdens of judges and particularly of supreme courts, with the objective that they concentrate on adjudication.

Financial autonomy also determines the level of independence of the judiciary for various reasons. First, financial autonomy in the management of the judicial budget is necessary to ensure judicial independence and impartiality. There is little available information (and research) on how judicial budgets are allocated and spent, so that discussions of the financial aspects of the judiciary are often impressionistic. The difficulty of obtaining information on the judicial budget and its administration is in itself perhaps indicative of the lack of transparency with regard to the internal workings of the judiciary. Generally, where there is no judicial council, the judicial budget is administered at the level of the supreme courts, thus implying a considerable degree of political autonomy in the internal allocation of resources. However, how the budget is determined varies from country to country. Certain constitutions in the region establish a fixed percentage of the national budget that is to be allocated to the judiciary (interestingly, these percentages are in practice often disregarded).[16] The general impression is that judiciaries are underfinanced.[17] However, more resources do not necessarily improve court services; comparative data reveal that the size of the budget is not necessarily correlative to judicial efficiency, which depends also on budgetary management and administrative skills, generally deficient throughout the region.[18]

More damaging is the fact that insufficient funding frequently implies low salaries of judicial staff and poor working incentives, which in turn produce an environment conducive to corruption and bribery. Low salaries lessen the public prestige of judicial appointments, particularly at the level of lower court judges, so that the better jurists will tend to move to more lucrative opportunities in private practice rather than remain in the public sector.[19] This is especially so for the appointment of judicial positions below the supreme court. Finally, low budgets lead to infrastructural deficiencies, as courts are understaffed and ill-equipped. This undermines judicial efficiency and aggravates the problems of case backlog and delays in court proceedings, further exacerbated by the highly bureaucratic and complex nature of legal procedures.

The general impression through much of the region is that a key difficulty within the judiciary is precisely the problem of judicial administration and the lack of transparency in how courts are run. Although this tells us little specifically about executive-judiciary relations, the broader problems of court services discussed here undermine the credibility of the judiciary in current democratic processes. Judicial processes are distrusted because citizens do not feel that courts operate with sufficient impartiality in either conflict resolution or rights protection.

Judicial Review Powers and Practices

Judicial review and how it is used will affect the political role of the judiciary. First, the scope of judicial review powers determines the political impact of court rulings on questions of constitutionality. However, it is possible that even if judicial review powers are fairly broad, judicial rulings may reflect a passive or nonconfrontational position by the courts. Again, overgeneralizations must be avoided, as the nature of judicial review varies from country to country. Moreover, lacking in the literature is systematic analysis of case statistics that can give reliable assessments of how supreme courts in Latin America have used judicial review powers.[20]

In much of Latin America, judicial review has normally taken the form of *amparo constitucional* or variations on it. This is a limited form of review by which the constitutionality or legality of a law or act can be contested by an affected claimant. If the court rules in favor of the claimant, the unconstitutional law is not applied to that individual, but legislation is not automatically revoked.[21] This limits the mechanism of judicial control on the other branches of power. Arguably, the limited nature of judicial review allows for judicial decisions to be taken more freely, as their political impact is not far-reaching.[22]

Although judicial review powers in much of Latin America are traditionally weak, this does not fully explain judicial subordination to the political needs of the executive. For even in this limited form of review, courts have been reluctant to confront the executive.[23] Judicial weakness is a function not only of institutional limitations, but also of the political, social, and cultural environment in which judicial legal structures develop. Recent discussion on the question of judicial review and its generally limited nature

in Latin America has prompted great enthusiasm for the creation of constitutional tribunals that would be separate from the supreme court and that
would have the exclusive task of reviewing the constitutionality of legislation and executive acts.[24] To some extent, this is prompted by the success
attributed to the Spanish constitutional tribunal. However, it is far from
clear how the creation of a special tribunal on constitutional matters would
be free of the vices of overpoliticization, the lack of independence and professional competence, and the absence of adequate resources that afflict
many of the supreme court systems in Latin America. Unless these problems are tackled, there is little reason to suppose that an additional institution in the form of a constitutional tribunal would be more suitably
equipped to make better decisions on matters of judicial or constitutional
review.

Again, more damaging than the limited nature of judicial review to the
rule of law are the reasons related to undemocratic traditions that have
inhibited the full development of judicial review practices and habits. It
should be remembered that the political importance and excellent public
reputation of the U.S. Supreme Court have taken decades of state building
to achieve. Moreover, it is not evident that Latin American countries should
aspire to the U.S. model; rather, they might do well to look to their continental European counterparts of the code law tradition, which, with a generally much lower political profile, nonetheless fulfill minimally the task of
constitutional control and legal accountability.

While these problems have largely inhibited the development of credible judicial branches, the pertinent question is what is required for this state
of affairs to change for the better in the current context of democracy building and institutional design? It would seem that the problem of judicial
independence and constitutional control goes well beyond constitutional
and legal prescriptions and reflects a deep-rooted lack of rule observance
and law-abidingness—and long-established habits of impunity and disrespect for the law. The passage of time and accommodation to institutional
continuity and constitutional habits (which are far from being achieved) go
a long way toward fortifying the judicial function.

For now, some optimism can be drawn from the growing presence of
judicial decisions and court activism in political affairs and from the growing public demand for improved legal and law enforcement mechanisms.
However, it would seem that judicial self-assertion and the establishment of
the rule of law needs a longer time span than the transition processes in
which actors arrived at political agreements on democratic procedures. I
cannot, however, overstress the differences that distinguish the judicial role
on politics in the different Latin American countries. I have merely tried to
present a few of the key problem areas that exist in some of the new
democracies.

Growing Demands for Judicial Reform in Latin America

Many of the obstacles I have described that hinder an adequate functioning of the judiciary are by no means new. What is novel is the current concern throughout the region with the failings of the institutions of justice. Another novelty is the introduction of various constitutional and legislative reforms regarding the judiciary. This current concern with reforming legal systems in Latin America is the fruit of a number of converging forces and causes of both a domestic and an international nature. The interaction of these forces and their relative strength will doubtlessly affect the nature of legal reforms when, and if, they take place. This section briefly explores some of these causes.

First, with democratization and the expansion of the franchise, there emerges the notion of citizenship and civil society. In the new democratic discourse, both citizens and civil associations are called upon to participate politically and to exercise democratic rights. As there is greater awareness of these rights and what they should entail, there is growing public pressure for effective rule of law. This is further encouraged by the mass media, more schooling, and a universal message of what the benefits of democracy should be. Because Latin American societies (with significant variations— Uruguay by no means shares common socioeconomic features with, say, Guatemala) represent highly complex and heterogeneous entities, there are enormous differences with regard to how different sectors are immersed or not in the formal and bureaucratic procedures of democratic citizenship. Social changes—which are both a result of and parallel to the establishment of market economics—while they appear to reflect a greater degree of social fragmentation and disintegration, also present a society that demands respect and the protection of certain basic rights. This is all the more so as "state-shrinking" cuts in the public sector and the weakening of old corporatist state structures have had the effect of diminishing other channels for articulating demands, normally of a social or economic nature. These demands were not necessarily adequately satisfied before, but the sense of loss is nonetheless felt by the "losing" actors. Nonetheless, while public opinion in general appears to be increasingly dissatisfied with the impunity and corruption that characterize public office at every level and demands for fairer justice mechanisms are growing, there is not necessarily a clearly articulated or homogeneous sense of what citizenship means, how rights should be defined, or what needs improving in the justice and law enforcement institutions. Much of the public demand for legal reform also stems from a growing concern with law and order and increasing levels of public insecurity.

In addition, new democracies face more complex and urbanized societies, which require more effective and fairer mechanisms of dispute settlement. Latin American societies are becoming more litigious, as is evident from increasing caseloads in the courts. It is also evident that the court systems are unable to meet these new challenges. At the root of this general diffuse demand for improved legal institutions is the problem of regime legitimization, which the new democracies are at pains to resolve. A second pressure for legal reforms stems from the demand for the effective protection of civil and human rights encouraged by the growing presence of international and domestic agencies, both public and private, that specialize in the subject. Nongovernmental organizations (NGOs) have played a key role in the denunciation of human rights abuses.[25] Much of this greater public visibility, and hence scrutiny of the courts, was to a large extent prompted by the denunciations of human rights violations under military rule in Latin America. This appears to be the case in Argentina.[26] It is also evident in the democratic process in Bolivia, where the Supreme Court gained considerable public prominence with the trial against General García Mesa. A corollary of this has been the creation of new public institutions that act as human rights ombudsmen (Mexico, El Salvador). These actions have had some impact on the process of consciousness-raising regarding the deficiencies of justice administration and the problems of impunity. Added to this is the official discourse of the United States, although by no means entirely consistent, which has taken on the promotion of human rights protection, legality, and judicial reform in Latin America.[27] This, however, has in part taken the form of anticorruption campaigns often linked to drug issues, with all the conditionality and political overtones that this implies.[28]

Perhaps a more important source of pressure, in terms of political and economic leverage, for the establishment of more predictable and reliable court systems and legality stems from certain business sectors (those more in tune with economic liberalization). This pressure is by no means consistent or representative of the entire business community of the countries in question; in fact, many businesses have benefited from discretionary practices of state capitalist development where judicial scrutiny was not effective.[29] The main concern here is with strengthening a legal framework that guarantees the protection of private property, gives greater stability to the legal boundaries of property rights and to contract law, and curbs the threat of state intervention.[30] This will find keen support among business sectors—ultimately key actors in the current democratic processes that are intimately linked to free-market politics. Surveys in the private sector throughout the region indicate that the judicial system is regarded as a major constraint to private sector development.[31]

The strategic position of these economic agents, all the more so in a context of privatization and economic liberalization, may prove to be the more compelling force behind any attempt at judicial reform in the region. It is evident that economic performance and long-term developmental possibilities cannot be taken in isolation from the institutional environment in which economic policies are implemented.[32] However, while it is evident that business sectors have not resisted democratization, it remains to be seen the extent to which they have fully internalized the benefits of democratic reforms. The dramatic uncertainties of political and economic crisis may well inspire temporary and indeed pressing demands for legal reforms by capitalist interests. But long-established habits, including informal codes of behavior in economic activities and a predatory attitude toward a vitiated state apparatus, are hard to kick.

A final source of pressure, and one intimately linked to the above, stems from the current global context of economic liberalization and internationalization of capitalist development. Not only international public financial agencies but also potential foreign investors encourage the establishment of regulated and predictable legal frameworks. International organizations, such as the World Bank, have become important actors in the promotion of judicial reforms specifically targeted at enhancing efficiency in justice administration. However, imported prescriptive reform projects risk being incompatible with local needs. In an era of globalization, the temptation to advocate universal reform packages is great. And although many of the problems identified in this chapter recur within the judicial structures of the region, country-specific conditions need to be considered and respected in order for reforms to be effective.

That some of these pressures will operate with greater effect on the reform of legal structures may, however, lead to a dualistic development of the justice system. It is possible to envisage considerable progress in legal reforms in some areas of litigation, such as those that concern the modernizing sectors of the economic elite in matters of an economic, financial, or commercial nature (benefiting those sectors that have greater lobbying power and leverage and that are perhaps more articulate in their specific concerns). Yet other areas of litigation and access to justice may remain untouched, corrupted, and persistently lacking in infrastructure and resources.[33]

There is no doubt that the legal institutions in Latin America, in spite of the pressing need for reform, are probably the institutional aspects most resistant to change. Effective rule of law requires not just the reform of the necessary legal and constitutional texts (sometimes those in existence are not necessarily bad but simply not abided by). In the long term, an effective reform of the legal system also requires substantive changes in the political culture, values, and expectations of a society and political class. Because of the complexity of Latin American societies, the latter point is of particular relevance.

Evaluating Judicial Reform

Latin American democracies in varying degrees, and largely as a result of the above pressures, have begun or are in the process of designing judicial reforms. Prominent in the political discourse throughout the region are issues of democratic rights and rule of law. The reforms are part of the process of institution building with a view to improved transparency, public accountability, and a more profound questioning of a behavior and tradition of impunity. This occurs amid corruption scandals and evident dissatisfaction with and public mistrust of the fundamental democratic institutions. However, as discussed above, the obstacles to be overcome are considerable.

It would appear that reforms are likely to take place in the following situations: where political elites face legitimation crises and the regime viability comes seriously into question; where (often a consequence of the preceding) the short-term political benefits of reform outweigh the costs of reform (for instance, concrete electoral benefits);[34] and where the pressures for reform are widespread or come from specific pressure groups that do have political or economic leverage, as discussed above.

A major issue is what kinds of resistance reform efforts will face. Elements that promote reform must take on interests that are threatened by reform. Resistance to reform can block reform initiatives, or, once reforms have been passed, resistance can make their implementation difficult. A powerful obstacle to reform stems from networks of patronage and clientelism that characterize many of the state systems of the region. This combines with strongly rooted habits of circumventing the law, inertial expectations of impunity, and a historical legacy of a predatory attitude toward public office. Reforms designed to enhance horizontal accountability will be seen as undermining the rent-seeking capacity of powerholders as well as their political patronage networks. There may also be fear that judicial reforms will lead to uncovering past acts of corruption. Resistance to reforms may also come specifically from the executive or legislative branches unwilling to relinquish control to judicial bodies.[35] Finally, resistance may come from within the judicial systems themselves.[36] Judicial personnel are likely to feel threatened by new rules enhancing internal mechanisms of accountability. It appears that in countries in which judges have not participated in the reform projects, implementation has been most problematic. Judges may feel that their areas of control will be reduced, and their authority undermined.

It is clear that legal reforms in Latin America are a complex matter and require more than redesigning formal mechanisms that will strengthen political independence and impartiality and enhance accountability and transparency. They also require resources, investment, and a transformation of illiberal habits based on political manipulation, clientelism, and inefficiency that pervade the public sector. Although judicial reforms have been taking place in Latin America, tracking their performance is complicated at best. In this section I attempt to categorize some of the recent reform efforts.

Perhaps two levels of reform can be identified. The first addresses problems of justice administration in general—that is, structural, administrative, and procedural. The typical problem areas that are contemplated here are the questions of resources and infrastructure, procedures for appointing lower court judges, and performance assessment criteria based on merit, training and legal education, court and case management, and internal disciplinary mechanisms. With regard to procedural reforms, the emphasis is on ways of simplifying legal procedures and court bureaucracy. The second level includes reforms that alter the "horizontal" relationship between the judiciary and the other branches of government. Here the predominant concerns are with enhancing judicial autonomy from the other branches, notably the executive, and with establishing an adequate scope of judicial review of legislative acts.

The two levels are intimately linked, as both are necessary for the advancement of rule of law and independent adjudication. Ideally, the two levels of reform should be complementary. Reforming legal structures with a view to enhancing both horizontal accountability and rights protection is complicated at best. To the extent that reforms have taken place, it would appear that more emphasis has been placed on the first level. Frequently the reforms have been partial and generally still require additional legislation before full implementation of the reforms is in place. Moreover, the reforms seem to involve a learning-by-doing process, in which as implementation takes place, new problems are identified that have not been contemplated or fully addressed by the reforms.

The main thrust of the reforms has generally been to address the administrative problems of the court systems—to some extent in response to specific pressures from international organizations such as the World Bank, whose main concern is the efficiency of court services. The outstanding feature of many of the reform processes is the creation of judicial councils or *consejos de judicatura* or *magistratura*. Countries that have recently incorporated these councils into their judicial systems are Costa Rica in 1989, Colombia in 1991, Paraguay in 1992, Ecuador in 1992, Bolivia in 1994, Argentina in 1994, and Mexico in 1994.[37] Ecuador has yet to fully establish these councils. It appears that the legislature is unwilling to give up some of its appointment powers to the judicial council.[38]

There is considerable variation between these councils in terms of how appointments to them are made and what the councils' main functions are. As regards appointment mechanisms, frequently the executive selects one or more of the council members, while the others are selected by the judiciary or the legislature. The aim has generally been to minimize political influence in the councils. The councils usually take on a number of administrative tasks. A first function is to recruit judicial staff and appoint lower-level judges (in some cases, such as Bolivia, the councils also participate in the appointment of supreme court judges). The councils are also in charge of establishing merit-based appointment procedures, promotion mechanisms, and disciplinary procedures to curb corruption within the courts. In many cases, the administration of the judicial budget will also be under the control of the judicial councils. The councils, therefore, are an attempt to resolve many of the administrative problems that characterize the justice systems in the region: chronic administrative backlogs, inefficiency, and lack of transparency.

Where judicial councils have begun to operate, evaluation of their performance can only be preliminary. Even where the judicial councils have been in place for a while (Mexico and Colombia), improvement in justice administration is still not evident. This reflects in part the fact that reforming the administration of justice is a complex process that involves different facets and stages. To the extent that reforms are being undertaken, they normally involve a staggered process, so that often the full implementation of the reforms is either not in place or not fully legislated.

Additional administrative reforms include such laws as the General Code of Procedure in Uruguay (1989), which attempts to shorten and simplify court proceedings to enhance judicial efficiency.[39] Some countries have introduced the use of professional managers on a trial basis with the aim of reducing the administrative tasks of lower court judges (in Bolivia, Chile, Costa Rica, El Salvador, Honduras, and Panama). World Bank–supported reform projects contemplate increasing support infrastructure, introducing training facilities to enhance the institutional development of courts, and improving courtroom productivity and efficiency. These are mainly targeted at streamlining judicial efficiency in the administration of justice.

Reforms that address the horizontal relationship between the judiciary and the executive range from changing the appointments procedure to reduce the power of the executive (Bolivia in 1994 and Mexico in 1994), to increasing the judicial review powers of the high tribunals (Mexico, Brazil in 1988)—in some cases through the creation of constitutional courts (Bolivia, Colombia in 1991). In Colombia, whereas the justice administration side of judicial reform has as yet neither improved the image of the judiciary nor made justice administration more efficient, the Supreme Court and the Constitutional Tribunal (the latter created in the 1991 Constitution) are fairly well regarded as independent branches capable of exercising autonomous constitutional checks on the other branches[40]—it is not clear, however, that this respectability of the high tribunal does not in fact predate the reforms. The justice system in Colombia thus reflects a dual reality in which the incapacity of justice administration is both a product and consequence of the complex process of social disintegration the state has been unable to resolve. And the relative respectability of the higher courts has not proved capable of filtering through to the justice system in general, so that the dramatic problems of lack of rule of law at a societal level continue.[41]

In Brazil, the 1988 Constitution strengthened the autonomy power of the high tribunal. Judicial rulings on matters of constitutionality, however, have become highly politicized.[42] This is in part a consequence of an ambitious constitution that addresses almost every aspect of social life, thus inviting frequent constitutional contestation of legislation. But the main problem of the justice system in Brazil stems from inefficiency in justice administration.[43] By contrast, in Argentina, reforms have concentrated on justice administration with limited results. With regard to the role of constitutional checks and control of legality of the other branches, the experience of the Supreme Court under Menem reveals not only a lack of autonomy but in fact a level of interbranch complicity that undermines any notion of judicial independence. In Mexico, the Supreme Court, following the constitutional reforms of 1994, should move toward a position of greater political autonomy from the executive; moreover, the court now has greater judicial review powers. However, the broader political context of regime transition renders any assessment of the Mexican case tentative at best.

Clearly, with regard to the problem of judicial independence from the other branches, it is not only a matter of institutional reform but also of shaking off traditions of judicial subordination rooted in the experience of authoritarian rule and the historic weakness of democratic institutions. The process of self-assertion of the judiciary depends not only on specific institutional reforms but also on the broader political process of democratic consolidation.

The reforms in Latin America reflect a complex combination of concerns with addressing a broad variety of problems of the judiciary, regarding not only its political independence and role as a check on the other branches of state, but also its role of justice administration and rights protection in general. Which reforms have been emphasized varies from country to country, largely determined by where the pressures for reform originate, what power structures are in place, whether executive interests concur with the goal of enhancing rule of law and judicial independence, and what the specific problems are of a given judicial system. Measuring the success of judicial reforms is further compounded, because the yardstick for one country context may not be applicable to another.

Test cases of institutional confrontation between the judiciary and the other branches may be a form of signaling change toward greater judicial independence. It would seem that there is a process by which there is a judicialization of politics, as supreme courts are playing a considerably more political role than in the past. Highly visible judicial decisions, such as the corruption cases of Carlos Andrés Pérez in Venezuela and Fernando Collor de Mello in Brazil, might seem political instances in which the independence of the courts is on trial. Whether they imply precedent-setting cases is difficult to assess. Both were extremely politicized moments in which the legal decisions corresponded to overwhelming popular support, rather than real test cases to judge a more consistent and structural autonomy of the legal system from executive interests. Moreover, greater political prominence of the courts tells us little about the quality of judicial independence. Autonomy from executive influence does not imply independence from conflicting parties or from plebiscitary pressures. It is possible that in their bid to appear as relevant actors in a new democratic setting, judges will bow to public opinion rather than make independent judicial decisions. However, it is likely that because judicial rulings do have a bearing on policymaking, where judicial autonomy is strengthened or in place, executive policy decisions and legislation will need to be more aware of constitutional limits. Where this has been most evident is perhaps in Brazil and Colombia.

In the case of Argentina, it is clear that despite reforms (and perhaps even as a result of the early 1990 reforms), the judiciary is more tied than ever to the executive's will, failing to represent a credible instance of legal and constitutional control and accountability. In Mexico (notwithstanding the still dubious democratic credentials of the regime), the reforms that have been potentially far-reaching do point to a reaccommodation of the role of the judiciary in the political system toward greater independence. In addition, it would appear that for the first time, the Supreme Court is actively reasserting a position of political independence. Recent friction between the executive-appointed attorney general's office (*procuraduría general*) and the judiciary, resulting from each laying the blame of corruption at the other institution's door, suggests that the problems of corruption are as great as ever—what has changed is the nature of interorgan relations from one of institutional complicity to one of conflict, as the rules of the political system are in a process of transformation. In the case of Bolivia in 1991, the most dramatic confrontation between the executive and the judiciary in fact preceded judicial reform. At best this suggests a process of judicial self-assertion vis-à-vis the executive; at worst it was merely an example of interpolitical elite conflict, in which the role of the judiciary in democratic politics was a tangential consideration, as the conflict was resolved between political parties and not with strict adherence to the law.

Perhaps rather than looking at precedent-setting cases, what we should be examining is longer-term consistency in court rulings that might suggest a move toward judicial independence. This requires careful analysis of court cases and case statistics, which is not readily available in the current literature on the judiciary in Latin America.[44] Only by examining court rulings over time regarding judicial review decisions can a more accurate conclusion about the effects of judicial reform be reached. Moreover, improvement in judicial independence not only will be the result of reforms, but will probably also be a product of the advancement and entrenchment of democratic rules within the broader political setting, which will involve redefining the role of the judiciary.

Finally, the benefits from judicial reform will be slower to come than from other political processes. In part this reflects the inertial or even active resistance within the legal institutions to implement the reforms. But also, the nature of many of the reforms requires the passage of time for the full benefits to be felt. For instance, new merit-based appointments and promotion systems would only gradually affect judicial personnel, as new attitudes and behavior could not immediately be imposed on existing generations of judicial personnel. Many of the reforms in Latin America are very recent and in most cases have been only partially implemented.

Conclusion

This is only a summary presentation of the complex reality of the judicial systems in Latin America. The differences that separate Latin American countries in the specificities of their judicial traditions cannot be overstressed. Constitutional prescriptions are only an initial guideline, for the same rules applied in different countries will develop along divergent paths in accordance with the complexities of political, social, economic, and cultural surroundings.

Judicial politics is highly relevant for the question of regime legitimation and consolidation. Without minimally effective mechanisms of rule of law, two fundamental tasks of constitutional government are not fulfilled: first, checking the state for abuse of power and subjecting government to controls of transparency, accountability, and constitutionality; and second, providing the necessary conditions for the minimum protection of rights through impartial, predictable, and accessible justice mechanisms. The former strengthens the foundations of constitutional legitimacy of the regime and the latter promotes the internalization of democratic values, as it contributes to making citizenship effective through rights protection.

While these are explicit principles in the constitutional texts of the region, the reality of judicial independence and rights protection in the new democracies leaves much to be desired. Far from achieving optimal standards of legal accountability and respect for constitutional rights, these countries face severe obstacles in realizing this goal. The prevailing image of impunity and corruption severely undermines regime legitimacy, and the lack of perceived rights and guarantees erodes the prospects for binding loyalties to democratic rule both within the political elites and at the societal level. Indeed, if we compare the progress made in the more formally procedural aspects of democratic rule, namely free and competitive elections, the judicial aspect lags noticeably behind in the consolidation processes. The danger lies in the implications this has with regard to the internalization and entrenchment of democratic values in the region. Without an operative rule of law, it is difficult to envisage the development of democratic "civil society" in terms of internalized perceptions of rights and obligations, or the consolidation of credible government bound by rules of legal and constitutional accountability.

Judicial processes, in all their complexity and the different aspects of social life they touch upon, evidently do not reflect an easily traceable or linear direction of development. Some areas progress while others deteriorate. Ideally, even if this is the case, the differentiated changes in justice mechanisms will correspond to the changing needs of society. However, this appears not to be the case in Latin America, and it is possible to envisage the uneven development of different areas of adjudication. In addition, even if progress may be detected at the level of supreme courts regarding growing judicial autonomy from political influence, this does not necessarily contribute to resolving some of the structural problems of justice administration that characterize court services.

Optimism can be drawn, nonetheless, from what appear to be genuine concerns with reforming the long-neglected justice apparatus in much of Latin America. Already many of the new democracies are undertaking gradual legal reforms in different areas of civil and penal procedures, strengthening the *ministerio público,* introducing police reforms, and so forth. Similarly, the increased presence of supreme court decisions in political events throughout the region might denote a process of judicial self-assertion in the political systems of the new democracies, such that we can speak of a gradual move toward a more effective separation of powers. Equally, greater public scrutiny and demands for accountability and transparency of government are arguably having a positive impact on the democratic process—and will continue as long as expectations are not completely dashed and regime legitimacy is not totally eroded before at least some progress is seen to take place.

It would seem that the process by which constitutional norms and rule of law becomes fully entrenched and binding in Latin American societies is bound to be slow. It involves not only actual formal reforms, but also profound change in illiberal habits and discretionary practices of "rule-bending" at all levels of state and society. It would be unreasonable to expect the new democracies to achieve this more rapidly than have the more developed countries where, after all, constitution and rule of law building has taken decades, and even centuries.

Notes

1. Even after democratization, rights are still alarmingly violated in a routine manner, to some extent reproducing a legacy of military repression that remains within, for instance, the police forces (see Rodley, "Torture and Conditions of Detention"). Pockets of rights violations persist, and impunity in the use of state force, combined with the current concern with law and order and increased crime

rates, does not augur well for reducing levels of violence in the treatment of this problem.

2. Waltman, "The Courts," p. 216.

3. See Fiss, "The Right Degree," Kahn, "Independence and Responsibility," and Shapiro, *Courts,* for discussions on the problems of achieving the right degree of independence.

4. Fiss, "The Right Degree."

5. Frankel, "Concerning the Role of the Judiciary."

6. See Dakolias, *The Judicial Sector,* p. 4, Ungar, "All Justice Is Local," and Sadek, "Perspectivas."

7. Rico and Salas, *Independencia judicial,* Verner, "Independence," and Rosenn, "Judicial Review."

8. Nino, "On the Exercise of Judicial Review."

9. Rico and Salas, *Independencia judicial,* pp. 18–19.

10. The Chilean example is one where excessive judicial independence has imperiled the democratic principle of the judicial function. See also Galleguillos, "Checks and Balances," and Correa, "The Judiciary."

11. This was the case in Argentina in the different regime changes, particularly after 1955, when the practice of replacing the entire Supreme Court became the norm (prior to this judges were replaced only selectively). Democratic rule has in this case not improved matters; in 1990, Menem assured majority support in the high tribunal through the addition of four members (see Smulovitz, "El poder judicial," and Nino, "On the Exercise of Judicial Review"). Bolivia, similarly, has an impressive record of Supreme Court turnover with every change of regime throughout its history (see Castro Rodríguez, *Historia judicial*). Military rule in Uruguay formally abolished judicial independence in 1977. In Brazil, habeas corpus was suspended for political offenses, and judicial competencies were transferred to special military tribunals (see Rico and Salas, *Independencia judicial,* pp. 14–15). By contrast, in 1973, Pinochet did not change the members of the Supreme Court in Chile, as the military did not perceive the judiciary as a threat.

12. The recent case in Mexico in which a judge was bought off by a financier to ensure that the fraud charges against him be kept within the confines of the local state judicial system and not remitted to the federal judiciary where his chances of leniency would be lessened is an example of corruption within the lower levels of the judiciary that affects the image of the legal institutions in general.

13. It is worth remembering that U.S. Supreme Court appointments, although controlled, are also highly politicized, but alternation in power between the two main parties generally works to balance ideological swings within the judiciary. Also, here it is a matter of ideological leaning rather than personal or political loyalties that link Supreme Court appointments to the executive.

14. Rico and Salas, *Independencia judicial,* p. 31; and Correa, "Capacitación y carrera judicial."

15. In Ecuador, administrative tasks take up to 70 percent of judges' time, in Brazil 65 percent, and in Peru 69 percent (see Dakolias, *The Judicial Sector,* p. 23; see also Casaus, "Court Organisation").

16. Six percent in Costa Rica, 3 percent in Honduras, 2.5 percent in Ecuador, and 2 percent in Panama. Invariably these percentages are not respected. In Costa Rica, the average real percentage of the national budget is 5 percent and in Honduras 1.4 percent (see Rico and Salas, *Independencia judicial*). In Ecuador, the judiciary received 0.96 percent in 1993, 1.4 percent in 1994, and 1.6 percent in 1995 (see Dakolias, *The Judicial Sector*).

17. In Mexico, the judicial budget is in fact lower than the budget allocated to the IFE (Federal Electoral Institute).

18. Dakolias, *The Judicial Sector*, p. 27.

19. Lynch, "Legal Roles."

20. Studies of this kind are few. On the whole, research has generally confined itself to examining constitutional provisions for judicial review, but this tells us little of the behavior of courts regarding constitutional review. Clearly, a major obstacle for research in this area has been the difficulty in obtaining reliable case statistics.

21. Rosenn, "Judicial Review," and Biles, "The Position of the Judiciary."

22. Jurisprudence is established in some countries more consistently than in others.

23. Verner, "Independence," classifies supreme courts in Latin America in the following manner: (1) independent activist (Costa Rica); (2) attenuated activist (traditionally Uruguay and Chile before military rule); (3) stable reactive (Mexico, largely as a function of the relative stability of the regime); (4) reactive compliant (Argentina, Brazil, Colombia and Venezuela); and (5) minimalist (Peru, Bolivia, Panama, Ecuador, El Salvador, Guatemala, and Honduras). Nino, "On the Exercise of Judicial Review," speaks of the Argentine Supreme Court as one that has followed different periods of activism in its relationship with the executive. It is clear that under Menem judicial independence has deteriorated, rendering a subservient court. In Chile, the Supreme Court confronted the executive under Allende. Its compliance with Pinochet appears to have been more a matter of common interest and ideological convergence than judicial subordination.

24. González, "Tribunales constitucionales."

25. Panizza, "Human Rights."

26. Smulovitz, "El poder judicial."

27. Carrothers, *In the Name of Democracy*.

28. Specifically related to this is the creation of special drug courts in some of the coca-producing countries, such as Bolivia and Colombia. In Bolivia, drug courts were created with specialist staff and are semi-independent from the formal justice system, although ultimately accountable to the Supreme Court. This, however, has not been free of considerable national concern on the questions of sovereignty, constitutionality, and rights protection (see Gamarra, "The System of Justice").

29. State-business relations, traditionally dictated by clientelist and protectionist informal codes, provided a comfortable setting for business interests to coalesce with state capitalism. Military rule upset some of these conventions as did growing economic crises and uncertainty, which prompted, in some countries more explicitly than in others, a demand for clearer and more formalized rules of the game.

30. Elster, "The Impact of Constitutions," stresses the importance of constitutional rule on sustained economic development in terms of stability, accountability, reliability, and predictable state regulatory capacity. See also Maxfield and Schneider, "Business," who stress the importance of two conditions that favor economic performance: credibility and trust in state-business relations—factors that undoubtedly would be favorably reinforced by strengthening a binding set of constitutional and legal norms.

31. Dakolias, *The Judicial Sector*, p. 3.

32. North, *Institutions*.

33. It is worth drawing attention to the unclear connection between the "ideological" premises of the current economic policies and the type of democracy these entail. This parallel process of democracy building and market economics implies, for instance, the necessary creation of a good "business climate," a consequence of which is the loss of rights on the side of labor. What needs to be questioned is that while good business conditions are desirable for economic growth, and by extension arguably conducive to democracy, we must forewarn against the inevitable

implied causal relationship between protecting the interests of capital and democratic consolidation. Free-market economics does not ensure democratic consolidation. And democracy surely involves more than providing a good business climate.

34. Geddes, "A Game-Theoretical Model," examines electoral conditions that make state reform likely: internal party and legislative structures and the distribution of patronage structures among the top political groups.

35. This has been the case in Ecuador, where some of the judicial reforms, such as the establishment of the judicial council body, have been delayed at the legislative level.

36. Geddes, "A Game-Theoretical Model" pp. 167–168.

37. Fix-Zamudio and Fix-Fierro, *El consejo.*

38. Dakolias, *The Judicial Sector,* p. 21.

39. Tarigo, "Legal Reform in Uruguay." Oral hearings have been introduced, and the number of courts has increased. Here the results have been positive in terms of reducing the average duration of a trial.

40. Franco, "Independencia judicial." Curiously, despite the relative success of the constitutional court, there have been legislative attempts to curb its judicial review powers.

41. The levels of violence in Colombian society have meant that lower court judges are subjected daily to pressures that inevitably undermine their capacity to make independent judicial decisions. Between 1980 and 1990, 230 judges were murdered and approximately 1,600 received death threats (see Parra Quijano, "La administración de justicia," p. 140.

42. Sadek, "Perspectivas."

43. Ibid.

44. There are a few isolated studies that examine the case history of supreme court decisions on matters of judicial review. See, for instance, Schwartz, "Jueces en la penumbra," and González Casanova, *La democracia en México.* But on the whole, this is an unexplored area of research in most of Latin America. In most countries, court statistics are only recently being collected and becoming reliable.

11

Building Judicial Independence in Common Law Africa

JENNIFER WIDNER

T his chapter is about the separation of powers. It tries to contribute to our general understanding of why courts are able to acquire and maintain significant independence from other branches of government in some countries, while in others, similarly situated, the judiciary has lost institutional autonomy. Its focus is common law Africa, a part of the world where the need to build rule of law is especially urgent and where considerable attention now focuses on the courts. The chapter draws out some of the distinctive features associated with efforts to build independence in the region and proposes an account of these.

In the search for insight and for reliable generalizations, it is often most edifying to engage practitioners to find out how they think about a problem and get them to reflect upon the experiences of others in different parts of the world, to arrive at a sense of the ways in which the task may be different in one time and place than in another. Who are the relevant players? What resources do they bring to bear? Which institutions and rules structure relationships among decisionmakers? In short, how do the people most directly involved understand this context, the stakes, the risks—and how negotiations in different spheres affect each other? This chapter distills the main elements of conversations with more than 130 lawyers, judges, and magistrates in Tanzania, Uganda, Botswana, and Kenya during 1995–1996. Many of its illustrations draw from the career of Chief Justice Francis Nyalali, of Tanzania, currently the world's longest-serving chief justice.

Assessing Judicial Independence

Judicial independence is here defined as the insulation of judges and the judicial process from partisan pressure to influence the outcomes of individual cases. At the center of attention is undue pressure from the other branches of government to decide cases in certain ways—the kinds of concerns that are associated with the separation of powers. Clearly, judges' education and social backgrounds may give them a subconscious predisposition to favor certain kinds of causes over others. Socially powerful litigants may seek to influence the judicial process as well. Yet such broader psychological and social concerns of independence fall outside the purview of this chapter.

Even after shedding many of its complexities, judicial independence is difficult to assess in practical terms for those who want to measure the performance of courts against each other. The concept is at once multidimensional and unobservable. It has many components, and it is something we cannot measure directly. To capture the different elements of independence, judges themselves have tried to develop indicators, embodied in the "Siracusa Principles," a set of standards published under the auspices of the International Commission of Jurists.[1] The lists of indicators the judges have put together are voluminous and touch on the very many ways people may exert, or feel, pressure to decide a case in a particular way. They include direct efforts to influence decisions, such as bribery and harassment, as well as intervention in other aspects of the judicial process, such as control over the assignment of cases to individual judges. They focus on whether the executive branch plays a formal role in administrative matters that affect judges' own fortunes—for example, in the determination of salaries, hiring, promotions, transfers, and dismissals. They include removal of cases from the jurisdiction of the courts and their placement in parallel tribunals that do not safeguard due process.

These lists are excellent heuristic devices, but they are not as useful for assessing whether a court is more or less independent than one would hope. It is one thing to try to identify the components of independence, and another to put these to practical use in assessing variations or trends. An index, which combines scores on diverse criteria to produce a single number, is the standard social science technique for reducing the data to a form that permits comparison; but information about the severity of violations and the relative importance of different measures is lost. More to the point, in many countries, the information required to assess performance on each individual criterion is often missing.

In studies of the United States and other industrial democracies, scholars often employ an alternative method of measurement. They count numbers of decisions in which the government loses. In those periods in which the government prevails more often, the courts are considered less independent. Although this method is common in current research, it is seriously flawed. Judges may rule in favor of government for any number of reasons, and this approach provides no means for determining which decisions are really instances of undue influence. Contextual information, rarely incorporated, would aid the reliability of inferences, but it cannot solve the problem completely. Moreover, the focus on decisions overlooks the capacity of other branches of government to influence outcomes in particular cases, not through the judges themselves but through intervention in the judicial process—in the flows of paperwork or pressure on members of the bar.

In the absence of the detailed information required to develop reliable indicators, the best method may be to allow those who have most contact with the judicial system, the lawyers, to offer their own evaluations of trends in their countries. The research that underlies this chapter uses a combination of open-ended interviews and small surveys of members of the bar to try to estimate the direction of change and to establish the reasons for increases and decreases in independence, so defined, across contexts. These data come from a survey I carried out in Botswana, Tanzania, and Uganda. The study drew small random samples of lawyers from lists of practicing members of the bar. Asked whether the judiciary is more independent, about as independent, or less independent now than it was ten years ago, 3.2 percent of lawyers in Botswana, but 73.9 in Tanzania and 78.9 percent in Uganda, said it was more independent; 64.5 percent of respondents in Botswana thought is was about the same, while only 17.4 and 19.3 percent thought so in Tanzania and Uganda, respectively. The remaining respondents, 25.8 percent in Botswana, 8.7 percent in Tanzania, and zero percent in Uganda, thought the courts had become less independent.

Standard Explanations

Like central banks, auditors, and election commissions, judiciaries bring little leverage to negotiations with the other branches of government. They have no army and no power of the purse. Their power resides mainly in the degree to which political elites and members of the public consider impartial resolution of disputes important to the conduct of their lives. For this reason, most of the prevailing accounts of judicial independence place the action outside the courts themselves. In Martin Shapiro's classic book, *The Courts,* he suggests that independent courts were developed to restrain a predatory monarchy and, later, a parliament with similar appetites.[2] Concerns about fair adjudication of land and tax disputes, first by nobles, then by the early parliament and powerful economic interests, were important causal factors. One of the legacies of past governmental centralization in Africa is the relative absence of such powerful domestic lobbies. Debates about judicial independence are commonplace, but there are few groups with both the intense commitment and the economic clout required to serve as a vocal constituency. Business, which has a stake in the impartial resolution of contract disputes, has long been weakly organized and has been divided by ethnic differences or affiliations with competing political leaders, or both. Often cited as an important pressure group, members of the bar have typically raised their voices on behalf of the judiciary only irregularly.

Other writings on separation of powers and judicial independence have treated independence as the product of legislative or executive delegation, echoing some of the themes of Shapiro's account. The judges themselves play no role in these explanations.

William Landes and Richard Posner, for example, note that legislation is the product of interest group competition; legislators favor the groups that make the greatest investment in lobbying activities. "A judiciary that was subservient to the current membership of the legislature could nullify legislation enacted in a previous session," creating considerable instability in the legal regimes.[3] Support for judicial independence results. Similarly, E. O. Salzberger argues that many issues before legislatures attract high levels of interest group lobbying. Individual legislators risk loss of at least some support and gains in other quarters. "The desirability of delegation, in the individual legislator's eyes and from the perspective of political costs, depends on the divergence between the credit shifts and the blame shifts that the delegation is likely to create," he writes.[4] Delegation to an independent judiciary is an effort to attenuate responsibility, reducing the chance of attack from those who oppose the legislator's opinion by saying, "We should let the courts decide."

Observing variations in the degree of judicial independence among industrial democracies, Mark Ramseyer amends the Landes and Posner argument. He suggests that independence is linked to the competitiveness of the party system. In single-party-dominant Japan, judicial independence is lower than it is in countries where there is a serious risk that the party in power will lose control of the legislature at each election.[5]

Although among themselves many African judges speak about the virtues of multiparty politics for separation of powers, theories of legislative delegation have little capacity to explain varying patterns of institutional independence where these judges work. In some of the countries where lawyers report increasing levels of judicial independence, multiparty systems are new and fragile; in others, such as Uganda, single-party systems are still in place.

Scholars who work outside the industrial democracies have also employed theories of delegation, focusing on the executive, not the legislature. For example, James Rosberg, in his recent dissertation on judicial independence in Egypt, has argued that successive heads of state worried about the politicization of the police and social services. Careful central supervision of bureaucratic agencies, on the model of a police patrol, was very expensive. Heads of state settled instead for decentralized monitoring, or a "fire alarm" model, which allowed those who felt they had been treated unfairly to sue in the courts. Executive branch leaders invested in measures to enhance judicial independence as part of this effort.[6]

On the ground, in Africa, the most common explanation for levels of judicial independence centers on the terms of appointment and removal. Constitutions lay out the terms of appointment, tenure, and discipline for judges and magistrates. Originally these provisions were similar across countries, produced by the same template at independence. Subsequent alterations in constitutions have produced some variation. Contrary to the hunches expressed, however, a careful review of the data shows no observable relationship between such provisions and patterns of judicial independence across countries.[7] Countries whose constitutions have similar language regarding separation of powers, judicial independence, and the appointment and tenure of judges display a range of actual outcomes.

Strategies for Change

A focus on choice and strategy yields more understanding of variation in judicial independence. Conversations in Africa suggest that the process of building judicial independence usually engages judges as important actors and encompasses a much broader range of tactics than conventional theories suggest. Chief justices in countries where judicial independence is increasing usually pursue several tactics simultaneously. Chief justices in countries where independence has declined in recent years have eschewed all or most of the same.

Offering Impartiality

Consistent with several of the conventional theories, the elites interviewed suggest that increases in independence usually start with a temporary "deal" between the executive and the judiciary. The reasons for these pacts vary. Some start in appeals to the head of state to consider his historical image. Does he wish to go down in the books as someone who established the rule of law or extinguished it? The desire of a head of state to distinguish himself from his predecessors may also provide an incentive. In some instances, these pacts have their origins in the need to root out corruption in the ruling party or a dominant faction. To save political capital, party leaders delegate responsibility for making decisions about who is guilty and who is not to the courts. Equally, however, the disregard for rule of law by anticorruption units has sometimes tiggered a crisis about the appropriate relationship between the branches and forced the issue of judicial independence onto the negotiating table.

In some countries, as in Tanzania and Uganda, growing independence has come in the first instance from changes in attitudes among the head of state and top officials of the ruling party. Judges have played a role in altering executive perspectives in some instances.

It is possible to trace a slow but steady movement toward greater separation of powers in Tanzania to 1983–1984. The late 1970s and early 1980s
were troubled times for the courts. Many officials dismissed the concept of
judicial independence as a colonial hangover. Party officials and district
officers regularly assumed the role of the courts; private militias held sway
in some areas, in the absence of a fair and effective police force or shared
agreement on norms. Lawlessness surged. Disruption in the enforcement of
customary laws, without the effective replacement of those laws by a new
legal system, was an important trigger. A sudden increase in corrupt practices was another. The response was rapid enactment of stringent anticorruption measures that removed a number of offenses from the jurisdiction
of the regular courts and threatened to undermine the judiciary once and for
all.

With the future of the judiciary under challenge, judges stepped out of
their usual roles and launched into negotiations with the president, and then
with party officials. Deeply concerned by the ouster of jurisdiction implied
by the new measures, several senior judges considered tendering their res-
ignations. They met together to discuss what to do. On the basis of their
deliberations, the chief justice, Francis Nyalali, approached the president.
The two men discussed the judges' concerns about the legislation just
enacted. Without amendments, the anticorruption act would widen the
scope for abuse of power, the chief justice suggested. If the concern was to
reduce corruption in government and business, then it was important to
guarantee impartial hearing and judgment of cases, lest one faction or political leader use the laws against others and the party collapse under the
weight of disagreement. The president intended to step down eventually.
What did he want his legacy to be?

President Nyerere listened to the appeal and suggested the chief justice
take his case to the party executive committee. With some trepidation, the
chief justice did so, speaking before the committee members in May 1984,
in the presence of the president. He emphasized that the law had been draft-
ed in a rush and its provisions were not clear. He then went on to explain
how the courts worked and why it was important, for the stability of the
country, that regional party chairs and others not try to do the courts' job.
The executive committee members were at first averse to the ideas proposed. Tanzania's constitution granted the party supremacy. Why should
the party leaders allow the courts to overrule them? Then they gradually
came around to the chief justice's point of view, with some prodding from
the president.

In the end, in Tanzania, the perceived threat the collapse of the rule of
law posed to party cohesion, coupled with the chief justice's initiative,
introduced new views at the top, although problems remained at the lower
levels and the new outlook was vulnerable to retraction. In other countries,

judges played a less central role in influencing the attitudes of the executive and the legislature. In Uganda, for instance, where Idi Amin's government had killed a chief justice and lawless behavior on the part of government officials was part of the motivation for Yoweri Museveni's rebel struggle, the openness of the National Resistance Movement to restoration of judicial independence was part of creating a new political base—a grounds for differentiation from previous regimes. Moreover, the Museveni government's interest in promoting commercial activity and investment made it easier for some of the judges, the solicitor general, and others to appeal for separation of powers, as well as increased financial resources for the courts. In Botswana, long-serving judges and magistrates speculate that low levels of executive interference come from the proximity to South Africa and the continual movement of well-trained antiapartheid lawyers from South Africa in and out of the courts, before which they often practiced, and in and out of the ranks of government.

In Kenya, where judicial independence has suffered in recent years, no "crisis" has impelled the other branches of government to invest in impartial dispute resolution. Fears of political violence run rampant, but opposition parties have fragmented and government leaders have succeeded in using the coercive powers of the executive to ensure that they need not fear competition.

Improving Effectiveness

Chief justices must ensure that lower levels of the judiciary respect admonishments not to allow partisan interference in legal proceedings. Hierarchical organizations are vulnerable to what social scientists call "principal-agent problems," in which officials who wield delegated authority, the agents, use their power for interests other than those of the chief, or principal. To keep tabs on the behavior of subordinates, a chief justice usually relies on private litigants to bring problems to the uppermost court's attention, through appeal of cases they believe were wrongly decided. Adherence to directives is monitored through a system of "fire alarms," or appeals, in lieu of regular monitoring, or the court equivalent of a "police patrol." Procedural reforms to enhance effectiveness are employed as elements of strategy. They are central in any effort to monitor influence and corruption in the judicial process. They are also important to cultivate support in an era when publics are dissatisfied with the delay, cost, and corruption often associated with the legal systems in their countries. In conversation, Chief Justice Nyalali has argued:

The people have to value an independent judiciary and be willing to defend it. And to win public affection, we, the judges, must do our jobs well. The courts must work. People must feel they can resolve disputes satisfactorily and in a reasonable amount of time. If they do, then the people will support us. You see, it is really the quality of justice that determines whether we remain independent.

With the help of the international community, courts in common law Africa are taking several steps to reduce delay, improve monitoring, and increase the salience of reputational factors. For example, one innovation tried in Tanzania is adoption of an individual calendar system, which prevents litigants or officials from playing one judge off against another, to drag out the proceedings by assigning each case to a single judge from the beginning of its life in the court system. Another is the creation of case-flow management committees that draw together representatives of the police, the prisons, the courts, and others whose actions must be coordinated to ensure that defendants and witnesses arrive in court on the same day.

Building Constituencies

Senior judicial officers try to "lock in" the new independence by molding popular opinion, on the view that public outrage, or having recourse to a powerful constituency, is the courts' only bulwark against interference. (1) They encourage and write columns on legal issues in the print media, take to the airwaves, or support legal literacy programs. (2) Some quietly lobby for multiparty systems they consider more conducive to the maintenance of a clear separation of powers. (3) Finally, some chief justices have sought to build a rapport with religious leaders, the other main arbiters of value. Typically, governments in Africa have allowed religious organizations greater autonomy than other types of groups. By highlighting the functional parallels, juxtaposing the images, and borrowing the grassroots networks of religious groups, the courts in some countries have sought to build their image in the popular imagination.

Promoting legal literacy. The judges themselves see their constituency as the public at large. Chief Justice Francis Nyalali of Tanzania commented that "the ultimate safeguard is really public opinion. Judges cannot force the military back to the barracks. They can't run for seats in parliament in order to influence the legislature. The people have to value an independent judiciary and be willing to defend it."[8] It has to be possible to muster outrage. To that end, the Tanzanian judges have taken several steps to enter into a dialogue not only with elite opinion but also with mass attitudes. They seek to forge a public opinion through tactics of persuasion.

Legal literacy initiatives are one tactic in the judges' arsenal. People are most likely to appreciate the role courts can play if they can take problems to judges and magistrates and have these resolved in a fair manner. Helping people get to know what the courts do and educating them in the law may lead more people to bring matters to the judiciary, allowing the judges to demonstrate their usefulness and to educate through the texts of their decisions. To that end, Tanzania's judges launched workshops on a variety of legal topics, including gender issues and labor laws. They started a newspaper column on the courts to explain decisions, and the chief justice took to the radio waves. Several judges wrote pamphlets on the courts and the law, and many took to giving speeches on legal issues.

Championing multiparty politics. To endure, separation of powers cannot be based on short-term preferences of executive or legislative leaders. In conversation, many of the judges interviewed for this project share the view that the best safeguard of judicial independence is party competition. They say that where there are real risks of losing office, legislators will try to ensure that there are impartial forums for resolving differences with those in power and for deciding election petitions. They offer these observations not as an explanation for increases (or decreases) in independence over the past decade but as an aspiration, a firmer ground for the institution of which they are part.

Very few judges are in any position to shape the character of a political regime, and even fewer would consider it part of their role to do so. The Tanzanian courts have ventured where many others will not go, however, and their efforts are interesting, if not necessarily replicable elsewhere. At the president's request, Chief Justice Nyalali led a commission to consider whether the country should move from a one-party state to a multiparty system. Under the chief justice's direction, the commission members traveled throughout the country, holding 1,016 private and public meetings in which an estimated 36,299 people participated. To further inform its deliberations, the commission drew on research papers, newspaper articles, over a thousand memoranda submitted by individuals and private groups, and 16,348 questionnaires.

The commission found itself confronted with a delicate task. As measured through the written questionnaires, public opinion on the Tanzanian mainland was 79.7 percent in favor of continuing the single-party system, while a slimmer majority of Zanzibaris polled similarly. The judge's instincts of the chief justice prevailed, however. He did not take the results of the questionnaires and the meetings as final. Rather, he probed further, to arrive at a different interpretation of the evidence before him. In addition to recommending a move to multiparty democracy, the chief justice used the commission as a way to draw attention to the role of a judiciary in a democracy. Much of the commission's report focused on the courts and on the need for legal reform to support multiparty competition.

Although such opportunities come along infrequently, there are some analogues in other common law countries. In Uganda, for instance, Justice Odoki, a senior justice on the Supreme Court, chaired a similar exercise to redraft his country's constitution. That constitution enhanced provisions for an independent judiciary, even if it did not move the country to a multiparty system.

Exploiting symbolism.   As a third tactic for building a public constituency, the Tanzanian courts have tried to borrow some of the aura surrounding those other arbiters of value: religious organizations. Most court systems have festivities to mark the opening of the legal year. In the past, advocates and politicians have spoken at these, as has the chief justice. Recently, however, the court has decided to invite religious leaders to attend and to bless the proceedings. They have asked that churchgoers pray for the judges—and for the fairness of their decisions. These prayer sessions provide another means of communication with rural majorities and create associations in people's minds that may help create a popular understanding of the separation of powers.

Refashioning Jurisprudence

In several instances, the effort to build independence rests in part on innovations in jurisprudence. In their efforts to define the sphere of the judiciary and to enhance the appearance of fairness, some judges have started to expand the rules of statutory construction, the rules used in interpreting legal materials. For example, they look to new types of evidence to assess purpose or legislative intent.

These innovations are more than an intellectual conceit. Although it is a far stretch from issues of legal philosophy to curbing partisan influence in particular cases, changes in these ideas help shape the authority of the court and the ability of judges to explain their decisions both to one another and to a broader community. They can provide courts with the vocabulary to create a basis for judicial review, if it is not specified in a country's constitution, much as John Marshall did in *Marbury v. Madison.* They can influence the meaning accorded ambiguous terms in a statute or directive or determine whether a statute is narrowly or broadly construed, providing rationales or justifications for interpretations that might otherwise appear arbitrary to a legislature, a head of state, or a broader public.

The principles that guide statutory construction vary across national contexts, depending on legal culture. In Africa, the norms that emerge from precedent do not necessarily resonate with local intuitions about what is fair or otherwise appropriate. Many laws in Anglophone Africa derive from the "Indian Codes," developed during the nineteenth century to help courts resolve disputes in the multiethnic Indian subcontinent. The common law is largely English in origin, adopted through Reception Statutes during the colonial period. Courts also borrow precedents and principles from other common law jurisdictions, such as India, Ireland, and the United States.

Thus, one of the enterprises of the innovative chief justices is to try to find analogous concepts or principles in local beliefs, identify differences, and ground the rules of interpretation used in the courts in principles with which people can identify. The source material is diverse. For example, the chief justice of Tanzania has turned to the documents of the nationalist movement in his own country. Several courts in common law Africa have ruled important laws unconstitutional in recent years, signaling their independence to a broader public. In the mid-1980s, after the encounter with the party's National Executive Committee over the Economic Crime and Corruption Act and upon the introduction of a bill of rights into the Tanzanian constitution, a few judges of the Tanzanian High Court began to depart from past restraint in this respect. Judges in Botswana, Zambia, and Zimbabwe have done the same. Kenya, again, is an exception. There, a decision in the mid-1980s determined that the High Court could not hear rights cases, because the chief justice had not promulgated procedures for the High Court when sitting as a human rights court. This decision deepened the popular perception of the courts as puppets of the executive and precluded any possibility of following the Tanzanian example.

Playing Nested Games

Finally, the judges' tactics include alliance with international organizations as sources of funding, bargaining power, and monitoring assistance. In the absence of domestic constituencies with economic power, the courts increasingly turn to donors, regional groupings, and nongovernmental organizations to provide incentives for governments to respect judicial independence. They participate in "two-level" bargaining games. Donor rule of law programs provide money to bring judges and lawyers together, increasing the value to individuals of possessing a "good reputation." On occasion they also fund essential items, such as law reports, which have low priority in most budgets. Conditions attached to loans can serve as very powerful incentives. Judges and lawyers have actively supported the renewal of the East African Community as a vehicle for improving the flow of information between court systems and for bringing attention to shared law reform problems.

Successful cooperation between judges and members of the international community requires great sensitivity and deftness on the part of a chief justice. To many politicians, the laws bequeathed at independence remain foreign. As the body that interprets and applies the law, the courts also remain alien in the minds of some. The continued presence of judges from other parts of the world, hired on contract, sharpens that sense. The legitimacy of the courts depends partly on making the institution less distant, not more so. Too much donor involvement with rule of law programs—or the wrong kind—can tip the balance against the courts.

It has been said that the move to multiparty systems in Africa during the early 1990s was domestically demanded but internationally supplied.[9] Political elites and majorities felt it was time for change but lacked the power to win reform from incumbent governments. Changes in the conditions on foreign loans and grants, and quiet lobbying behind the scenes, helped push leaders to liberalize. A similar argument has been made about judicial reform in Latin America.[10]

Although these accounts may be correct under such circumstances, they have less explanatory power with regard to judicial independence in common law Africa. Although many courts have forged relationships with members of the international community, the initiatives for reform came from within and predated donor interest. Moreover, outside involvement has remained limited and double-edged.

Distinctive Features

Is the process of building judicial independence different in common law Africa, compared to other regions or historical periods? The question is hard to answer. It depends partly on one's faith in the adequacy of accounts of what has taken place elsewhere. Can these be used as reliable benchmarks to distinguish the distinctive features of African cases? It also depends on the point of entry. A focus on necessary conditions produces one story; a focus on what is sufficient to sustain initial increases in institutional autonomy produces another.

Three main features appear to distinguish efforts to build judicial independence in Africa from comparable initiatives in other parts of the world. First, as in the United States, the struggle for independence, if not judge-centered, has historically featured judges as central actors. That has not been so in many other regions, where the pushing and prodding of political parties and business leaders have made a greater difference. Second, judges accord exceptional importance to public opinion in their efforts to develop and preserve the separation of powers. Third, although few of those involved would call it such, changes in jurisprudence are also central to many of the more successful strategies.

The Key Role of Judges

In Latin America, the pressure for independence has often come from economic elites and economic reformers, who desire impartial forums for the resolution of contract disputes and often act as a result of international pressure. In Mexico, for example, "justice politicians" had captured the courts, and businesses resolved disputes outside their confines. Internationalization of the economy conferred higher value on impartial and effective dispute resolution, and managers of large firms, allied with a new breed of lawyer, chose to rely on alternative institutions that bypassed the traditional legal system. The competition created pressures for change that are now working their way slowly through the system.[11]

By contrast, in African contexts, judges often play central roles in initiating bids for greater independence. In Uganda, judges and government lawyers have teamed up to make the case to the country's president that independent and effective courts could be useful for attracting investors and improving economic conditions. Business has remained less vocal. In Tanzania, senior judges have emphasized the utility of an independent judiciary for helping to rebuild rule of law.

The differences have several roots. A small and divided business community means that a constituency important elsewhere has remained inarticulate in common law Africa. Foreign businesses monitor rule of law as a general indicator of political risk, but their stake in effective courts is more limited than that of domestic counterparts; they can insure against risk and write into their contracts that major disputes will be resolved in their home countries. Bar associations have not wielded much power, although their ability to speak out has increased with the advent of multiparty rule.[12] In short, there are few if any constituencies with bargaining power.

Moreover, the distribution of ideas varies across societies. In most countries, there are grassroots complaints about courts, but popular demands are too diffuse and hard to sustain to bring effective pressure to bear on key decisionmakers. It is the distribution of ideas among policy elites that matters most. In Latin America, neoclassically trained economists and young lawyers who have studied in U.S. law schools bring ideas about judicial independence to policy circles. In most parts of Africa, there are many fewer people who meet this description. Neoclassical economists can be uncomfortable allies, too; their ideas meet with more suspicion in Africa than in Latin America. Arguments about the desirability of judicial independence are more current in the better-traveled, upper ranks of the judiciary than among politicians or the business community.

The Importance of Public Opinion

The strategies for building judicial independence in common law Africa accord public opinion considerable prominence. Public opinion looms as a bulwark against encroachment. The specter of public outrage over infringements by the legislature or executive is a disincentive to partisan interference in particular cases. Less often stated, but equally important, is the need to keep people sufficiently happy with the courts and the decisions they make that they do not give an interfering legislature or executive their support. In African contexts, with high levels of legal pluralism and a limited rights culture, independent courts that rely on international covenants or nondiscrimination clauses embedded in constitutions may find themselves frequently out of step with majority sentiment. Public relations are thus especially important.

To an outsider, this aspect of judicial strategy is puzzling, however. It is curious first because it is not clear whether there really is something one can call public opinion, defined as the product of social interaction and not the mere aggregation of opinions, in most African settings. Judges and social scientists differ with each other. The social scientists have typically argued that in African contexts, barriers to mass communication created by limited infrastructure and poverty mean that it is often hard to share information or views over a large territory. Moreover, publics tend to form around institutions that command authority. In Africa, to a greater degree than in most other parts of the globe, the institutional world of which the courts are part operates in parallel with other systems of governance that often retain greater authority. As scholar Peter Ekeh has written, in Africa, most people are members of two publics, and the civic public that forms around state institutions is of secondary importance.[13] Finally, the hypothesized tendency to confine conversation, and thus the flow of information, to people related by birth or place means that there are multiple "publics" instead of the civic public or national constituency at the focus of public opinion studies.

The premise is also puzzling because relatively few people monitor decisions and have informed views about what takes place in courtrooms— or so social scientists usually assume, wherever they work. Despite the tremendous attraction court television seems to hold for Americans, academicians typically claim that the public knowledgeable in legal matters includes a comparatively small group of people, including litigators, their clients, and members of an urban elite.

The steps some courts have taken to appeal to public opinion focus partly on the much smaller "relevant public." For example, efforts to promote better legal journalism and to hold periodic press conferences for journalists target urban communities. This public is believed to have greater knowledge; there is also historical evidence that the urban public has sometimes risked armed retaliation by police forces by mobilizing around issues its members have cared about, such as entrance to universities or electoral irregularities.

Some of the judges' other appeals to public opinion go beyond what social scientists would identify as the relevant public, however. Radio broadcasts and support for legal literacy campaigns that some courts provide open a dialogue with a group of people, both urban and rural. Many senior judges, such as Chief Justice Nyalali, consider these measures very important in their institution-building strategies.

The judges' emphasis could be misplaced. Legal training in common law countries predisposes advocates and judges to imagine themselves engaged in a dialogue with a community. Indeed, many concepts in law are based on the notion that there can be shared norms of acceptable behavior among people who do not know each other personally. Without such, the "reasonable man" standard so important in the common law would have no basis. Education may then encourage judges to accord public opinion more importance than it really has in safeguarding institutional independence.

The Centrality of Jurisprudence

The faces of most judges and lawyers turn blank at the mention of the word *jurisprudence*. Yet jurisprudential innovation is increasingly common in Africa. The hesitancy to call it such comes partly from the fact that the pressures of the job rarely allow practitioners to step back and survey the work they do. It derives partly from uneasiness about exactly what is entailed. Whether building judicial independence in Africa is distinctive in the importance of this kind of innovation is not clear. Indian and Israeli courts have done the same. Latin American courts, such as Mexico's, may have accorded it less significance, although that could be a function of the civil law system, not conditions particular to a region.

There are reasons to think that the interest in new principles of interpretation may respond to special needs. For example, to the extent that law is supposed to be an expression of community norms, as represented in an elected legislature, the intentions of members of parliament in passing laws are important. Legislative intent as a basis of interpretation has suffered attack in industrial democracies, where it is evident that a bill is often as much a product of log-rolling as it is of a clear set of policy objectives. In Africa, where the legitimacy of single-party legislatures has generally collapsed and where many laws from the colonial era, when citizens had no voice, remain on the books, judges try to reach for other principles to assess the meaning of an ambiguous passage.

Many governments have also signed international covenants, some of whose provisions may depart from widely shared community norms or from existing law. Judges find themselves in the position of needing to reconcile these differences. They reach for new principles of interpretation as part of that endeavor. At a time when African communities are undergoing rapid change, careful explanation of the grounds for a decision have special social importance. The background norms that usually provide members of the public with intuitions about the reasoning behind an opinion are in disarray. For the courts, the risk of giving the appearance of arbitrariness is all the greater as a result. Members of the public look to the judges for guidance not only about the grounds for the court decisions but also for help in constructing a common sense that will guide them through the new political institutions put in place.

Finally, the effort to clarify rules of interpretation is part of a dialogue with elected officials, many of whom are new to their roles. To enhance the legitimacy of the courts and thereby develop and protect their independence, it is important that judges' power not stem primarily from an ability to strike down laws that are unconstitutional. The ability to instill understanding of the way the courts work and the broad principles that need to underlie lawmaking is crucial. Speaking at the bicentennial celebration of the birth of Chief Justice John Marshall, Henry Hart captured perfectly the challenge that judges face in a new democracy. In words Chief Justice Nyalali would appreciate, he observed that "[i]t is a delusion to suppose . . . that if only you can prevent the abuse of governmental power everything else will be all right. The political problem is a problem also of eliciting from government officials, and from the members of society generally, the affirmative, creative performances upon which the well-being of the society depends."[14]

Conclusion

Judicial independence in common law Africa remains volatile. It is simply too early to engage in an analysis of which strategies or which sequence of tactics generally produce higher levels of institutional autonomy. Social science can perform a service nonetheless by eliciting a better understanding of the way people on the ground perceive the relevant players, the stakes, and the risks. That enterprise is essentially ethnographic. It rests on extended conversations and debates with judges and lawyers. I have tried in this chapter to provide the beginnings of such an ethnography. I have sketched the main elements of strategy, as those I interviewed perceive them, along with the calculus that lies behind them. I have also tried to point out what is distinctive about efforts to build judicial independence in Africa, compared to other regions—and why.

Notes

I would like to acknowledge the advice and assistance provided by the many people involved in aspects of the larger book project on judicial independence on which this chapter is based, most especially the Honorable Chief Justice of Tanzania, Francis L. Nyalali; the Honorable Chief Justice of Uganda, S. W. W. Wambuzi; and the Honorable Chief Justice of Botswana, Moleleki Mokama, as well as the judges and magistrates of their courts. Members of the bar in all three countries provided invaluable help. Special thanks are due to the president of the Uganda Law Society, Solomy Bossa, and the president of the Tanganyika Law Society, Mohamed Ismael. Professor Bojosi Otlhogile, Professor Ahthalia Molokomme, and Professor Joe Oloka-Onyango provided helpful direction and advice. Betty Munabi, Sadique Kebonang, and Geoffrey Ijumbe provided research assistance. USIS public affairs officers Judy Butterman, Kiki Munshi, and Steve Lauterbach facilitated my efforts to stretch the limits of a Fulbright grant to accommodate this research. The Honorable Nan R. Shuker, the Honorable Susan R. Winfield, the Honorable Nathaniel Jones, Rozann Stayden, Harlow Case, and Professor William Burnett Harvey offered invaluable direction. All errors are my own.

1. International Commission of Jurists, "Draft Principles."

2. Shapiro, *Courts.*

3. Landes and Posner, "The Independent Judiciary," p. 879.

4. Salzberger, "A Positive Analysis," pp. 361–362.

5. Ramseyer, "The Puzzling (In)Dependence."

6. Rosberg, "The Rise of an Independent Judiciary."

7. For some portion of the postindependence era, these countries also employed judges from other parts of the Commonwealth, on contract. Although many lawyers suggest that use of contract judges undermines independence, the data show no relationship, positive or negative.

8. Interview with Chief Justice Francis Lucas Nyalali, conducted during the U.S.-Africa Judicial Exchange, Washington, D.C., May 1995.

9. Bates, "The Impulse to Reform."

10. Dezalay and Garth, "Building the Law."

11. Ibid., p. 71.

12. Surveys in 1995–1996 of lawyers in Botswana, Tanzania, and Uganda revealed that lawyers perceive they have increasing influence but feel that their activism has followed political change and the initiatives in the courts, not led these developments. In Botswana, whose court is considered more independent than many others, there was no law society at the time of the survey and lawyers considered that they had little voice. In Kenya, not represented in the survey, lawyers have played a much more active role than they have elsewhere, but to no avail. To the question "How much influence does the law society have over public policy?" 12.9 percent of respondents in Botswana, 13 percent in Tanzania, and 14 percent in Uganda said it exercises an "important" influence. The figures for those who think the law societies exercise only "sometimes" political influence are 16.1 percent, 52.2 percent, and 54.4 percent in Botswana, Tanzania, and Uganda, respectively. The rest think they are "rarely" influential (67.7 percent in Botswana, 30.4 percent in Tanzania, and 29.8 percent in Uganda).

13. Ekeh, "Colonialism."

14. Hart as quoted in Harvey, "The Rule of Law."

12

Surprising Success:
The New Eastern European
Constitutional Courts

HERMAN SCHWARTZ

It is rare that a new political institution performs beyond expectations, especially where one of its main tasks is to enforce horizontal accountability against power-seeking governmental forces. Yet, among the many astonishing events of the last decade, the performance of the new Eastern European constitutional courts in that task is that rare case. And that unexpected piece of good news has come in what have been almost everywhere inauspicious, and even aggressively hostile, environments. This is not to say that the record is unblemished. Some of these new constitutional courts have been mere tools of the regime. This is hardly surprising given the odds against success. But overall, these tribunals have done remarkably well. In this chapter I explore that experience and offer some tentative reflections on the nature and reasons for that success.

The Contrast with the
United States Supreme Court

It is obviously more than coincidence that the nations that moved quickly to establish constitutional tribunals to ensure governmental accountability were those that had been under authoritarian or worse regimes. Germany, Italy, Spain, and Portugal all established constitutional courts as soon as they became nascent democracies, as did Hungary and the other Central European nations. The weakest of these courts was in Romania, and appropriately enough, until the end of 1996, Romania had had only a partial revolution.

Before turning to the discussion and analysis of how these courts have performed and why, it may be useful to explore the many significant differences and similarities between the U.S. Supreme Court and the new European courts.

Despite the European courts' origin in U.S. notions of the propriety and need for judicial supervision over the actions of the popularly chosen branches by a basically nondemocratic institution, the two systems are quite different in many important aspects. These differences are reflected in how they go about fulfilling their respective missions.

The U.S. Supreme Court is a conventional appellate court that presides over a hierarchy of general courts, both federal and state, to ensure that the U.S. Constitution and laws are adhered to by all courts. Like any other court, its primary (and indeed almost sole) function in the U.S. national court system[1] is to adjudicate disputes presented to the general courts in a traditional legal form: one natural or legal, private or public entity—the "complainant"—bringing another such public or private entity—the "defendant"—before a court to use the power of the state to order and, if necessary, force the defendant to do or not to do something. For the complainant to persuade the court to issue such an order against the defendant, the complainant must show that the defendant violated some legal norm that represents a valid exercise of state power. That legal norm may be a principle of private law, such as a rule of contract law; an administrative regulation or practice, such as a health and safety regulation; or a constitutional mandate, such as a bar to improper governmental interference with freedom of speech.

The prerequisite for a decision in favor of one side or the other is, of course, that the winning party be on the right side of a valid legal norm. The validity of that norm can always be put in question, and since modern law is a hierarchical system, all norms must comport with the highest and most basic legal norm—the Constitution. Thus, in the U.S. system, any court that deals with a case, no matter how lowly, may decide a constitutional question if necessary to a decision of the case before it. For example, in a traffic court, a motorist may claim that the police officer's stop was unjustified and violated the motorist's constitutional right to privacy.

What must be kept in mind is that all the decisionmaking—whether it be adjudicating a private dispute over an automobile accident, interpreting and applying a low-level administrative rule affecting only a few people, or deciding a fundamental constitutional question that affects the lives or welfare of millions—is for one purpose and one purpose only: to decide the specific dispute between the interested parties that is before the court. Nothing else. If, for example, the parties settle the case before the court issues a decision, or the complainant drops the suit or disappears, the court will dismiss the case regardless of the importance of the constitutional question or how many people want the court to decide it.[2]

Moreover, the court charged with deciding a constitutional question— that is, whether the norm or defendants' behavior comports with the

Constitution—is always aware of the special delicacy of the task. It involves overseeing and possibly annulling the action of a popularly elected institution by an institution that, by design, is not accountable and whose members may have life tenure, which in the U.S. federal system means until they die, resign, or become incompetent. Also, if that norm violates the Constitution, it cannot be applied at all without changing the Constitution, which is, by design, very difficult.

For these reasons, U.S. courts try to avoid deciding questions on constitutional grounds if they can legitimately resolve the case on some non-constitutional basis. Techniques for avoiding a decision on constitutional questions have been developed, including limiting the class of those who may sue to those with a very specific kind of direct injury, creating "political questions" the court deems not appropriate for judicial treatment and, at the Supreme Court level, having virtually complete discretion over which cases it will hear. Thus, whereas the U.S. Supreme Court decided approximately 140–150 cases up to a few years ago, now it hears no more than 75–85. In sum, the U.S. Supreme Court is in the business of resolving specific disputes. Its jurisdiction to decide constitutional questions is purely incidental to that task and exists only because the Constitution is seen as establishing legal norms that are at the hierarchical apex.

This is very different from the European system designed by Hans Kelsen. The great difference results from both the different nonconstitutional legal systems and a different conception of the constitutional tribunal. U.S. constitutional law came out of a legal background in which judges had a great deal of what was really legislative power, the common law. This is a set of legal norms created by judges alone, which because of the doctrine of precedential authority, *stare decisis,* become governing legal norms for future cases to as great a degree as legislative lawmaking. Judges also exercised very significant executive and legislative powers in prerevolutionary America.[3] Partly for this reason, the link between political activity and appointment to the bench was established quite early, and judges were awarded the great deference accorded to successful political actors. Ultimately they came to be seen as exalted beings exercising great powers. It was thus not a major leap for judges to assert judicial control over legislative activity, particularly as disenchantment with legislative behavior developed in the United States in the 1780s.[4]

In Europe, the post-1789 period saw the establishment of a very different kind of judiciary: a career civil service staffed largely by low-status and low-income functionaries who were supposed to stick closely and mechanically to the text of very detailed codes and were subjected to close appellate supervision to make sure they did. As in most bureaucracies, promotion depended on a combination of seniority and acquiescence. The communist system, which subordinated everything to the interests of the working class or, more realistically, the Central Committee of the Communist Party, went even further and snuffed out whatever sparks of judicial independence might have survived the preexisting system. The position of the judge in communist countries was totally subordinated to the procurator and the secret police. "Telephone justice" was the name given the system, and what that means needs no explanation.

For all these reasons, even though many of the supreme courts in some of the emerging Central and Eastern European countries sought the new power of constitutional judicial review for themselves, only in Estonia were they successful, and there only because it was anticipated that there would not be enough constitutional cases to warrant creating a new institution. Everywhere else, a new institution was created to resolve the many constitutional questions that were anticipated, an institution that was not to be an adjunct to the regular general court system staffed by general court judges, who usually had life tenure. Instead, the judges of this new separate institution were to be largely new people, who might have a broad vision and who would serve relatively brief, and usually nonrenewable, terms. For this reason, most of the new constitutional court judges are legal scholars and academics of great prestige, many of whom had already devoted a good deal of time and thought to constitutional questions before they were appointed. Some general court judges were also put on these new tribunals, but not too many. Only in Bulgaria has there been a paucity of academics: no more than two or three at a time.

Of equal importance were the many functions given the new courts that the U.S. Supreme Court has either lacked or refused to take on. Whereas the latter decided constitutional questions only as an incident to lawsuit resolution, the constitutional court was set up specifically to decide such questions. It was not supposed to avoid or discourage them, like the U.S. Supreme Court. Quite the contrary. Some of these European tribunals were authorized to reach out and decide constitutional questions that had not even been submitted to them. And even where the constitutional court could consider only cases submitted to it by others—while the U.S. federal courts have been shrinking the classes of complainants who are allowed to make such a submission—the Hungarian court, for example, was authorized to consider a constitutional challenge to an existing law from anyone at all, even a foreigner. One of its first decisions and a very courageous one at that—its decision striking down capital punishment in Hungary despite strong public support for the penalty—was at the behest of an anti–capital punishment group of law professors.

A particularly striking example of this difference is in the treatment of legislators and other government officials who are dissatisfied with some law or other legal norm and want the court to test its constitutionality. Whereas U.S. courts have made it almost impossible for representatives or senators to challenge a law in their official capacity, all the European constitutions and laws virtually encourage such submission. They authorize not only the chairs of the parliamentary chambers and the president or prime minister to challenge a legislative enactment, as Kelsen had suggested, but also a relatively small group of deputies or senators, thus ensuring that political defeats will be the stuff of constitutional questions that the constitutional courts will have to decide. For example, in Bulgaria, one-fifth of the members of the National Assembly can challenge a law. Indeed, in Russia, one deputy could challenge a law until 1993. The result is obvious and inevitable: every not-insubstantial parliamentary faction that loses a fight on a controversial bill turns promptly to the constitutional court to try to win constitutionally what it lost politically. That court is thus continually drawn into politically charged controversies, which raises a fundamental question about all these courts: How should they deal with politically volatile issues without becoming or seeming to become just another politically partisan institution? How can they maintain both the reality and the appearance of an independent tribunal dedicated solely to law and justice?

The problem is aggravated by the fact that the members of these tribunals are always composed of people chosen by political entities—parliaments, presidents, and governments—all of whom are involved in partisan politics and fully aware of the power of these tribunals.

One further indication of a vital difference is that European constitutional courts are given very little discretion to turn away cases that fall within their jurisdiction, though some, as we shall see, have succeeded in devising such avoidance techniques.

There are, of course, numerous similarities with the U.S. system:[5] in both cases, the constitutional courts can often decide constitutional questions in ongoing litigation, though in the continental system, the constitutional court does not decide the case but only the constitutional question—the case itself is suspended by the regular court until the question is answered and then ultimately decided by that court. In the United States, the Supreme Court decides the whole case. And in some places, like Russia, the regular Supreme Court has taken to deciding constitutional issues alongside the constitutional court, which raises conflict and uniformity problems.[6]

Perhaps most important is that nothing in the U.S. Constitution authorizes the Supreme Court to exercise judicial review over legislative and executive action. The authority was asserted by the courts and has been acquiesced in by the American people, who now wholeheartedly support it. Despite this popular support, the lack of explicit constitutional authority has cast a shadow over the Supreme Court's exercise of judicial review so that "judicial activism" has become an epithet. The European courts, by contrast, all have a specific constitutional mandate to impose their views, and they have been extremely activist, without hesitation.

Other differences include the terms of office, which in Eastern

Europe—except for Russia, where there is life tenure—are typically limited to one or two eight- , nine- , or ten-year terms. Also, in Romania, as in France, a law can be challenged by members of the legislature only before it is promulgated, though in Romania, if the constitutionality of a law already on the books is relevant to deciding a lawsuit, the ordinary court can refer the constitutional question to the constitutional court. In the United States, a case is considered not "ripe," and will be dismissed, until the law or other action goes into effect and adversely affects someone's specific interest. And in many countries, the court can be required to interpret the constitution or a law even without an active dispute or challenge. Nothing could differ more from the U.S. Supreme Court, which has a strict rule against hearing anything that smacks of an advisory opinion and that is not necessary to decide the specific controversy being litigated.

One of the greatest variations among these new courts is with respect to individual citizen complaints. In Hungary, Russia, and now Poland under its new constitution, individuals may complain about a law directly to the constitutional court; in Romania, they can raise such an issue before the constitutional court only in connection with an existing lawsuit; in Bulgaria, however, individual citizens cannot get to the constitutional court at all.

It should be noted that many of the constitutional courts in the Eastern European countries are not limited to judicial review of legislative enactments. Many may also review administrative regulations and, in some cases, even administrative practices and acts. For example, in Poland and Slovakia, the court reviews administrative regulations; and in the Czech Republic, the court reviews any alleged interference by public authorities with constitutionally guaranteed rights and freedoms.

The Eastern European Experience, 1986–1997[7]

Issues of accountability in the exercise of executive power and indeed of governmental power in general can be raised in at least three contexts: by one branch of the national government intruding on the prerogatives of another and thereby violating *separation of power* principles, of which a subcategory is an administrative unit exceeding its constitutional or statutory authority; by the national government intruding on the prerogatives of lower-level units and thereby violating *federalism* and *local autonomy* principles;[8] and by any branch of government violating the *individual or group rights* of the people. Constitutional courts have been involved in all of these situations and, with notable exceptions, have vigorously and effectively upheld the rule of law.

It is difficult and probably misleading to try to characterize a whole region containing many different countries with different histories and problems, despite the many similarities. It may therefore be best to summarize the experience with these new tribunals by providing thumbnail sketches of some of them, noting both successes and failures.

Counterintentional Independence: The Polish Constitutional Tribunal

The oldest of these new constitutional courts is the original Polish Constitutional Tribunal. Established by statute in 1986 by the then governing Communists as a result of earlier Solidarity and other pressures, the tribunal was not intended to be a very significant institution; its adoption was really for Western consumption. To ensure that the tribunal would remain under control, the regime made its decisions subject to a two-thirds override by the Parliament, the control of which the Communists did not then expect ever to lose.

From the first, however, the tribunal moved far beyond what the legislature had intended and expected. In its first four years, it limited itself to exercising tight control over what the executive could do by administrative decree, which had been the favored form of early Communist lawmaking. Few political conflicts were involved.

In these early years, the tribunal issued some forty rulings on administrative rules and regulations, of which twenty-eight concerned human rights and twenty resulted in nullification of the norm, as the two leading scholars of the tribunal summarized it:

> By 1989, after almost forty decisions, the Tribunal had established several guidelines for judging the law-making powers of the executive branch. First, agencies could issue regulations only with explicit statutory authority and in conformity with the specific subject matter of the statute; they could not rely on implied delegations. Second, an agency could not delegate regulatory powers to other bodies absent explicit authorization in the statute's delegation clause. Third, substatutory acts had to conform to all parliamentary statutes. . . . The Tribunal successfully limited the well-established law-making practices of state bureaucrats, while gaining the acceptance or tolerance of other political actors.[9]

As grounds for its decisions, the tribunal court invoked constitutional provisions calling for equality and "social justice," both of which had existed as virtual dead letters in the 1952 Polish Constitution as well as in the unwritten *Rechtsstaat* principles. The specific cases covered many areas and included, for example, nullification of increases in apartment rents and of quotas on women in medical school, among many others. The tribunal has since also ruled that the government may not tap phones or screen letters except in certain temporary situations. Starting in 1989, the tribunal began to review statutes, and its ax fell just as heavily as it had on administrative action: from 1 January 1989 through 30 June 1994, of some sixty statutes reviewed by the tribunal, forty were found unconstitutional. Much of the tribunal's work, both in the early years and later, focused on the effects of Poland's economic "shock therapy." In the name of equality, social justice, nonretroactivity, and vested private rights—the latter two drawn from general *Rechtsstaat* principles that were not even in the constitution—the tribunal struck down many of the laws and regulations adopted in this program. The tribunal also nullified the repeated efforts by former president Lech Walesa to extend his power beyond constitutional limits. In the course of these decisions, the court was drawn deeply into many of the political and social conflicts of those early years.

Among the more sensitive decisions were several between 1990 and 1994 protecting former Communist officeholders against vengeful denial of pension and other measures that smacked of unfairness. Polish animosity toward Russians is of ancient vintage, and communism was always an alien growth. The desire for vengeance among Solidarity supporters and others was intense, but as an outside observer commented, "[A]ll Poles are anti-Communist, but no one [is] so disliked as the staunch anti-Communist."[10] It nevertheless took courage for the tribunal to take these positions. The one area where the tribunal seems to have been too fearful is in matters relating to the Catholic Church and abortion, where it has upheld the church's position almost every time, particularly with respect to abortion, much to the dismay of most commentators and large majorities of the Polish people.

In recognition of the popularity and strength of the tribunal, the new constitution that was approved by referendum on 27 May 1997 and went into effect in October 1997, removes certain restraints and limitations on the current tribunal. After two years, all the tribunal's rulings will be final, while before it could be overruled by two-thirds of the Sejm;[11] such overrulings occurred only five times, and only with respect to economic measures. The Sejm's nervousness about the tribunal's activism obviously made it hesitant about giving up its power over the tribunal's judgments, and it therefore postponed full finality to the tribunal's rulings until October 1999. The tribunal will be able to consider individual citizen complaints, which will probably bring it closer to Western European courts, where the bulk of the work consists of human rights issues raised by individual citizens, and it is also allowed to take international law into account in its decisionmaking.

Overall, the tribunal has been one of the most significant success stories in Poland's post-1989 history. It has served as the effective check on executive excesses with respect to both the citizenry, where the danger was primarily from long-standing Communist administrative arbitrariness, and the president's effort to expand his power at the expense of the parliament and the government. Time and again it was plunged into the conflicts between Lech Walesa and the Sejm, and by and large, its decisions were accepted as fair. It has also tempered some of the harshness of Poland's successful "shock therapy" approach to economic change.

Popular Boldness: The Hungarian Constitutional Court

It is possible that a key element in the Polish tribunal's success was the lack of forceful retaliation against it by those adversely affected by its rulings, such as the president, the government, or the parliament. The same holds true for Hungary, where the establishment of the constitutional court in 1989 was the result of roundtable discussions between the Reform Communists and the opposition. Going far beyond any other country in the region and perhaps in the world, the court was given the authority to entertain complaints by anyone about the "abstract" unconstitutionality of laws and other legal norms, though not of specific concrete acts by government officials. This "abstract norm control," as it is called, gives an excessively political cast to the court's decisions, making it appear less like a court and more like a legislative chamber.

Nevertheless, the court has been immensely popular in the country. Right from the beginning, it has been vigorous and forceful. Most of its work has focused on statutes enacted by the parliament, both pre-1989 laws, like the capital punishment law it struck down as one of its first acts in 1990, and post-1989 laws. Like the Polish tribunal, the court has often relied on general *Rechtsstaat* principles against retroactivity and in favor of legal security. It has developed the notion of human dignity as a core value, using it in its case on capital punishment. It has tried to protect free speech against excessive executive interference, a perennial problem in all these countries, particularly in the radio and television media. The court has shown itself particularly solicitous of the rights of those against whom vengeance has been directed for the abuses and cruelties of the past, particularly those related to the 1956 uprising.

All constitutions that adopt separation of powers principles are necessarily vague about the division of power. Hungary's is worse than most, however, because it is not a new constitution but a patchwork that contains a great deal that is new, but also much that is old. As a result, there are many inherent contradictions and ambiguities in it. Among the most ambiguous lines of authority was the division of powers between President Arpad Goncz and the government, led by Prime Minister Joszef Antall, who became political and institutional adversaries. One of the most heated disputes between them was over control of the radio and television media.

The public broadcast media are the most politically powerful of the communications media, and virtually every government in the region has tried (usually successfully) to control them, particularly television. On 9 July 1991, Prime Minister Antall, unhappy with radio and TV criticism of his government, submitted nominations for six vice-presidents of Hungarian television and radio in order to undercut the broadcast presidents whom he considered hostile to him and his party, even though he had originally nominated them himself. Goncz refused to confirm the nominations. He read the constitution as requiring agreement between the president and the prime minister on the nominations, whereas Antall saw the president's role as ceremonial and regarded the decisionmaking authority as lying solely with the prime minister. On 23 September, the constitutional court ruled that the president has no power under the constitution to veto candidates submitted by the prime minister for high state posts; there were three dissents.[12] Relying primarily on the nature of parliamentary government and the president's lack of political accountability, the court agreed with Prime Minister Antall in reading the constitution as establishing a weak presidency.[13] The only case in which the president could block an appointment, ruled the court, was if the appointment threatened the democratic order, since Article 29 of the constitution makes the president its guardian.[14]

Many of the court's decisions have been severely criticized, particularly its 1995 decisions striking down some twenty-three provisions of the post–Communist government's economic austerity package, which was said to cost the treasury $300 million.[15] Nevertheless, none of the critics, including the government itself, even questioned the court's right to decide as it did, or suggested any defiance.

The Hungarian court has been perhaps the boldest of all the constitutional courts, particularly in the area of human rights, including economic and social rights. This may be due to the outstanding qualities of its president, László Solyom, who has become a major figure in the international constitutional community.

Checks and Imbalances: Russia's Constitutional Court

Because the post-1989 movement from communism to parliamentary democracy in Poland was so smooth as to be almost consensual, there was little need to cope with blatant or violent abuses of power, as in other countries where the transition was much more troubled.

One example of a troubled and imperfect transition was Russia, where there was both an aggressive executive seeking major change and facing a resistant legislature and a vigorous constitutional court. Ultimately, the president and the court clashed, with the inevitable result that the court lost, though not entirely.

Russia's tradition is one of "legal nihilism," in which arbitrary executive action, whether czarist or Communist, has been the norm. An effort to establish a rule of law, which many Soviet legal theorists had been thinking about since the late 1950s during the brief Khrushchev thaw, failed. Citizens had no recourse against the exercise of illegal state power.

A few years after Gorbachev took power in 1988, he created a committee on constitutional supervision with limited powers over laws and regulations; its actions could be ignored by the issuing body. It actually performed rather well, reflecting perhaps a hunger for a check on arbitrary power. During its brief tenure, it decided twenty-three cases, mostly on its own initiative. Hobbled (1) by a patchwork Soviet constitution from which it was often difficult to determine what rights were in fact granted, (2) by deliberately stunted powers, (3) by an ambiguous status in the governmental structure (not being a court but only an adjunct to the legislature), and (4) by the lack of public support or even awareness, the committee focused on human rights violations and produced a remarkably positive record in its short life, consistently favoring citizen rights.[16]

The Soviet Union disappeared in 1991 before establishing a true constitutional court, but in 1990 and 1991, the Russian Republic did so. That court went into operation in December 1991, headed by a strong-minded academic, Valery Zorkin, who had been chair of the constitutional commission. The court was given very wide ranging jurisdiction to oversee governmental activity, including the power to take up constitutional problems on its own initiative. Within weeks after it went into operation in December 1991, it struck at executive power, in the first of many confrontations with President Boris Yeltsin.

In October 1991, before the court actually went into operation, the Communist Party threw a very hot potato into the court's lap by challenging Yeltsin's post-coup decrees outlawing the party, banning its activity, and confiscating its property, all of which were considered by most legal observers to be beyond Yeltsin's legal powers. Before the court could act on the Communist Party case, shortly after the court convened, the parliament challenged a Yeltsin decree merging what was left of the KGB with the MVD, a move that revived memories of a similar merger in 1936 that had preceded Stalin's murderous purges.

Yeltsin was still immensely popular, but the court did not hesitate: within weeks, on 15 January 1992, it unanimously set aside the decree on the ground that the merger could not be affected by an executive decree but only by parliamentary action. Yeltsin grumbled but complied, apparently after a one-hour conversation with the court chair, Zorkin.

This was the first of many decisions in 1992 checking executive and legislative power that were widely applauded. The Communist Party case was resolved in November 1992 by a Solomonic compromise. A few months after the KGB-MVD case, in April 1992, the court slapped down parliamentary chair Ruslan Khasbulatov when he had the Supreme Soviet Presidium, which he headed, create a copyright bureau to succeed a Soviet agency that had had a terrible reputation for political censorship and KGB ties.

During the court's pre-October 1993 phase, it issued twenty decisions involving legislative and executive powers, in which ten executive decrees and ten parliamentary acts were annulled. Among the court's actions was a decision blocking Yeltsin's effort to ban the National Salvation Front, a right-wing political party, and a decision frustrating the parliament's effort to take over *Izvestia,* which had become a respected independent journal. Most of the court's decisions appeared to be sound and well reasoned.

Throughout this period, Chairman Zorkin gave numerous interviews and made numerous appearances on television and elsewhere. He became a very public personality. To many, he clearly overstepped the bounds of judicial propriety, seemingly involving himself in politics. Nevertheless, because the court seemed to be doing a good job, his national popularity was very high.

The struggle between Yeltsin and the parliament grew increasingly bitter and personal, and the court was drawn in again and again. In late March 1993, Yeltsin announced that he had signed a decree establishing presidential rule and would hold a referendum on presidential power a month later. Without seeing the decree, Zorkin convened an all-night session of the tribunal, after which a bitterly divided court decided that Yeltsin's actions violated the constitution (which by then had at least 320 amendments). The die was cast. Yeltsin and a few of the judges on the court saw Zorkin and the majority as implacably hostile to Yeltsin and an ally of Khasbulatov and of Vice-President Alexandr Rutskoi, Yeltsin's prime foe, even though the court continued to rule against Khasbulatov and the parliament as well.

The last straw came during the September 1993 crisis. On 14 September, Yeltsin issued Decree 1400 disbanding parliament, suspending parts of the constitution, and forbidding the constitutional court to meet, clearly unconstitutional acts. Despite Yeltsin's decree, within hours Zorkin called an emergency session of the court, which several of the judges boycotted. Those who showed up condemned the decree as unconstitutional and called for Yeltsin's impeachment. Yeltsin thereupon cut off the court's phone lines and withdrew its guards.

Tuesday, 5 October, marked the end of the first Russian constitutional court. It was not to resume decisionmaking again for another eighteen months. Yeltsin's chief of staff, Sergei Filatov, went to Zorkin "advising" him to resign and threatening criminal proceedings if he did not. The next day Zorkin, who was suffering from high blood pressure, resigned. The court was not to meet again until February 1995. When it did, its powers had been clipped and it thereafter avoided any confrontations with Yeltsin, probably an inevitable result given that it had been enlarged and many of the new members were Yeltsin supporters. The prime example of this increased caution was its ruling in a challenge to Yeltsin's decision to invade Chechnya with armed force. In a very divided decision, the court upheld his actions.

A Champion of Constitutionalism: Bulgaria's Constitutional Court

Until October 1993, it looked as if Yeltsin would tolerate and indeed accept the court's various adverse rulings. There were no signs of any threats or really serious pressure, except that after Zorkin started to appear in public alongside Yeltsin's opponents, Yeltsin withdrew some of Zorkin's *nomenklatura* privileges like a dacha and a big car. But nothing more. And his December 1993 Constitution did reinstate the court, somewhat weakened, even though there had been some thought in October 1993 of turning over its constitutional jurisdiction to the more compliant Supreme Court.

In Bulgaria and Slovakia, the governments have been much more open in their hostility and have either tried to undermine the court or have threatened to do so. The Bulgarian constitutional court's efforts to establish and maintain horizontal accountability have been handicapped in several ways: it does not handle individual citizen complaints, since only public officials have standing before the court; it has no jurisdiction over the constitutionality of administrative norms but only of legislative and presidential acts; and it became the target of the 1994–1996 Videmov post–Communist government campaign to undermine if not actually destroy its authority.

Bulgaria has had two ideologically rigid governments: one by the anti-Communist opposition, the Union of Democratic Forces (UDF); and the other by the Communists, renamed the Bulgarian Socialist Party (BSP). When the UDF was in power, in 1991–1992, it used its parliamentary majority to purge and punish Communists in a series of laws designed to deny them banking posts, pensions, and senior university administrative positions. Although the twelve-member Bulgarian constitutional court was sharply divided six to six between "Reds" and "Blues," the first two laws were easily struck down as violating constitutional rights to work and to social security. In the third, known as the Panev Law after its author, there was a six-to-five vote on Blue-Red lines to strike down the law, but this was not enough to void the law under the Bulgarian Constitution, which requires at least seven of the twelve.

In early 1994, even before the BSP won its majority, it took advantage of a UDF boycott of parliament to pass a law requiring judges, prosecutors, and law professors to have five years of experience. This, of course, meant that current judges or prosecutors had to have held that position under the old regime. The law was reportedly aimed at unfriendly judges and at the procurator, General Ivan Tatarchev, who had been vigorously prosecuting former Communists. In a sharply split vote, the constitutional court struck down the five-year requirement when applied to incumbents, as well as other provisions that would have allowed parliament to remove judges "if they violate the ethical and professional rules of the profession."

After the BSP took power in December 1994, it launched a full-scale attack on the judiciary. Shortly after taking office, it tried to cut the constitutional court judges' salaries and abolish their right to retire with a pension. Using its budgetary powers, the government also cut salaries of the Supreme Judicial Council, which has the power of appointment, promotion, demotion, discipline, and oversight over the judiciary. Later it tried to remove the constitutional court from its building, but that effort failed when the electoral commission, which was supposed to move in, denied that it needed the building. The government then decided to "save electricity" by suspending service on the court's elevator, forcing the judges to walk up the stairs. That was not very successful either, and finally the government gave in.

During this period, the court continued to act vigorously and independently, overturning numerous efforts by the BSP to reverse the reform process that the UDF had started, including measures to control the national media. As constitutional court judge Todor Todorov told an interviewer in the face of BSP attacks on economic reform, the media, and the courts,

> "The Court rather abruptly emerged as the true champion of the principles of constitutionalism. . . . Given the configuration of forces here, none of the political parties could afford to disregard the Constitution without harming their public prestige. . . . The Constitution itself . . . stipulates that the Court is the sole institution authorized to interpret constitutional norms [and] this prerogative turned out to be the Court's greatest power."[17]

Curbing Cronyism: The Slovakian Constitutional Court

In Slovakia, the forces of reform and the rule of law, supported by the constitutional court, and the regressive forces, led by Prime Minister Vladimir Meciar and his nationalist coalition, are still bitterly locked in the struggle that began when Meciar regained power in the fall 1994 elections.

As soon as Meciar was reelected, he and his parliamentary troops moved to destroy the opposition. They first tried to deny them seats in parliament, but the constitutional court blocked that. In some eight other cases, the court held that citizens' rights had been violated in one way or another by the Meciar government and its parliamentary supporters. The court ruled in one that parliamentary fact-finding commissions do not have the power to start criminal prosecutions or interfere with personal liberties; in another, that restrictions on the right to medical care may be imposed only by parliament and not by executive bodies through regulation; and, in a third, that the prosecutor general may not refuse to implement the decision of the president to grant a pardon.

In a particularly important decision, the constitutional court struck down the government's effort to use so-called golden shares to give the government a veto on key decisions in dozens of key privatized companies. It also overturned a 1994 law shortly after Meciar returned to power that transferred privatization power over large enterprises to the National Property Fund, run by Meciar supporters and suspected of cronyism in direct privatization sales to investors; in more than a few cases, the fund had sold large stakes in major Slovak companies to their friends at prices far below market value. As of March 1997, the court had issued some thirteen legal decisions knocking out all or part of laws since Meciar took over. Thereafter, in May 1997, in one of its most significant decisions, the court ruled that the nation had the right to vote on the direct election of the president. The Meciar government refused to print the question on the ballot. This produced a widespread boycott of the referendum, which had also included questions on NATO. Because of the boycott, the whole process was rendered void, raising fears that Meciar would try to steal the 1997 parliamentary elections. This was but one of the many similar actions by Meciar and his government in defiance of the rule of law and human rights, which led the European Union to deny Slovakia's application for membership at this time despite a relatively good economy.

Despite Meciar's own relatively high public standing, the constitutional court remains an immensely popular institution. In a January 1997 poll, the Slovak public ranked the constitutional court just below the army and even with the commercial television station: 70 percent trusted the army, while the constitutional court and the television station received 63 percent. The government drew only 35 percent trust.

Although Meciar has tried to strike back at the court in various ways, by and large, and with some notable exceptions, the government has complied with court rulings. As Slovak constitutional court judge Jan Drgonec told an interviewer recently, "[S]o far, all our decisions, although after some hesitation, have been respected."

The Failures

These are the success stories; there are others—in Slovenia, the Czech Republic, and the Baltics. There are also many failures, in some cases after courageous and independent decisions the local strongmen could not accept. In Kazakhstan, the constitutional court struck down several presidential decrees issued by President Nursultan Nazarbayev, and in the summer of 1995, it commented negatively on his proposed constitution. In reprisal, Nazarbayev simply wrote the court out of the new constitution and submitted the redraft to a referendum. It was adopted.

In Belarus, it was a slightly different story. The would-be Stalinist Alexander Lukashenka, in his drive to eliminate all opposition, continually clashed with the constitutional court, several of whose members had studied in the West. A divided court struck down one presidential decree after another. Lukashenka, however, had popular support (as did Nazarbayev) and continued to defy the court, often ignoring its decisions. As a result, in January 1997, seven of the eleven justices resigned. Lukashenka replaced them with his own people, who promptly reversed some of the earlier rulings.

In Albania, the constitutional court supinely followed former president Sali Berisha's orders and has exercised no independent judgment. In 1997, for example, the court overturned the new prime minister's dismissal of the deputy security minister, who is a former police chief often accused of using the police against political opponents.

Finally, one of the more ambiguous tribunals, in keeping with the more ambiguous nature of the transformation in that country, is the Romanian constitutional court. Although vigorous in striking down parliamentary enactments (even though until November 1996 the parliament was controlled largely by adherents of President Ion Iliescu), the court has rubber-stamped everything Iliescu has done. For example, it ruled last fall that President Iliescu could run for the presidency a third time, even though it had earlier ruled that his 1992–1996 term was his second, and the Romanian constitution imposes a two-term limit. According to some, "the Court has turned itself into an obsequious institution, at President [Iliescu's] beck and call."[18] Whether it will behave more independently now that Iliescu has been ousted from the presidency and is in opposition, remains to be seen.

Conclusion

How great a role has this new institution, the constitutional court, played in promoting horizontal accountability and the rule of law in these new states? Insofar as some of these courts have helped to establish or maintain such accountability, what has made that possible? Insofar as some or all of these have failed in that task, why?

It is obviously difficult to make such judgments definitively, but it seems clear that at least some of these courts have made a significant positive contribution, even when the circumstances were unfavorable to their efforts, such as political attacks on the courts, retaliation, stringent national economic circumstances, and lack of public awareness, to mention but a few problems. Why and how are much less clear. A few tentative thoughts have occurred to me, after a good deal of time working with and studying these courts.

In the first place, a new institution like a constitutional court with the power of judicial review over legislative and executive acts seems necessary in today's world: leaders indifferent to human rights and legal limitations no longer act exclusively or primarily through executive ukases. Instead, in a bow to democratic forms, they often have their puppet legislature and administrative agencies enact the appropriate legislation and regulations. Without an institution free from the stifling judicial deference to legislative supremacy and timidity vis-à-vis legislation that are still common among the general judiciary in most of these Eastern European countries, this legislation would remain unchallenged. There must be some vehicle for checking these laws, and the existing judiciary is simply not up to the task, at least not at this time.[19]

What factors made for success where it existed? If success is measured by the scope of decisions, the degree to which those decisions affected public life, and the public support the courts have developed, then unquestionably two of the most successful of these institutions are the Polish and Hungarian courts. They achieved their success despite having to work with internally inconsistent and indeed contradictory patchwork constitutions; Hungary still has such a patchwork. It seems more than coincidence that these two countries also had probably the smoothest of transitions: a negotiated agreement between the Communists and the opposition at extended roundtable meetings that was almost consensual.

By the same token, failures like Kazakhstan and Belarus and even partial failures like Russia and Romania occurred in nations that, despite new constitutions in some of them, really had either no transition or very turbulent ambiguous changes. The near-consensual nature of the transfer of power in Poland and Hungary and the later evolution of the Communist parties in those countries away from hard-line communism, in contrast with Kazakhstan and Belarus where governing power is in the hands of a hardline regressive element that resists any genuine political change, means that an institution like a constitutional court, which checks power, faces trouble in the latter countries. Russia may well be a special case, in keeping with the unique evolution of the Russian constitutional court. Because of the bitterness of the conflict over the transition, even Yeltsin, the "reformist" winner—who in the eyes of many retains a strong authoritarian streak—could not tolerate too independent a court. Yet he did not abolish it entirely when he obviously could have, and this itself may be considered a partial success, since the court does live to fight another day.

The most interesting cases are, of course, Slovakia, where Vladimir Meciar, whose leanings toward Soviet-style authoritarianism are all too obvious, is continually being checked by the constitutional court; and Bulgaria during the Videnov BSP regime from 1994 to February 1997. There the transition has been very troubled, and the Videnov government had deliberately tried to destroy judicial independence. Why and how did these tribunals manage to act courageously and independently despite continual attacks by a democratically elected executive? Neither court was considered particularly impressive when first appointed and both are still considered inadequate by academic scholars and others in those countries. Moreover, many of the judges were successful products of the Communist regimes.

Perhaps the Slovak case can be ascribed in part to the democratic traditions of the interwar period and the inherently Western orientation of much of the Slovak elite. It is no coincidence, I think, that Slovak politics reflects a clash between, on the one hand, nationalism and traditionalism, concentrated in provincial areas where Meciar and the extreme nationalists have their strength, and, on the other hand a Western-oriented urban class concentrated in cities like Bratislava. Obviously the judges, many of whom are academics, are drawn from the latter. Another factor may be that while the nationalist parties that support Meciar have a working majority in parliament, the opposition has very substantial popular support, which is reflected in the high approval rating for the constitutional court, noted earlier.

The Bulgarian case is more puzzling. Even the Videnov government did not try to defy the court's adverse decisions, despite its hostility to the court. Part of the reason may be that half of the twelve judges had been chosen by the opposition. Moreover, at least some of the so-called Red judges were distinguished academics. And it may also be that democracy and a respect for the rule of law have really taken hold in Bulgaria, despite the lack of a democratic tradition and its cultural and other forms of closeness to Russia and the Soviet Union.

Related to these considerations is the nature of the regimes in Kazakhstan, Belarus, Romania, Albania, and, to a lesser extent, post-1993 Russia. There, as elsewhere, the president plays a very great role, directly and indirectly, in choosing the constitutional court judges. But in all those places, the regimes were based on overwhelming executive power in the person of a strongman—Nazarbayev, Lukashenka, Sali Berisha, somewhat less so Iliescu, and the coup d'étatiste Yeltsin. In many cases, as in Albania, Belarus, Romania, Kazakhstan, and Russia, the strongman was democratically elected and supported, at least initially, as in Albania, Belarus, and Russia. Strongmen do not like checks and often make sure in advance that they will not have any. They therefore choose judges who would not be overly independent.

Finally, there may be a more intangible matter: the courts' apparent independence and objectivity. These courts are seen as trying to decide on legal, not political, grounds, though everyone knows that politics and law are inextricably intertwined. If a court relies primarily on legal discourse and reasoning, text, demonstrable legislative intent, precedents, common sense, other courts, logic, basic and widely accepted principles of fairness, human dignity, and similar values—if the court's explanations for its decisions are couched in these terms, the myth of the separation of law and politics will have enough of a kernel of truth as to be accepted and available for the tribunal to rely on. And experience shows that if reasoning this way also leads to the exercise of courage and independence, the court's position will be even stronger. For in the long run, the court's authority depends on the people's acceptance of this Platonic myth.

If there is substance to these tentative suggestions, then the key factor in the success or failure of constitutional judicial review is the overall political situation in the country. In the places where it has succeeded, the constitutional court may well have played a largely secondary and incidental role, though often an important one, in promoting horizontal accountability, whereas in the failures, it played an ineffective one. To political scientists, that probably comes as no surprise, but to those of us concerned with actively trying to nurture democracy and the rule of law by working with these courts, it is an important if troubling reminder.

Years ago, one of the greatest of modern U.S. judges, Learned Hand, wrote,

> I often wonder whether we do not rest our hopes too much upon constitutions, upon laws and upon courts. These are false hopes; believe me, these are false hopes. Liberty lies in the hearts of men and women; when it dies there, no constitution, no law, no court can save it; no constitution, no law, no court can even do much to help it. While it lies there it needs no constitution, no law, no court to save it.[20]

If that spirit has indeed died, then it is true that no court can save it. But if that spirit still flickers, albeit feebly, and if the threats to it are resistible and not overwhelming, then courts can do a great deal toward helping it grow and flourish.

Notes

1. Apart from issuing search warrants and similar dispute-related activities; some state courts have additional responsibilities.

2. There is an exception to this rule for those special situations, such as temporary residency or abortion requirements, where time may moot a question that is important and likely to recur.

3. Wood, *Radicalism*, pp. 81–82.

4. Indeed, there was a basic legal principle that statutes in derogation of the common law were to be strictly, i.e., narrowly, construed. The power of the common law continues today, even after statutes and codes have come to govern most transactions. As Supreme Court justice Antonin Scalia has recently written, it is still true that "American lawyers cut their teeth on the common law" (Scalia, "Common Law Courts," p. 4).

5. Louis Favoreu has highlighted some of the similarities (see Favoreu, "American and European Models," pp. 105, 115–119.

6. Krug, "Departure."

7. The constitutional courts are not the only judicial institutions charged with maintaining the horizontal accountability of the executive. In France, Germany, and Austria, as well as in prewar Czechoslovakia, there were administrative courts, but except in Poland this has not caught on in post-1989 Eastern Europe.

8. This issue requires a separate conference all to itself and will not be discussed here.

9. Brzezinski and Garlicki, "Judicial Powers," pp. 13, 30.

10. Manne, "Poland."

11. The Sejm is the lower and more powerful house of Parliament.

12. Judgment of 26 September 1991 (power distribution case),

Alkotmánybíróság (constitutional law court), No. 48/1991 (IX.26)AB (Hung.) (translation on file with author).

13. For a brief description of the reasoning, see Brunner, "Preface."

14. For criticism of this decision, see Arato, "Constitution and Continuity," pp. 271–273.

15. See Sajo, "Rule of Law," pp. 31–41.

16. Among other things, the committee ruled that consumers should be protected against poor-quality goods; compulsory treatment of alcoholics and drug addicts violates basic human rights as reflected in international treaties; residence permits are unconstitutional, a ruling that had virtually no effect; immediate loss of citizenship for those emigrating to Israel is unconstitutional; certain criminal procedures violated the presumption of innocence; and more. The court also ruled that all rules and regulations that affect citizens' rights and responsibilities must be published within three months or they would become ineffective; it was estimated that some 70 percent of about 210 regulations then in effect were secret (see Hausmaninger, "From the Soviet Committee," p. 316, n. 80).

17. Ganev, "Interview," pp. 65, 67.

18. "Constitution Watch," p. 20.

19. This need is obviously less in a system of truly separated powers as in the U.S. presidential system, where there is the possibility of different parties controlling each of the two lawmaking branches. Even when both the branches are of the same party, their different institutional interests and the increasing weakness of party structures, with the concomitant increase in television-driven personality politics, are separate checks. For proof of that, one need only examine President Clinton's first term, when his party had solid majorities in each house of Congress.

20. Learned Hand, *The Spirit of Liberty,* p. 190.

Part 4

Corruption Control

13

A Brief History
of Anticorruption Agencies

MICHAEL JOHNSTON

A s concern over corruption and horizontal accountability grows, the idea of pursuing reform through powerful, permanent, and politically independent anticorruption agencies has attracted great interest. Such agencies—often called ICACs after the best-known such body, the Independent Commission Against Corruption in Hong Kong—have produced significant, sustained reductions of corruption in societies where that once seemed unlikely; they have also been effective barriers against corruption in countries where moderate corruption seemed likely to grow.

ICACs are relatively new elements in the fight against corruption. While the oldest such agency—Singapore's Corrupt Practices Investigation Bureau (CPIB)—dates back to 1952, it did not begin to acquire its current powers until after independence in 1959, and the top-level political backing so critical to its success did not develop until even later. Hong Kong's ICAC, with its innovative public education programs and its extensive powers to investigate the private sector, is the best known and broadest based, but it did not originate until 1974, and its future is very much an open question. The two newer ICACs considered here—one in New South Wales, Australia, and the other in Botswana—have even shorter track records. Thus, a full assessment of ICACs must await the passage of time and considerable research. Still, initial indications of success are promising and, as we shall see, ICACs also raise important questions of second-order accountability. For these reasons, a preliminary survey of their history and activities may set the stage for further analysis.

Anticorruption Agencies: The Range of Options

Anticorruption organizations come in forms too numerous to catalog here. Virtually every country has had commissions of inquiry, parliamentary or judicial investigations, and "blue-ribbon commissions" that investigate a particular episode of corruption, recommend reforms, and then wind up their work. These bodies, with their prestigious members and their origins as responses to scandal, may enjoy widespread support for a time. Their recommendations can produce legislation, prosecutions, and political defeat for those linked to corruption, but they cannot provide permanent oversight. Moreover, their reforms tend to be aimed at particular corrupt practices, rather than at underlying problems, and can do more harm than good to effective government.[1] As a result, one-shot commissions may do more to dissipate political will for reform than to institutionalize it. Eventually corruption returns, often in forms more difficult to detect and uproot.

More effective are commissions that not only investigate corruption but also create new supervisory bodies. Britain's Committee on Standards in Public Life, chaired by Lord Nolan, investigated "cash-for-questions" deals and other forms of "parliamentary sleaze," ministerial conflicts of interest, and corruption in the National Health Service and various "quangos."[2] It also produced institutional changes, including the creation of the independent Parliamentary Commissioner for Standards—the first external accountability agency for the House of Commons in its more than 900 years of existence. The Nolan Committee's mandate ended in 1997, however.[3] The supervisory bodies it created perform limited functions on tight budgets. Should new corrupt practices come to light, or should inquiries into broader concerns such as donations to political parties be deemed necessary, new legislation would be needed to establish another body.

More lasting anticorruption activities can be delegated to prosecutors. But in those agencies, corruption competes against other kinds of crime for priority status. Action against corruption can thus depend more on the personal ambitions of prosecutors than on the scope of the problem itself. Even if particular investigations are successful, systematic oversight and corruption prevention are only indirectly aided by arrests and convictions.

The ICAC Model: Four Characteristics

ICACs are distinctive not only because of their independence, but also because of their permanence, broad mandates, and efforts at prevention. *Independence,* as we might expect, is fundamental: a genuine anticorruption effort cannot initiate or cancel investigations, or impose, withhold, or modify punishments, because of the interests of powerful individuals or factions. It must be free to investigate corruption anywhere it is suspected and to follow the trail of evidence wherever it may lead. *Permanence* is also essential if corruption is to be reduced over the long term, and if reformers are to deal with evolving techniques of misconduct.

ICACs possess broad mandates in several respects. First, they are not restricted to investigating particular institutions or events, but rather are empowered to investigate and punish corruption wherever it occurs. The Hong Kong ICAC's powers extend into the private sector as well as throughout the local government. Finally, most ICACs have a corruption prevention mission that complements their investigative work. Prevention involves working with public agencies and private firms to improve staff training and internal management. It also can include efforts to change social values and expectations through educational and public relations programs and to encourage citizens to report suspected corruption to the commission. These efforts can counteract the sense that corruption is inevitable and can create a climate of opinion in which it is not tolerated. Established ICACs also exhibit contrasts reflecting their countries' political and social cultures, legal systems, and the specific circumstances surrounding their creation. Indeed, any listing of the world's ICAC-style anticorruption agencies is open to disagreement. In this discussion I focus on Singapore, Hong Kong, New South Wales, and Botswana. But Angela Gorta, research director of the New South Wales ICAC, has suggested (in response to my query) that a broader list could also include agencies in Macau, New Zealand, Nigeria, the Philippines, Sri Lanka, Thailand, Zambia, and the state of Western Australia. These organizations have widely varying titles, powers, and anticorruption strategies. Others attempt to draw on the ICAC tradition in unconvincing ways: Kenya's announcement of an ICAC has been greeted with skepticism, in part because of doubts about the real independence of any agency under the rule of President Moi.

Four Historical Illustrations

Let us consider four major examples of the ICAC model, in order of their founding. Singapore's Corrupt Practices Investigation Bureau gradually developed into the prototype. Hong Kong's ICAC is the best-known and most widely imitated. More recent creations include the ICAC of the Australian state of New South Wales, and Botswana's Directorate of Corruption and Economic Crime.

Singapore's CPIB: Expertise and Political Will

Corruption was long a fact of life in Singapore, particularly following World War II. British colonial governments were well aware of the problem; indeed, anticorruption efforts date back sixty years.[4] The Prevention of Corruption Act of 1937 was the first attempt to regulate the problem, but its provisions were weak and there was no independent agency to enforce it. In any event, anticorruption efforts were quickly sidetracked by war and Japanese occupation.

Postwar reform efforts were complicated by the fact that the police played a central role in investigations and enforcement. This meant not only that corruption competed with all other forms of crime for priority; at a more basic level, there was a conflict of interest, as the police themselves were frequently implicated in corruption. Although the CPIB was founded in 1952, vigorous action was unlikely as long as the police played a central role. Independence brought the People's Action Party to power in 1959, and with it renewed commitment to reduce corruption. The 1937 law was amended in 1960 and again in 1963. The eight-member CPIB was expanded and made independent of the police. The 1963 amendments made it possible to convict an individual of corruption even if he or she did not personally receive a bribe, and they mandated that "Singapore citizens would be liable for corrupt offenses committed outside Singapore and would be dealt with as if such offenses had been perpetrated within Singapore."[5] As the latter provision applied primarily to government officials working abroad and based jurisdiction on nationality rather than territorial claims, it was not exactly a precursor of the United States Foreign Corrupt Practices Act or the recent anticorruption convention of the Organization for Economic Cooperation and Development. Still, it remains one of the earliest explicit attempts by any country to control corruption abroad. In 1981, further amendments supplemented criminal penalties with restitution requirements.

For a time, the CPIB moved back and forth among ministries, but in 1970 it was placed within the prime minister's office. It has benefited from strong political support ever since. Unlike Hong Kong's ICAC, whose powers extend to private businesses, the CPIB deals only with the public service. It can, however, pursue any other criminal offenses discovered in the course of its investigations. In addition, CPIB provides advice and training on corruption prevention. Its strategy has two main elements: reducing *opportunities* for corruption through investigation and prevention, and reducing *incentives* to corruption through periodic pay raises for civil servants. While small compared to Hong Kong's ICAC, the CPIB has helped make Singapore one of the least-corrupt countries in Asia and perhaps the world. There is little doubt, however, that it has been made more effective by strong support from the very top levels of Singapore's tightly controlled political and legal system.

Hong Kong's ICAC: Ending the Culture of Corruption

The former British Crown Colony of Hong Kong also had a long history of corruption. Indeed, corrupt dealings there were as systemic and broadly tolerated as anywhere in the world because of the unceasing flow of people, goods, and capital through the colony. After World War II, rapid economic growth and immigration contributed to a wide-open climate in which corruption flourished, despite amendments to anticorruption legislation in 1948 and 1971.[6] As in Singapore, anticorruption activity was the responsibility of the police, creating a conflict of interest that erupted into a crisis in 1973.

In that year, Peter Godber, chief superintendent of the Hong Kong Police, became the focus of a major investigation by the Anti-Corruption Office. Godber fled Hong Kong, allegedly through police connivance and in possession of substantial amounts of bribe money. The resulting public outcry made it clear that new anticorruption arrangements were required. Then Governor MacLehose appointed a commission of inquiry charged with investigating not only the Godber fiasco but also current anticorruption policies. The result was the establishment of the ICAC on 14 February 1974. The new agency made bringing Godber to justice its first priority, and indeed he eventually served four years in prison on a bribery conviction.

The ICAC has grown considerably both in size and reputation.[7] In addition to an administrative branch, three arms of the agency report to the commissioner, who in turn reports to the chief executive of the new Special Administrative Region. The Corruption Prevention Department analyzes the workings of public agencies and provides advice and training, while the Operations Department conducts criminal investigations. The innovative Community Relations Department educates the public, encourages reports of corruption to a special hotline, and builds public support for anticorruption efforts. Its activities include television programs (the ICAC is written into dramatic series and presents its own public service messages), educational programs, and sponsorship of sporting, cultural, and entertainment events, often aimed at youth and emphasizing anticorruption themes. These efforts have helped reduce public tolerance for corruption.[8]

The Hong Kong ICAC differs from other agencies in its extensive powers to investigate private business. It is also empowered to require those under investigation to demonstrate their own innocence. Both powers are facilitated by extensive access to business and bank records that would be difficult to obtain in many other countries. Some of these procedures might not fit well into the legal systems of many democracies; on the other hand, it must be said that given Hong Kong's tradition of wide-open business practices, an anticorruption agency barred from the private sector would have been much less effective.

Like Singapore's CPIB, Hong Kong's ICAC has become a model for anticorruption activity elsewhere and is widely credited with significantly reducing corruption. Now that Hong Kong has been returned to China, the ICAC's future will depend on new political realities whose consequences are difficult to predict. The agency remained active right up to the date of the handover, however: while the number of Operations Department investigations peaked at 3,836 in 1994, declining to 3,710 in 1995 and 3,257 in 1996, the total for the first six months of 1997 was 2,166—more than the annual totals for any full year from 1986 through 1990.[9] Prosecutions totaled 393 in 1996 (271 involving private sector figures), and 147 for the first six months of 1997 (113 from the private sector).[10] Current ICAC officials emphasize their determination to carry on with the agency's work.

New South Wales: Reform and Controversy

The Australian state of New South Wales (NSW) might seem an unlikely home for an ICAC. While hardly free of corruption, NSW and its main city of Sydney experienced few of the problems seen in the two city-states after World War II. Moreover, it has a competitive parliamentary political system rather than a colonial or one-party regime—thus raising new questions about accountability and independence. NSW's ICAC has been caught up in partisan controversy at times but balances political independence with accountability to the people. In its structure, operations, and basic anticorruption strategy, the NSW ICAC has much in common with our first two cases, offering a fascinating case study of how the ICAC model can be applied to more competitive political systems.[11]

Concern over corruption was growing in the early 1980s in New South Wales, particularly surrounding perceived abuses within the Labour Party state government. Among the issues were bribery of cabinet ministers, attempts to influence judicial functions improperly, and police corruption involving senior officers. The Liberal–National Party opposition coalition used corruption as a major issue against Labour in 1984, and although Labour returned to power, corruption issues continued to surface. The coalition ousted Labour in 1988, and the incoming government promised action. The ICAC Act was adopted in 1988, and the NSW ICAC formally began operations in March 1989.

Like its Hong Kong counterpart, the ICAC strategy has three elements: investigation, prevention, and education. Four branches—Investigation, Corruption Prevention and Education, Legal, and Corruption Services and Research—employ 140 staff members and receive an annual budget of about A$13 million (about U.S.$8.7 million). Under its public education function, the NSW ICAC conducts a variety of anticorruption programs and also carries out sophisticated opinion research among officials and the public. Its remit is limited to the public sector—no small mandate, as it places 386,000 individuals under ICAC jurisdiction[12]—but as in Singapore, the NSW ICAC can investigate private parties' dealings with the public sector. It can require public authorities or private individuals to produce information; search private premises; enter the premises of any public authority or official and inspect and copy documents; and compel witnesses to testify and produce documents at public hearings, even if such witnesses object (evidence taken over such objections is limited in its uses). NSW's competitive political system and free news media make public hearings a considerable weapon indeed.

Some critics have portrayed the ICAC as a Liberal-National creation aimed at discrediting Labour, but it has taken up cases involving individuals from across the political spectrum. Moreover, the ICAC is held accountable to the citizens through the multiparty Parliamentary Joint Committee, which monitors its activities; through the Operations Review Committee, which includes members of the public and of various government agencies; through its obligation to report to the public annually as well as on its major investigations; and through the State Supreme Court, which can review commission findings on certain grounds.

In the decade since its founding, NSW's ICAC has conducted numerous hearings and inquiries and developed a considerable body of research. It has also navigated the cross-currents of parliamentary politics with considerable success, although some of its key figures have become controversial. However, it is difficult to imagine an ICAC-style agency in a democracy that would *not* encounter such problems; and such contention in a way discourages the abuse of commission powers. Systematic evidence on actual trends in corruption in the state has yet to emerge, but ICAC opinion research provides solid evidence that the agency and its work enjoy broad public acceptance.

Botswana: Guarding Against Complacency

The small country of Botswana is in many respects an African success story: since independence in 1966 it has not only maintained democratic politics and respect for human rights, but it also has avoided the devastating corruption found in many other countries on the continent.[13] Indeed, through the end of the 1980s, the general view both in and outside of Botswana was that whatever the country's other challenges might be, serious corruption was not among them.

In the 1990s, however, a series of scandals both shattered that impression and fueled demands for reform. In 1990, for example, the first Presidential Commission of Inquiry on corruption in Botswana's history found fraud in the supply of textbooks amounting to about U.S.$15 million. Two further presidential commissions found significant corruption in the distribution of lands surrounding the capital, Gaborone (1991), and in the management of the Botswana Housing Corporation (1992). Most disturbing was the fact that much of this corruption involved not poorly paid, low-level bureaucrats, but prominent officials who were very well paid by Botswana's standards. Corruption on that scale was clear evidence for many that systems of accountability and supervision had broken down and that the perception of corruption as an unusual event needed revision. As Frimpong put it, "Corruption became a problem in Botswana as a result of political complacency."[14]

The response was to establish the Directorate of Corruption and Economic Crime (DCEC) on 19 August 1994. Like other ICACs, the DCEC is politically independent, possesses extensive investigatory powers, and pursues the threefold strategy of investigation and prosecution, public education, and prevention. The first of these tasks, delegated to the Investigation and Prosecution Unit, covers all government departments and parastatal organizations, which it can unilaterally require to produce evidence and to assist in investigations. Private businesses and other organizations, by contrast, must consent before the DCEC can investigate them. The Corruption and Prevention Group not only recommends preventive procedures but can conduct investigations of its own. A Public Education Group conducts research and public relations activities; like the Hong Kong ICAC, it seeks to end public tolerance of corruption and to build support for DCEC efforts. This unit reports that it has persuaded a majority of the public that a significant corruption problem exists and that the DCEC deserves its support.[15]

As the DCEC has only been in operation since 1994, it is difficult to assess effects on corruption itself. Annual reports, however, document considerable activity: as of the end of 1996, the DCEC had handled 536 cases, producing 141 prosecutions and 59 convictions. By September 1997, the cumulative totals had risen to 3,468 cases; 1,197 investigations, of which 675 were complete; and 173 prosecutions.[16]

Botswana is of particular interest because the DCEC is attempting to reestablish previously low levels of corruption. Moreover, it must do so in a small state (population about 1.4 million) with an economy dependent on such exports as diamonds—one particularly vulnerable, therefore, to international economic trends and interests. The work of the DCEC will bear close attention over the next several years; it may well be that regional cooperation and international assistance will be particularly important to its success.

Conclusion

I have been able to consider only a few elements of the ICAC story in this brief history. Detailed assessments of success or problems in fighting corruption or in changing public opinion must await further study. A few tentative generalizations are still possible, however. First is that no matter how powerful and independent the agency, it cannot reduce corruption alone, nor can it do so through investigations and prosecutions only. Any government serious about fighting corruption must commit major resources for the long term, and must regard prevention and education as just as important as the law enforcement activities that produce headlines.

Prevention is by definition preferable to waiting for corruption to happen. Corruption is an adaptive process, and its potential rewards often far exceed likely criminal penalties (particularly when the likelihood of discovery is perceived as low). Combating only known corrupt practices will mean that reformers will always be "fighting the last war" while corrupt interests devise new and better-concealed techniques. Prevention efforts, by contrast, can institutionalize anticorruption values, procedures, and incentives and help investigators become more aware of the realities of daily life, where public officials and private interests meet. Citizens too can become a force for reform—at the polls, in the marketplace, and within the values of a culture—once it has been shown how corruption harms *them* as well as the orderly functioning of government and once they have been persuaded that resisting it is not futile. Education on these issues must continue as new generations come along but can build a lasting base of support critical to an ICAC's survival and success.

At another level, it is striking that two of these ICACs were established in nondemocratic systems and that all four operate within relatively small jurisdictions—two of them city-states and all with populations under 8 million. Can the ICAC model and, in particular, its public education and prevention functions succeed in larger societies? New South Wales provides hopeful evidence, but we may never know whether ICACs can be "scaled up" to the size of, say, a European country until it has been tried. Also, is the ICAC model compatible with democracy? New South Wales, again, is accumulating valuable experience in reconciling independence and extensive investigatory powers with accountability and due process. Botswana too has begun an ICAC-style initiative in a relatively open political setting; here, the small scale of society might enable it to build more informal bases of legitimacy and accountability. Still, "second-order accountability"[17]— "guarding the guardians"—is not to be dismissed lightly: a powerful independent agency, even when pursuing the laudable goal of combating corruption, can commit abuses of its own unless accountability and due process are carefully maintained.

ICACs are unlikely to be right for every country. Still, these cases show that permanent, independent agencies addressing corruption as a deep-rooted problem, making society a partner in reform, and developing careful strategies for prevention may be a promising way to confront serious corruption.

Notes

1. See Anechiarico and Jacobs, *Pursuit of Absolute Integrity.*
2. See HMSO, "Standards in Public Life."

3. Ibid., p. 3.

4. This discussion draws on Quah, "Singapore's Experience," Quah, "Controlling Corruption in City-States," and Makhdoom, "Government of Singapore."

5. Quah, "Singapore's Experience," p. 844.

6. This discussion draws on Clark, "Dirigisme," Klitgaard, *Controlling Corruption,* Manion, "Policy Instruments," de Speville, "Hong Kong's War on Corruption," Hong Kong ICAC, "Operations Department Review," and Hong Kong ICAC, website.

7. I use the present tense here because both ICAC leadership and the government of the new Hong Kong SAR have promised continuity in anticorruption and many other aspects of government. This does not, of course, preclude extensive changes in the commission's structure, function, and political role in the future.

8. See Clark, "Dirigisme," and Manion, "Policy Instruments."

9. Hong Kong ICAC, "Operations Department Review," p. 76.

10. Ibid., p. 80.

11. This discussion draws on Gorta, "Strategies."

12. Ibid., p. 1, at footnote 1.

13. This discussion draws on Frimpong, "Analysis of Corruption."

14. Ibid., p. 25.

15. Ibid.

16. DCEC *Annual Report 1996,* sections 3.3.1, 3.3.2; and unpublished DCEC figures, all as quoted in Frimpong, "Analysis of Corruption," p. 25.

17. See Schedler, "Conceptualizing Accountability," this volume.

14

Corruption, Democracy, and Reform in Benin

John R. Heilbrunn

C orruption poses a particularly nettlesome problem for emerging democracies in Africa. In the public sector, African governments provide a range of services; yet most lack an efficient "Weberian" bureaucracy characterized by merit-based recruitment, performance as a criteria for promotion, adequate pay, and accountability, with state employment representing an honorable career.[1] Civil servants in these circumstances are generally demoralized; many seek additional employment, and most demand bribes to perform their basic duties. Uncontrolled corruption is symptomatic of poorly defined political and economic institutions. Consequently, individuals in private enterprises are encouraged to offer bribes to secure contracts, to access information necessary for licenses, or simply to improve the circumstances under which they conduct business. As a consequence, the general public pays for venal bureaucrats with lost state revenues and insecure markets. Reducing venal behavior is a challenge to democratizing governments whose mandates are often insecure and whose legitimacy often means little more than the capacity to provide benefits for supporters.

In this chapter I describe attempts to curb bureaucratic corruption undertaken by a new African polyarchy, namely the Republic of Benin.[2] Among the governments that have initiated serious efforts to control corruption, Benin's unfortunate status as one of the world's poorest countries makes its multiple policies unique and noteworthy.[3] Despite economic conditions that would militate against substantive reforms, the Beninese government has implemented an innovative strategy of conferences, the organization of an anticorruption commission, and legislation to discourage corrupt behavior. I explain why the government of Benin has chosen these strategies and assess their potential for success.

Corruption and Democracy

The relationship between corruption and development is controversial, and some have argued that bribery may even help a country develop economically.[4] By contrast, I depart from assumptions that corruption in its myriad forms (for example, rent-seeking, extortion, bribery, embezzlement) curbs political development and economic growth.[5] The very fact that the state controls funds makes it a target of "distributional coalitions" that perpetuate a system of undefined political rules, poorly paid civil servants, and information asymmetries.[6] Creating institutions of "horizontal accountability" limits the capacity of actors within and outside the state to capture monopolies and consume rents.

Bureaucratic corruption, whether high-level, "grand" corruption or low-level, "petty" corruption, has long permeated African governments. In contemporary Africa, Jean-François Médard has suggested that opportunistic officials behave according to the norms of traditional authority while exercising the powers of the modern state.[7] In some countries—notably, Nigeria, Cameroon, and Sudan, among others—malfeasance has assumed such proportions that some have labeled them criminal states.[8] Jean-François Bayart has asserted that corruption in Africa reflects cultural norms that extol the gains of a resourceful thief: when poverty is endemic and hope low, a culture of corruption accepts criminal acts of bribery and extortion as legitimate coping mechanisms.[9]

Whereas revelations of corrupt acts constitute a scandal in a representative democracy, in other governments, different groups compete for limited state resources and their "capture" may be seen as a "coup" for a particular group. In a new democracy, a transition government may find that prosecuting corrupt officials legitimates its rule and distinguishes it from the previous regime. Leaders of new polyarchies who act to limit venality demonstrate the sense of obligation that Guillermo O'Donnell ascribes in Chapter 3 to the republican tradition. However, reducing bureaucratic corruption requires commitment from actors both within the state and in society. For example, the media are critical elements of any anticorruption effort. In combination with government agencies, the media increase information and expose abuses of power. In a society undergoing a transition from authoritarian rule, newspapers can pressure leaders to enact effective legislation against bribery and establish credible agencies to enforce horizontal accountability. Even where voters are able to impose vertical accountability on a government, establishing effective anticorruption agencies may encounter strong resistance. Opposition to reform is especially strong when a culture of corruption has become so entrenched that the informal rules that structure transactions between the government and its citizens command a bribe.

A "culture of corruption" emerges when, increasingly, actors find it less costly to make illicit payments to agents of the state than to comply with laws and contracts. Paying bribes therefore becomes an equilibrium: a reputation for corruption creates expectations, social norms then militate against efforts at reform, and corruption persists over time.[10] To reverse this culture, a new set of social norms must emerge that condemns venal behavior.[11] It is the domain of politics from which these new social norms must emerge. Controlling corruption therefore requires the political will to facilitate a shift from one equilibrium to another that is economically and politically more efficient. Often this shift results from a precipitating event that has preceded a democratic transition and pushes a majority of political actors to seek a new equilibrium to control corruption. However, any redefinition of social norms will often be opposed by individuals within the ruling coalition who stand to lose as much from new rules as those who had operated within the ancien régime.

A Culture of Corruption

Corrupt practices had infected practically every branch of Benin's government after a military dictatorship cloaked in Marxist-Leninist ideology took power and established a multitude of public enterprises. Its leader, Major Mathieu Kérékou, distributed the directorships of the new state-owned monopolies to cronies who openly solicited bribes or embezzled funds. Corruption continued unabated until November 1988, when all three state-owned banks crashed, leaving the country without savings or foreign exchange. The ensuing economic crisis can hardly be exaggerated: throughout 1989, Benin essentially operated as a barter economy. Although Kérékou appointed a commission to investigate the bank crash, he was incapable of prosecuting the perpetrators who had plundered the banks, most of whom were high-ranking members of his regime.[12]

The bank crash may have been predictable; Kérékou had been managing Benin's economy poorly for some years. Salaries to civil servants and teachers had almost always been late, because the government lacked sufficient revenues to pay its civil service. These shortfalls resulted in part from a policy that offered government appointments to graduating students, by far Benin's most fractious population. Each cohort demanded entry into a civil service that consumed a growing share of Benin's revenue and distorted the state's capacity to provide basic services. By 1990, Benin had a civil service that employed approximately 45,000 people and revenues that could pay for only a fraction of that number. Salaries declined, promotions lagged, and agents of the state used their positions to demand the bribes that effectively replaced their salaries. The government was paralyzed, and ministers competed fiercely with other officials for a shrinking pool of development assistance and revenues.

A culture of bureaucratic corruption evolved wherein people *expected* officials to demand a bribe, and payment for services became a social norm. Predatory practices undermined any institution of private property, and enforcement of contracts ceased to apply. What had saved Benin's economy from collapse before was the Nigerian oil boom between 1977 and 1982. Indeed, during those five years, the Beninese economy actually grew by 4 to 5 percent in real terms.[13] Private traders accumulated significant wealth from the transit trade with Nigeria; their activities encouraged venality among high- as well as low-level government officials. While peasants paid police and customs officers small bribes to smuggle 50-kilo sacks of yam *cossettes* on the back of motorcycles to Nigeria, high-level government officials received large sums from merchants importing shiploads of champagne, liquors, cigarettes, and other luxury items through the port of Cotonou. After 1985, however, political authorities in Nigeria clamped down on the cross-border trade, which staggered the Beninese economy and slowly revealed the extent of corruption.

Fewer available rents from smuggling forced officials to seek other sources of income. The bank crash of 1988 was a consequence of a culture of corruption that had permeated Kérékou's government. After the economy collapsed in 1989, popular protests erupted against the regime. People resented having to endure the ramshackle hospitals and schools, heaps of garbage, and unpaved roads, while members of the regime constructed palatial villas in Cotonou's exclusive neighborhoods of Les Cocotiers, Haie Vive, Quartier Jacques, and Les Ambassadeurs. Construction around Cotonou attested to an extraordinary increase of wealth in the private sector while the state grew more and more destitute. A popular backlash found expression at the National Conference of Living Forces of the Nation in February 1990 that removed Kérékou from office and began a transition to representative government.

The (Perceived) Return of Corruption Under Soglo

Ironically, the extraordinary corruption in Kérékou's Marxist-Leninist regime set the preconditions for democratic rule. The story of Benin's national conference is well known: Kérékou pleaded for reconciliation, a High Council of the Republic oversaw the drafting of a new constitution, and elections concluded a transition from Marxism-Leninism.[14] Corruption was the root cause of the crisis that ushered in the 1990 conference. In many respects, Benin was a unique example of an unambiguous transition from authoritarian rule in Francophone Africa. In the 1991 presidential elections, voters selected Nicéphore Soglo over Kérékou by a margin of two to one.

Nicéphore Soglo's background was impressive: he had graduated from the prestigious École Nationale d'Administration in Paris, served as minister of finance, and later was a representative for Africa on the World Bank board of governors. Soglo's understanding of the international community helped him secure relatively large transfers of bilateral and multilateral assistance to reconstruct the Beninese economy. The administration dutifully enacted a set of reforms prescribed as part of a World Bank structural adjustment loan (SAL). Overall, the policies succeeded and the Beninese economy grew during Soglo's administration. However, Soglo was far more successful at managing economic reform than building a sustainable and effective political machine.

Representative government optimally provides all social groups a voice in the affairs of state. In Benin, a country where strict controls had stifled speech for fifteen years, freedom of expression and the liberty to join associations unleashed a cacophony of voices. Literally hundreds of voluntary associations emerged to represent the interests of people and groups around the country. In the enthusiasm that characterized the aftermath of Benin's national conference, popular rejection of corruption was evident in a vibrant press that published stories exposing incidents of official venality. Although the press had enthusiastically supported Soglo during the 1991 elections, it increasingly criticized alleged nepotism and corruption in his administration.

Individuals rapidly organized new groups or used existing organizations to oppose and destabilize Soglo's administration. Many of these people had occupied influential positions in the Kérékou regime and felt threatened by the new government's anticorruption position. An early challenge came from the civil servants' trade union that launched strikes to demand unpaid wages and protest the package of programs under negotiation in the SAL. The Soglo administration weathered the strike, but later conflicts over constitutional issues concerning budgets and presidential prerogative soon disrupted political stability.[15] As the budget crisis unfolded, allegations of bribe taking, the appropriation of government properties, and embezzlement by individuals at the highest levels of Soglo's government began to percolate. Despite Soglo's attempts to defuse the scandals, accusations of nepotism and corruption eroded confidence in his government.[16]

Soglo's electoral mandate had been first to reconstruct the Beninese economy, curb bureaucratic corruption, and recover the funds stolen from the state-owned banks. The arrest and incarceration of Mamadou Cissé, the most infamous member of Kérékou's regime, was a highly popular act. Subsequent policies to replace as many as 80 percent of high-ranking civil servants demonstrated a resolve to control corruption.[17] Newly appointed officials expressed contempt for their corrupt predecessors. Public support for the government's attempts to recover embezzled funds demonstrated an awareness of the difference between public and private finance.[18] However, the honeymoon ended; Soglo had been politically unable to prosecute the villains of the bank crash, and petty corruption resurfaced in proportions that recalled the worst years of the previous regime. Allegations of high-level corruption circulated throughout the capital without any investigation of whether they were true or false. Indeed, their veracity was unimportant; Soglo's detractors succeeded in portraying the president as a nepotistic and venal leader.

Voicing Discontent:
The National Conferences Under Soglo

For the Soglo government, the main procedure that established some sem-blance of public accountability was articulated in the various meetings called national conferences and estates general. The National Conference of Living Forces of February 1990 set an institutional precedent by defining a method for people to interact with the state and express their sentiments about the government. Unfortunately, the December 1990 Constitution made no provi-sion for an ombudsman, auditor-general, or *médiateur de la république*. The government was subject to only vertical accountability, as manifest in elec-tions. Conceivably, it ignored the issue of horizontal accountability, because President Soglo perceived that his priority was to rebuild the Beninese econ-omy. In a reconstruction scenario, creating offices to impose horizontal accountability presented just one more burdensome task.

Yet, optimally, the meetings gave the populace a means to impose cer-tain limits on the government and to obtain more information about their state's activities.[19] Increased transparency resulted from the relative regu-larity with which the conferences occurred. The national conferences helped define rules governing interactions between citizens and the state. In this sense, the conferences established new structures in which citizens debated politics. Continuity was crucial: participants recognized that anoth-er assembly would follow. Indeed, the national conferences enhanced polit-ical efficacy and improved popular awareness about specific problems con-fronting the government. Each conference thereby reinforced sentiments that the government was committed to engage in a dialogue with its con-stituents.

Although the assemblies carried considerable symbolic importance, they hardly constituted a tool to impose accountability on the state. Few of the specific recommendations delegates decided at the meetings were enacted as policies afterward. One conceivable explanation was that bud-getary constraints limited the options of the leadership to enact meaningful, sustainable reforms. Under Soglo, the Beninese government remained dependent on foreign aid, which strongly affected the reforms proposed at the assemblies, in spite of a deficient institutional and financial capacity for their enactment. Hence, resolutions at each conference resulted in superficial actions and requests for further assistance from multi- and bilateral donors. Whereas it would be too strong to dismiss the conferences as simply window dressing, it would similarly be a mistake to accord them too great a role as agents of restraint. Their impact has been largely symbolic, and their contribution has been to educate the public about the problems confronting their government.

It is crucial to recall that the 1990 national conference built on experiences from Benin's history to remove a venal Marxist-Leninist regime that had governed between 1972 and 1990.[20] After the transition, subsequent conferences assembled a wide representation of civic organizations to engage the government in dialogue. These organizations included trade unions, women's organizations, school leavers, the unemployed, leaders of religious congregations, and members of voluntary associations. Informal groups joined mainstream organizations in an iterated debate that shifted calculations of competition among Benin's ethnic groups and improved the government's legitimacy. Broadcasts of the debates on national television and radio, and reports in the press, contributed to a sense that the Beninese people could impose some accountability on their government.

The two meetings that occurred during Soglo's tenure as president suggested a recognition that the state lacked any organized mechanism of public accountability. Reforms proposed at the 1993 États Généraux de l'Administration Territoriale recommended a new policy of administrative decentralization: the government would reallocate political power to provincial and local governments.[21] The French Ministry of Cooperation guided delegates toward these recommendations, ostensibly because local responsibility for policies would deepen democracy.[22] A decentralized administration would improve vertical accountability, since local elected officials and civil servants would be more accountable to the populations they serve. To a great extent, the proposed model of administrative decentralization reflected the influence of François Mitterrand's socialist government that had implemented quite similar policies in France.[23] In Benin, however, administrative entropy and resistance from individuals who stood to lose from the reforms added to the cost of decentralizing the territorial administration. Accordingly, little actual progress was made in the realization of these goals during Soglo's administration.

In December 1994, a second forum, called États Généraux de la Fonction Publique, similarly recommended administrative decentralization to overcome problems of ghost workers, dual employment, patronage, and bribery. During the proceedings, numerous speakers voiced concern that Benin had not yet established a state of law. Some speakers blamed popular apathy for a seeming lack of an accountable state.[24] Others called for increased civic participation by individuals and voluntary associations to balance government abuses. Accordingly, one speaker complained that "there can be no democracy without responsible citizens, nor can an administration perform its functions without a constituency aware of its rights and civic duties."[25] These considerations presaged popular demands for institutions to impose some measure of accountability on permanent agents of the state.

To organize and maintain an adequately paid civil service recruited on the basis of merit proved a daunting challenge for the impoverished Beninese government. At the États Généraux de la Fonction Publique, delegates articulated two fundamental proposals: first was the familiar theme of administrative decentralization; second, greater civic participation was proposed to oversee the state's efforts to police itself. These proposals reflected the recommendations issued in five audits contracted early in the Soglo administration. As a preliminary step, a census of civil servants was suggested. Unfortunately, inefficiency and corruption militated against a census of permanent civil servants, and attempts by the government to enact administrative decentralization encountered resistance from various ministries.[26] As Soglo became increasingly paralyzed by scandal, entrenched interests grew bolder in their opposition to the administration, and his attempts at substantive reform failed.

Crises and Miscalculations

The paralysis that frustrated Soglo's last years in office was aggravated by a convergence of domestic and international events. Regional conflicts in Togo and Liberia and the currency devaluation of 1994 were primary among the external events. Civil war in Liberia and political instability in Togo discouraged foreign investment and hindered economic growth. When more than 100,000 refugees fled into southeastern Benin to escape violence in neighboring Togo, Benin had to accommodate their humanitarian needs for food and shelter. Meanwhile, the ongoing civil war in Liberia occupied much of Soglo's time in his capacity as chairman of the Economic Community of West African States (ECOWAS).[27] President Soglo recognized that foreign investors would continue to avoid West Africa as long as war and instability were common. Accordingly, he worked to bring an expeditious end to both conflicts.

Short-term fiscal disturbances resulting from the 1994 devaluation politically damaged Soglo, even though their negative impact had been far less than his opponents implied. Recall that in January 1994, finance ministers from the various countries in the monetary union, the Communauté Financière Africaine (CFA), announced that the CFA franc would be devalued from one French franc equaling CFA 50 to a 1:100 ratio. The devaluation damaged merchants who imported manufactured goods either for domestic use or to trade in Nigeria. At the same time, primary exports in agriculture (cotton) increased as farmers received more for their products.

Although the economy quickly stabilized from the devaluation's effects, the government suffered a considerable loss of popularity. Soglo's opponents successfully portrayed him as a lackey of the Bretton Woods institutions and France. Hence, debtors to the failed banks rejected his demands for repayment of loans and blamed him for any losses they incurred from the CFA devaluation.

Unfortunately, while Soglo understood complex linkages between regional stability and economic growth, he had difficulties communicating this knowledge to the Beninese people. Soglo compounded his problems during the electoral campaign by underestimating the Beninese people's exasperation with his leadership style (especially the perceived role of his wife), Kérékou's talents at coalition building, and French resistance to his administration. These miscalculations allowed domestic rivals to divert his attention and undermine his electoral campaign. Perhaps Soglo might have been more effective in his dealings with domestic coalitions had he been more sensitive to Benin's ethnoregional conflicts that underlie practically all questions of reform and distribution. Impressively high growth rates were forgotten, while allegations of nepotism and corruption dogged his administration. Whereas the highly trained and technocratic Soglo understood the complexities of economic adjustment, he failed to master the political intricacies of conveying his successes to the Beninese people.[28]

Soglo's considerable achievements were obscured by popular perceptions that he was arrogant and his wife overbearing. This perception was reinforced when he rejected forging agreements with possible coalition partners. Perhaps had the president been more open to coalitions with competing parties, he could have united an otherwise divided country. However, he firmly believed that the growing economy and resulting prosperity would convince voters to support him for a second term. This belief had some clear merits but ultimately proved wrong. He entered the 1996 presidential campaign with a tarnished reputation and confronted a set of powerful opponents in Kérékou; the speaker of the National Assembly, Adrien Houngbedji; French president Jacques Chirac; and Chirac's adviser for Africa, Jacques Foccart.[29] Rumors in Cotonou alleged that the French government financially supported Soglo's opponents and clandestinely did everything it could to ensure his defeat. Whatever the configuration of opposition, the efforts succeeded, and Kérékou narrowly defeated Soglo in the 1996 bid for the republic's presidency.

The Presidential Election Campaign, 1996

Corruption was a major issue in the 1996 electoral campaign. Popular sentiment held that corruption had regained its previous proportions. Business leaders complained that since the transition, venality within the judiciary had increased the costs of doing business in Benin. Complaints about a wildly corrupt civil service and a judiciary for sale to the highest bidder were common. The extent of corruption and its acceptance as a norm aggravated ethnoregional cleavages, since it was perceived that bureaucrats favored those from their own groups or regions over others. Even prosecution of criminals who had been officials in the Marxist-Leninist regime encountered stiff opposition. Consequently, any transitional jurisprudence became mired in interest group politics, and the crimes of the previous regime had gone largely unpunished.[30] Such developments compounded allegations of numerous irregularities during the elections that brought the entire transition into doubt.

Politicians and citizens alike recognized that corruption represented a threat to Benin's fragile democracy. The incapacity of the Soglo administration to prosecute corrupt members of the previous regime diminished governmental legitimacy. Indeed, bribery became so pervasive that a general sense of apathy characterized attitudes about extortion by agents of the state. Early in his administration, Soglo contracted external audits of five ministries to diagnose problems that impeded the government's effective operation. Conclusions from the audits were that Benin's ministries actively competed for funds, rarely communicated with one another, and never coordinated operations. The audits noted that corrupt practices had resumed proportions that indicated an extraordinary depth of venality in Benin. Indeed, the persistence of corruption in the Beninese government recalled Yves Mény's observation that "the existence of corruption is a translation of a social and political malaise."[31]

The 1990 national conference had been a major force in Beninese politics and contributed to a significant mobilization of political participation. Soglo tried to reanimate politics through the États Généraux de l'Administration Territoriale and at the later Conférence Nationale de la Fonction Publique. Convoking a series of assemblies was a means to overcome a growing antipathy to his regime and, optimally, to demonstrate a commitment to creating some elements of public accountability in the government. However, continuing accusations of corruption at the highest levels of the administration had undermined Soglo's efforts, and his popularity plummeted in the weeks before the election.

Accordingly, Soglo lost the 1996 elections to a rehabilitated Kérékou, a newly born-again Christian who professed guilt for his earlier transgressions. In April 1996, Benin experienced only its second peaceful transfer of power since independence. When Kérékou assumed office as an *elected* president, it attested to the strength of Benin's democracy and the vertical accountability that the polls may impose in emerging polyarchies. However, institutions of horizontal accountability had remained tentative and poorly organized under the Soglo government. Among the challenges facing the coalition that had formed around Kérékou's candidacy was to decrease bureaucratic corruption and to reverse the dilemmas of reputation facing the government.

Defusing Criticism:
The National Conferences Under Kérékou II

Although legislative and presidential elections postponed conferences for two years, Kérékou understood better than most the power of the assemblies in Beninese society. Almost immediately upon assuming the responsibilities of office, he announced an États Généraux de la Justice, a Conférence Nationale de l'Économie, and a Conférence Nationale des Forces Militaires. National conferences had a great symbolic impact and helped the administration avoid accusations of ethnoregional favoritism. Participants came from all over the country to share their opinions about specific policies. During the election, Kérékou had promised to reform the civil service and reduce corruption; the meetings thereby served to defuse criticism that the new government was aloof.

The Kérékou government convened the États Généraux de la Justice in November 1996. Delegates discussed issues of human rights and judicial reform. The president opened the meeting with a speech in which he remarked that a state of law cannot exist without an independent and nonpartisan judiciary. His revealing comments acknowledged a widespread sentiment that the judiciary was corrupt and ineffective. The minister of justice, Ismaël Tidjani Serpos, confirmed that "if economic liberalism is to succeed in a democracy, it requires a judiciary that is independent, easily accessible, and operationally functional."[32] A later speech by the head of the bar association, A. Pognon, critically stated that in Benin "the judiciary is not independent. It is vulnerable to the power of money, social considerations, and diverse pressures. And this vulnerability effectively puts justice on the auction block."[33] These speeches recognized that the rule of law operates when the judiciary is autonomous from the other branches of government. Without the rule of law, horizontal accountability cannot emerge to enforce sanctions and maintain responsible government.

At the Conférence Nationale de l'Économie in December 1996, delegates explicitly condemned corruption as an obstacle to "good governance." This conference debated the privatization of remaining state-owned enterprises, private sector development, and corruption control, among other issues. As during the other conferences, debates were widely covered by the media. Discussions at the conference placed a particular emphasis on the need to attract investment; speakers identified the rule of law as a primary means to improve the investment environment. Accordingly, numerous recommendations explicitly called for an elimination of corruption at all levels of the state.[34] Despite a call to end venal practices in the civil service and judiciary, the workshop on governance made no specific recommendations but left suggestions for reform to a new anticorruption agency, La Cellule pour la Moralisation de la Vie Publique (CMVP), that Kérékou had impaneled in December 1996.[35]

The Presidential Commission on Corruption

Benin's legislation against corrupt practices follows a number of other African governments that have specifically outlawed the solicitation or acceptance of bribes. However, bureaucratic corruption is a symptom of a larger problem for African governments. As a result, anticorruption agencies have been generally ineffectual in all but a handful of cases. Typically, an anticorruption agency has been a response to a particularly egregious scandal by public officials. In order to quell the uproar, the government organizes an agency to draft a report, educate the public, and investigate allegedly corrupt officials. Some governments have taken Hong Kong's Independent Commission Against Corruption (ICAC) as their model. For instance, Botswana's Directorate for Corruption and Economic Crimes, Tanzania's Warioba Commission, and the efforts in Uganda all follow the Hong Kong model. However, in the African context, these organizations' accomplishments have been highly ambiguous.

Experiences have demonstrated that a government must enact a mix of policies to reduce the incentives as well as opportunities for corruption. Sanctions and oversight committees are effective only when officials are adequately paid and their careers hold real promise. Benin's anticorruption efforts have significant potential; the national conferences and the CMVP present a mixture of policies and programs that may effectively curb corruption in the civil service. However, chronic budgetary problems remain a possible impediment to reforming the civil service, which means both trimming its size and paying its members an adequate wage. Yet, an incremental approach to curbing corruption cannot follow any magic formula. In Benin, the use of assemblies and the establishment of a watchdog agency may be viable strategies to diminish bureaucratic venality.

The CMVP's official goal has been to eradicate corruption in public life and widen efforts to reform the civil service. The CMVP's responsibilities include the investigation of alleged incidents of corruption and assistance in the prosecution of accused officials. To achieve its goals, the CMVP received an autonomous budget and instructions to report directly to the president. However, locating the commission in the executive's offices may ultimately undermine its effectiveness; the president can use the agency as a potential weapon to punish opponents and protect supporters. This pattern of prosecution and protection has occurred in other African cases, notably Côte d'Ivoire.[36] Even an appearance of favoritism toward the government can fatally undermine an anticorruption agency's effectiveness.

Although the CMVP faces many challenges to its effectiveness, the organization has received substantial support from the media, business community, and religious congregations. The extent of support reflected a popular fatigue with the constant problem of corruption. Hence, the CMVP has received critical support from business leaders who complained about the extra costs of bribery and the constant uncertainty of contracts. As with other anticorruption agencies, the commission has a mandate that goes beyond simply investigating incidents of extortion and bribery that affect the business community; its responsibilities also include initiating prosecution and educating the public.

Second, the CMVP has received the support of Benin's dynamic media. As in similar cases, the role of a reform-minded media cannot be overstated. In Tanzania, for example, exposés in the *Daily News* provided President Benjamin Mkapa the political will to fire his finance minister for accepting bribes. In Benin, beginning with the *Tam-Tam Express* in 1988, newspapers have acted as watchdogs over government misconduct and constrained the president's activities. After the 1990 national conference, journalists and editors (often the same people) criticized the government for being so long in responding to corruption. For example, when police shot and killed a pregnant woman riding in a taxi that had failed to stop and pay the requisite bribe of CFA 200 in October 1996, newspapers uniformly asked how long the Beninese people must endure such abuses from their security forces. Subsequent editorials criticized the government for permitting corruption at grand and petty levels and forced Kérékou to condemn the police as little more than gangsters. It was against this backdrop that the CMVP emerged. Although complaints were common that journalists irresponsibly wrote articles that violate libel laws, the media have been among the most vocal voices demanding anticorruption reforms.

The Commission's Ethnoregional Bias

The CMVP deviates from the legislated controls common in other Francophone African countries, such as Côte d'Ivoire and Senegal.[37] Its structure more closely resembles the anticorruption agencies found in Botswana, Hong Kong, and Singapore.[38] The commission intends to operate through a number of divisions to investigate allegations of corruption. In principle, each of the codirectors will have critical input into the communications division; the studies and strategies division; and an investigation, monitoring, and oversight division. In turn, the divisions have a particular competence that enhances the CMVP's effectiveness and overall goals of diminishing corruption in Benin. Yet, what remains to be demonstrated is whether Benin's government has the political will to investigate, prosecute, and punish individuals accused of corruption. The prosecution and punishment of corrupt officials is unquestionably the critical feature of horizontal accountability. And in the case of Benin, it is the most problematic.

Certain aspects of the CMVP may limit its success. Above all, the CMVP leadership is from only one ethnic group: Berthaire Babatounde and Anne Adjai belong to the Yoruba ethnic group, which counts about 15 percent of the population. This ethnic factor is critical in a country divided among regions that host numerous groups. The appointment of two people from the same group presents a serious problem of credibility. If, on the one hand, the CMVP investigates individuals from one of the other major ethnic groups, its motives will come under attack as regionally determined. On the other hand, if the directors of CMVP investigate a member of their own group, they will come under attack as traitors. In short, the commission faces formidable constraints that may potentially undermine its role as a watchdog agency. The appointment of two people from the same subgroup and region makes the CMVP also vulnerable to accusations of being blatantly partisan. Any links to the coalition of political parties that support Prime Minister Adrien Houngbedji would suggest that the CMVP is nothing more than an extension of political influence of Porto-Novo.

Despite these obstacles, the two commissioners have cultivated close links to the donor community, particularly the multilateral donors and the French. These relations have been critical in helping the directors raise funding for the initiative. The lack of funding is among the most serious constraints facing the CMVP, and the financial support provided by multilateral donors can hardly be ignored in assessing the commission's long-term prospects. In addition, Adjai's inclusion as codirector recognizes the importance of women in Benin's political economy. Women dominate much of the country's retail trade, especially in small- and medium-scale enterprises.[39] Thus, the problems confronting the CMVP are somewhat offset by its positive attributes.

Conclusion

In this chapter I have described various innovations the Beninese government has used to control corruption. Institutions that modify behavior are unquestionably the most difficult to create; yet in numerous African governments, the executive has sought to change the rules about corruption. Part of changing the rules is shifting social norms so that the resourceful tax collector who builds a magnificent villa is perceived as nothing more than a common thief. Civil servants would no longer have free rein to embezzle funds, expect bribes, and extort payments from the populace.

Anticorruption initiatives point to a deepening of democracy and a popular acceptance of representative government as the political norm. In a democracy, consumption of government revenues by corrupt civil servants becomes a theft from the collective citizenry. Hence, "agencies of restraint" (Paul Collier) reflect an expansion of democracy even if through semicompetitive elections. In Benin, the second round of elections more firmly entrenched the institutions of democracy and, as a corollary, opened up new perspectives of horizontal accountability.

Democratic governments must answer to their populace at the polls at regular intervals. The governments must therefore respond to certain needs if it expects to return to office. In politics, economic hardship is a fundamental reason for electoral defeat. While a democratic African government must improve the country's economic performance, it must also define political rules that legitimate its tenure in office. Soglo learned this lesson when he lost the 1996 elections; his successor (and predecessor) must now satisfy the same needs. Conceivably, the various national conferences and États Généraux support that goal; however, the scourge of corruption lurks behind each budgetary shortfall and relaxation of administrative control.

The resurgence of bribery during Soglo's last years in office raises some questions about the sources of corrupt behavior and the capacity of any government to bring it under control. Coalitions within the Beninese state undoubtedly profited from corrupt arrangements and may even have used bribery to protect their access to illicit gains. Conceivably, the absence of prosecution of individuals implicated in the 1988 bank crash suggested that those who had profited from the previous corruption forestalled government action. Indeed, fears of a stillborn transition to democracy were founded in a lack of transitional jurisprudence; individuals supported Kérékou's candidacy quite possibly because he promised to forgive unpaid debts. A lengthy trial would have recalled the various crimes of Kérékou's previous regime; the newly elected president had an incentive to forget the embezzlement and unpaid loans of his previous regime.

Given a past filled with venality and scandal, the creation of an anticorruption agency represents considerable irony. Indeed, the question arises whether the coalition that supported Kérékou for president will enfeeble the commission and never allow it to operate effectively. When a government relies on uneasy coalitions, as in Benin under Kérékou, the use of an anticorruption commission to control bribery may mask grand corruption by individuals who are essentially untouchable. Conflicts within the Coalition des Forces Démocratiques suggested that Kérékou would resort to shifting appointments to still critics and hold onto power.[40] Although no such realignments occurred in 1997, the precedent of moving opponents out of positions of influence was one of Kérékou's distinctive features of rule during the turbulent 1980s. The anticorruption commission may enable the president to unsettle opponents and create new coalitions as needed. This possibility remains as a fundamental threat to any agency of public accountability in Benin as well as to the country's general prospects for sustainable democracy.

Notes

The opinions expressed in this chapter are solely my own and do not reflect the opinions of the World Bank, its board of governors, or its member nations.

1. Evans, "State Structures," p. 66.
2. On polyarchy, see Dahl, *Polyarchy.*
3. Benin's 5 million inhabitants have an average per capita income of U.S.$370 a year (see World Bank, *World Development Report 1997*).
4. Huntington, *Political Order,* pp. 59–71; Leff, "Economic Development," p. 389.
5. I agree with current arguments of Murphy et al., "Why Is Rent-Seeking So Costly," Mauro, "Corruption and Growth," and Shleifer and Vishny, "Corruption."
6. Olson, *Rise and Decline,* pp. 43–47; Olson's work builds closely on the rent-seeking literature that was pioneered by Krueger, "The Political Economy of the Rent-Seeking Society."
7. Médard, "Corruption in Africa," p. 115.
8. Bayart et al., "De l'état kleptocrate."
9. Bayart, "Le 'capital social,'" p. 61.
10. Tirole, "A Theory of Collective Reputations," p. 2; Tirole, "Persistence of Corruption," p. 5.
11. Elster, "Social Norms."
12. CADR, *Le livre rouge.*
13. Westebbe, "Structural Adjustment," p. 84.
14. Heilbrunn, "Social Origins."
15. Magnusson, "Benin," pp. 39–42.
16. Soglo had appointed his brother-in-law as minister of state for governmental coordination, his son as presidential counsel, and his spouse as secretary-general of his political party.
17. Thomson et al., *Benin Macro-Governance Assessment,* p. 29.
18. Rose-Ackerman, "Democracy," p. 365.
19. A chronology of the conferences includes the following: National Conference of Living Forces, February 1990; National Education Conference, October 1990; Estates General for Territorial Administration, January 1993; Estates General for the Reform and Modernization of the Civil Service, December 1994; Estates General for the Judiciary, November 1996; National Economic Conference, December 1996; and Estates General for Defense, July 1997.
20. The first national conference in Benin occurred in 1969 under then president Émile Derlin Zinzou. Ten years later, Kérékou's Marxist-Leninist regime held a similar national conference (see Heilbrunn, "Authority," pp. 379, 666).
21. République du Bénin, États Généraux de l'Administration Territoriale.
22. République de France, *Réflexion.* See also Banégas and Quantin, "Orientations," p. 122.
23. Schmidt, *Democratizing France.*
24. République du Bénin, *Plan de réforme.*
25. Ibid.
26. Gletton-Quenum, "Bénin: Nouvelle chasse," pp. 18–19.
27. Heilbrunn, "The Flea on Nigeria's Back."

28. Soglo, "Pourquoi," pp. 18–20.

29. On the French support of Kérékou, see Gaillard, *Foccart parle,* p. 391.

30. On the concept of transitional jurisprudence, see Teitel, "Transitional Jurisprudence."

31. Mény, *La corruption,* p. 231.

32. Tidjani, "Allocation du garde."

33. Pognon, "Communication."

34. République du Bénin, "Conférence économique nationale."

35. République du Bénin, "Portant création."

36. Rose-Ackerman, "Democracy," p. 373.

37. For example, the government of Côte d'Ivoire passed an anticorruption law in 1979; the Senegalese government passed *la loi sur l'enrichissement illicite* in 1988 as part of Abdou Diouf's presidential campaign.

38. Klitgaard, *Controlling Corruption.*

39. Heilbrunn, "Commerce."

40. Gletton-Quenum, "Bénin: Secousses," pp. 32–33.

15

Combating Corruption in South Korea and Thailand

Jon S. T. Quah

There are two recent important trends affecting many countries: a positive trend toward democratization and a universal tidal wave of corruption scandals involving countries from all the continents. Dubbed the "Year of the Great Cleanup," 1995 saw "high-profile corruption probes hitting corporate suites and ministerial offices from Paris to Seoul to Mexico City."[1] Moreover, "a survey of the *Economist*, the *Financial Times,* and international coverage in the *New York Times* revealed that articles mentioning official corruption . . . quadrupled between 1984 and 1995."[2] Similarly, in Asia, "corruption was the year's biggest story" in 1996, the Year of the Rat, according to the Chinese lunar calendar.[3] There are two reasons for the global corruption epidemic. First, the end of the Cold War and the emergence of civil societies in many countries have contributed to the disclosure of corruption. Second, the trend toward democracy and markets has paradoxically "increased both the opportunities for graft and the likelihood of exposure."[4]

According to the Corruption Perception Index developed by Transparency International (TI), South Korea and Thailand were ranked twenty-seventh and thirty-seventh by businesspeople surveyed in fifty-four countries in 1996.[5] The rankings for South Korea and Thailand in 1997 were thirty-fourth and thirty-ninth, respectively, among the fifty-two countries surveyed.[6] In this chapter I analyze these two countries' experiences in curbing corruption as their political systems gradually move toward democratization after many years of military rule. First I compare and evaluate the effectiveness of the anticorruption agencies in South Korea and Thailand, then ascertain whether democratization has increased or minimized corruption in these countries.

Combating Corruption in South Korea

Corruption has been a serious problem in South Korea since the sixteenth century, when the participation of the king's relatives in politics led to "increasing nepotism and corruption in administration."[7] The corruption scandals in recent years have led to the description of South Korea as "a[n] ROTC (Republic of Total Corruption) by the people and mass media."[8]

Since attaining independence in 1948, South Korea has experienced several stages of political development, beginning with the "First Republic" under the government of President Syngman Rhee (1948–1960) until the present regime of President Kim Young Sam, who assumed power in February 1993 after winning the December 1992 presidential election.[9] After twenty-six years of authoritarian rule under the military from 1961 to 1979 under President Park Chung Hee, and from 1980 to 1988 under President Chun Doo Hwan, South Korea adopted democracy on 29 June 1987, with Roh Tae Woo's Democratic Declaration.

The battle against corruption was initiated by President Park, who had assumed office in May 1961 after ousting the government of President Chang Myon, officially because of its involvement in corruption, its inability to defend the country from communism, and its incompetence in initiating economic and social change.[10] Park began by forming the Board of Audit and Inspection (BAI) in 1963 to act as a "direct check on the economic bureaucracy."[11] Thus, the BAI was the first de facto South Korean anticorruption agency.

In March 1975, Park introduced the Seojungshaeshin (or general administration reform) movement to ensure "a National Restoration through enhancement of administrative and political efficiency, elimination of corruption in officialdom, clean-up of social waste and injustice, and valuational [sic] and mental revolution."[12] As punishment of corrupt personnel was emphasized, the number of civil servants prosecuted increased substantially from 331 in April 1974[13] to 21,919 in 1975, and 51,468 in 1976.[14] Even though the Seojungshaeshin movement had more impact than previous anticorruption efforts because of Park's commitment, its broader scope, the longer duration of the remedial measures, and the provision of feedback mechanisms for evaluating its effectiveness,[15] the Park government "failed to address such critical weaknesses as inflation, corruption and alienation between the privileged rich and the repressed poor."[16]

Park's assassination in October 1979 led to the assumption of power a year later by his successor, President Chun, who reaffirmed his government's anticorruption stance by purging corrupt public officials and introducing such measures as requiring senior bureaucrats to register their properties and a system for providing information on proposals and requests for political or administrative favors. The government also enacted an ethics law to reward honest officials and to enhance the structures for civil service reform.[17]

However, Chun's government "lacked legitimacy and was beset with opposition" from rival political parties, "dissident student leaders, intellectuals, and progressive Christians."[18] Roh Tae Woo's Democratic Declaration of 29 June 1987 pacified Chun's opponents, as it "embodied a wholesale acceptance of the opposition's demands" and initiated the democratization process because of Roh's support for the popular election of the president.[19] As he was unpopular, Chun retired as promised after his seven-year term on 26 February 1988.[20] Gerald Caiden and Jung Kim have criticized the past anticorruption campaigns of former presidents Park and Chun for being "sporadic, periodic, episodic, incidental and improvisatory," "too cosmetic and lip-serving," and for being implemented quickly and without careful preparation.[21]

The peaceful transfer of power to President Roh enabled him "to investigate political abuses and corruption under the Chun regime" during the five years of his presidency, which have been described as a period of democratization in South Korea.[22] During the parliamentary hearings in November and December 1988, Chun, his two brothers, and his wife's family were accused of massive corruption. On 23 November 1988, Chun and his wife apologized for their misbehavior and returned 13.9 billion won (U.S.$20 million) to the government. In July 1989, his two brothers were convicted for corruption and sentenced to between four and seven years imprisonment. The relatives of Chun's wife were also found guilty of corruption and were fined heavily.[23]

While Roh remained committed to the establishment of democracy during his presidency, he was nevertheless plagued by the long-festering problem of political corruption, as six legislators were found guilty of extorting funds from the business community. The Hanbo scandal of 1992 shocked the country when Chung Tae Soo, chair of Hanbo Construction Company, was accused of contributing substantial funds to the ruling and opposition political parties for favors involving land development.[24] However, Roh was not immune: it was discovered in October 1995 that "the major business conglomerates and numerous individuals had contributed almost [U.S.]$600 million" to his private political fund, which he had used to reward supporters and kept for himself and his family.[25]

As President Kim had "campaigned on a promise to end the 'Korean disease,' namely corruption," he attempted to "change the culture of corruption which had dominated Korea for so long" by voluntarily declaring his personal assets of 1.7 billion won (U.S.$2.1 million) after assuming office, giving up golf—which "had become a symbol of corporate-government cronyism and the exchange of corrupt gifts"—and issuing a presidential decree in August 1993 for Koreans to use their real names for all financial transactions, especially bank accounts—the "anonymous or false-name account had been the backbone of the black economy and massive fraud, corruption and tax evasion schemes."[26]

However, the most important reforms introduced by Kim were the strengthening of the BAI into the first de jure anticorruption agency in South Korea, and the creation of the Commission for the Prevention of Corruption (CPC), which is an advisory body of private citizens formed to assist the BAI's chairman in the task of fighting corruption. In March 1993, the government set up a team of 100 special inspectors within the BAI to implement Kim's anticorruption campaign by focusing on "officials handling taxes, government contracts, procurement, military conscription and licences who are suspected of being corrupt."[27]

The BAI's chairman is appointed by the president for four years with the consent of the National Assembly. Similarly, the BAI's commissioner is appointed by the president for four years on the recommendation of the chair. According to the Korean constitution and the BAI Act, the BAI performs three functions: confirming the closing accounts of the state's revenues and expenditures, auditing those organizations subject to its audit, and inspecting the administrative duties of government agencies and public officials.[28]

In August 1993, the BAI had 776 officials involved in audit and administrative inspection. Its broad audit function includes the accounts of the state, local autonomous bodies, the Bank of Korea, and government-invested organizations. Article 24 of the BAI Act enables the BAI to conduct anticorruption activities by inspecting the behavior of civil servants. If it finds something illegal or unjust after an audit and inspection, the BAI may request the minister concerned to rectify the problem. It is required to inform the public prosecution authorities if it suspects that a crime has been committed after an audit and inspection.[29]

In contrast, the CPC's role is advisory in nature, as it was formed on 9 April 1993 to analyze the causes of corruption and formulate preventive measures; develop ways of correcting defects in laws, decrees, and institutions that breed irregularities; recommend measures to improve BAI's anticorruption activities; and deliberate on other matters referred to it by the BAI's chair. In addition to the chair, the CPC has nineteen nonstanding members, who are appointed for one year and are mainly prominent citizens.[30]

Combating Corruption in Thailand

Democracy was first introduced in Thailand in 1932, when a military coup replaced the absolute monarchy with a formal constitutional democracy.

However, it did not survive because there was limited public interest in the 1932 revolution and the coup leaders refused to give up their power. Bureaucrats became the "dominant political group monopolizing the power of the state," and for the next forty-one years, Thailand became a "bureaucratic polity."[31] The military became the most powerful institution, and as military coups "became an institutionalized means for political leaders to alternate in power" and "to keep popular participatory political institutions under control,"[32] it was not surprising that nineteen coups occurred between 1932 and 1992.

Corruption is also a serious problem in Thailand. Like in South Korea, its origins can be traced to the sixteenth century, when civil servants withheld revenue collected for the king for themselves (they were not paid regular salaries) and sent only a small amount to the king.[33] This tradition of officials retaining part of the royal revenue was difficult to eradicate, and it remained even after the creation of the Revenue and Audit Offices in 1873 by King Chulalongkorn, who later introduced a salary system and ordered all tax collections to be returned to the king regardless of the quantity.[34]

The Board of Inspection and Follow-up of Government Operations, created in September 1972, was the first de jure anticorruption agency in Thailand. However, it was not effective, because its five members were guilty of corruption themselves, and it was dissolved after the October 1973 revolution. In May 1974, Prime Minister Sanya appointed the Counter Corruption Committee to investigate charges of corruption against civil servants and to report its findings to him. In addition to investigating corruption cases, this committee was also required to prepare an anticorruption draft bill to supplement the inadequate penal code. The cabinet approved the draft bill and sent it in December 1974 to the National Legislative Assembly, which passed it, and the Counter Corruption Act (CCA) was enacted in February 1975.

The CCA transformed the Counter Corruption Committee into the Commission of Counter Corruption (CCC), which consists of a chair and five to nine members. The CCC members are appointed by the king with the approval of the Senate and House of Representatives. Apart from investigating allegations of corruption against public officials, the CCC also submits proposals for preventing corruption and for revising administrative practices to the cabinet and sends a report of its performance to the prime minister, the Senate's president, and the speaker of the House of Representatives.

In their analysis of Thai politics, Elliott Kulick and Dick Wilson contend that the Thai concern for saving "face" or self-respect and their acceptance of corruption as a way of life have caused difficulties in implementing democracy in the country.[35] Consequently, the Thais "practice by fits and starts a kind of halfway democracy" or "zigzag democracy," as Thailand does not have a high score for "the four planks in any democratic system—representation, participation, openness and equity."[36]

Although democracy was introduced in Thailand in 1932 and universal suffrage was granted to its citizens before it was in many Asian countries, Clark Neher and Ross Marlay have pointed out that for "80 percent of the time since 1932 Thailand has been ruled by undemocratic regimes dominated by the army."[37] The military's predominance in Thai politics was interrupted by the October 1973 student revolt, which resulted in a civilian government and the "most democratic Constitution in Thai history"[38] in 1974 and the introduction of the CCA and CCC in 1975. However, this democratic interlude was short-lived, as military rule resumed after the October 1976 coup.

Military power was constrained by the government of Prem Tinsulanond from 1980 to 1988, as Thailand "evolved from an authoritarian state to a more democratic one" during this period. While the election of Chatichai Choonhavan as prime minister in 1988 was the "clearest sign of democratization in Thai politics," the military coup of February 1991 disproved the popular belief that the military would no longer intervene in politics. The coup leader, General Suchinda Kraprayoon, became prime minister after the March 1992 election, but his government survived for only forty-eight days; he "was driven from power by massive demonstrations" throughout the country.[39] Thus, unlike Kulick and Wilson, Neher and Marlay are more optimistic about Thai democracy, as "by late 1992, Thailand's government met our criteria for democracy in citizen participation, electoral competition, and civil liberties."[40]

Comparative Analysis

Corruption is a serious problem in Thailand and South Korea, as it is a way of life in both countries. Unfortunately, the erosion of military rule and increasing democratization since mid-1987 in South Korea and late 1992 in Thailand has not reduced corruption significantly, because two of its main causes—vote buying and low salaries of civil servants and political leaders—have not been eliminated in either country.

Economic growth and democratization in South Korea and Thailand have exacerbated the problem by increasing the opportunities for corruption. Corruption was a minor problem in South Korea in 1945 when the country was still poor. However, corruption became a serious problem during the country's rapid economic growth in the 1970s and 1980s. President Kim's anticorruption drive beginning in 1993 not only confirmed that corruption is a way of life in South Korea but also exposed its pervasiveness in the country. "As Kim turned the spotlight on such [corrupt] practices, it exposed more dirt than the Korean people had ever imagined or are comfortable with."[41] Indeed, many Koreans were shocked to discover the unprecedented scale of former president Roh's graft while in office.

Corruption is also an endemic disease in Thailand, and academic studies confirm that it is not only pervasive but also a key aspect of the Thai political process. Nearly two decades ago, a Thai political scientist, Thinapan Nakata, warned that as "the problem of corruption in the country is more widespread with each passing day," the existing administrative system would not survive if urgent solutions were not found.[42] Corruption in Thailand is a serious problem that "affects the very heart of the democratic process because of the wide extent of vote-buying and vote-selling." A poor farmer in northeastern Thailand admitted frankly that "a general election is a time for collecting money. Democracy? I must pay off my debts first before thinking about it."[43] The Chart Thai Party was reported to have spent U.S.$120 million on buying votes in the 1990 election.[44] The November 1996 general election was the "dirtiest" election, as vote buying was widespread and politicians spent more than U.S.$1 billion on buying votes.[45]

The scandalous revelation that both former presidents Chun and Roh had secretly amassed vast slush funds of U.S.$1.2 billion and U.S.$654 million respectively while they were in office confirmed the widespread practice of money politics in South Korean politics. Indeed, both Chun and Roh justified "the practice of the slush funds as essential for paying the high costs of democratic politics in South Korea with its expensive elections.[46]

Apart from vote buying and money politics, the other major problem requiring redress in both South Korea and Thailand is the low salaries in their civil services. "When civil service pay is too low, civil servants may be obliged to use their positions to collect bribes as a way of making ends meet, particularly when the expected cost of being caught is low."[47] The solution to this problem is obvious but expensive: the governments in both countries have to increase the salaries of civil servants to minimize corruption.

According to Robert Leiken, "[W]hen the people pay government functionaries decent salaries, they are buying a layer of insulation against patronage and bribery," and "the official gains the security and the self-respect of a civil servant, subverting patrimonialism."[48] One lesson drawn from Singapore's experience is "the importance of reducing the incentive for corruption by keeping the salaries of civil servants and political leaders competitive with the private sector," for they will be more vulnerable to corruption if their salaries are low.[49]

In South Korea, Meredith Woo-Cummings has suggested that civil service salaries, which constitute only 70 percent of private sector wages, should be improved to reduce corruption.[50] Similarly, Jong Sup Jun and

Jae Poong Yoon have recommended that it is unrealistic to expect South Korean civil servants "to show dedication without providing adequate remuneration and changing the administrative culture."[51] In his study of the Thai civil service, Kasem Suwanagul contended that the low salaries of civil servants during the postwar period gave rise to more bureaucratic corruption, as their low salaries were insufficient to meet inflation and below those offered in the private sector.[52] Unfortunately, the salaries of Thai civil servants are still inadequate today, and they usually take a second job or resort to corruption to make ends meet. Thus, the need for reforming civil service compensation is perhaps greater in Thailand, where civil servants earn lower wages than their South Korean counterparts. In short, corruption will continue to plague both South Korea and Thailand as long as their governments do not reform their electoral systems to eliminate vote buying and money politics and to improve the salaries of public officials.

Thailand's lower scores on TI's Corruption Perception Index for 1996 and 1997 imply that for the businesspeople surveyed, the level of corruption is perceived to be higher in Thailand than in South Korea. There are three reasons for this difference in perception. First, the political leadership in South Korea, especially President Kim Young Sam, has been much more committed to combating corruption than the Thai political leaders, as manifested in the various anticorruption measures Kim has introduced. The most important lesson to be drawn from the effective anticorruption strategies of Singapore and Hong Kong is that "the political leadership must be sincerely committed to the eradication of corruption" by demonstrating exemplary conduct and punishing anyone found guilty of corruption, regardless of his or her position or status in society. An anticorruption strategy will fail if it protects the rich and powerful from prosecution for corruption and focuses instead on arresting the poor and powerless.[53]

Young Jong Kim, one of the pioneers in studying South Korean corruption, has lamented the lack of political will in his country's efforts to curb corruption, especially under the regimes of Presidents Rhee, Park, and Chun.[54] Even though Kim's anticorruption campaign has been hindered somewhat by the 17 May 1997 arrest of his son for bribery and tax evasion in the Hanbo loan scandal and his sentencing to three years imprisonment five months later,[55] Kim has clearly demonstrated his commitment to eliminating corruption by not obstructing or preventing the legal arrest and sentencing of his son. Nevertheless, the Hanbo scandal and his son's arrest and imprisonment for his involvement in the scandal have seriously undermined President Kim's legitimacy and jeopardized the continued success of his anticorruption drive. Whether Kim's commitment to curb corruption will be continued by his successor remains to be seen.

In contrast, most Thai political leaders (with few exceptions, such as Prime Ministers Anand Panyarachun and Chuan Leekpai) are not committed to tackling corruption. Pasuk Phongpaichit and Sungsidh Piriyarangsan found that the rate of political corruption was "highest in the Chatichai period at 633.3 million baht per year, as compared to 86.3 million [baht] for Sarit, and 60.0 million baht in the case of Thanom-Praphat."[56] As a percentage of GDP, political corruption was at its peak during Sarit's period and was "higher under military-dominated governments than under the elected government of Chatichai." Finally, King Bhumiphol's concern with the pervasiveness of corruption in Thailand was reflected in his lament that "if all corrupt persons were executed, there would not be many people left."[57]

Second, South Korea's anticorruption strategy appears to be more effective than Thailand's because of the reforms introduced by President Kim, especially the strengthening of the BAI and the formation of the CPC to assist the BAI in 1993. As the first civilian to become president, Kim received popular support for his anticorruption campaign, and his legitimacy was not challenged before the outbreak of the Hanbo scandal[58] and the revelation of his son's involvement.

In contrast, Thailand's anticorruption strategy was described as "hopeless" by Quah sixteen years ago, as its anticorruption measures were inadequate and its political leaders unconcerned "about alleviating the problem of corruption."[59] Unfortunately, the situation has not changed significantly in the 1990s, as "corruption has escalated quickly and vigorously, beyond anyone's ability to stop its spread";[60] the CCC and CCA lack the power to prosecute corrupt public officials, and most Thai political leaders have not been concerned about curbing corruption. More specifically, there are three reasons for the CCC's ineffectiveness. First, according to the anthropologist Niels Mulder, "[T]he idea of corruption, meaning that the external world should not be exploited for personal gain because it constitutes the public interest" is "so baffling [to the Thais] that it lames all Anti-Corruption Commissions at the outset."[61] He explains that there is no equivalent word for corruption in the Thai language, as "nobody had apparently conceived of the practice before," because the external world was viewed as "a field of opportunity." The closest Thai equivalent is *choo rat bang luang,* which means "to defraud the state," or stealing from the king, which is risky but not perceived as an erosion of the public interest.[62] In other words, corruption is perceived by Thais to be a way of life and not against the public interest. Moreover, "unlike Westerners, they expect their leaders to be corrupt too, and accept the fact as part of life."[63]

Second, the CCC was unable to curb high-level corruption because of the constant conflict between the cabinet and bureaucracy.[64] A former director of the CCC has admitted that "a third of the national budget was being pocketed by corrupt officials," with most of them cheating on their housing allowances.[65]

Third, the CCC was viewed by its critics as a "paper tiger" without real teeth, as "it could only send reports to the prime minister and the cabinet" since it lacks "direct authority to punish public officials." Consequently, very few civil servants have been punished for corruption. The CCC's ineffectiveness led to the CCA's amendment in 1987 to give it more power.[66] In spite of this amendment, the CCC still cannot take action against politicians, and it "only has the power to investigate a bureaucrat following a complaint." If the complaint is valid, the CCC reports it to the accused official's superior, who can order a second investigation to decide whether the case should be sent to the public prosecutor for criminal charges or settled through departmental disciplinary action. Officials found "guilty" by the CCC are usually reprimanded or disciplined within the department, as the public prosecutor does not use the evidence collected by the CCC and initiates new investigations.[67]

The final reason for the perception that Thailand has a higher level of corruption than South Korea is that any incumbent Thai government will encounter more obstacles than its South Korean counterpart in combating corruption, because Thailand is a bigger country, with a larger population and civil service, but with fewer resources to devote to anticorruption efforts given its lower GNP per capita. Thailand is five times bigger than South Korea and has a larger population (60.2 million in 1995) and civil service (1.14 million civil servants in 1994) than South Korea, which has a population of 44.8 million (1995) and nearly 900,000 civil servants (1993). Thailand is also poorer than South Korea, as its GNP per capita of U.S.$2,765 is less than one-third of South Korea's U.S.$10,158 (1995).[68]

In short, the transition from authoritarian military rule to democratization in South Korea and Thailand in recent years has not minimized but widened the scope for corruption, which is already a way of life because of the prevalence of vote buying and low salaries of civil servants and political leaders. Thus, democratization in South Korea and Thailand has not resulted in effective control over corruption, as their governments have not removed these two causes.

However, democratization in South Korea and Thailand has also given their citizens the power and opportunity to punish governments that fail to curb corruption. Pye has contended that money politics in South Korea has paradoxically made its politics "more pluralistic and competitive," as the "shock of the public exposure of the scandals has had the same effect of enhancing views more compatible with democracy."[69] Similarly, in Thailand's case, Prime Minister Banharn "paid the price for the public perception that he was presiding over a corrupt government" when he was defeated in the November 1996 general election.[70]

Notes

1. Rossant, "Dirty Money," p. 25.
2. Leiken, "Controlling," p. 58.

3. Ghosh et al., "Corruption," p. 18.
4. Leiken, "Controlling," p. 58.
5. Transparency International, *The Fight Against Corruption,* p. 65.
6. Transparency International, "Transparency International," p. 3.
7. Rahman, "Legal and Administrative Measures," p. 119.
8. Kim, *Bureaucratic Corruption,* p. 215.
9. Bedeski, *The Transformation of South Korea,* pp. 54–55.
10. Han, "South Korea," p. 273.
11. Hart-Landsberg, *The Rush to Development,* p. 54.
12. Oh, "The Counter-Corruption Campaign," p. 324.
13. Jun, "The Paradoxes of Development," p. 63.
14. Rahman, "Legal and Administrative Measures," p. 122.
15. Oh, "The Counter-Corruption Campaign," p. 344.
16. Kim et al., *Administrative Dynamics,* p. 3.
17. Jun, "The Paradoxes of Development," p. 63.
18. Han, "South Korea," pp. 283–284.
19. Ibid., p. 288.
20. Macdonald and Clark, *The Koreans,* p. 120.
21. Caiden and Kim, "A New Anti-Corruption Strategy," pp. 137–139.
22. Ibid., p. 60.
23. *Asia Yearbook 1990,* "Korea—South," pp. 155–156.
24. *Asia Yearbook 1992,* "Korea—South," p. 138.
25. Macdonald and Clark, *The Koreans,* pp. 159–160.
26. Sheridan, *Tigers,* pp. 13–15.
27. "Special Team to Root Out Graft."
28. Kim, *Bureaucratic Corruption,* p. 218.
29. Ibid., pp. 219–220.
30. Ibid., p. 220.
31. Riggs, *Thailand.*
32. Chai-Anan and Sukhumbhand, "Thailand," p. 125.
33. Chai-Anan, "Problems of Bureaucratic Corruption," pp. 1, 4.
34. Ibid., p. 7.
35. Kulick and Wilson, *Thailand's Turn,* pp. 34–39.
36. Ibid., pp. 39–40.
37. Neher and Marlay, *Democracy and Development,* p. 29.
38. Ibid., p. 32.
39. Ibid., pp. 32–35.
40. Ibid., p. 49.
41. Genzberger, *Korea Business,* p. 25.
42. Thinapan Nakata, "Corruption," p. 102.
43. Kulick and Wilson, *Thailand's Turn,* p. 38.
44. Ibid., p. 39.
45. Ghosh et al., "Corruption," p. 20; Vatikiotis and Fairclough, "Thailand," p. 16.
46. Pye, "Money Politics," p. 220.
47. Mauro, *Why Worry,* p. 5.
48. Leiken, "Controlling," p. 68.
49. Quah, "Singapore's Experience," p. 850.
50. Woo-Cummings, "Developmental Bureaucracy," pp. 455–456.
51. Jun and Yoon, "Korean Public Administration," p. 107.
52. Kasem, "Civil Service of Thailand," pp. 79–80.
53. Quah, "Controlling Corruption in City-States," p. 408.
54. Kim, *Bureaucratic Corruption,* p. 207.
55. "South Korea Leader's Son."

56. Pasuk and Sungsidh, *Corruption,* pp. 39–41.
57. Kulick and Wilson, *Thailand's Turn,* p. 36.
58. Hwang, "Administrative Corruption," p. 165.
59. Quah, "Bureaucratic Corruption," pp. 175–176.
60. Quoted in Ockey, "Political Parties," p. 251.
61. Mulder, *Inside Thai Society,* pp. 173–174.
62. Ibid., p. 174.
63. Kulick and Wilson, *Thailand's Turn,* p. 36.
64. Dalpino, "Thailand's Search for Accountability," p. 66.
65. Kulick and Wilson, *Thailand's Turn,* p. 37.
66. Amara, "Bureaucracy vs. Bureaucracy," p. 240.
67. Pasuk and Sungsidh, *Corruption,* pp. 180–181.
68. Euromonitor, *World Economic Factbook,* pp. 382–383, 412–413; Jun and Yoon, "Korean Public Administration," p. 100.
69. Pye, "Money Politics," p. 221.
70. Ghosh et al., "Corruption," p. 20.

16

The Global Coalition Against Corruption: Evaluating Transparency International

FREDRIK GALTUNG AND JEREMY POPE

S ystemic corruption was long held to be a cultural, moral, and historical problem; by the 1990s it has clearly become an institutional one as well. There are few newly elected governments in Latin America, Africa, and Asia that do not promise sweeping legal and administrative reforms to reduce corruption. International financial organizations and bilateral development agencies have recently begun to support this trend and to link corruption control to the disbursement of aid or loans.

Before corruption became "depoliticized" with the fall of the Berlin Wall, such policies would have been impossible. Then, tyrants on every continent were shored up by Western governments anxious to secure and retain support for their own agendas in international forums. Much of this support was channeled through international organizations. With the Cold War imperative gone, the scope for action against corrupt governments, wherever they may be, greatly widened. Previously overlooked in favor of a so-called trickle-down theory, systemic corruption has at last come to be understood as a major impediment to sustainable development.

The Founding Period

In 1990, the World Bank representatives stationed in Africa met in Swaziland to discuss the Bank's long-term perspective study on improving governance as a condition for economic development.[1] Drawing on more than two decades of experience at the Bank, Peter Eigen, then the regional director for East Africa based in Nairobi, described corruption as a "powerful enemy of good governance,"[2] with significant economic and social repercussions. The response was enthusiastic, and it was agreed that the time had come to develop an anticorruption agenda within the World Bank.

At the Bank's Washington headquarters, doubts quickly emerged about the possibility of taking on this agenda. The Bank's legal department was implacably opposed, repeatedly citing the Bank's *Articles of Confederation* as prohibiting it from being involved in a member government's political affairs and claiming that corruption was therefore beyond the Bank's legal mandate. This viewpoint seemed to dominate senior and middle-management circles. In spite of encouragement from the field (very likely generated from what staff there were experiencing), from within the Bank itself, and from some (but by no means all) political leaders in the African region, it was felt at the time that to tackle corruption would so clearly interfere with the Bank charter's claimed "requirement" to abstain from "political" considerations in lending decisions as to completely rule out explicit action on its part.[3]

Frustrated by the Bank's unwillingness to change from within, Peter Eigen took early retirement and set out on an arduous odyssey to concretize the anticorruption concepts floated in Swaziland.[4] With support from the German technical assistance agency (GTZ), which had encountered corruption in its own development assistance projects and was anxious to confront what seemed to be a growing menace, Eigen literally crisscrossed the world, holding a seemingly endless succession of small meetings with those who expressed interest and drumming up support for the enterprise.[5]

A number of Eigen's friends and colleagues supported the idea of creating a structure independent of the constraints of an intergovernmental framework. They formed a working group that met at regular intervals throughout 1991–1992: first in Eschborn (near Frankfurt), then in Kampala, London, Washington, D.C., and, finally, The Hague. By the end of 1992, a substantial group of supporters formed the initial board of directors and advisory council of Transparency International (TI).

It was clear from the outset that TI would be a "one-issue non-profit organization"[6] aimed at curbing corruption in the South as well as in the postcommunist countries in transition in Eastern and Central Europe and the former Soviet Union. Corruption is, of course, found everywhere, but while "countries of the North may be able to 'afford' the luxury of corruption . . . those elsewhere cannot."[7] In addition to working in those countries where systemic corruption was prevalent, TI would also focus on the countries in the North whose business community was fueling corruption as they bribed to obtain export orders. It was felt that international "grand corruption"[8] had the most devastating impact on the economic and social development of countries in the South and countries in transition. International corruption also took place in a legal vacuum, since only one country, the United States, criminalized bribery by its multinationals abroad; and international mutual judicial assistance arrangements were not geared to indict leading political figures.[9]

Finally, international corruption, whatever its source, was determined to be a legitimate agenda of an international nongovernmental organization (NGO). Petty corruption within countries, in culturally specific contexts, remained an issue that was thought best left to local institutions. TI's motto in the first few years described the organization as "the coalition against corruption in international business transactions."

Precisely how these ambitions were to be realized was unclear. Initially, some supporters advocated an organization devoted to exposing cases of corruption throughout the world, much like Amnesty International (AI) does for human rights abuses. Ian Martin, AI's former secretary-general, was among those who convincingly argued that this model would not suit TI. An exposing role would be incompatible with the coalition-building function of reforming corrupt systems. These two approaches were determined to be mutually exclusive. One could not seek to work with the government and private sector in strengthening the procurement system of a country, for example, and at the same time expose the corrupt practices of the very same companies and public officials one was working with. Nor could TI claim any obvious competitive advantage in this area of exposure, which was the legitimate concern of investigative journalists.[10] Furthermore, an exposure/investigative role would entail considerable personal risk and the threat of ongoing libel actions.

Over and above all these objections, the governments most amenable to the TI approach were likely to be those who were far from the world's worst. Resources would have greater impact in countries where change was likely to have an effect than in countries whose governments were at the top of the corruption league and demonstrated no sign of mending their ways.

It became clear that the TI approach would need to be evolutionary and focus on reforming systems. To this end the name Transparency International was decided upon, in preference to earlier names such as the International Business Monitor.[11] TI working group consensus was that while corruption was undoubtedly a moral issue, a sufficiently broad coalition of interests could only be built around the social, political, and economic costs of corruption. The issue could not be sold on moral grounds alone. Different messages of self-interest would need to be generated and targeted at different areas of activity. In May 1993, TI held its launch conference in Berlin with more than seventy participants from all continents. They included people from the three sectors that are the core international stakeholders in this anticorruption process: national governments in the South, the international development community, and transnational corporations (TNCs).[12]

In the five years since the launch conference, TI has been widely rec-ognized for its leadership role in influencing and setting the agenda for cor-ruption reform. It has played a considerable role in raising public, govern-mental, and private sector awareness of the importance of corruption control. TI has influenced intergovernmental organizations and the drafting of conventions; national chapters have been formed or are in formation in more than seventy countries; and programs have been undertaken in more than two dozen countries.

This chapter is an initial assessment of TI's activities and its effective-ness. At this stage it would have been ideal to draw on a critical secondary literature on TI. Unfortunately, while TI is cited in innumerable articles and books on corruption in recent years, only one aspect of TI's work, the annu-al Corruption Perception Index, has been subject to critical review (see below).[13] This review of TI's approach and activities will hopefully prompt outsiders to undertake analysis of other dimensions of TI's work in coming years.

In its 1997 mission statement, TI broadened its purpose from a rela-tively narrow initial focus on international bribery. Inspired by the demands of its national chapters, TI now aims "to curb corruption by mobilizing a global coalition to promote and strengthen international and national integrity systems." There are two distinct aspects to this sentence. The first is the objective: "to curb corruption." The second describes the means by which this might be done. In this chapter we focus on TI's record and abili-ty to do the latter. TI's current approach contains four constitutive ele-ments: (1) building national, regional, and global coalitions—embracing the state, civil society, and the private sector—in order to fight domestic and international corruption; (2) coordinating and supporting national chap-ters to implement this mission; (3) assisting (in conjunction with national chapters) in the design and implementation of effective integrity systems; and (4) collecting, analyzing, and disseminating information to raise public awareness on the damaging impact of corruption on human and economic development (especially in low-income countries).[14]

An Analytic Framework

In the standard legal definition of bribery there is a bribe giver and a bribe taker.[15] If we leave aside scenarios in which there are multiple recipients, the essential point is that it takes two parties for a transaction to qualify as bribery: a corrupter and one who is corrupted. One of Robert Klitgaard's most interesting contributions to the study of corruption was to depart from this notion and to point out that there are not just two but *three* actors involved in any corrupt transaction: a principal (P), an agent (A), and a client (C).[16] To take an example from corruption in the tax administration, a tax collector (A) abuses the power given by the state (P) when accepting money from a taxpayer (C) to reduce his or her tax burden.

Most definitions of corruption cover both transactions between A and C (e.g., bribery, extortion) and the direct abuse of A's relationship to P (e.g., internal fraud, theft of government property). If C abuses his or her relationship with P (e.g., through tax fraud or illegal capital transfers), this is not considered to be corruption, because it does not include the active (or passive) collusion of an agent of the state. It is straightforward theft.

In Klitgaard's work, P plays the determining role in any reform process: P selects and is responsible for the actions of A; P sets A's rewards and penalties; and P affects A's and C's costs of corruption.[17] In any fundamental institutional reform, it is important to appreciate that if political will is lacking—both for change and for rigorous implementation at all levels of government—no legislative or administrative changes can be effective in containing corruption.[18] And if existing laws are being ignored, merely introducing new ones is unlikely to effect any meaningful change.

While the Klitgaard model is a useful analysis in many ways, its reliance on a principal reveals one of the greatest obstacles to reform, which lies at the very heart of government—with the politicians and the political interests in power. These will almost invariably perceive the introduction of greater transparency and accountability as an erosion of their own power, as indeed it is. A principal, like the former president of Mexico, might on the one hand take initiatives to curb corruption, while on the other hand continue to engage in grand corruption for his political party and his personal benefit.

In other words, a president can be both principal and agent, depending on the circumstances. The principal in Klitgaard's sense has the power to define and influence both its relationship to agents and clients as well as their relationship to each other. P (e.g., a minister) can also become an agent, however, either by assuming this role illicitly (e.g., by interfering in public contracts) or because another P (e.g., a head of state) redefines its position. The principal-agent-client model of corruption needs to be extended to include these distinctions and account for the roles of all key stakeholders in the process.

Forging Coalitions Against Domestic and International Corruption

NGOs tend to favor the creation of networks.[19] Some claim that the effectiveness of NGOs depends almost entirely on their ability to network and build coalitions "with other NGOs and with other public and private actors."[20] From the beginning it was clear that the coalition-building approach would be at the center of TI's strategy. Whether it would succeed or not, no one could predict. İt is helpful at this stage to recall the state of affairs prevailing in 1992–1993 when TI was formed.

With the exception of U.S.-based corporations, with their hands partially tied by the 1977 Foreign Corrupt Practices Act criminalizing corruption abroad, TNCs were more often than not opposed to international standards and regulations against corruption. The International Chamber of Commerce's 1977 "Rules of Conduct to Combat Extortion and Bribery" were widely recognized as a toothless and unenforceable instrument.

As late as 1994, a BBC World Service program, featuring several TI-UK members, included a contribution that has been quoted frequently in TI literature. Lord Young, then chair of Cable and Wireless and former UK minister for trade and industry, stated that "[w]hen you're talking about kickbacks, you're talking about something that's illegal [in the UK], and of course, you wouldn't dream of doing it here. . . . But there are parts of the world I've been to where we all know it happens. And if you want to be in business you have to do [it]."[21] Father Rupert Lay, a leading German theologian and management consultant on business ethics, stated in the same year that the only "moral issue pertaining to corruption in international trade is jobs"[22]—German jobs.

As the 1990s progressed, most European countries continued to allow for the tax deductibility of bribes as business expenses. This was done on the basis of a tacitly agreed "sliding scale," according to which exporters could pay up to 15 percent in tax-deductible illicit commissions in high-growth/high-corruption countries and even up to 3 percent for expenses incurred within the European Union (EU).[23]

Some leading economists made it clear that, in their view, the solution to systemic corruption at the interface of the public and the private sectors was simple. Gary Becker argued that "the only way to reduce corruption permanently is to drastically cut back government's role in the economy."[24] In other words, governments should privatize state holdings and public services. The experience of many countries over the past few years indicates that the privatization process can in itself be a significant source of corruption.[25] In one particularly telling example, after a coup in Nigeria, the military rulers used the cover of a war on corruption to "speed up the privatization of the state companies, whose profitable shares could be sold to loyal servants of the new regime."[26]

Some economists have also viewed corruption as a means of cutting red tape in public administration and speeding up the process of acquiring permits and paperwork. Underlying this "grease-is-positive"[27] hypothesis is the notion that corruption allows supply and demand to operate in the public sphere to the benefit of the highest bidder. Experience shows that this systematically increases the costs of public procurement.[28] Moreover, there are public goods, like old-growth forests, where a "highest-bidder principle" in contravention of environmental laws can have disastrous consequences.

Social scientists fared no better in their ability to assess the damage done by corruption and its implications, not only in developing countries, but also in Europe. Robert Putnam's 1993 book *Making Democracy Work,* the outcome of a twenty-year study of the relative effectiveness of Italian public institutions, is one of the most influential works in political science this decade. *The Economist* referred to Putnam's book as "a great work of social science, worthy to rank alongside de Tocqueville, Pareto, and Weber."[29]

There is no doubt that Putnam's research has produced significant findings. What is striking for the student of corruption, however, is that the only references to corruption in his work are the clientelism and patrimonialism prevalent in the south of Italy. The systemic corruption of the north that some argue is behind the Italian economic boom of the 1980s, and that came to a dramatic halt with the advent of *mani pulite* in 1992, is missing from his analysis.[30]

When TI was launched, the World Bank had just published *Governance,* a treatise on the four constitutive elements of "good governance": (1) public sector management, (2) accountability, (3) the legal framework for development, and (4) information and transparency.[31] Very little specific reference to corruption was made in this document, although it is a key symptom of the failure of these governance dimensions and a variable undermining the process as well. An internal memorandum referred to corruption as the "C" word, symptomatic of the taboo within this institution and much of the multilateral development community for this issue.

It would be misleading to argue that TI grew on ground that was entirely infertile. The most significant social factor contributing to TI's early recognition was the popular movements against corruption in so many countries beginning in the late 1980s. People power contributed to bringing down corrupt rulers in the Philippines. In Bangladesh, protesters choked the streets to Dhaka to force down President Ershad. In Brazil, thousands of "painted faces" took to the streets and deposed President Collor.[32]

Throughout 1992 and 1993, significant corruption scandals reaching the highest political echelons in countries as diverse as Belgium, Spain, Italy, Japan, France, and Russia also made it clear that corruption was not a problem limited to developing countries. These scandals effectively exploded the myth of the cultural superiority of the North and helped demonstrate to the South that the North could no longer preach from a position of virtue. More important, these problems made it clear that corruption was not merely a difficult but a necessary stage in state formation and capital accumulation that countries pass through on the road to modernization.

The significant corruption problems of some modernized countries provided strong evidence against any such assumption.

The end of the Cold War and the wave of democratization in the South and the East must also be mentioned in this context.[33] These events implied at least three things for the anticorruption agenda. First, they reduced the international protection numerous authoritarian rulers had enjoyed for long periods of time. Second, with some people calling for an end to history and ideology, this was an ideal time to challenge corruption as a prima facie "postideological" issue. Third, the United States had more leverage than in the past to influence the agenda in international forums, like the Organization for Economic Cooperation and Development (OECD) and the Organization of American States (OAS), to press for regional anticorruption conventions.[34]

From its discussions with sympathetic business leaders, TI knew that there was a significant business lobby ready to change corporate conduct. Critically, this would be possible only if controlling corruption could be achieved without conceding competitive advantages to business rivals. It was a classic case of the prisoner's dilemma: businesspeople did not trust their competitors; yet unless they did, they could not escape from the corruption scenario. The rules, TI concluded, must change for everyone and all at once, so that there were no "winners" and no "losers."

With very limited means, TI decided from the outset against lobbying for a global convention against international bribery. The risks would be too high. Past experience indicated that this process would take years of consultation to draft and many more years to come into force. Reluctant countries would find it easy to set the threshold at a high level in terms of the number of countries acceding to the convention. Even if this were not the case, there would be a continuing need for monitoring (not a feature of most international conventions). Without determined monitoring, compliance would be minimal.

Subsequent events proved this assumption right. In December 1996, the UN General Assembly approved a declaration calling on member states to "take effective and concrete action to combat all forms of corruption, bribery, and related illicit practices in international commercial transactions"; the UN is not attempting to draft a universal convention.

At the first meeting of the World Trade Organisation (WTO), in Singapore, Southeast Asian nations effectively vetoed the WTO—the only other relevant body that could have introduced global rules against corruption—from including corruption on its agenda.[35] TI scored its first major triumph when a number of TI national chapters, working with the then chair of the TI advisory council, vice-president of Ecuador Alberto Dahik, lobbied to place the issue of corruption on the agenda for the Summit of the Americas, held in Miami in 1994. It was important that the voice of the South be heard as being behind such a move. In an official communiqué, more than thirty elected heads of state and government from countries as diverse as Colombia and Canada and the United States and Uruguay, unanimously agreed that corruption was a problem in all of their countries and required concerted action, both at the national and international level, to remedy the situation. This was a landmark declaration, representing the first time that leaders had so clearly laid the groundwork for a regional convention.[36] Furthermore, their declaration specifically addressed the need to incorporate civil society in any anticorruption effort. The taboo was shattered in Miami.[37]

The other prospect was to lobby the Paris-based OECD. Mechanisms emerging from the OECD would have the potential of curbing the export of international corruption; they could also be extended to include non-OECD countries once the process was ratified. When the U.S. Congress amended the Foreign Corrupt Practices Act (FCPA) in 1988, it met critics of the legislation by calling on the U.S. government to launch an effort to require the OECD to prohibit bribery of foreign officials. This began during the Bush administration but did not go beyond the level of committee discussions.

International corruption reform was given much higher priority in 1993, at the beginning of the Clinton administration. Dan Tarullo, who became assistant secretary of state for economics and business affairs in 1993, became actively involved and was strongly supported by the secretary of state, Warren Christopher. Their combined efforts led to the adoption of the first OECD recommendation on corruption at the May 1994 ministerial meeting. Because the U.S. diplomatic initiative coincided with the launch of the TI movement, TI lobbied support for the proposed initiative, with chapters in OECD countries such as Australia, Belgium, Britain, Canada, Denmark, France, and the United States maintaining continuing dialogue with their governments and missions at the OECD.

In November 1997, the twenty-nine industrialized member countries of the OECD, along with five additional non-OECD countries, completed a treaty requiring all signatories to ban overseas bribery, going well beyond the original objective of ending the tax deductibility of bribes paid abroad. This was a process TI followed closely; and through its network of national chapters in key OECD member countries that lobbied their governments at opportune moments, it played a role advancing the process. Editorials in the *New York Times, Washington Post,* and *International Herald Tribune* have credited TI for this contribution.[38]

In the future, TI national chapters in the North will need to ensure that their national legislatures codify and enforce the terms of the convention, making the necessary changes in their national criminal legislation. National chapters in the South, especially in rapidly developing regions, can also lobby their governments to adhere to this convention, which has a specific outreach focus to non-OECD member countries. Several Latin American governments are already signatories to the convention. In addition to the convention, the OECD is considering equally important "soft law" measures to bring taxation and auditing practices into line.

TI-Brussels was instrumental in encouraging the European Commission to issue directives against intracommunity, transborder corruption, encompassing areas previously outside the bounds of legal prosecution. TI-Brussels (which is both a national chapter for Belgium but, as its name acknowledges, also has a role in the EU) prepared and circulated a detailed discussion document that outlined areas in which the EU could move in ways consistent with its general mandates. The presence of senior retired EU officials in the chapter gave the paper particular weight and helped to ensure that it would receive serious attention at the highest levels.

This regionalization of international corruption control is not merely a pragmatic compromise between unilateral action and a global convention. Regional controls set the stage for developing appropriate instruments and jurisprudence within a smaller group of countries, which is necessary if international cooperation is to be made to work.

At the time of the diplomatic push at the OECD, leading U.S. corporations pressured the International Chamber of Commerce (ICC) to revise and give teeth to its 1977 "Rules of Conduct to Combat Extortion and Bribery." U.S. corporate interests sought a "level playing field" for the conduct of export business and the removal of the competitive disadvantage the FCPA was seen to impose on its members.

TI was also interested in convincing the World Bank and the International Monetary Fund (IMF) to adopt a more assertive posture against corruption. Brown-bag lunches at the World Bank in Washington, D.C., from 1993 onward consistently drew crowds that often extended down the corridors outside. In the field, a partnership was being created between TI and the World Bank's Economic Development Institute (EDI) in the form of Peter Langseth. Langseth had been the World Bank adviser for civil service reform in Uganda in the early 1990s and had excellent contacts in and out of the Ugandan government. TI's 1995 work in Uganda and Tanzania quickly attracted his interest, and thereafter EDI has been able to magnify the scope and impact of TI's in-country work. For example, EDI published the proceedings of the first Arusha National Integrity Workshop, held in Tanzania in 1995.[39] This book included the integrity pledge adopted by Benjamin Mkapa when he was elected president of Tanzania a month after the workshop.

Within EDI, Langseth was able to demonstrate to skeptics in the Bank that it was possible to become engaged in anticorruption work without courting controversy, provided the work was implemented with a partner NGO. In addition, EDI published, translated, and widely disseminated the TI publication *National Integrity Systems: The TI Source Book*.[40] The book has assumed a central role in much of TI's and the EDI's in-country work. James Wolfensohn's 1996 appointment as the Bank's new president brought in new opportunities. If the EDI was carrying out its experimental role, Wolfensohn was determined to mainstream the issue within the core of Bank activities. During his first year in office he invited a TI group to Washington, D.C., to conduct a half-day seminar on corruption for him and his senior staff; thereafter TI was engaged as a consultant to assist the World Bank in developing its own new strategy against corruption.[41] Several TI national chapters now work actively with the World Bank in the Bank's member countries, and there is a relatively free flow of information between the international financial institutions and TI.

In some ways, the most telling expression of TI's leadership internationally in the anticorruption sphere has been its more recent role as the secretariat for the Council of the International Anti-Corruption Conference (IACC). The IACC has been held biannually since it was started by the Hong Kong Independent Commission Against Corruption (ICAC) in the 1980s. Originally the main international meeting for public officials engaged in corruption and fraud control, it now embraces multilateral organizations, the private sector, academia, and NGOs. At the 1995 IACC in Beijing, TI was invited to act as a facilitator ensuring that future conferences were not held in a vacuum but that there was continuity and follow-up. Some 1,200 participants from more than ninety countries attended the 1997 conference in Lima (the first meeting for which TI played this facilitating role). On that occasion, the Lima Declaration was issued, setting out the actions and responsibilities that need to be taken in the coming years. The declaration will be assessed when the IACC reconvenes in South Africa in 1999.

This international coalition of interests would never have been possible without individual leadership and commitment. TI has relied heavily and benefited enormously from a large network of voluntary supporters. This has instilled a unique culture that places it quite clearly in the NGO community, distinct from the multilateral organizations or a private sector consultancy. This starts with Peter Eigen, who has worked as a full-time "volunteer" chair of the organization. It includes an activist board of directors, with thirteen people from all continents, a number of them contributing a substantial part of their working day to TI's ongoing activities—again, on a pro bono basis. TI also has the volunteer services of two "support groups," one based in Washington, D.C., and the other in London.[42]

The involvement of these high-level professionals, and the access they have to key decisionmakers, means that TI can be more effective than many traditional advocacy groups. It has also formed small expert working groups of lawyers and of accountants dedicated to developing approaches that can be used in implementing both the abolition of tax deductibility and the effective criminalization of foreign bribery.

Academics also contribute actively to TI's work in research and dissemination. TI consults a steering committee of leading academics and professionals for its work on the annual corruption indices. A group of more than thirty academics from some twenty countries contributes to the TI Council on Governance Research. This network of volunteers helps to explain how TI was able to operate during its first four years with only a minimal professional capacity in its Berlin office. It was only in 1998 that TI grew to four senior staff members, in addition to eight program officers (from six countries).

The original founding members of TI thought that in order to safeguard the independence of the organization, it should be careful to avoid becoming overly dependent on funding from any one source or any one category of sources. Particular effort was to be made not be overly dependent on funding from the public sector. As the annual accounts show, TI receives significant grants from several government and institutional sources.[43] Its fundraising in the private sector has been slower than had been hoped but is presently on the order of about 10 percent of its budget. The funding comes from more than a dozen countries.[44]

Building Effective National Chapters

A central element of TI's institutional strategy has been to build coalitions of a diversity of interests. This emphasis on coalitions reflects TI's conviction that anticorruption programs will succeed only if there is broad-based support, and if a wide cross-section of civil society has specific reasons (beyond the general public good) for containing corruption. Corruption impinges, for example, on the protection of human rights; on the enforcement of property rights (essential for business); on the development of professional standards (e.g., in law, accounting, and engineering); on the protection of children against exploitation; and on environmental protection.

The very diversity of the appeal of containing corruption means that actors who are normally strangers to each other can be brought together. TI tries to ensure that the core group that seeks to form a new national chapter includes representatives from a broad range of groups. The TI board emphasizes the importance of a national chapter chair's ability to reach out and work with diverse interests in the accreditation process. The national chapters are the backbone of TI's activities. They define TI both as an international NGO and as an entity entirely distinct from a multilateral body. It is clearly located in the civil society of the countries in which it operates, and it will define the means by which TI is able to be sustainable over the medium to long term.

Media coverage of TI in its first year was extensive and generally favorable. As a result, the secretariat in Berlin received hundreds of letters

and faxes in its first year alone with inquiries about the possibility of forming affiliated national chapters in their countries. This network grew to
more than seventy chapters by the beginning of 1998.

TI's goal is to form coalitions of the state, civil society, and the private
sector. This notion of civil society is implicitly Gramscian, where it is jux-
taposed conceptually not only against the state but also against the economy and the private sector. In practice, the national chapters and the coalitions they seek to forge do not follow such narrow distinctions. As the
examples in the following paragraph illustrate, national chapters draw on
people from all segments of society. In essence, they aim to be Gellnerian
"non-governmental institutions which [are] strong enough to counterbalance the state [without] preventing the state from fulfilling its role of keep-
er of the peace and arbitrator between major interests."[45]

In Belgium, the chair of the national chapter is Baron Jean Godeaux,
former president of the central bank; in Benin, it is Monseigneur de Souza,
archbishop of Cotonou; and in Malawi, it is an Anglican bishop, the Right
Reverend Bvumbwe. In Brazil, Canada, Egypt, Germany, Poland, New
Zealand, Russia, Singapore, and South Korea, university academics lead
the chapters. In Colombia, The Gambia, Mali, and Panama, it is newspaper
editors and publishers. In numerous countries (e.g., Denmark, Hungary,
Italy, Kenya, Malaysia, Mauritius, Paraguay, Tanzania, Uganda, the UK,
and the United States), the initiative has been taken by members of the private sector representing companies of all sizes. Current and former public
officials have also taken leadership positions in Bolivia, Ecuador, France,
Jamaica, Namibia, Papua New Guinea, Peru, and Zambia. And in some
countries, existing NGOs with an anticorruption agenda have been accredited to TI as national chapters (e.g., Argentina, Pakistan, Panama, and
Venezuela).

In the taxonomy of chapters used in TI's *Annual Report*, the distinction
is made between those chapters that have been formally accredited by the
TI board of directors, chapters that are in formation, and countries for
which there is only a contact person but an insufficient basis to start a chapter. Of the seventy chapters currently being developed, about thirty are
effectively implementing their own activities.

The diversity of people engaged in the formation of national chapters
indicates that TI has been largely demand-driven. TI has not followed a
blueprint process for the formation of local NGOs but has rather awaited
local expressions of interest. National chapters are wholly sui generis and
develop their own national programs in the light of their own perceptions
of needs and possibilities. Two restricting principles, however, are articulated in TI's "Guidelines for National Chapters." First, national chapters must
be politically nonpartisan. Prominent members of the opposition or the
governing political party cannot occupy leadership or board-level positions

in the national chapter. In Ecuador, TI learned the hard way how mistakes can occur if this is not taken seriously enough. The founding chair of TI's advisory council was the former vice-president of Ecuador, Alberto Dahik. In an initial phase, he took personal initiative in bringing together prominent members of the Ecuadorian establishment to form a national chapter in his country. Irrespective of his policies at the time, civil society groups in the country were justifiably skeptical about the credibility of this national chapter's independence vis-à-vis the government. In a second instance, Dahik was himself accused of bribing members of parliament using a secret slush fund. Ironically, while this was an unfortunate practice of long standing, the crucial piece of legislation Dahik wished to pass through parliament in this instance was new anticorruption legislation. In 1995, Dahik's party did not control the legislature, and the latter thereupon turned on Dahik and used the judiciary (which the opposition legislature had appointed) to order his arrest. Dahik left Ecuador and sought political asylum in Costa Rica. He immediately resigned his post with TI, expressing concern that the events might reflect adversely on the organization.

TI learned two lessons from this experience: first, active politicians should not be members of TI's international board or advisory council; second, national chapters must be both perceived to be and in fact independent of the governing party and politicians.[46]

The second restriction on national chapters is that they do not "undertake investigations of individual allegations of corruption."[47] As mentioned earlier, such activity would undermine TI's efforts to build coalitions that can strengthen anticorruption systems.[48]

With these two caveats in mind, national chapters are free to develop any activities that might contribute to the movement's objectives, as the following examples illustrate: commission a touring street theater to take anticorruption messages to rural areas (e.g., Uganda); organize and participate in national integrity workshops (e.g., India, Malaysia, Malawi, Tanzania, Uganda); adapt the TI sourcebook on national integrity systems to local circumstances and jurisprudence (e.g., Uganda); organize national integrity surveys and publicize the results (e.g., Bangladesh, Denmark, Tanzania, Uganda); provide training programs for investigative journalists to strengthen the role of the media in containing corruption (e.g., Russia, Tanzania, Uganda, Zimbabwe); campaign for leading politicians to sign specific anticorruption pledges during electoral campaigns, with built-in follow-up mechanisms (e.g., Argentina, Papua New Guinea, Tanzania); and promote a national competition for schoolchildren to write essays on bribes and cheating (e.g., Argentina).

Multilateral organizations that have embraced the notion of cooperation with civil society organizations are often keen to enlist the support of national chapters. The World Bank and, particularly, its Economic Development Institute are forging partnerships with local national chapters—for example, in Tanzania, Uganda, Mauritius, and Bolivia—recognizing that civil society has a crucial and creative role to play in the development, implementation, and monitoring of national anticorruption strategies. The UN Development Programme (UNDP) has also worked with several national chapters and is developing a broader strategy with the TI movement. In some cases, multilateral donors admit that the cooperation with a recognized local NGO provides a legitimacy the institution would not have on its own. In the best of cases, national chapters can provide "local knowledge" that might otherwise be difficult to grasp for an international organization, whether governmental or nongovernmental. In Zimbabwe, for example, a workshop was held with the police fraud squad. It emerged that they were unable to read balance sheets and did not know what the term *debit* meant! Assuming that funds could be organized, the logical response might be to provide some form of training for these inspectors. The police commissioner objected, pointing out that if his officers were trained in accounting, they would immediately leave the police force for better pay in the private sector. Under these circumstances, there are no ready-made solutions. They have to be found locally. TI's national chapters have been spreading across the globe, but many are new and relatively fragile. In some countries, they operate in environments that have been traditionally alien to civil society asserting its values and operating freely. In others, creating new NGOs has become a cottage industry, attracting unscrupulous individuals.

NGOs are often criticized for seeing growth as a "duty." Biggs and Neame claim that "some NGOs view an increase in their activity as synonymous with greater impact."[49] This issue has been a matter of real concern for TI. As the movement has spread rapidly, the maintenance of quality control over national chapters, combined with active and sustained support, is crucial. There is a certification process, which involves careful and discreet examination of credentials, especially of the chair of the new national chapter. This is done not only to check his or her good standing but also to ensure that the rules of nonpartisanship and the prohibition against investigations and exposures are being followed.

Because each national chapter is sui juris and because each is required to be transparent and democratic, and especially because each national chapter is an independent organ of civil society, there are limits as to the control a secretariat can exercise. A process TI has recently introduced will involve national chapters being required to meet additional criteria before being affiliated; they will be affiliated in the first instance only for two years (as a form of probation); and for affiliation to be kept "alive," they will be required to meet continuing performance targets, including the provision to the secretariat of audited annual accounts and a work plan.

In a few countries, opportunistic individuals have seized on the current interest in the donor community for governance and corruption by claiming to be accredited national chapters when they were not. In Burkina Faso, an NGO calling itself "Faso Transparence" wrote to bilateral and multilateral donors based in the country claiming to be the TI national chapter. After a TI staffer had visited the country to attend a regional conference, Faso Transparence representatives also claimed that they had been with him to see the prime minister, when the staffer had seen neither them nor the prime minister. One bilateral donor checked with its head office and upon receiving the message that the TI secretariat receives support from them, they thought the "national chapter" could be trusted. They did not check with TI in Berlin.

Similar scenarios have been repeated in other countries. However, thus far it has only been in Zambia where a government has moved to establish a "stooge" national chapter. Fortunately, news of this reached Berlin and the donor community was quickly alerted. This indicates that in addition to coalition building, coordination among various funding agencies would be useful. In a review of the literature on development case studies, Milton Esman and Norman Uphoff come to two conclusions. The first is that "a vigorous network of membership organizations is essential to any serious effort to overcome mass poverty."[50] In fact, they cannot imagine significant development taking place without it. Second, to be effective, these NGOs have to have local roots and cannot be implanted from the outside. TI's experience confirms these observations.

Designing National Integrity Systems

It is a sobering reflection on the utility of the law that most countries in the world provide criminal sanctions against those involved in corruption, yet when corruption is systemic, the laws are widely flouted and sanctions are infrequently imposed. When they are, they tend to be directed against small fish rather than big fish. Reforming corrupt institutions is therefore both a critical and a necessary step.

TI has taken two complementary approaches to reforming public institutions. One is comprehensive and the other is highly limited in scope and time. The comprehensive approach includes the national integrity systems (NIS).[51] The more restricted approach embraces the integrity pacts.

The TI–Integrity Pact

Transparency International has developed an anticorruption mechanism called the Integrity Pact (TI-IP) that would also have the effect of engaging key stakeholders, while creating a level playing field for those companies caught in a classic prisoner's dilemma: if one company commits itself not to pay bribes, it cannot trust its competitors to do likewise.

The TI-IP would function as follows: A government, when inviting contractors or suppliers of goods and services to tender for a specific, usually large public contract, informs the potential bidders that their tender offer must contain a commitment signed personally by the bidder's chief executive officer (CEO), not to offer or pay any bribes in connection with this contract. The government on its part commits itself to prevent extortion and the acceptance of bribes by its officials and to follow transparent procurement rules. The monitoring and compliance process is accompanied by the principal, the agents, and the clients (i.e., the competing companies), as well as NGOs active in this field (e.g., TI national chapters).

Although critics say that the TI-IP is nothing more than a commitment to respect and invoke the existing laws of the country, there is a vital difference. The bidders who violate their commitment not to bribe are subject to significant sanctions, such as loss of contract, liability for damages (to the government and the competing bidders), and forfeiture of the bid security. The government could also blacklist the offender from all government business for an appropriate period of time. In other words, all the sanctions are commercial. This creates the strongest incentive for the bidders to enforce the sanctions themselves, through the courts or by international arbitration. The TI-IP also involves the CEOs personally. This procedure requires them to certify the amounts of payments to third parties so they will not be able to disclaim knowledge of malpractice as is now often the case. At present, the TI-IP is being introduced in eight countries in Central and South America, Asia, and Africa at the request of the national governments and with the technical support of TI and the national chapters in the respective countries.

In 1997, TI worked with the Global Coalition for Africa (GCA) to introduce the TI-IP in six African countries at the invitation of the heads of state. Despite some internal opposition, the World Bank has moved cautiously toward this approach and has joined in the GCA-TI initiative.

The National Integrity System

The national integrity system captures a concept that has caught the imagination of activists and reformers around the world. It is that instead of viewing the various facets of governance in isolation, they should be seen as a single entity with various "pillars" sustaining the whole.[52]

The National Integrity System approach involves reviewing, strengthening, and supporting the five main pillars (public programs, civil service reform, law enforcement, public awareness, and the institutions to prevent corruption) to create a "holistic" anticorruption strategy. This approach is summarized in *National Integrity Systems: The TI Sourcebook*, first published in 1995 and now in its second edition. The sourcebook has a companion volume containing over a thousand pages of best-case legislation, codes and standards of conduct, draft conventions, and the like. Now in its ninth language, the sourcebook has been used in several "adaptation workshops" to suit national needs. Drawing on the expertise of national participants from the pillars of the integrity system, local standards and experience are introduced so that the book can serve as a national handbook on integrity.

National Integrity Workshops

An additional instrument that is attracting widespread attention is the holding of "integrity workshops." These workshops draw on all the stakeholders within the integrity system (executive office, public service, investigations, prosecution, judiciary, education, information, and key vulnerable departments such as customs, procurement, revenue collection, and local government), together with coalition partners from outside government (NGOs, religious leaders, the private sector, relevant professional bodies, and others).

Analyzing the existing framework and identifying areas for reform, the working group develops short- , medium-, and long-term goals and assigns responsibilities for follow-up action and reporting back to the working group. Contributions by outsiders are minimal or, where possible, nonexistent. Papers are written by participants, and the whole event is locally planned, driven, and owned. In Tanzania and Uganda, the establishment of the working group and its overall plan have been publicized, and inputs from the wider public have been solicited. All this has taken place with the endorsement of the political leadership. This approach is also being adopted by other organizations as a creative approach (for example, by UNDP and the World Bank).

Raising Public Awareness

TI's primary goal in terms of awareness raising was to crack the taboo that surrounded open discussion of the issue. This clearly had its roots not only in the aberrations caused by the Cold War, but also by a feeling that the North could not discuss corruption without seeming morally superior (as, indeed, many living there thought they were), nor could the South and East without feeling that they were under attack.

The fundamental point had to be made that the leading exporters, say from Europe, given the opportunity, were likely to be just as corrupt as everyone else. Certainly their integrity systems were older and working better, and in most countries corruption was viewed as a high-risk, low-profit undertaking. But the fact remained that their governments actively connived in the corruption of politicians and officials in the South by giving tax deductions for bribery, by refusing to countenance corrupt conduct abroad as constituting criminal conduct, and by providing advice and comfort in corruption matters through the good offices of diplomats stationed in their missions abroad.[53] At the same time, public opinion in the North had to be aroused to the fact that their taxes were going not only to pay for programs of official overseas aid, but also to subsidize the bribery elements in corruptly obtained contracts. This was potentially difficult territory for TI, as it would have been all too easy for efforts in this field to have fueled the anti-aid lobby and to be used as a weapon against the provision of any aid at all to the developing world—which was precisely the opposite of what TI was trying to achieve.

Press coverage since TI was launched has been remarkable, with the TI Corruption Perception Index in particular ensuring that hardly a day passes without reference to the organization in the media somewhere. Indeed, such has been the media profile that TI has been concerned that its appearances (and so expectations) were running well ahead of its reality.

The Corruption Perception Index

TI's most effective public awareness tool by far has been the TI Corruption Perception Index (CPI), published annually with Johann Graf Lambsdorff of Göttingen University since 1995. The TI CPI is a "poll of polls" that captures the perception of thousands of international business leaders, risk analysts, and business journalists on the relative degree of corruption in more than fifty countries. Countries are included in the CPI if they are covered by at least four polls. Their score is averaged on a scale of 0 to 10, where 0 would be an entirely corrupt state and 10 a perfectly "clean" state. In the 1997 CPI, Nigeria (1.76) and Denmark (9.94) ranked as the most and the least corrupt countries. Thomas Lancaster and Gabriella Montinola recommend this index because it is "robust" and "captures more than a single indicator" and "combines several measures of political corruption for each country."[54] There is a widespread recognition that this is perhaps the most useful indicator of corruption we currently have.[55] There are few recent scholarly publications on corruption that do not cite it or use it in some manner.

The impact of the CPI goes well beyond the academic world. It extends, for example, to jokes by taxi drivers in Pakistan. Jeff Stein quotes his Pakistani driver in an article on corruption in Pakistan:

> "You know," asked Ahmad, swerving around a crater that could have swallowed his little taxi, "how Pakistan was No. 2 in the world in corruption?" I said that I'd heard something about it. Pakistan had been ranked second only to Nigeria in a 1996 "global corruption index" by an outfit called Transparency International. "Actually," Ahmad went on, "we were No. 1. But we bribed the Nigerians to take first place."[56]

Shortly after the publication of the 1996 CPI, opposition members of parliament confronted Prime Minister Benazir Bhutto with the results of the survey. She erupted angrily, claiming that hers was the "most honest administration in Pakistan's history." Street demonstrations followed and only days later she was dismissed from office by a president who was reportedly influenced in his decision by Bhutto's response to the index. Bhutto lost the ensuing elections in a landslide, and the evidence of rampant corruption in her administration and her personal and family affairs is considerable.

In Malaysia, the government initially reacted strongly against the index. Prime Minister Mahatir Mohammed called the index another example of Western "cultural imperialism."[57] He added it was now time to set up watchdog agencies to monitor the West and their export of corruption. This was followed by a serious effort to understand the methodology of the index. A delegation of the Malaysian Anti-Corruption Agency was sent to Berlin, where the mechanics and methodology of the index were explained to them.

The government then started an anticorruption campaign, continually pointing to the TI index in its public statements and parliamentary debates as the reason why all Malaysians needed to be mobilized to counter corruption. The government bolstered both the powers and the budget of the Anti-Corruption Agency. The net outcome is that the index is forming the focal point for an official national awareness-raising program and is often referred to in public speeches. This provided an excellent precondition for the future work of the nascent national chapter of TI in the country. Initially viewed with suspicion, TI-Malaysia is now seen as an independent partner in the push to enhance the country's integrity.

The examples from Pakistan and Malaysia are indicative of the influence the CPI can have. The former president of a country is so incensed at the poor results of his country in the index—he claims they have had a negative effect on foreign direct investment and even on aid—that he has threatened to mount a legal action against TI.

Even countries that do not figure in the ranking of the index provide interpretations. In Ecuador, for instance, the absence of the country from the index was taken as a sign that the country is so corrupt that it does not even deserve to be included.[58] In Kenya, the government claimed the country's absence was a bill of clean health for their anticorruption program.[59]

Because of the considerable impact of the Corruption Perception Index, TI is under pressure to improve and expand on its original methodology. At best, however, this survey type can measure two things: trends over time and relative positions vis-à-vis other countries. It does not capture the absolute amount of corruption in any one country, nor does it go much into detail. Also missing from this index is the role of the bribe givers in international trade. The CPI measures perceived levels of corruption in the public sector, but it says nothing about the export behavior of the leading industrialized countries. TI plans to develop a "bribery index" that should capture this behavior in the near future.

National Integrity Surveys

In a number of countries, efforts are under way to do in-depth integrity surveys based on samples of the general population. This approach has the advantage of moving well beyond the one-digit-per-country data of the CPI to provide detailed surveys of all the pillars of the national integrity system that are of much greater use for national reformers, both within and outside government. TI national chapters in Tanzania, Uganda, Bolivia, and Bangladesh have already done surveys of this kind, some of them with support of the World Bank's Economic Development Institute.[60] In the first three countries, the data has fed right into the national integrity workshop consultations between the public administration, the private sector, and civil society. Tanzania and Uganda are already undertaking their second and third national integrity surveys to measure the impact of follow-up activities. Other national chapters are likely to follow. For academics and for multilateral organizations interested in knowing more about the social and economic context of corruption and its reform, this will also provide a unique set of comparative data.

"Big Mac Indices"

Public awareness of the cost and intensity of corruption is now widespread. The taboo has definitely been broken at the multilateral level, where earnest efforts are being made to counter corruption. At a national level, countries where a public debate of corruption cannot or does not take place are becoming rare. Until recently, there were numerous apologists for corruption in Southeast Asia, for example. They argued that corruption in Asia "spurred growth,"[61] but they neglected to predict the economic collapse it could bring with it.[62] Even high-ranking public officials in China now speak of introducing greater transparency and freeing the press as a means of controlling corruption—not just using the death penalty as an ineffective means of dissuasion.[63] At present, the Gulf states are perhaps the last region in which corruption cannot be debated publicly, a symptom of a weak civil society and a general lack of accountability of public officials.[64]

Since public awareness is now so widespread, the incipient new phase is to add the collection of "harder" data to this growing body of opinion polls, thereby prompting concrete administrative reforms. In a pilot study in Argentina by Rafael Di Tella and Luis Moreno Ocampo, an effort is under way to create a data-monitoring and collection process of public procurement costs.[65] This goes beyond a specific measure of corruption in the public administration, but it has the potential of reaping substantial benefits for reform. The aim is to work with data that are (1) not subject to complex technical specification variations; (2) subject to public sector provision in most developing and emerging economies; and (3) procured by the public sector in a decentralized fashion via multiple institutions throughout the country. Generic drugs, such as dextrose, are cases in point, since hospitals throughout the country need to procure them.

Another example is standard school lunches in primary education. In Argentina, this case showed how powerful the collection and dissemination of simple "hard" data can be: a simple check indicated that in the province of Buenos Aires, the average cost paid for a school lunch was the equivalent of U.S.$5. In the province of Mendoza, where a reformist governor was implementing an anticorruption campaign with TI's national chapter, Poder Ciudadano, the unit cost for essentially the same lunch was only 80 cents to the dollar! Within days of such a "discovery," the procurement price for school lunches in Buenos Aires more than halved.

The tremendous benefit of this approach is that it did not have to appeal to cumbersome legal procedures—the reforms could be implemented before putting anyone behind bars, since the policy change would be measured in dollar terms, not by the number of prosecutions. This type of data has the potential of producing an administrative waste index similar to *The Economist*'s annual "Big Mac Index." It is currently being reproduced throughout Latin America and will extend to other TI national chapters by 2000.

Conclusion: The Globalization of Corruption Control

The Spanish sociologist José María Tortosa's book on corruption opens with the observation that to analyze corruption in any one country, one has to understand the world system in which it functions.[66] Corruption is no longer a strictly local issue. In recent years, there does seem to be an international dimension to most cases of grand corruption: the bribe giver might be a transnational corporation; a corrupt politician might seek refuge from prosecution abroad; and, most common of all, the proceeds of corruption can be secreted to numbered accounts in foreign destinations.

Nonetheless, most anticorruption activity and a substantial part of the literature on corruption focus almost exclusively on the use of national measures to control a national or local problem. Transparency International has been part of, and in many instances in the lead of, a move to internationalize the efforts to curb corruption. In our view, this element goes a long way toward explaining TI's relative success in five years of activities.

If we distinguish between national and international corruption (restricting the term *international corruption* to cases where an international company or organization is a party to a corrupt deal either with a public official in a given country or with an international civil servant), and between actions against these forms of corruption that are either national (and in some cases local, e.g., at the level of a province or municipality) or international (and regional) in scope, we may appreciate the international dimension of TI's work. TI combats both international and national corruption, and it does so acting on the international as well as the national level. In Save the Children–UK, a leading development NGO, there has been an ongoing debate in the 1990s to define the purpose and structure of the organization: "[S]hould the agency be operational in the field, a funder of Southern partners, an advocacy and campaigning organization, a think-tank, or all four?"[67] TI, in a way, tries to be all that. If there is a criticism that can be made of TI, it is that it tries to do too much, not too little.

In the end, TI's most significant contribution, however, has been to identify and assert the role of civil society—in a broad sense—as the missing factor in previous efforts to contain corruption (in other words, C in the principal-agent model). By challenging the monopoly previously claimed for governments and international agencies, TI has forced a rethinking on the part of many actors. Overwhelmingly they have come to see the force of the TI position. The coming years will begin to show whether or not TI has provided the means with which to disentangle the Gordian knot of corruption control.

Notes

We wish to express gratitude to Peter Eigen, Zeev Emmerich, Sam Gibson, Joe Githongo, Fritz Heimann, Dani Kaufmann, Valeria Merino-Dirani, George Moody-Stuart, Mark Robinson, and José María Tortosa for their helpful comments and suggestions. The views expressed here remain our own.

1. World Bank, *Sub-Saharan Africa.*
2. Eigen, "Combating Corruption," p. 158.
3. The prohibition against taking political considerations into account in lending decisions was clearly designed to provide protection for countries with one-party state systems of government—monarchies and the like—and to prevent discrimination on constitutional grounds. In our view, it cannot reasonably be read as excluding the Bank from taking into account the likelihood that elites would loot the treasury and distort public decisions, leaving the people of the country to meet the costs. We see their view as substantiated by the Bank's 180-degree U-turn on the issue, and this without any amendment to the charter.
4. Conversations with Peter Eigen.
5. One of the authors, Jeremy Pope, was approached in his then capacity as legal counsel to the Commonwealth secretary-general and director of the Legal and Constitutional Affairs Division of the Commonwealth secretariat.
6. *Washington Post* editorial, "Banning Bribes," 28 November 1997.
7. Pope, "Strengthening the Role of Civil Society," p. 1.
8. The expression *grand corruption* was coined by George Moody-Stuart, originally in "Grand Corruption in Third World Development."

9. Most international mutual legal assistance treaties contain a "political exemption" clause that can be used to block the provision of assistance where it is claimed that a case is being pursued for political reasons. Because a fallen politician in exile is almost invariably not of the political persuasion of those seeking assistance either to extradite the politician or to confiscate assets, the arrangements (designed for more ordinary crimes) were generally ineffective. Allied to this, the insistence on bank secrecy in such havens as Switzerland posed insuperable barriers to investigators seeking to trace assets internationally.

10. Curiously, it was journalists who from the outset criticized TI for adopting the noninvestigative approach it did. However, these critics generally came to understand the legitimacy of the approach, and a number have joined the TI movement. Membership in the TI does not, of course, impose fetters on individual actions.

11. A further indication that the time was becoming ripe for action was the notion circulated in the UNDP's *Human Development Report* of 1992 for the creation of an "Honesty International" to fight corruption.

12. In early 1993, there were only a handful of national NGOs active in this area, but they are now the fourth group in this process. Among the participants from the South at the launch conference were Olusegun Obasanjo, former president of Nigeria; Nobel laureate Oscar Arias from Costa Rica; Festus Mogae, vice-president of Botswana; Ronald MacLean Abaroa, then foreign minister of Bolivia; Alberto Dahik, then vice-president of Ecuador; and former chief justice Enoch Dumbutshena of Zimbabwe, among others. Numerous bilateral and multilateral donors were represented, including Germany, the Netherlands, the UK, and France. The World Bank and UNDP also attended; private sector participation included General Electric and Boeing.

13. One of the few critical reviews of TI is Espinosa's "Corrupción: Una agenda necesaria." He claims (p. 82) that, while there is no doubt that corruption is morally deplorable, one has to be aware that TI is

hija legítima de padre neoliberal y de madre modernizadora tanto porque la transparencia es una condición de credibilidad para el proceso privatizador, para la inversión extranjera y para la ayuda internacional al desarrollo, como porque los neoliberales han hecho de la afinidad y mutua apetencia entre Estado omnipotente y corrupción un eficaz instrumento de propaganda sobre la necesidad de reducir el tamaño del estado.

14. From the "TI Mission Statement," 24 April 1997.
15. Bribery is evidently only one manifestation of corruption.
16. Klitgaard, *Controlling Corruption.*
17. Ibid., p. 73.
18. Schedler, "Credibility."
19. Gordenker and Weiss, "NGO Participation."
20. Biggs and Neame, "Negotiating Room for Manoeuvre," p. 33.
21. *TI Newsletter,* June 1994.
22. Lay, "Einem Stern folgen."
23. Based on conversations with European exporters, in particular with French arms exporters. See also *Le Monde,* 17 March 1995.
24. Becker, "To Root Out Corruption," p. 10.
25. Rose-Ackerman, "The Political Economy of Corruption."
26. Naylor, *Hot Money,* p. 361.
27. Kaufmann, "Corruption: The Facts," p. 17.

28. Ibid.

29. From *The Economist,* cited on the back cover of the paperback edition of *Making Democracy Work.*

30. Tarrow, "Making Social Science Work."

31. World Bank, *Governance.*

32. This process of civil action, of course, continued. For example, during the supreme court hearings of President Pérez, the housewives of Caracas beat their pots and pans every evening in protest because they feared the trial was rigged. And when the *mani pulite* judges in Milan were to have their authority undermined by the very politicians they were investigating, some of the largest demonstrations in Italy's postwar history came to their support.

33. The notion of the "South" and "North" draws on the South Commission's report, *The Challenge to the South.* The "East" refers to the countries of transition in Eastern and Central Europe and the former Soviet Union.

34. The change in climate was timely. For some years there had been strong dissatisfaction on the part of corporate America with the FCPA, and successive administrations had been lobbied to repeal the legislation on the grounds that no one else had such a law and it was imposing a competitive disadvantage on U.S. exporters. To their credit, the Reagan, Bush, and Clinton administrations all resisted this pressure, opting instead for a policy to "export" the FCPA and so level the playing field in that way. Just what the present situation would be had the United States opted to repeal the FCPA is food for thought, particularly for those who consider that the United States has pushed too hard in international forums on this issue.

35. Ironically, in 1997, it emerged that several of the Asian Tigers sustained an economic collapse, induced to a significant degree by corruption. See, for example, *Bangkok Post,* 14 February 1998, p. 3: "Graft Is to Blame for Economic Crisis."

36. By the end of 1997, almost all OAS member countries had signed the anti-corruption convention, and it had been ratified by almost a dozen countries. TI national chapters in the region are lobbying to ensure that the necessary changes in national legislation are implemented and used.

37. In 1990, at the Commonwealth Heads of State meeting in Auckland, an official declaration on the need to curb corruption was also made. It was not followed up by concrete measures, however.

38. *Washington Post,* 28 November 1997; *International Herald Tribune,* 2 December 1997.

39. Langan and Cooksey, *The National Integrity System in Tanzania.*

40. The book, funded by the Ford Foundation, was to all intents and purposes a first attempt by TI to articulate what it was actually trying to do on the ground. Edited by Jeremy Pope, a number of individuals and national chapters assisted in the undertaking, most preeminently TI vice-chair Frank Vogl, and Susan Rose Ackerman of Yale. The text of the book is on the Internet at www.transparency.de.

41. World Bank, *Helping Countries.*

42. A number of former senior World Bank officials, as well as a former director-general for development cooperation of the European Commission, Dieter Frisch; Michael Wiehen, a retired senior World Bank official; and Peter Rooke, a former senior partner of Clifford Chance, all work pro bono, and most full-time.

43. See www.transparency.de.

44. Reflecting a considerable growth in activities and institutional support, TI's budget has increased substantially in four years: in 1995, expenses totaled U.S.\$570,000; in 1996, \$730,000; and in 1997, \$1.1 million. In 1998, the projected budget exceeds \$2.5 million.

45. Gellner, *Conditions of Liberty,* p. 5.

46. A third lesson has subsequently been made. It is all too easy for a national chapter to become a de facto opposition political party or movement. In Zimbabwe, for instance, the leader of the opposition party, former chief justice Enoch Dumbutshena, sought membership in the nascent chapter. The national chapter indicated that they would welcome him as a member provided he could bring with him a member of similar stature from the ruling ZANU-PF Party.

47. "Revised TI Guidelines for National Chapters," 1998.

48. Eigen, "Combating Corruption."

49. Biggs and Neame, "Negotiating Room for Manoeuvre," p. 36.

50. Esman and Uphoff, *Local Organizations,* cited in Putnam, *Making Democracy Work,* p. 90.

51. The notion of the "national integrity system" is now used quite widely, for example, in the World Bank literature on corruption control. The concept is described in detail in Pope, *National Integrity Systems,* and Langseth, "The Role of a National Integrity System."

52. The notion of the "pillars" was coined by Ibrahim Seushi, chair of TI-Tanzania.

53. Moody-Stuart, *Grand Corruption.*

54. Lancaster and Mantinola, "Toward a Methodology."

55. All the leading econometric work on corruption in recent years is based at least in part on the TI index; see, for example, Elliott, *Corruption,* and Wei, "How Taxing Is Corruption."

56. Stein, "In Pakistan, the Corruption Is Lethal."

57. "Mahathir Tells West: 'Don't Tell Us How to Run Our Country,'" *Straits Times,* 5 June 1996.

58. Conversation with Valeria Merino Dirani, managing director of TI-Ecuador.

59. Conversation with Joe Githongo, chair of TI-Kenya.

60. See, for example, TI-Bangladesh's *Survey on Corruption in Bangladesh,* available at www.wordsmith.demon.co.uk/tib.html.

61. Backman, "The Economics of Corruption."

62. Chang, "Reform for the Long Term in South Korea."

63. "China Official Urges Political Reforms," *International Herald Tribune,* 18 February 1998.

64. Saudi Arabia's *Arab News* published a strongly worded editorial, "Survey Mania," against the Corruption Perception Index (2 August 1997):

What do those who publish this survey, a self-appointed watchdog organization called Transparency International, understand by the notion of corruption? It is a hopelessly subjective concept. What might be considered corruption in Denmark and Sweden, or indeed Berlin, might be standard practice in some other countries. The practice of introduction payments is a notoriously difficult one to pin down, and a great deal of hypocrisy surrounds those who try to make political mileage out of it.

65. Di Tella, "Volver a Sarmiento." This section draws on Kaufmann, "On the Transparency International Corruption Index."

66. Tortosa, *Corrupción.*

67. Edwards, "Organizational Learning," p. 242.

Part 5

Central Banks

17

A Brief History of
Central Bank Independence
in Developing Countries

Sylvia Maxfield

C entral bank independence is a relatively new phenomenon in global
history, especially for nonindustrialized countries. Countries ranging
from Eritrea to Malta, France, Kazahkstan, New Zealand, England, and
Chile have recently approved, or have contemplated, new central bank legislation. Between 1990 and 1995, at least thirty countries, spanning five
continents, legislated increases in the statutory independence of their central banks. This represents a rate of increase in central bank independence
many times greater than in any other post–World War II decade.

This brief survey of the current history of central bank independence in
emerging market countries discusses definitions and measurements of central bank autonomy, patterns of twentieth-century central banking in developing countries, recent changes in central bank independence, and debates
over the consequences of central bank independence for growth, distribution, and democracy.

Defining and Measuring Central Bank Independence

Accepting the most common conceptual usage of central bank independence vis-à-vis the executive branch, definitions and indicators still vary
considerably. An important distinction is between independence *from* and
freedom *to*. Analysts separate freedom from the executive branch from the
freedom to choose policy instruments. At its extreme, freedom from the
executive implies the central bank need not comply with stipulations for
monetary policy designed to keep economic outcomes in line with voter
preferences. Another important distinction in the conceptual understanding
of central bank independence is between discretion over the goals of mone-

tary policy and discretion over the tools with which to reach goals set by others. The latter captures the more widely accepted definition of central bank independence: freedom to choose policy instruments with which to conduct policy that accords with directly/indirectly determined electoral mandates for economic policy.

Another issue concerns whether the term *independence* captures the situation of mutual consultation between the monetary and fiscal authority. In particular, fiscal authorities closely consult with many of the central banks thought of as most independent. For example, during much of its history, the Bank of Thailand enjoyed a virtual veto over government fiscal policy.[1] The conceptual distinction here is whether or not the central bank has authority to shape decisions tangential to, but nonetheless affecting, its discretion over the goals or tools of monetary policy.

Quantitative indicators used to measure central bank independence vary widely. Japan's ranking places it anywhere from the bottom to the third quartile, depending on which set of legal independence measures one follows.[2] The standard components of legal independence include some or all of the following categories of statutory stipulations: personnel appointment (most important, proportion of central bank policy board members appointed by the government and length of term); government finance (nature of limits); policy process (specifically relations with government); policy objectives and instruments; mechanisms for resolving bank–executive branch conflict; and extent of constitutional guarantee. Inconsistency in quantitative measures of legal central bank independence stems in part from emphasis on different aspects of central bank legislation, leading scholars to code the same legal texts differently. De jure independence is a questionable proxy for behavioral independence. History is replete with cases of formally independent central banks, like Weimar Germany's Reichsbank, that presided over galloping inflation because politicians demanded it.

Important theoretical findings are implicit in the different results obtained by scholars using different concepts and indicators of central bank independence. Although never complete, law, for example, appears to be a better explanation of behavioral central bank independence in industrialized countries than in nonindustrialized countries.[3]

Paths to Central Banking in Developing Countries

There are two stereotypes about central bank origins. "In every Western setting," writes John Woolley expressing one of these stereotypes, "central banks emerged as a response to needs for a central institution to serve other banks."[4] If this is the predominant reason for the birth of central banking institutions, why would such institutions ever have emerged in developing countries where, in contrast to advanced industrial countries, private financial markets have always been under developed? The typical answer is that central banking institutions in developing countries are born in response to the financial needs of government.[5] In reality, there is more diversity in patterns of central bank founding, although—as these two stereotypes suggest—two key variables shape emerging central banking institutions: the nature of private financial markets and the sources of public finance. In other words, the greater a government's need for financing beyond what private financial markets offer, the less conservative and authoritative the central bank.[6] Financial structures, which often reflect a nation's historical propensity to inflation, create incentives for political leaders to encourage or discourage the emergence of authoritative central banking institutions. Where domestic financial markets are weak, an important source of noninflationary government finance is eliminated. Where governments must print money to finance expenditures, the resulting inflation inhibits development of strong private financial institutions. The nature of early central banking institutions reinforces the existing financial structure and inflation propensity, which in turn reinforces politicians' incentives. Once it is embarked on, it is hard to deviate from the path of inflation, poorly developed domestic financial markets, and large need for central bank financing of government.[7]

Central banking institutions, or their precursors, founded by states seeking to resolve their own fiscal problems, can anticipate a future of bailing out the government and/or weak commercial banks overburdened with increasingly devalued government bills and bonds. The government's financial prospects dictate its willingness to delegate authority to the central bank. Where government deficits relative to revenue are high, government typically seeks a central bank that is subject to close executive direction and unrestrained in its ability to finance the state and other favored actors. This is consistent with Alex Cukierman's hypothesis that the greater a government's financial needs relative to resources and/or the larger its internal debt, the less likely there is to be an independent central bank.[8]

Where government deficits relative to revenue are low, government has less need for a suppliant central bank. There is then greater likelihood that the private financial community will be robust and will take the lead in founding a central bank designed to serve its interests by maintaining overall monetary stability, guaranteeing private bank transactions, and restricting excess competition among private banks. As with politicians, the financial position of private banks shapes their preferences for central bank policy and authority. Private banks that are financially sound are interested in an authoritative, conservative central bank, a suggestion that echoes Cukierman's hypothesis that the more robust private financial markets are, the more likely is central bank independence. For Cukierman, the causal logic behind this correlation is as follows: the more developed private financial markets are, the most costly is inflation; and central bank independence is perceived as a bulwark against inflation.[9] In other words, the more robust private financial markets are, the more private financiers will feel they have to lose if they do not work to establish and/or preserve central bank independence.

The more financially vulnerable banks are, the more they depend on central bank largesse—in the form of loans, regulations, or reduced reserve requirements—to keep them afloat, and the greater their preference for loose monetary policy and state intervention in financial markets. In contrast to a financially autonomous banking sector, a financially dependent banking sector tends to prefer a central bank unrestrained in its ability to print money and subsidize private actors.

Continuity in central bank authority is also reinforced in another way. The financial situation of industrialists and their preferences regarding central bank policy and authority are likely to evolve differently depending on the original circumstances under which the central bank was founded. Where private financial markets are relatively weak, industrialists are likely to rely on government credit. In this case, industrialists have an interest in a central bank that is suppliant to government mandate, and politicians can easily curry favor with industry through direct or indirect provision of subsidized credit. Government inducement of banks to lend according to nonmarket criteria is likely to reinforce weakness of the private banking sector.[10]

Global Trends in Central Bank Independence

The different patterns in central banking among emerging market countries are ending slowly under the weight of international pressures. International economic integration is an increasingly powerful conduit for the spread of central bank independence. More and more emerging market countries have central banks that come closer to the historical model typified by Thailand. The trend toward central bank independence in developing countries has been most pronounced in Europe, but it is also evident in Latin America. Change in Asia and the Pacific has been moderate, and in the Middle East and Africa, it has been minimal.

Need for international financial resources and international creditworthiness has been great in Eastern and Central Europe in the 1990s. In many cases, legal protection for central bank independence was a condition of multilateral financing. New-found nationhood and a strong desire to emulate Western institutions are also behind the trend toward legal protection of central bank independence in the central and eastern parts of Europe. But de jure independence is not de facto independence. In many cases, the demands of concomitant political and economic liberalization still constrain central bank practice. Government leaders face high uncertainty in these fledgling democracies. For many of these leaders, protecting the central bank from the pressure of credit-hungry financiers and industrialists in order to maintain international creditworthiness pales by comparison with the demands of building and maintaining a political mandate to remain in office. These cases, where democracy is barely institutionalized, illustrate the importance of politicians' tenure security in their prioritization of central bank independence.

Five Latin American countries enacted new central bank legislation between 1989 and 1992: Chile, Argentina, Venezuela, Colombia, and Mexico. The departing Pinochet government granted the Banco Nacional de Chile significant new legal authority in December 1989. Pinochet's concern was to protect Chile's economic progress, including international creditworthiness, against the potentially poor judgment of successor governments. Between 1989 and 1992, the Peronist government of Argentina also drew up several plans to give the central bank more independence in handling monetary policy. A 1989 standby agreement with the International Monetary Fund included provisions for increased central bank independence.[11] Congress finally approved a new central bank law in mid-1992.[12]

The new Colombian constitution of 1991 included a commitment to future legislation of increased central bank independence. Congress approved a new central bank statute in December 1992. The Venezuelan government also approved a new central bank statute in December 1992. This statute gave the central bank complete independence in the formulation of monetary policy. In practice, after 1993, government mishandling of the domestic financial sector crisis that broke in 1994 and continued for several years severely compromised Venezuelan central bank autonomy. In May 1993, Mexican president Salinas sent new central bank legislation to the Mexican legislature designed to increase the autonomy of that country's central bank, the Banco de México. The new statute passed into law in December 1993. Even in strongly antiliberal Brazil, the country's constitution, rewritten in the 1980s as part of Brazil's democratic transition, opened the door to unspecified reform of the central bank. Since then, there have been a variety of proposals to increase central bank autonomy.

In Latin America, central bank independence came after considerable progress had already been made in stabilizing inflation and consolidating democracy. From the point of view of official creditors, such as the Inter-American Development Bank, improvement in governance institutions was the second stage in the fight to build healthy economies in the region.

The Impact of Central Bank Independence

Central bank independence (CBI) is politically controversial. U.S. congressional representatives periodically complain that their nation's central bank, the Federal Reserve, is "undemocratic." Academics echo this concern. The current trend toward CBI, John Freeman contends, "is antithetical to popular sovereignty," because independent central banks and the owners of mobile capital they essentially "represent" are usurping national power to "decide the distribution of power and wealth."[13] Central bankers emphatically deny this claim. For example, in an assertion often repeated in other European countries, Carlos Ciampi (of the Bank of Italy) justifies CBI on the grounds that "a sound currency is a cornerstone of just democracy."[14]

Another argument invoked against central bank independence is that it hinders policy coordination with the executive branch. In his popular critique of the U.S. Federal Reserve bank, William Grieder used the analogy of a "car with two drivers."[15] CBI leads to "over-steering," because the fiscal policy driver compensates for anticipated actions of the monetary policy "driver" and vice versa. This could aggravate business cycles. William Clark and his colleagues find that OECD countries with more independent central banks are less prone to political business cycles.[16]

Others argue that central bank independence systematically biases economic policy toward lower inflation and higher unemployment than preferred by the average voter. This is because central bankers are likely to be more conservative than the average voter and are not directly accountable to the electorate. Supporters of CBI argue that it fosters growth.

What does current history tell us about the desirability of CBI in developing countries, as measured by its impact on growth, distribution, and democracy? Empirical research has moved farthest in addressing questions about growth, although almost all the research focuses on industrial countries. Cukierman and his colleagues find a positive effect on growth in developing countries but no effect in industrial countries.[17] My own findings corroborate Cukierman's; for developing countries, the greater the CBI the higher the private investment.

Even if there is some uncertainty over the extent of the contribution of CBI to growth in developing countries, unless there is reason to fear that the impact might be growth-reducing, the potential benefits might well outweigh the costs. The costs are more likely to stem from distributional consequences of CBI and its impact on employment.

One of the problems in evaluating the distributional impact of central bank independence stems from the mixed nature of wage bargaining in most nations. The rationale for CBI is stronger the greater the pressure for employment-motivated inflation in monetary policy as presumably exists with highly unionized work forces. Adding nuance to this debate, Robert Franzese suggests that CBI is of little need in the context of centralized wage-bargaining systems such as Austria's.[18] The more decentralized the wage-bargaining system, the greater the inflation-fighting rationale for central bank independence. These findings suggest that in countries with firm-level wage bargaining (such as Japan), inflation will be lower to the extent the central bank is independent. This argument is hard to extend to non-industrialized countries. Korea has enjoyed relatively low inflation rates under a dependent central bank. But one could hardly imagine effective centralized wage bargaining in such an authoritarian political environment as Korea's has been for most of the post–World War II era. Brazil and Mexico have suffered high inflation under a dependent central bank with a relatively centralized wage-bargaining system, which is supposedly a recipe for good macroeconomic performance.

Clearly the impact of central bank independence on employment in developing countries is an important area for future research. Nonetheless, at the present time, engaging in debate over the employment costs of CBI could well be viewed as an unrecognized luxury for those operating within an industrialized country reference frame. In 1999, the cost of a history of macroeconomic instability in many middle-income industrializing countries greatly outweighs any possible employment benefits from subordinating the central bank. Furthermore, financial expertise is so thin in many of these countries that independent central banks arguably provide a net social benefit simply as a training ground for policy-oriented economists.

Concern over the threat central bank independence may pose to democratic accountability could also be somewhat misplaced in a developing country context.[19] For example, as the 1987–1988 Korean CBI movement illustrates, in an authoritarian political context, central bank independence is more likely to be democracy-enhancing than democracy-detracting. Many also interpret the increased legal independence of the Mexican central bank, legislated in 1993, as a positive contribution to the slow process of political liberalization by reducing the authority of the Mexican presidency, one of the most powerful national presidencies in the world.

Notes

1. Maxfield, "Financial Incentives," pp. 556–589.
2. Bernhard, "Legislatures, Governments, and Bureaucratic Structure," p. 20.
3. Cukierman et al., "Central Bank Independence."
4. Woolley, "Central Banks and Inflation," p. 319.
5. Davies, *Central Banking*.
6. Pointing to the nature of private financial markets and government financial needs echoes a version of "domestic structures" political economy arguments that attribute multifaceted explanatory power to the structure of financial markets. Hall, for example, argues that the likelihood of political leaders adopting Keynesian economic ideas and policies is shaped by "the kind of financial instruments that each state developed to fund its debt, the regulatory regime imposed on the banking sector and the general character of the capital markets" (see Hall, *The Political Power*, p. 380).
7. "Once a financial system is created," Henning writes, "the capacity for

rapid change is severely limited. The developmental state is the prisoner, in all but the long run, of its past decisions on financial structures" (see Henning, "Finance," p. 55).

8. Cukierman et al., "Central Bank Independence," p. 450. Under these circumstances, the government will delegate authority to the central bank only to the extent it perceives the need for credibility in the eyes of potential private creditors who in turn seek central bank authority as a signal of government intentions. See Maxfield, "International Sources of Central Bank Convergence."

9. Cukierman et al., "Central Bank Independence," pp. 449–450.

10. For a more extensive discussion of sources of central bank independence and a comparative study of four contrasting cases (Brazil, Mexico, South Korea, and Thailand), see Maxfield, *Gatekeepers of Growth.*

11. Fidler, "The IMF."

12. Miller, "Constitutional Moments," pp. 1073–1074.

13. Freeman, "Banking on Democracy," p. 14.

14. Quoted by Volcker, "The Independence of Central Banks."

15. Grieder, *Secrets of the Temple.*

16. Clark et al., "Central Rates and Central Banks."

17. Cukierman et al., "Central Bank Independence."

18. Franzese, "Central Bank Independence."

19. McIntyre and Medley, "Democratic Reform of the Fed," pp. 156–162.

18

Misguided Autonomy: Central Bank Independence in the Russian Transition

Juliet Johnson

O ver the past several years, scholars and policymakers have increasingly come to emphasize the importance of creating insulated, independent central banks to safeguard the currency and lead macroeconomic policy during postcommunist transition periods.[1] As Joan Nelson states, "[R]esponsible, ongoing monetary policy is probably best protected by a largely autonomous central bank . . . there is considerable agreement [on this point]."[2] This proposition stems from the view of an independent central bank as one that can restrain government officials from manipulating the economy in pursuit of short-term political goals in defiance of the state's longer-term interests.[3] It receives further support from mainstream economists who argue that, in general, the more independent the central bank, the lower the inflation rate.[4] Therefore, an independent central bank, although undemocratic itself by definition, successfully compensates for one of the major weaknesses of democracy by serving as an "agent of horizontal accountability."

The argument is a compelling one. Radical economic transformation requires a strong state that can implement sometimes unpopular reforms. Democratization demands just the opposite: that the state become more responsive to and representative of the diverse interest groups in society. If an independent central bank can provide economic stability and serve as a scapegoat for painful yet vital economic reforms, the chances for a successful dual transition should intuitively be greater. Western scholars and advisers thus encouraged postcommunist countries to adopt measures to raise the independence level of their central banks, with the expectation that this would lead to anti-inflationary monetary policies.

However, as this chapter demonstrates, Russia's experience in the 1990s did not bear out this thesis.[5] Although the Central Bank of Russia

(CBR) was able to develop a significant degree of freedom from political interference during its early years, its monetary policies at that time were anything but conservative and anti-inflationary. Then, when the CBR's political autonomy began to erode after mid-1993 while its technical capabilities improved, its increasingly monetarist actions began to appear more typical of an "independent" central bank and inflation receded accordingly. An autonomous central bank, it turns out, was no panacea for ensuring stable monetary policy during Russia's dual transition.

Central Bank Independence in Theory and Practice

The advocates of central bank independence would have failed to predict Russia's combination of political autonomy for the central bank with highly inflationary central banking policies, and vice versa, for two principal reasons: their reification of "autonomy" and the limitations of current conceptions of central bank independence.

First, although the CBR had a great deal of political autonomy by 1992, it had also inherited command-economic values and technical capabilities from its Soviet predecessor. These characteristics naturally take much longer to change. For the CBR, this meant that its increasing political autonomy was not matched either by technical competence or by an internal or external consensus on the economic goals that the bank should pursue. Therefore, during the period of time when the Russian executive branch most wanted to carry out macroeconomic reforms, the central bank was both unable and unwilling to cooperate.

Second, the theoretical confusion stems from academic assumptions about the independence of central banks that inadvertently obscure our understanding of the CBR's role in Russian economic policymaking. These assumptions conflate formal and informal political autonomy with the technical capacity for carrying out particular kinds of monetary and regulatory functions. Moreover, they presume that an independent central bank will always have inflation fighting as a primary goal and that central bankers will always care more about restraining inflation than will politicians. These assumptions simply do not hold in the postcommunist context. We must take into account exactly what an "independent" central bank actually has the power and desire to do.

Therefore, traditional definitions of independence must be unpacked and reevaluated in order to understand the policy choices and roles of central banks in transitional postcommunist economies.[6] The key components of central bank independence include formal legal autonomy (the bank's independent legal status), political autonomy (the bank's freedom to set its own goals and to implement its desired policies despite outside pressures), and technical capacity (the bank's practical ability to act on the goals it sets). In doing such an evaluation, it is important to remember that no precise "tipping point" exists beyond which we can say that a particular central bank is definitively politically autonomous or has been captured by outside forces, or is technically incapable or adept. Moreover, no central bank can be completely separate from politics. Scholars across the board acknowledge that central banks need political support in order to maintain their independence and that central banks never act without taking politics into consideration.[7]

The first section of the analysis evaluates the CBR's level of formal legal autonomy, demonstrating both that the CBR has enjoyed a high and rising level of formal legal autonomy and that this kind of autonomy is not particularly indicative of the actual power of a central bank. The next section focuses on the development of the CBR's political autonomy and technical capacity during two discrete periods. The first covers the period from 1992 through mid-1993, exploring the high political autonomy and low technical capacity of the bank and demonstrating the perverse effects that this combination had on two key events during that era: the attempt at shock therapy and the breakup of the ruble zone. The second covers the period from mid-1993 to the present, explaining how the CBR lost much of its political autonomy from the government while gaining in technical capacity, leading to comparatively stable monetary policy in Russia but not to deeper structural economic reform.

Formal Legal Autonomy

Many studies measuring central bank independence focus primarily on the legal protections the central bank enjoys, finding that in developed market economies the extent of the central bank's legal independence correlates well with its political autonomy in practice.[8] The CBR has enjoyed extensive formal legal autonomy since its inception, for reasons rooted in its emergence as a result of the 1990–1991 struggle between the Russian and Soviet governments. This formal autonomy has, moreover, continually been strengthened throughout the transition period; the CBR's formal autonomy today compares favorably with the German Bundesbank (widely considered to be the most independent central bank in the world) on all of the accepted measures of formal legal autonomy.

The CBR's formal autonomy from the government was enshrined in the 1990 RSFSR Law on the Central Bank, enhanced by the 1993 Russian Constitution and confirmed in the 1995 revised Law on the Central Bank, which states that "[t]he Bank of Russia . . . is independent in its activities. Federal organs of state power, organs of state power of the subjects of the Russian Federation, and organs of local self-government do not have the right to interfere in the activities of the Bank of Russia." According to the law, the head of the CBR, who must be nominated by the president and confirmed by parliament, controls the board of the bank and makes many decisions autonomously.

In addition, the CBR has jurisdiction over a wider array of areas than do most other central banks. It completely controlled the exchange rate regime until late 1995, when it introduced a ruble corridor in cooperation with the government. In contrast, most governments reserve control over their country's exchange rate regime for themselves. The CBR decides on emission levels for cash and credit and sets the discount rate. It also regulates commercial bank activities, including some securities operations, and issues and repeals commercial bank licenses. By contrast, many Western central banks (such as those in Switzerland, Chile, and Germany) do not regulate commercial banks at all; this power is reserved for separate banking supervisory institutions.

However, as Sylvia Maxfield points out, in developing countries formal legal autonomy is a poor measure of a central bank's actual behavior.[9] While granting a central bank formal legal autonomy may be a necessary first step in the process of establishing a trusted, competent central bank, it is far from a sufficient condition. Where the court system and the rule of law have not traditionally been strong, where corruption and clientelism reign, and where the entire political and economic framework of a society is undergoing upheaval, autonomy granted on paper provides little comfort to central bankers. Therefore, to understand the CBR's role in the Russian economy during the transition period and the obstacles it faces in the future, we need to evaluate the CBR's political autonomy and technical capacity.

The Era of Autonomy

Before mid-1993, although the CBR lacked many technical capabilities, it regularly exercised its political autonomy in a way that would be impossible for central banks in more developed market economies. Most Western central banks make headlines by adjusting interest rates by fractions of a percentage point. The CBR, in contrast, introduced a new currency without informing the executive or parliament, attempted to save and then inadvertently destroyed the ruble zone, introduced a new and unpopular payments system, cleared the interenterprise debts of thousands of state enterprises, and printed money almost at will. In short, the CBR often formulated and carried out its own policies and, in doing so, demonstrated the capacity to act much more radically than almost any other central bank in the world.

Measuring a central bank's level of political autonomy is, of course, always somewhat problematic because of the unavoidable difficulties inherent in analyzing informal channels of authority. This problem becomes even more severe in transitional economies, where alliances, preferences, and the relative power of actors can change fairly quickly. In addition, because postcommunist economies have only recently created true central banks, many measures of informal autonomy based on time-sensitive data remain unhelpful in these cases. For example, although Maxfield found that the extent of turnover of central bank governors in developing countries during the period 1950–1989 adequately predicted a bank's corresponding level of political autonomy, the seven-year existence of the CBR is too short for this to be a reliable measure.[10] For this reason, my analysis of the CBR's political autonomy relies on a deeper case-specific look at what Maxfield calls "classic indicators of power: the number of instances in which a central bank achieves compliance with its policy preferences from those opposed and, more subtly, the number of instances in which a central bank manages to keep opposing policy options off the policy agenda entirely."[11]

The CBR's high level of political autonomy during 1992 to mid-1993 can thus be demonstrated by examining both the president's and the parliament's continual and vociferous complaints that the CBR ignored their wishes and directives.[12] The CBR's actions in contradiction of the president's wishes, most notably the monetary and credit emissions in July 1992 and the introduction of new ruble notes in 1993, are discussed extensively in the next section. The CBR, though, just as regularly defied the wishes of parliament.[13] For example, from 1990 to 1992, the Russian Supreme Soviet, according to the 1990 Law on the Central Bank, was supposed to confirm members of the CBR's board, but then CBR head Matiukhin ignored this law and appointed them personally without seeking confirmation.[14] A May 1992 Supreme Soviet memorandum criticized Matiukhin for arbitrary, autonomous, and dangerous actions in the areas of monetary and credit policy, clearing, budget operations, and relations with commercial banks.[15]

In 1992, parliament could not get any reports on the CBR's balance sheet or on its monetary and credit principles and complained that "the leadership of the Central Bank of Russia systematically refuses to fulfill the decisions of the Russian Federation Supreme Soviet and its Presidium."[16] In May 1992, experts with the parliament's subcommittee on banking affairs stated, among other criticisms, that "monetary policy, for which the Russian Central Bank is mainly responsible, is in need of serious adjustment."[17] In January 1993, well after the CBR directorship had passed to Viktor Gerashchenko, the same subcommittee experts published an extensive article in the influential journal *Den'gi i kredit* (Money and Banking) again charging that the CBR was accountable to the parliament in name only. Among the CBR's offenses: not providing information on the bank's operations, strategizing and taking decisions without the input of parliament, regularly violating the Law on the Central Bank of Russia, and not allowing the parliament to confirm members of the board of directors.[18] In addition, under Gerashchenko the bank's board did not meet regularly and decisions were often not taken in consultation with the entire board.[19]

This political autonomy becomes a key issue when we realize that at this time Russia's central bankers had very different conceptions of the proper role of a central bank than a typical central banker in an established market economy. Gosbank was designed to disburse centralized credits, and after Russia became independent, the first CBR leaders continued to see this task as vital for shoring up Russia's failing industrial and agricultural enterprises.[20] Moreover, some central bankers, especially in the early years of reform, did not accept the tenets of Western economic theory.[21] They saw, for example, no inherent incompatibility between controlling inflation and supporting enterprises with subsidized credits. Many CBR officials simply did not believe that inflation could be caused by expanding the money supply. As an International Monetary Fund (IMF) official observed, "There was a widespread view, including within the central bank, that inflation in Russia resulted from the high degree of monopolization of the economy."[22]

Gerashchenko, the second, longest-serving, and most influential director of the CBR, particularly supported an active CBR role in enterprise policy and became infamous for claiming that it was "impossible to apply economic theory to Russia."[23] Most fundamental, Gerashchenko saw no necessary connection between monetary emission and inflation. According to Izvestiia, "the Chairman of the Central Bank himself considers credit emission to be the main financial source for the conversion [of military industry to civilian production] and the structural reform of industry."[24] As late as September 1994, Gerashchenko stated that the fall in production and the related catastrophic drop in long-term investment by commercial banks could not be solved by monetary-credit methods and that the government should impose a state investment policy in order to turn it around.[25] These policy preferences that prioritized employment and production over lowering inflation strongly affected the CBR's actions, especially during 1992.

Why did the CBR enjoy this high level of political autonomy from 1992 through mid-1993? Primarily because the CBR was at the nexus of the ongoing duel between Boris Yeltsin and the Russian parliament. In practice, the CBR did not have to answer to or cooperate with the president, parliament, or any other policymaking institution, which heightened the level of tension among these groups. As the CBR's first leader, Georgii Matiukhin, put it: "despite the widely stated suspicion of parliament that I was subordinate to the executive and of the executive that I was subordinate to the parliament . . . the Central Bank was in actuality independent."[26] No coordinating institution to resolve conflicts over high-level macroeconomic policy existed. Although numerous decrees, resolutions, and laws were sent down requiring the creation of such a coordinating body, this did not occur. Indeed, even though the revised Law on the Central Bank passed in April 1995 explicitly required the creation of a National Banking Council, this institution was not formed until 1997.

But more important, the president and the parliament had deeply conflicting ideas about the proper conduct of monetary policy, with the parliament preferring a loose policy and the executive a tight one. Both sides realized that the CBR represented the key to Russian macroeconomic policymaking. As former finance minister Boris Fedorov put it during his own unsuccessful campaign to be named director of the CBR, "If you can control the Central Bank, you can control a dozen other things."[27] Because of its importance, neither president nor parliament could allow the other to gain control over the CBR. For example, the parliament firmly blocked Yegor Gaidar's November 1991 attempt to subordinate the CBR to the executive. This standoff led to a string of initiatives on the part of both president and parliament to enshrine the CBR's institutional independence in law, even as each tried (and usually failed) to undermine the CBR regarding specific policies. This conflictual relationship between the equally powerful president and parliament gave the CBR wide latitude in implementing its own preferred policies in the face of political opposition.

Technical Difficulties

This politically powerful CBR began its life with limited technical capabilities due to its constrained responsibilities under the Soviet system. In its early years, the CBR had little control over the money supply because of the existence of the ruble zone and burgeoning interenterprise debt; it also suffered from poorly trained staff, had few tools of monetary policy, had no choice but to lend money to the government, and suffered under an extremely weak payments system. This section covers the technical problems of the CBR in more detail, making clear that in its early years it would have been all but impossible for even an inflation-averse CBR to prevent the meltdown of Russia's economy.

First, when the USSR broke up at the end of 1991, the CBR found itself saddled with many of the institutional legacies but none of the all-Union power of Gosbank. Suddenly, the CBR faced fourteen other "independent" central banks, all using the ruble as their sole currency. Although their central banks could not print rubles like the CBR (since all of the printing presses were on Russian territory), the banks could and did emit large quantities of ruble credits to local enterprises, dramatically increasing the money supply. For example, in 1992, Ukraine's government issued credits totaling 1.3 trillion rubles, which led to 2,000 percent inflation in Ukraine and adversely affected other states in the ruble zone.[28] A lack of coordination also snarled the payments systems among the former republics, because clearing a transaction required it to be routed through two central banks instead of one. To further complicate matters, the Russian Federation had always subsidized the other republics, and the other republics naturally preferred to continue that arrangement. This transitional legacy put the CBR in a unique position as compared to the postcommunist central banks in Eastern Europe—a position that was not taken into account by Yeltsin's radical reform team in 1992.

Second, as Douglass North notes, "the incentives that are built into the institutional framework play the decisive role in shaping the kinds of skills and knowledge that pay off."[29] The skills that central bankers developed under communism were entirely different from those necessary to function within a market economy. Georgii Matiukhin flatly stated that "the problem of cadres was and remains to this day one of the main problems for the Central Bank of Russia."[30] Former finance minister Boris Fedorov echoed this frustration, saying that "the problem with the Central Bank is that there are practically no central bankers over there."[31] CBR staffers, the great majority of whom were holdovers from the days of Gosbank, were in no way technically prepared to take the leading role in guiding Russia's monetary policy and regulating its commercial banks.

In Soviet times, the poorly paid, lowly regarded Gosbank staffer had little to do besides shuffle papers in fulfillment of orders from above. When Matiukhin's CBR took over the Russian Republic branch of Gosbank in 1990, he noted that only 17.4 percent of the employees had any higher education at all.[32] Central bankers, with only a few exceptions, did not know how they might use different tools of monetary policy to affect the money supply and inflation rate, did not know how commercial banks ought to be licensed and regulated, and did not understand how security markets worked. As a central banker in Riazan admitted, "[P]roblems arise that no one can solve. . . . Our work used to be easier."[33] To make matters worse, as Matiukhin pointed out, "the most qualified specialists began to leave the Central Bank for commercial banks, inasmuch as the commercial banks offered them a significantly higher salary."[34] This left the CBR, especially in Moscow, with an unstable and comparatively inexperienced staff just when the CBR's new responsibilities began to mushroom.

The early 1990s gave Russia's central bankers a painful crash course in financial policymaking and market economics. They had to learn their new roles while on the job, through trial and error. Many took classes at one of the numerous new financial academies that sprouted up around the country or visited banks overseas. As early as 1991, Matiukhin opened a training center in the CBR and sent many of his staffers abroad for training. Nevertheless, such skills take time to accrue, and most central bankers only gradually began to feel comfortable in their positions. In the interim, experimentation and on-the-job training lent a large degree of unpredictability to the CBR's policy decisions, from top-level judgments on credit disbursement to local-level decisions on how to sanction commercial banks for infractions of CBR regulations.

Third, the limited tools of monetary policy in the CBR's arsenal constrained its policy options. The central bank never needed such tools under the command economy, when monetary output, exchange rates, and so on were determined by the government. For example, instead of using the discount window as an expensive source of short-term liquidity for the commercial banking system, the CBR continued the Soviet-era practice of using it as a way of disbursing centralized credit. Directed credits from the CBR or the federal budget still formed about half of all commercial bank loans granted in 1992, and their level remained high through 1994. Moreover, the CBR's discount rate was actually negative in real terms until October 1993. Neither Matiukhin nor Gerashchenko wanted to cut off credits to industry or shock industrialists by raising rates to what would appear to be, in nominal terms, extremely high levels in order to compensate for the 2,500 percent yearly inflation in 1992.[35] As then deputy prime minister Boris Fedorov exclaimed in March 1993, "[Because of the] abyss between [commercial bank rates] and the Central Bank's rates . . . seekers of free credit are flocking to Moscow."[36] Therefore, during this period the banking system continued to act as an allocator of resources, not as a guardian of money.

Another serious problem was the CBR's inability to use the open market to control the money supply, due to the previous lack of instruments such as treasury bills in Russia. The U.S. Federal Reserve, for example, can buy or sell U.S. treasury bills on the secondary markets in order to affect the money supply—a much more effective instrument of control than simply printing (or not printing) money. But, as Stephen Lewarne explains, "One of the underlying rationales for [relying on open market operations] is that people have faith in the government's ability and willingness to honor these contracts. Such a contractual relationship does not exist in the transitional economy."[37] Treasury bill sales require time to prepare, a certain level of economic and political stability to carry out, and a domestic financial sector with the desire and wherewithal to support the market. In Russia, the CBR did not carry out its first, experimental treasury bill (GKO) auction until March 1993.

Fourth, partial CBR financing of the government's budget deficit was unavoidable in the early years of the transition for structural reasons. The government had no other way in which to finance its expenditures. It lost much of its traditional revenue sources through privatization, exchange rate liberalization, and the falling value of private deposits in Sberbank. At the same time, it could not instantaneously develop the tools that market economies use to acquire government revenue, such as tax collection, treasury bill sales, and foreign loans.[38] Russia entered the transition period with no infrastructure for collecting taxes—no equivalent of the IRS, no tax code, and no legal system within which to punish tax offenders. Moreover, Russians, who had never been expected to pay direct taxes and who had become quite adept at getting around officialdom in Soviet times, felt no moral compunction to pay up. Foreign loans were also not an immediate option because of Russia's previous separation from the world economy and the contentious issue of the repayment of debts from the Soviet Union. Until these structural economic reforms were put into place, it would have been impossible to finance the Russian government without funds from the CBR.

Finally, another institutional legacy that proved to be nearly catastrophic for the CBR was the almost complete lack of a payments and clearing system in Russia to handle the financial traffic of the commercial banks.[39] To make matters worse, the persistent Soviet-era separation of rubles into *nalichnye* (cash) and *beznalichnye* (noncash) in effect necessitated two kinds of payments systems. For example, an enterprise that received noncash rubles (i.e., state credits) in the planning process could use these credits to purchase inputs from other state enterprises but could not take this money out of the bank as cash to pay wages or to make purchases from private firms. This dual monetary circuit allowed Gosbank to give so-called soft credit to enterprises with few adverse macroeconomic consequences in the command economy and created a relaxed attitude on all sides toward completing timely payments transfers. The old payments system transferred money from one bank to the next, and "it did not matter in particular to whom the money belonged. It belonged to the state."[40] However, in 1988–1989, cooperatives began to figure out how to turn noncash rubles into cash by purchasing goods from state enterprises (often enterprises affiliated with the cooperatives) for low, noncash payments and then turning around and selling these goods for cash.[41] As inflation began to rise and cash (but not credits) became hard to come by, the CBR came under increasing pressure to streamline the payments system, unify the dual monetary circuit, and expedite the increasing volume of credit transfers.

So on 1 April 1992, in an effort to increase its control over payments transfers, the CBR began to require that all commercial bank payments be processed through the CBR itself. This unpopular move caused incredible backlogs, contributing to the parliament's May 1992 decision to call for a vote of no confidence in CBR chair Georgii Matiukhin and leading to his subsequent resignation.[42] Payments got especially backed up in July and August 1992; former acting CBR director Tatiana Paramonova "remembers with terror" the mountains of sacks filled with different bank payments documents that piled up in the CBR during that time.[43] In a 1993 survey of commercial bankers, 77 percent named the payments system as the problem most in need of immediate resolution for the successful development of the banking system.[44]

Policy Consequences

The political autonomy and technical incapacity of the CBR from 1992 through mid-1993 combined to affect concrete policy outcomes in two significant issue areas, with major consequences for the Russian political and economic transition. I am referring to CBR's actions during Russia's shock therapy attempt in 1992 and during the breakup of the ruble zone in 1993.

The Unpredictable Money Supply

After the failure of the coup, Yeltsin began to advocate Russia's adoption of a kind of radical economic reform known as "shock therapy." Directed by economist Yegor Gaidar and pushed by the IMF and Western economic advisers, this strategy aimed to "shock" the Russian economy into modernity by simultaneously liberalizing prices and trade, eliminating the budget deficit, and rapidly privatizing state enterprises. Shock therapy represented an ill-defined economic program with an explicit political strategy. Yeltsin and Gaidar adopted shock therapy hoping to take advantage of the purported window of opportunity that existed after the failed coup had discredited old Soviet institutions.[45] Yeltsin promised that this decisive blow, although causing some brief economic pain, would tame inflation rapidly and restore the productive power of the Russian economy.[46] After much debate, the Russian parliament granted Yeltsin emergency decree powers for one year to allow him to whip the economy into shape. Accordingly, on 2 January 1992, Russia freed prices and set the wheels of shock therapy into motion.

The results proved to be disastrous, as the shock therapists' utopian plans clashed brutally with the entrenched institutional framework of Russia's economy. Higher-than-expected inflation wiped out people's life savings, cash became scarce, capital flight and the dollarization of the economy both skyrocketed, the ruble's value fell, and the level of mutual debt among enterprises reached billions of rubles. Perhaps worst of all, shock therapy accelerated the long-term decline in economic production, starting with a 25 percent drop by the end of 1992 and continuing to decline each quarter through mid-1996, when it exceeded 50 percent.[47]

The CBR played a pivotal role in the progress of the Russian shock therapy attempt, epitomizing the political and institutional barriers to the success of such a policy at that time. When Yeltsin and Gaidar tried to introduce shock therapy into Russia, they had no choice but to implement their monetary policies through the CBR. The CBR, however, was not willing or able to control cash and credit emissions. The inefficient interbank payments system, the CBR's lack of tools of monetary policy, and the persistence of the credit-hungry ruble zone left the CBR technically unable to control the levels of cash and credit in the economy. Moreover, not only did

Matiukhin and Gerashchenko (the two CBR chairs during this era) disagree with the executive's policy, they had the ability to act on their views. To attempt to deal with the cash shortage, Matiukhin printed money as fast as possible, day and night. He introduced higher-denomination notes, increased the capacity of the printing presses, and did away with the lowly kopek. As for interenterprise debt, Matiukhin and Gaidar had tentatively worked out an agreement for mutual debt offsetting under which net debtors and creditors would have been referred to an Agency for the Settlement of State Enterprises' Debts. Net creditors would have received "shares" in this agency instead of new credits. But when Gerashchenko took over the CBR in July 1992, he unilaterally voided this agreement with his 28 July telegram on canceling debts among state enterprises. The CBR reached the high-water mark of credit release in mid-1992. Supported by the parliament, the CBR used the autonomy it had forged during its struggles with Gosbank to carry out its own preferred monetary policies aimed at supporting production and maintaining the ruble zone.

Shock therapy proved to be impossible to implement in Russia, not because of a lack of political will on the part of Russia's leaders but because it assumed that microlevel economic practices could be changed rapidly by making a few macrolevel economic policy adjustments. With the executive and the CBR working at cross-purposes, Russia had no consistent macroeconomic policy throughout this entire period. Its painful results initiated hostilities between the formerly agreeable president and parliament, later culminating in Yeltsin's forcible dissolution of the same Russian Supreme Soviet that he had previously led.

Razing the Ruble Zone

The breakup of the ruble zone also demonstrates how the CBR's political autonomy and technical incapacity combined to lead to undesirable events for both the executive and the CBR. The CBR preferred to retain the ruble zone because of its traditional view that the union structure provided some economies of scale and because of its desire to recentralize the unionwide banking system under its own control. The Russian government's views were mixed. Although the parliament favored preservation of the ruble zone, as it became clear that the other ruble zone members preferred to move their economic reforms forward at a slower pace, the Yeltsin government increasingly began to regard the ruble zone as an economic liability. The executive and the CBR quickly clashed over this issue, undermining each other's policies.

To keep the ruble zone together, the CBR maintained its high levels of financial support for the other former republics' economies. So, despite numerous presidential decrees that attempted to limit these former republics' access to Russian financing, the CBR managed to find ways to undercut Yeltsin. The CBR continued to give credits to the states of the Confederation of Independent States (CIS) until the Russian government, under pressure from the IMF, shut credits down completely in April 1993. To soften this blow, in 1993, the CBR delivered 1.5 trillion rubles of cash to the former republics, a move that proved to be extremely unpopular in increasingly nationalistic Russia.[48]

The CBR, though, continued its efforts to increase its own control over fiscal flows within the ruble zone. Because of the dual monetary circuit, other central banks had been able to release credits to their own national enterprises without CBR coordination or approval. Therefore, the CBR announced in mid-1992 that in order to import or export within the ruble zone, an enterprise had to be able to pay or receive payment in the noncash ruble of the region. Noncash rubles lent by the central bank of Ukraine, for example, were Ukrainian rubles, with which an enterprise could not buy Russian goods. Naturally, a market in which to trade these ruble credits grew, and the differentials among the rates of exchange began to widen. This effort allowed the CBR, which already controlled the printing presses, to gain the same kind of control over the circulation of noncash rubles.

Meanwhile, some nervous republics had already started to issue parallel currencies. Cash shortages in other republics after Russian reforms began led some to introduce coupons to circulate in parallel with the ruble—in effect printing their own money. In an attempt to force these states to remain in the ruble zone under complete CBR control, the CBR announced in July 1993 that within one week all pre-1993 ruble notes would become invalid. This action took the Russian ministry of finance, the parliament, and President Yeltsin completely by surprise. Rather than negotiating or ceding some authority to the other republics, the CBR played a trump card with which it was very familiar. It was a policy straight out of the Gosbank handbook—administrative, confiscatory, and secretive. Indeed, it explicitly broke the CBR's own agreements with the other former republics that required the CBR to inform them before adopting any currency reforms. The Russian parliament and executive, the former republics, and international organizations all decried the move as illegitimate but were powerless to stop it. All Yeltsin could do was promulgate a decree extending the length of the original three-day exchange period.

Ironically, however, the CBR had misjudged the other republics. It underestimated both the symbolic importance of national currencies to these newly independent governments and their reluctance to accelerate their own economic reform programs to match Russian efforts. Rather than submitting to the will of the CBR, the republics responded by accelerating the introduction of their own currencies. By late 1993, most former Soviet republics had at least begun the process of issuing their own currencies. This solved the technical problem of CBR control over cash and credit emission but in a messy way that pleased no one. Not only did the CBR's refusal to consider the creation of a higher, coordinating authority preclude the establishment of a federal reserve–type system in the former Soviet Union and the preservation of the ruble zone (a system many economists were advocating), but from 1992 until the currency exchange in mid-1993, Russia lost a great deal of its precious currency due to the CBR's back-handed attempts to keep the ruble zone together. Moreover, this unwanted exercise of political autonomy by the CBR convinced Yeltsin and his economic team that something had to be done to bring the uncooperative bank to heel.

The Era of Stabilization

From mid-1993 on, the institutional characteristics of the CBR continued to evolve as the level of its political autonomy receded and its technical capacity rose. Its technical capacity increased because of the destruction of the ruble zone and the drive toward boosting its professional expertise with the help of the IMF. During 1993–1997, the CBR introduced credit auctions (cutting off subsidized credits for enterprises and commercial banks), developed a treasury bill market, improved the payments system, enforced stringent reserve requirements on commercial banks, achieved positive real interest rates, and introduced a "ruble corridor" to stabilize the exchange rate. In addition, the IMF's training programs and Yeltsin's influence began the process of socializing the central bank's staff into accepting more monetarist viewpoints. Although the CBR remained technically challenged in a number of ways, these developments helped the CBR gain greater control over the money supply, control the exchange rate, and reduce monthly inflation to single digits.

At the same time, though, its political autonomy fell due to two primary factors: the increased power of the executive in relation to the parliament, and the influence of the IMF. Importantly, because both of these forces preferred the CBR to restrain its level of cash and credit emission, this decline in the CBR's autonomy in fact led it to adopt more conservative monetary policies. In other words, a less "independent" CBR proved to be a better guardian of the currency. As a result, the CBR brought inflation under control but was left vulnerable to political intervention.

Because much of the CBR's political autonomy had rested on the mutual antagonism of the equally powerful president and parliament, it suffered serious blows during 1993 when Yeltsin used a variety of extralegal measures to put down the cantankerous Supreme Soviet. Yeltsin's bid to increase his power began with the 25 April 1993 referendum, in which people were asked whether or not they trusted the president's economic course. Yeltsin's victory gave him additional leverage in his battle with the parliament and the CBR.

In addition, at the same time, the IMF offered Russia a U.S.$3 billion loan under the new Systemic Transformation Facility, with the condition that the CBR adopt more restrictive monetary policies. Under this pressure from both the IMF and the ministry of finance, in May 1993, the CBR agreed to set up a credit policy committee run jointly by the ministry of finance and the CBR, leading to the introduction of credit ceilings for the CBR in May and the elimination of subsidized credits to enterprises in September. In May 1993, the CBR and the government also signed agreements to limit the CBR interest rate to no less that 7 percent below the interbank rate. Although Gerashchenko would have preferred not to have his autonomy limited in this way, the combination of coinciding pressures from the executive and the IMF forced his hand.

This escalating battle between Yeltsin and the parliament, with Gerashchenko's CBR often in the middle, prompted Yeltsin's fateful decision in September–October 1993 to abolish the Supreme Soviet and indeed the entire network of popularly elected soviets throughout Russia. The subsequent December elections to the new lower house of the Russian parliament, the state Duma, resulted in a triumph for nationalist and communist parties; however, Yeltsin's draft constitution, ratified by referendum at the same time, reserved so much power for the president that the new parliament found it difficult to oppose him effectively. Through the end of the year, interest rates continued to rise and inflation fell.

Although the newly ratified constitution guaranteed the CBR's "independence" from both the executive and the parliament, this victory for Yeltsin in fact transferred much control over monetary policy to the executive branch. While the CBR continued to defy the executive and the IMF at times, particularly through 1994, its days of regular, politically autonomous actions had ended. This was perhaps most tellingly illustrated by the November 1994 dismissal of Viktor Gerashchenko as CBR director after the ruble's value fell 40 percent against the dollar on "Black Tuesday," 13 October (in part due to Gerashchenko's defiant loosening of monetary policy). Although according to Russian law the CBR director's firing was the joint responsibility of the president and parliament, Yeltsin successfully dismissed Gerashchenko without even asking the parliament for its acquiescence. The subsequent appointment of Tatiana Paramonova, who remained only an acting director of the CBR through her year-long tenure due to parliament's refusal to confirm her as director, further eroded the CBR's autonomy.

The overwhelming power of the executive in Russia as compared to the parliament since the dissolution of the Supreme Soviet has made the legal independence of the CBR from the executive questionable in practice. As the primary example, the Communist-dominated parliament overwhelmingly confirmed commercial banker Sergei Dubinin as the new CBR director in November 1995, in part in the hope that his noted economic conservatism would prevent him from aiding Boris Yeltsin financially in the upcoming presidential campaign. However, immediately before the June 1996 presidential elections, Yeltsin forced the CBR to transfer $1 billion to the government to cover his campaign promises. Under severe protest, but preferring to aid Yeltsin rather than contribute to a potential Communist election victory, the CBR relented. Ironically, when I had asked Dubinin just two months earlier whether or not he considered the CBR to be independent, he replied, "We have a very, very strong ruling and supervising capacity. We operate in the political context of my country, but by the law we have two main items as the basis of our independence . . . nobody [alone] can fire the chief of the central bank . . . and no one can ask me or anyone at the central bank to give credit to the government."[49] This move by Yeltsin opened the door for further violations of the CBR's political autonomy in the future, in particular since the CBR backed down on its initial intent of taking the government to court over the matter.

The Complexity of Change

Although we should be cautious about drawing general conclusions from a single case study, three tentative lessons emerge from this exploration of the CBR's institutional development and its effect on the course of the political and economic transition in Russia. First, even a legally and politically autonomous central bank cannot be expected to produce predictable policy preferences and outcomes. Although central bank autonomy can be important in encouraging inflation-dampening macroeconomic policymaking in postcommunist states, autonomy in a postcommunist central bank can also lead to uncoordinated, contradictory monetary policy. In other words, the creation of a politically powerful, unaccountable central bank does not necessarily ameliorate the contradictions inherent in simultaneous democratization and economic reform. In fact, in this case it exacerbated them.

Second, it confirms that granting a postcommunist central bank formal legal autonomy is a necessary but not sufficient condition for insulating the bank from government interference. In fact, the CBR's actual political autonomy declined at the same time that its formal autonomy increased, after the ratification of the constitution. For the central bank to act as an effective "agent of restraint," it needs to have all three aspects of independence in place: formal legal autonomy, political autonomy, and technical capacity.

Third, it paradoxically demonstrates both the importance of structural institutional constraints and of individual central bank directors to central bank policymaking and implementation during a transition period. This should lead us to rethink our theories on central bank independence—both how we define independence and what we can and cannot expect of an "independent" central bank. Given the CBR's continuity of personnel, historical objectives, and technical capabilities, even a politically autonomous CBR could not be expected to internalize and implement new policy goals overnight. The broken economic promises that Yeltsin's reform team made to the Russian public as a result of such expectations bear some responsibility for the procommunist, antimarket backlash that swept Russia after 1993. Instead of narrowly focusing on the issue of autonomy, therefore, we need to be thinking about how institutions created to serve the needs of a command economy can develop the desire and ability to operate according to market principles in a changing, politicized environment.

Notes

1. By "independent" or "autonomous," they primarily refer to formal and informal insulation of the central bank from political pressure from the government (both the executive and legislative branches) or from other societal interest groups (such as credit-hungry industrial lobbies). See, for example, Nelson, "The Politics of Economic Transformation," Sachs and Lipton, "Remaining Steps," Kessides et al., *Financial Reform,* Federal Reserve Bank of Kansas City, *Central Banking Issues,* and Willett et al., *Establishing Monetary Stability.* See also the critical discussion of the growing consensus on the desirability of central bank independence in Bowles and White, "Central Bank Independence."

2. Nelson, "The Politics of Economic Transformation," pp. 441, 460.

3. For example, Nordhaus, "The Political Business Cycle," Williams, "The Political Manipulation," Tufte, *The Political Control,* and Goodman, *Monetary Sovereignty.*

4. Recently, several scholars, most notably Posen, have begun to question the independence/low inflation correlation for developed market economies. See Posen, "Why Central Bank Independence."

5. In the interest of brevity, this chapter focuses only on the CBR's role in conducting monetary policy and thus does not deal with the equally important and intriguing issue of the CBR's regulation of and relationship to Russia's emerging commercial banking sector.

6. While the term *independence* is in itself problematic (since no governmental institution is ever really independent from all of the others), I use it in this chapter and attempt to clarify its meaning because it is the term central bankers themselves use to describe their desired relationship with the government. For works on measuring central bank independence, see Cukierman, *Central Bank Strategy,* Alesina and Summers, "Central Bank Independence," Swinburne and Castello-Branco, "Central Bank Independence," Cukierman, Webb, and Neyapti, "Measuring the Independence," and Toma and Toma, *Central Bankers.*

7. For example, Goodhart, *The Central Bank,* p. 64; and Swinburne and Castello-Branco, "Central Bank Independence," p. 421.

8. For example, Goodman, *Monetary Sovereignty,* p. 9.

9. Maxfield, "Financial Incentives."

10. Ibid. However, for comparison's sake, the CBR emerges from such a calculation with an average level of political autonomy. There have been two official turnovers in CBR directors in Russia since the CBR's inception: Matiukhin to

Gerashchenko in May 1992, and Gerashchenko to Dubinin in 1994–1995. If we count Tatiana Paramonova's stint as acting director from October 1994 through November 1995, there have been three turnovers. Therefore, without Paramonova, the average turnover per year figure is .29; with Paramonova the figure is .43 per year. Maxfield, "Financial Incentives," examines, in part, the exceptionally strong political autonomy of the central banks of Thailand and Mexico, with respective turnover ratios of .21 and .15 per year.

11. Maxfield, "Financial Incentives."

12. For example, Yegorov in *Moscow News,* "Roundtable Discussion," p. 10.

13. For example, Vysman, "The New Banking Legislation."

14. Chugaev, "Central Bank," p. 6.

15. *Nezavisimaia gazeta,* "Explanatory Memorandum."

16. Ibid.

17. Lavrushkin and Mirkin, "Russia's Central Bank."

18. Lavrushkin and Mirkin, "Dolgosrochnaia konseptsiia," p. 6.

19. Chadajo, "Independence," p. 27.

20. Lewarne, "The Russian Central Bank," p. 174.

21. Aslund, *How Russia Became a Market Economy,* p. 220.

22. Hernández-Cata, "Russia and the IMF," p. 20.

23. Quoted in Rosett, "Obstacle to Reform."

24. Irina Demchenko, "Central Bank Chairman."

25. Gerashchenko, "Denezhno-kreditnaia sistema," p. 2, and "Address to the Fourth Annual Congress," pp. 7–8.

26. Matiukhin, *Ya byl glavnim bankirom Rossii,* p. 71.

27. Quoted in Roth, "Fedorov."

28. *The Economist,* "Ukraine," p. 56.

29. North, *Institutions,* p. 78.

30. Matiukhin, *Ya byl glavnim bankirom Rossii,* p. 67.

31. Quoted in Rosett, "Obstacle to Reform."

32. Matiukhin, *Ya byl glavnim bankirom Rossii,* p. 67.

33. Morozova, interview with author.

34. Matiukhin, *Ya byl glavnim bankirom Rossii,* p. 54.

35. Both CBR chairs did continually raise interest rates, however, antagonizing the parliament, commercial banks, and enterprises outraged at the "obscene" rates they were being charged. For example, see Mark Masarskii's comments in *Moscow News,* "Roundtable Discussion," p. 10.

36. Fedorov, "Fedorov Confronts Gerashchenko," p. 14.

37. Lewarne, "Legal Aspects," p. 200.

38. Indeed, 47 percent of government debt in developing countries and 12 percent in developed countries is financed by direct borrowing from central banks because of shallow domestic financial markets (see World Bank, *World Development Report 1997,* p. 62).

39. For the most detailed information available on the development of the Russian payments and clearing system, see Berezina and Krupnov, *Mezhbankovskie raschety.*

40. Vinogradov, in *Moskovskaia pravda,* "Payments Crisis."

41. Mikhail Leontiev noted in May 1992 that "the CBR has in recent times been implementing a policy which hinders the transfer of noncash money into cash. It is always trying to create some kind of barrier with purely fiscal methods. . . . The CBR is today conducting a counter-revolutionary policy. There is an entire industry of cash conversion" (*Nezavisimaia gazeta,* "Former Finance Minister").

42. Conventional wisdom holds that Matiukhin was asked to resign by the

Supreme Soviet because of his unacceptably tight monetary policy, but this was only one of many reasons. In fact, Matiukhin's monetary policies were tight only in comparison to Gerashchenko's. Many of the Supreme Soviet's complaints focused on issues of competence, including the CBR's secrecy, its continual flouting of the Law on the Central Bank, the payments system fiasco, its interference in the work of commercial banks, and late wage payments. See the summary of Supreme Soviet complaints about Matiukhin published in *Nezavisimaia gazeta,* "Explanatory Memorandum," p. 4.

43. Paramonova, Remarks, plenary session.

44. Survey by Cassandra research service. Results reported in the ARB *Informatsionnyi bulletin* 6 (1994).

45. For example, "Price liberalization or exchange rate unification can be decreed overnight. . . . If reformers want to use their political window of opportunity wisely, they should press ahead with those measures that can be promptly executed" (Banerjee et al., *Road Maps,* p. 64).

46. On this point, see Gaidar and Matiukhin, "Memorandum," pp. 4–5. In three separate places, including at the beginning and end of the memorandum, Gaidar and Matiukhin made clear that the success of the program depended on significant external financing from the international community. Although much of the expected support did not materialize, Gaidar and his reform team later blamed institutional constraints rather than the IMF for the failure of shock therapy in Russia.

47. Nelson and Kuzes, *Radical Reform,* p. 26.

48. Illarionov, "What Is the Price."

49. Dubinin, interview.

19

Learning from Failure: The International Financial Institutions as Agencies of Restraint in Africa

PAUL COLLIER

Until the 1990s, Africa had low private investment because the returns on investment in Africa were atypically low.[1] However, several African governments have now implemented considerable economic policy reforms, almost invariably linked to donor conditionality. There is some evidence that the returns on private investment in Africa are now well above the world average.[2] The response of output to policy reform has usually, however, been less than had been hoped. Probably the main reason for this poor response is that private investment has usually remained at low levels despite high returns.

In turn, probably the main reason for low supply response is that African governments are not trusted by investors. Africa is perceived by investment-rating agencies as the riskiest region in the world. The governments that have made the most progress with policy reform tend to be those that, even among African governments, had acquired the worst ratings prior to reform, forcing them to face huge reputational problems.[3] Recent survey evidence of actual and potential foreign investors in Africa shows that risk is the most important deterrent to investment. Among the risks, the single most important one is the fear of policy reversal, followed by fear of social disorder and civil war. There is also econometric evidence that risk as measured by the risk ratings significantly deters private investment.[4]

A government that faces a credibility problem can overcome it through one of two mechanisms: signaling or lock-in. With signaling, a government attempts to reassure investors by revealing its true preferences for reform. The standard approach here is for the government to signal with some action that is so politically costly that only a highly committed government would do it. Here, however, I am going to concentrate on lock-in. With lock-in, a government constructs a system that inhibits it from certain actions, either by the creation of penalties or by divesting itself of authority. This is arguably more important because, if a government can construct an effective way of locking itself into a policy reform, the very act of constructing the mechanism is itself a signal. Lock-in thus works with investors twice over. The institutional arrangement whereby a government locks itself into a policy I term an *agency of restraint*. My diagnosis of the disappointing investment response in Africa's reforming states is that governments have lacked effective agencies of restraint.

To date, the most important policy lock-in arrangement that African governments have used has been the conditionality negotiated with the international financial institutions, ostensibly covering a very wide range of economic policies. The high-risk, low-investment environment in Africa is an indication that this conditionality as it has been practiced for the past decade has failed to establish a credible policy environment. That is, to date, donor conditionality has not constituted an effective agency of restraint. In this chapter I attempt to explain why the conditionality relationship has failed to provide restraint and why it may have exacerbated the credibility problem. My argument is that in order for conditionality to deliver credible restraint, it would have to abandon the other objectives that have been more important to donors to date. African governments have not been alone in facing a problem of living down the past. Most obviously, the formerly communist countries have an even worse legacy to live down. However, in most of these countries, reforming governments were able to exit from history by revolutionary political change. The past was seen as irrelevant to the estimation of future political risks. By contrast, Africa has not had revolutionary political change. A few formerly communist governments, such as China and Vietnam, are in an analogous position, and it is illuminating to see why they have nevertheless faced a less severe credibility problem with investors. There are, I think, two reasons.

First, at least compared with China, potential investors are less knowledgeable about current political circumstances in the typical African country and rely instead for their assessment of policy risk on popular knowledge of major aspects of the country's history and the current events in neighboring countries. For example, in assessing the current risks of investment in Uganda, both the quite distant historical events associated with Amin and the more recent coup d'état in Sierra Leone, on the other side of Africa, would typically be seen as pertinent. They would receive greater weight than analogous events elsewhere—for example, the Cultural Revolution in China or the riots in Jakarta. There is nothing sinister in this; it simply reflects the fact that good information is costly and that the scale of investment in the typical African economy is too small to warrant the expense.

The second reason Africa has a more severe credibility problem than China and Vietnam is the much greater involvement of donors in Africa. By the 1990s, Africa was receiving around 12 percent of GDP in aid inflows, and most of these were at least ostensibly conditioned on some process of policy reform. One of the main themes of this chapter is that this attempt by donors to use aid as an incentive for policy change has considerably worsened the credibility problem African governments now face: investors do not believe that policy change has been internalized by African governments. By contrast, however opaque the political process in China, investors cannot seriously imagine that policy reform has been purchased by the World Bank.

A useful comparison is between the risk upratings of Mauritius since its reforms at the beginning of the 1980s and of Uganda since 1987. Mauritius has improved its *Institutional Investor* rating by 2.5 points per annum, whereas Uganda has achieved an average of only around 1.1 point per annum. One of the many reasons for this is certainly that Mauritius was not contaminated by a "bad neighborhood" effect. Nadeem Haque and his colleagues show that the risk ratings, such as *Institutional Investor*, systematically rate African countries as more risky than is explicable on economic criteria.[5] Further, Mauritius did not reform in response to an aid flow. It did, however, receive important international assistance in reducing risk when it received a guaranteed textile export quota under the Multi-Fibre Agreement. The challenge is to use the international financial institutions (IFIs) to construct for mainland Africa agencies of restraint that can accelerate the process of risk reduction from the rate Uganda has experienced in the past decade. At that rate, it will take Uganda a further twenty-five years to reach the risk ratings currently enjoyed by Mauritius and South Africa, at which level international investment can be attracted in large amounts.

Henceforth, taking as given that Africa currently faces a severe and costly credibility problem, I focus on how its relationship with the international financial institutions can exacerbate or alleviate this problem. I first set out the rationale for a government to lock itself into certain policies. I then ask how a government that wishes to bind itself can do so: how can it construct "agencies of restraint"? I then narrow the focus to donor conditionality, arguing that conditionality has five distinct rationales, one of which is as an agency of restraint, and that not all five are compatible. Finally, I discuss how conditionality might be redesigned to be a more effective agency of restraint and compare it with other options for restraint.

The Rationale for Agencies of Restraint

A government might wish to bind its future actions for a variety of reasons. However, the rationale that is most pertinent for Africa at present is that potential investors do not regard policy reforms as sufficiently credible or political regimes as sufficiently stable to warrant large irreversible investment commitments. Among the policy reversals investors typically fear are the reimposition of exchange controls, the nationalization of businesses, the sudden increase in taxation, and changes in regulations that make it impossible to operate. Potentially, agencies of restraint can reduce the probability of each of these policy reversals. They can also reduce the probability of unconstitutional political change—for example, by safeguarding opportunities for democratic protest. In this chapter, I discuss the use of donor conditionality as a means of reducing the perceived risk of the economic policy reversals that investors fear. However, in principle, there is nothing to stop the same approach from being applied to the safeguarding of democratic freedoms. A government that wished to defend itself against unconstitutional political change might well wish to reassure its opponents that they would have continuing constitutional opportunities for challenging it.

The best-known type of investor fear judged as an analytic problem, though not necessarily the most important fear among potential investors, is the "time consistency" problem. A policy is time inconsistent if, were private agents to act on the belief that it would be maintained, it would then become rational for the government to reverse it. For example, successive governments of Ghana taxed cocoa so heavily that it was not economic to replant cocoa trees. Gradually the trees died and the yield from cocoa taxation dwindled. Eventually, tax receipts were so low that the government lost little by removing the tax in the hope that farmers would replant cocoa and revive production. However, were farmers to replant cocoa on a sufficient scale, the government would face the same decision problem as when it first taxed cocoa. Since cocoa trees last a long time, were farmers to plant, the government would be rational to reimpose the tax. Knowing this, rational farmers will not trust the low-taxation phase to continue and so will not replant cocoa. The government would be better off were it able to bind itself from imposing heavy cocoa taxation.

Whereas in this simple time consistency problem everyone can be made better off by the government binding itself, there is an important variant in which there are some losers. Suppose that donors offer aid in return for policy reform (the aid supposedly to cover "costs of adjustment"). Three types of government will accept this offer. The first, for which it is intended, are those that regard the eventual effects of reform as beneficial but for which these benefits are in themselves insufficient to overcome the short-term costs. Such governments will accept the aid and maintain the reforms. The second type of government would have implemented the reforms even without the aid but accepts the aid as a pure windfall. The third type of government regards even the long-term effects of policy reform as negative. Such governments accept the aid in return for reform but then reverse the reforms once the aid ceases. Investors may not know which type of government has implemented the reforms and hence whether the reforms will persist. Their fear is that the government has preferences of the third type. The first two types of government would be better off were there some mechanism for binding policy, whereas the third type would be worse off: it would either have to forgo the aid or lock itself into the policy it would rather have reversed.

Another fear of investors is that government preferences will change as a result of either a change of government or a change of ministers. Whereas the time consistency problem is about an endogenous change in the choice made by a rational government with a single set of preferences, this kind of fear depends on competition for the control of government between agents with different preferences, the preferences of the current opposition group being such that policy would be reversed. The government would be better off were it able to bind its successor governments or personnel. In this case, there are losers and gainers within the country if the present government is able to bind itself: one set of preferences becomes permanently disregarded. Lock-in mechanisms thus have the potential to frustrate democratic choice. At one extreme, the costs of investor uncertainty are so large that even the group with the preferences for policy reversal may agree that binding would be better because, say, the chances of implementing the policy change are low. At the other extreme, investors may completely discount the policy change, but opposition supporters may attach great symbolic importance to the possibility of policy reversal. Both these views could be found, for example, in the British Labour Party's abolition of "clause 4" of its constitution, which called for widespread nationalization.

In each of the above cases a government committed to policy reform will gain by being able to lock itself into the reforms. However, only in the first case will there be no losers. In the second case, only nongenuine reforming governments will lose. In the third case, lock-in gives the current government the power to perpetuate its policies against the wishes of future governments that might indeed come to power through democratic means.

In all the above cases, lock-in makes reform more credible and so increases its effectiveness. A rational, well-informed government would therefore be more inclined to implement reform were it able to lock into it. That is, for a given set of costs of reform, the benefits would be contingent on credibility so that governments might rationally choose not to reform unless lock-in mechanisms were available. This argument would imply that the provision of lock-in mechanisms would increase the supply of reforms.

However, there is a counterargument: lock-in would inhibit experimental learning. Suppose that governments know that they have little knowledge of the consequences of policy reform. In this case, they may be willing to try the reforms for a period to learn about both the costs and the benefits. However, if the government has to lock into the reforms, it will lose the experimental approach. A risk-averse government will therefore hold off from reform because of fears of locking into costly policies. Although such governments have the option of reforming without using lock-in mechanisms, the very existence of such mechanisms might adversely affect the calculus of costs and benefits for them. By choosing to reform without using a lock-in mechanism, a government would inadvertently transmit to private investors a signal of its lack of commitment to the policy. By revealing this information, the government will attract less investment during reform because the policies are revealed as atypically vulnerable to reversal. An example might be useful here. The government of Zimbabwe embarked on the reform of trade policy during the 1990s. At the conclusion of the Uruguay Round, the government had the opportunity to bind its tariffs through the General Agreement on Tariffs and Trade (GATT). However, trade liberalization was highly controversial within the Zimbabwean government: the government did not know its fiscal effects and whether it would need to raise tariffs in order to meet a fiscal deficit. The government compromised by agreeing to bind its tariffs at the level prevailing on the day the Uruguay Round came into effect but on that day raised all its tariffs to 100 percent, lowering them back to their initial levels on the following day. The government thereby achieved liberalization without lock-in, leaving itself the freedom to raise tariffs should it wish to do so. The price the government paid for this policy flexibility was that its trade liberalization was even less credible than if the GATT binding mechanism had not existed.

Many African governments are probably characterized like that of Zimbabwe: having insufficient information to know whether reform would be wise but being persuadable into an attempt as long as the reforms can readily be reversed. Such behavior has demonstrably low credibility to investors and so will have a low supply response. Further, given that investors infer behavior by reference to experience around the continent, each such reform that is reversed is costly even to those governments that are committed to reform but that lack lock-in mechanisms.

Were lock-in mechanisms readily available, those governments that were convinced of the value of reform would use them. This would make their own reforms more effective but would further reduce the efficacy of reforms without lock-in. The provision of lock-in mechanisms would therefore reduce the attraction of experimental reform and increase the attraction of committed reform. To the extent that experimental reform has been the dominant mode of reform in Africa, the short-term net effect of the introduction of lock-in mechanisms might be to reduce the pace at which reforms were adopted.

However, experiment is not the only way a government that is uncertain about the efficacy of reform can learn. Indeed, given the downward bias in supply response implied by experimental reform, the information governments get from it is biased toward the erroneous inference that the reform was a mistake. The alternative to learning through experiment is learning through observation of similar experiences elsewhere. By increasing the efficacy of committed reform, lock-in mechanisms can accelerate the pace of reform on the continent through a sharper demonstration effect. Because even committed reformers are currently contaminated by the high reversibility of the experimenters, learning through copying ("social learning") is similarly biased downward. Thus, although the provision of effective lock-in mechanisms would reduce experimentation, it might overall increase the pace of reform as a by-product of increasing the efficacy of a given amount of reform.

Restraint Through Penalties

A government that wishes to lock itself into particular policies can sometimes construct an agency of restraint. The simple taxonomy of such agencies is that they can be domestic or external and can work either by means of penalties or by the shedding of authority. To give examples, an independent central bank is a domestic agency of restraint, whereas the World Trade Organisation (WTO) is an external one. Both the North American Free Trade Agreement (NAFTA) and the European Union (EU) are external agencies of restraint on their members, but NAFTA is enforced entirely by penalties, whereas the EU works predominantly by authority shedding. That is, what prevents Mexico from reimposing trade restrictions on the United States is the fear of retaliation from the U.S. Congress, whereas what restrains France from reimposing trade restrictions on Britain is that it has, to a large extent, shed the authority to do so to the European Commission. The euro is a striking case of authority shedding in the field of monetary policy.

Although agencies of restraint are solutions to credibility problems, they may themselves face credibility problems. If an agency is robust and effective, it will eventually establish its credibility by virtue of its record. However, if the agency initially lacks credibility, it will solve the government's policy credibility problem only gradually, by demonstrating that it has removed the reason for the fear of reversal. Further, if the agency works through penalties rather than authority shedding, then the process by which it establishes credibility will be costly, since the penalties are liable to damage the economy as well as the government. Thus, the ideal agency of restraint is one that achieves credibility at its creation or, failing this, that works by authority shedding. Donor conditionality is an external agency of restraint that works through penalties, the penalties being the suspension of aid flows. Its record of having failed to prevent policy reversals means that it now has low credibility. However, much of this was predictable in the design of the institution: that is, donor conditionality was incredible from its inception.

The credibility of a penalty-based agency of restraint depends on it having the incentive to inflict penalties that are sufficiently severe to deter the behavior they are intended to prevent. Donor-inflicted penalties were incredible in three respects: they lacked moral legitimacy, the punishment was excessive relative to the "crime," and the imposition of penalties was not in the financial interest of the donors. I consider these in turn.

Illegitimate Penalties

The infliction of penalties on an offending government must be seen as legitimate by two audiences. The actions of any Western public agency will come under moral scrutiny with the Western electorate and so must be morally defensible in its eyes. Western electorates regard the basic rationale for aid as charitable: Africa receives aid because it is poor. Linking the intrinsically threat-making activity of a penalty-based agency of restraint to a flow of money essentially based on charity is not easy: charity and threats sit uncomfortably together. This problem can be overcome, as I discuss below, but the most effective way would be for the recipient of the threats demonstrably to volunteer for them. Without some transparent moral basis, penalties inflicted by Western agencies on Africa can be made to look rather ugly, so investors can doubt whether they will actually be inflicted for any length of time. The second audience that will judge whether penalties are legitimate is the domestic African electorate. This is because the extent of the penalty to the government will in part depend on whether the government is seen by its own electorate as being to blame. External penalty-based agencies of restraint are at an obvious disadvantage because governments can attempt a populist-nationalist defense. A classic instance of this was the Nigerian debate over structural adjustment in 1986. The focus of the debate became not the overvaluation of the exchange rate, but the involvement of the IFIs. A more recent example is the repudiation of sound fiscal management by President Mugabe of Zimbabwe, which was packaged as a struggle against the intrusive power of the IFIs. Thus, far from reinforcing sensible policies, the involvement of the IFIs can provide populist governments with a defense for their own incompetence. This can only be avoided by an environment in which there is no question but that the government determines policy. A corollary is that for penalties to be credible, the IFIs would need to forsake trying to impose a detailed policy agenda of their own.

Excessive Penalties

The main instruments of conditional lending—the Structural Adjustment Program of the World Bank, the Enhanced Structural Adjustment Facility of the International Monetary Fund (IMF), and the Structural Adjustment Support Programme of the European Commission—have been designed so that release of large tranches depends on the fulfillment of many conditions. Agreements reflected in the Policy Framework Paper (the statement summarizing the IMF–World Bank–government discussions) may typically contain sixty conditions. It is understood that not all of these will be trigger points for the withholding of aid (that is, they do not appear in the Letter of Intent signed by the government), so that many "conditions" are not really conditions at all. However, of those that remain, each is potentially capable of holding up the entire aid flow. This is the problem of the "nuclear deterrent": the only responses available to the donors have been either to forgive breaches of the conditions or to inflict penalties that are often disproportionate to the policy failure. This problem has become more acute as the reform agenda has moved on from "stroke-of-the-pen" reforms, such as devaluations, to those that require a high level of capability in the government administration, such as privatizations. The IFIs risk plunging a country into crisis over some administrative failure.

Costly Penalties

The final credibility problem faced by the IFIs in inflicting penalties is defensive lending. In Africa, one of the main uses of gross aid flows is to repay past debts to the IFIs. An aid cutoff is very likely to trigger a suspension of debt service payments by the government. While the net financial impact on the IFIs may well be the same whether they lend money with which they are repaid or suspend lending and are not repaid, the impact on staff careers is liable to be radically different. People do not build careers in financial institutions on default and a lack of loan disbursements. To give an example, I was working in Kenya in 1990 at the time when a U.S.$100 million World Bank loan for trade liberalization was being processed. As part of the agreement the government had signed, the central bank had ended foreign exchange rationing for imports. While working in the central bank, I realized that it had already reverted to rationing and reported this to the local World Bank office. The response was that I was asked by the locally based officials not to tell Washington, since the loan was about to be approved by the board and the government needed the fast-disbursing money. More generally, as a result of defensive lending, aid flows are likely to signal the attempt to cope with an impending crisis. Dani Rodrik finds that private capital flows actually respond negatively to IMF programs: the programs are more likely to be treated as a signal of a crisis than as a signal of a solution.[6]

Defensive lending is not just a corruption of the original intentions of conditionality; rather it was a central part of its original rationale. Conditionality was introduced by the World Bank in the early 1980s at a time of rapidly deteriorating African terms of trade. Debt service was becoming a problem for many countries. At the time, the only instrument of lending was project aid, and the gross disbursement of project aid was constrained by the complex administrative procedures that governments had to follow (for example, competitive international tendering). The World Bank found itself unable to increase disbursements to countries approaching debt service crises because government bureaucracies could not increase the flow of projects. The invention of Program Lending, which was the vehicle for conditionality, was in part motivated by the ease of disbursement. A government need only sign a document promising specified reforms in order for very large disbursements to be made. The whole paraphernalia of project preparation, competitive tendering, and procurement was thereby avoided. Given the centrality of defensive lending to conditionality, it is not surprising that the penalties have had little credibility with governments.

The Uses of Conditionality

In the previous section I argued that the use of the aid relationship as an agency of restraint is intrinsically problematic. However, the main reason conditionality has failed to date is that it has been overburdened with other objectives.[7] Conditionality has not primarily been used as an agency of restraint, but rather for objectives that are often incompatible with it and sometimes incompatible with each other.

Conditionality as Incentive

The main use of conditionality to date has been not as a restraint but as an incentive for policy change. The conditionality is ex ante in the sense that governments promise to change policies in return for aid. This can be contrasted with a restraint function in which the focus is on the preservation of an existing set of policies. The use of conditionality as an incentive is about policy change, whereas its use for restraint is about policy stability. The technical design of the aid instrument is evolving to make the incentive function of conditionality more explicit. In place of the large adjustment loans conditioned on many requirements for policy change, reforms are now sometimes "priced" piecemeal. This gets round the "nuclear deterrent" problem, but it makes transparent the fact that the reforms are "owned" by the donors: donors are buying reforms at negotiated prices from governments. A revealing instance of it was the response of President Moi of Kenya to donor pressure for improvements in civil rights. Exasperated, he threatened that if the donors did not desist from criticism he would reverse the economic policy reforms. This was only meaningful if all parties understood that the reforms belonged to the donors and not to the government. Such a lack of ownership on the part of governments obviously accentuates the credibility problem. Investors can hardly help but have concluded in Kenya that the reforms were precarious.

The use of conditionality as an incentive for reform generally conflicts with the use of conditionality as an agency of restraint. The former is concerned with inducing policy change, whereas the latter is concerned with preventing it. The former focuses on a wide range of policy details, whereas the latter, to be effective, would focus on the maintenance of a few policies of central concern to investors. The former explicitly places ownership of policy with the donors. The latter depends on the government demonstrating such a high degree of ownership of its key policies that it chooses to create penalties against itself should it alter them. More severely, the former is credibility destroying, whereas the latter is credibility enhancing.

Incentive-based conditionality is credibility destroying because it induces governments to promise more than they are likely to be able to deliver. No Western government would commit itself to a detailed program of sixty policy changes over a two-year period, because there are too many uncertainties and default would burn up valuable political capital. One reason the credibility of African governments is so low is that they have been lured into promising more than they can deliver. Finally, incentive conditionality places African governments in the role of negotiating *against* policy reform. The IFIs will always want a low unit "price" of reform, the governments a high unit "price." They will therefore be inclined to exaggerate the cost of reform. Reforms will tend not to be done on the initiative of the government outside the context of an aid negotiation because they can then not be sold. It is even possible that a government might reverse a reform in order to sell it again later. Lest this seem fanciful, the government of Kenya has sold the same policy reform to the World Bank four times in fifteen years. This could surely only arise due to the conjunction of an IFI desperate for defensive lending, and a government that came to realize that the reversal of reforms was at worst costless and at best could actually increase the future flow of aid. Where governments implement reforms the IFIs are quick to claim the credit. For example, for years (until policy reversal), the World Bank claimed Ghana as *its* success. The only policies African governments are clearly identified as owning are those that are bad.

At present, the only way a government can avoid these negative effects of aid on credibility is by choosing to reform without aid. This is essentially what Vietnam did in the early 1990s and what South Africa is doing now. Vietnam was anomalous because at the time of its reforms, the U.S. Congress was still blocking aid and this prevented the World Bank from lending. As a result, for the first four years of the reforms the government of Vietnam was able to signal that it was reforming from choice rather than as the price for aid receipts. It is now receiving very large inflows of private capital.

Although the predominant use of aid has been as an incentive, it has been remarkably ineffective in inducing sustained policy change. Craig Burnside and David Dollar find that there is no econometric relationship from aid flows to policy change: aid has simply not bought policy improvement despite donor intentions.[8] Less formally, the World Bank's study of adjustment lending in Africa found the same result.[9] Dividing the twenty-three countries in its analysis into a matrix formed by whether aid had increased or decreased and by whether policy had improved or worsened, there was an embarrassing preponderance of observations on the "wrong" diagonal—that is, in the cells "aid increase, policy worsening" and "aid decrease, policy improvement." Thus, using conditionality as an incentive has had an opportunity cost in making it less suitable as an agency of restraint, while not achieving any compensating benefits.

Conditionality as Paternalism

Conditionality has also been used to influence the composition of government spending. I term this *paternalism*. While it is quite understandable that donors should wish to stipulate how their money is spent, the objective conflicts with that of restraint. By constructing an agency of restraint, a government is ceding power over some of its actions to another entity. It will choose to do this only if it is confident that the agency of restraint shares the preferences of the government. The more dissimilar are preferences the more dangerous it is to cede power to the agency. By using conditionality for paternalism, the IFIs signal that they regard their preferences as different from those of the government. Ulysses would not have instructed his crew to tie him to the mast had he suspected the crew of wanting to sail to Bermuda.

Although conditionality has been used for paternalism, like the incentives objective it has been remarkably ineffective. Tarhan Feyziolgu and his colleagues show that aid has been almost completely fungible.[10] With the exception of large transport projects, a dollar of aid is used by the government in the same way as its own unrestricted resources regardless of how it is ostensibly earmarked. Thus, again, using conditionality for paternalism has had an opportunity cost in making it less suitable as an agency of restraint while not achieving any compensating benefits.

Conditionality as Signal

Conditionality can also be used for purposes of rating and selectivity. By rating, I mean the assessment of economic policy performance for use by investors; by selectivity, I mean the criteria by which aid can be allocated between potential recipient countries.

With rating, the disbursement of aid is used as a signal of policy approval by the IFIs to private investors. This is a sensible role, since the

IFIs have far better knowledge of the policy environment than the average investor. Whenever aid is used as an incentive, it will fail to signal the level of the policy environment since it is concerned with purchasing change. Yet the investor is concerned not with whether the policy environment is improving but whether it is satisfactory. Recall that to date IFI flows appear actually to have discouraged private capital flows so that any rating function has been perverse. With selectivity, conditionality is used to direct aid to those environments in which it can be most effective. Burnside and Dollar find that aid is effective in raising the growth rate only in good policy environments. In bad policy environments it actually reduces the growth rate.[11] Hence, if the objective is to maximize the benefits of aid, taking the policy environment as given, aid should be allocated predominantly to countries in which the policy environment is already good. Since in such environments there is the least scope for policy improvement, this conflicts with using aid as an incentive for policy change; but recall that the latter is ineffective.

Used in this way, to target aid on good policy environments, the selectivity and rating objectives of conditionality could be met simultaneously. Since aid flows would be largest in the best policy environments (for a given level of income), the scope for the agency of restraint function would be strongest in such countries. That is, were a government to choose to subject itself to conditionality to maintain key policies, it would be imposing larger penalties on itself the more favorable the policy environment. It would thus be the best African policy environments that became the most credible. The use of conditionality for restraint in conjunction with its use for rating and selectivity would thus tend to accentuate differences within Africa. The best policy environments would be signaled as such by the rating role of conditionality and would gain enhanced credibility through the restraint role. They would also directly receive more money as a result of selectivity.

Conditionality has to date barely been used for selectivity. Burnside and Dollar show that for the bilateral donors there is virtually no relationship from performance to aid disbursements (controlling for the per capita income of the recipient country) and that for the IFIs there is only a weak relationship.

Effective Conditionality

The accentuation of differences in performance implied by a switch to using conditionality for selectivity, rating, and restraint is probably what is currently needed in Africa. To date Africa has lacked star performers, with the exception of Botswana and Mauritius, which are seen as too small and special to benefit the rest of Africa either as role models or through reputational spillover. The IFIs have radically overestimated their own power in attempting to induce reform in very poor policy environments. They have, in effect, ignored domestic politics. A more realistic vision might be that policies are determined by domestic political processes over which the IFIs can have little or no influence. An aid-for-reform package might temporarily disturb the political equilibrium but is unlikely to shift it permanently. Christian Morrisson and his colleagues show econometrically that policy reforms in Africa have tended to be aborted by the protests of urban interests: socially damaging economic controls are locally stable in the face of aid-induced policy perturbations.[12] This is not to argue that Africa is stuck with poor policies. The very experience of economic failure sometimes sets off a learning process, which is probably why Africa's strongest reformers started out with the worst risk ratings. However, it implies that the IFIs should treat the occurrence of policy reform as an exogenous event the credibility of which should be enhanced by their intervention, rather than as endogenous to their own activities.

In the process of attempting to induce reform in a political context in which it was unsustainable, the IFIs have reduced the credibility of reform in the few strong-reforming countries. Investors are unable clearly to distinguish between those governments that are genuinely committed and those that probably think of their actions as a contrivance, quite possibly in collaboration with IFI staff, to facilitate defensive lending. By concentrating their resources on strengthening the finances and the credibility of the strong reformers, the IFIs would be working to a more realistic assessment of their own strength and would be more effective. It is also quite possible that they would indirectly accelerate the pace of reform in those countries in which policies are currently poor. The main mechanism whereby these environments will be improved is probably emulation of neighbors rather than aid incentives. If the new Congo has better policies than the old Zaire, this will owe more to the emulation by Kabila of Museveni than to the inducements of the donor community.

Redesigning Conditionality

In the previous section I argued that conditionality could have multiple objectives but that for some of these objectives there was a trade-off. Using it for incentives and paternalism weakened its scope for use as an agency of restraint. Using it for rating and selectivity was compatible with its use as a restraint. I am therefore advocating a switch from the incentives-paternalism uses of conditionality to the selectivity-ratings-restraint uses. I now turn in more detail to what it would mean to use conditionality as an agency of restraint.

First, as I have already noted, the principle behind an agency of restraint is that it is something a government chooses to do in order to close off options that investors fear but that it does not in fact wish to do. Thus, paradoxically, by imposing on itself a restraint that is nonbinding (in the technical sense that it does not alter the planned behavior of the government), the government relaxes a constraint that is binding—namely, the low level of private investment. An agency of restraint is thus something a government chooses to build for itself.

For conditionality to be genuinely voluntary would require a huge cultural change in the IFIs. At present, the conditions are voluntary only in the sense that the government signs up to the reform program it has negotiated with the IFIs. Usually these programs are largely or even entirely designed by the IFIs. For conditionality to function as an agency of restraint, governments would have to take responsibility for the design of their policies. Further, the aid flow would not be conditioned on promises of policy improvement but on the level that policies had already attained. The donors would then unconditionally commit a flow of resources deemed appropriate for the present level of policy, over a horizon of perhaps two years. Only at this stage—that is, once the aid flow was determined—would voluntary conditionality enter as an option. The government would have the opportunity to make all or part of the flow of resources conditional on the maintenance of some policies, depending on where it felt it had a credibility problem. A shrewd government would survey potential investors to identify where its credibility was most in doubt. However, were a government to decide not to construct conditionality-based restraints, this would not affect the aid flow. Only with such a design would the conditionality be genuinely voluntary so that penalties would have credibility. If a government breached its own conditions, there would be a powerful moral case for the IFIs to implement the sanctions. The moral case would not be that the government had offended the IFIs by breaking its promises to them, but that without the infliction of penalties the commitment mechanism would itself lose its credibility and therefore its effectiveness for other governments.

The IFIs would have a right to refuse to accept proposed conditionalities, and it is important that this right should be exercised. The IFIs should refuse two types of conditionality. The first are those in which the government proposed penalties that were likely to be too severe for the donor to implement. The second are those by which the government proposed to bind the hands of a successor over a domain of policy that was domestically highly controversial and distributionally sensitive. For example, no government should be able to bind its successor with respect to income tax rates without the agreement of the opposition party. Democracy requires the periodic ability of electorates to change policies, and so lock-in commitments must be scrutinized for their compatibility with the democratic process.

There would need to be some coordination of IFI aid flows with bilateral aid flows. If the bilaterals were thought likely to offset penalties, then the conditionality would lose credibility. Conditionality so redesigned need not have a particularly long life to be useful. The reforming African governments are currently in the difficult position of having very limited options for policy lock-in. Any domestic agencies of restraint they construct will have little credibility until they prove themselves. They will thus not be able to provide a fast track to greater credibility and higher private investment. Eventually, African governments will, like other governments, rely for credibility on a mixture of reputation based on past performance, and domestic and external restraints, but in the phase in which credibility building is most crucial, they will need to rely largely on external restraints. The range of options among such restraints is not considerable. African governments have been very slow to use the commitment mechanisms available through the WTO. It is notable that a shrewd government such as that of China places a higher priority on gaining and using WTO membership. However, even if used, these commitment mechanisms are weak because the penalties for breaches of agreements are modest. The main reason member countries do not breach WTO conditions is that it would damage their reputations. However, if a government starts with a poor reputation, this holds little threat.

A final option is to link aid conditionality with the reciprocal policy threat structure of customs unions and free trade areas such as NAFTA and the EU. One opportunity is the renegotiation of the Lomé agreement.[13] Lomé V could offer an option of reciprocal freeing of trade between the EU and an African country (or regional group), and the agreement could be reinforced by making the aid flow that is one part of Lomé conditional on the maintenance of the agreement. An African country could thus lock into a commitment to free trade with Europe with penalties of loss of market access and loss of aid. A similar arrangement might be made between Africa and the United States.

Conclusion

Reforming African governments face a credibility problem of unusual severity. At present this is an important constraint on African growth because of its deterrent effect on private investment. African governments are not unique in facing this problem, but they have atypically few options for overcoming it. For example, the Labour government of Britain, which came to power in 1997 after eighteen years of opposition, was well aware that it would face a credibility problem in fiscal and monetary management. It needed commitment mechanisms. It solved the fiscal problem by making a high-profile electoral commitment not to raise income tax rates and to maintain the spending ceilings set by the previous government. The monetary problem was not so easily solved by an electoral commitment because monetary policy is intrinsically complex. The new government therefore chose to create an agency of restraint by shedding authority over the setting of interest rates to an independent central bank. This was sufficiently credible to cause the largest one-day increase in the price of government bonds in postwar history. Both of these commitment mechanisms were domestic. African governments currently lack this option because of their history of subverting national institutions and ignoring their electorates. Some African governments will gradually live down this reputation and thereby create for themselves the option of building domestic agencies of restraint. However, the need to reassure private investors is pressing, and so governments that wish to tackle this problem must depend on those agencies of restraint that would command instant credibility. These are likely to be largely external.

To date, the IFIs have been the agency of restraint in Africa. The very poor risk ratings for Africa indicate how badly they have fulfilled this role. To an extent, this was inevitable. Agencies based on the motivation of charity and established by Western, often former colonial, powers are intrinsically incredible as penalty-inflicting enforcers of commitments. African governments should therefore seek to participate in the external agencies of restraint that Western governments have created for their own use, notably the WTO, the EU, and NAFTA. However, IFI conditionality could be far more effective as a commitment mechanism than it has been to date. It has been flawed because the provision of a restraint mechanism has not been the main priority of donors. Conditionality has been used for other purposes, most notably as an incentive for reform, which have undermined the effectiveness as an agency of restraint that conditionality might have had. The use of conditionality for restraint has been undermined by a lack of moral legitimacy, by the failure to match the scale of penalties to the magnitude of breaches of conditions, and by the need for defensive lending. By far the most difficult of these three problems is the lack of the moral legitimacy essential for an effective agency of restraint. I have suggested that this can be rectified only by conditionality becoming truly voluntary and delinked from aid allocations. It should become a strategy that a shrewd government chooses to adopt in a few specific policy areas of the greatest importance for investors: typically, exchange rate convertibility, the avoidance of large fiscal deficits, the avoidance of high corporate tax rates, and the avoidance of nationalization.

The problem of "making the punishment fit the crime" can be resolved by breaking up the reform packages: each commitment to the maintenance of a specific policy would carry an aid penalty the IFIs felt able to inflict. The IFIs are indeed adopting this strategy of breaking up the reform packages. However, when the agreements are about the purchase of future reform rather than the locking-in of existing policies, the strategy accentuates the ownership problem: policies come to be sold piecemeal to the donors.

The problem of defensive lending is linked to the debt overhang. If debt service becomes too large, aid reductions trigger default. The aid relationship then becomes a source of risk for investors rather than a source of reassurance. Partial debt forgiveness should therefore be part of the selectivity exercise. Only when debts are manageable are aid penalties credible.

So redesigned, conditionality would provide selectivity, rating, and restraint instead of attempting to induce reform in the context of paternalistic interventions on budgetary composition, which has been its rationale to date. The selectivity-rating-restraint model would enable the few African governments that are currently serious about accelerating economic growth to alleviate their severe credibility problems. Were this to raise the growth rate of four or five African countries to the 8–10 percent range, it would transform perceptions of the continent and provide role models for other governments.

Notes

1. Collier and Gunning, "Explaining African Economic Performance."
2. Bhattacharya et al., "Private Capital Flows."
3. Collier and Pattillo, *Risk and Agencies of Restraint.*
4. Jaspersen et al., "Effects of Risk on Private Investment."
5. Haque et al., "Creditworthiness Ratings."
6. Rodrik, "Multilateral Lending."
7. For a fuller discussion of the rationales for conditionality, see Collier et al., "Redesigning Conditionality."
8. Burnside and Dollar, "Aid, Policies and Growth."
9. World Bank, *Adjustment in Africa.*
10. Feyzioglu et al., "Foreign Aid's Impact on Public Spending."
11. Burnside and Dollar, "Aid, Policies and Growth."
12. Morrisson et al., "Adjustment Programs."
13. Collier et al., "The Future of Lomé."

Part 6

Conclusion

20

Restraining the State: Conflicts and Agents of Accountability

ANDREAS SCHEDLER

D oes every book have the conclusion it deserves? No, definitely not. While this book invites an extensive analytical synthesis that would take up a wide array of theoretical issues, its concluding chapter faithfully obeys the message it wants to bring across to the democratic state official: practice self-discipline—which in this case does not imply a restraint on power, but one on thematic breadth. This chapter limits itself to two specific issues: the question of conflict versus consensus and the identification of relevant actors in the construction of institutional accountability.

Conflictive Accountability

Some institutions are public goods. They are coordination devices that resolve collective action problems. Their absence hurts everybody, while their creation benefits everybody. By contrast, other institutions look more like private goods. They are instruments of power that resolve distributive struggles. Some people favor and others oppose their emergence, and once in place, some win and others lose from their existence. At the current point of debate, drawing this analytic distinction—between institutions that generate collective benefits versus institutions as sources of privilege and discrimination—makes no headlines anymore. It has long been acknowledged that some social choice variants of the "new institutionalism" in political science have tended to privilege the former perspective while basically ignoring the latter.[1] However, the relevant question here is: how should we classify institutions of accountability? And which perspective should we adopt when we study their genesis?[2]

One possible (even if counterintuitive) answer is: we should treat them as collective goods, since both "sovereigns" and "subjects" share a common interest in their establishment. Some historical neoinstitutional studies that reconstruct the emergence of secure property rights in Western Europe adopt this perspective.[3] For example, Avner Greif, Paul Milgrom, and Barry Weingast explain the rise of merchant guilds in late medieval Europe by their capacity to act as "countervailing powers" to potentially confiscatory and predatory states and thus to enable trade to expand "to the benefit of merchants and rulers alike."[4] Similarly, Douglass North and Barry Weingast describe the new balance of power and the innovative constitutional design brought about by the Glorious Revolution in seventeenth-century England as institutional transformations that introduced "credible restrictions on the state's ability to manipulate economic rules," thus "making possible economic growth and political freedom."[5]

In empirical terms, the key question here is whether governments benefit from the institutionalization of political accountability the same way they do from the institutionalization of economic rights. The latter restrains the state's access to societal resources in the short run, but it sets the basis for prosperity and thus augments the taxable base in the long run. The former lays restrictions on the arbitrary exercise of power as well, but the long-run compensations it provides are much less transparent. "Any government wants to be free," after all, and its "desire to be as unconstrained as possible is a constant fact of politics."[6] Who is eager to respond to nasty questions in public? Who yearns for punishment for misbehavior? Governments usually do not. They understand that institutions of accountability limit their freedom of action and that they contain the potential to bring them into painful and embarrassing situations. So why should they be interested in establishing them?

In liberal democracies, the most plausible answer derives from the "electoral connection": rulers develop an interest in binding themselves through institutional mechanisms of accountability if voters punish them at the polls should they fail to do so. In the language of this book: horizontal and vertical accountability are interconnected. Governments may discover the beauties of horizontal accountability if voters open their eyes through the effective exercise of electoral accountability.

This sounds entirely plausible. We should note, however, that the linkage between electoral and horizontal accountability does not work automatically. To be effective it presupposes a series of restrictive conditions. First, voters have to value retrospective over prospective voting, and in their evaluations of past performance, they must give priority to institutional issues rather than to policy issues, valence issues, character issues, or party labels. Second, the incumbent party must be neither a dominant party (which is unlikely to lose an election) nor a pivotal party (which is unlikely to stay outside any possible government coalition).[7] Third, public officials must be in a position to anticipate voters' (potential) assessments; they must perceive their eventual punishment at polls as a credible threat. In brief, voters must be both able and willing, and able to signal their willingness, to "throw the rascals out" of unaccountable office.[8]

If and only if these three demanding conditions hold, we can conceptualize institutions of horizontal accountability as public goods, valued by officeholders as much as by citizens. But even if these conditions hold (which will never fully be the case, given the irrepressible margins of uncertainty that characterize popular elections), they do not add up to a sufficient explanation of eventual institutional reform initiatives. The reason resides in the possible gap between politicians' "best interest" and their actual courses of action. As we all know, neither collective interests nor enlightened self-interests are "self-enforcing" in the sense that "rational" utility-maximizing actors would always follow their wise advice. Officeholders may depend on their electorate (in the medium term) and be aware of their dependence. Still they may prefer to put their reelection at risk and pursue conflicting goals, be they of a short-term or a long-term nature, rather than consent to mechanisms of accountability that compress their margins of maneuver. If politicians can win elections only if they promise to tie their hands afterwards, they may well choose to either avoid such a promise beforehand or break it afterwards.[9] They may be deaf, or feign deafness, to the voice of reason even with citizens shouting themselves hoarse.

We should emphasize that the same "rationality gap" may open as well in situations where the expected societal benefits of institutional reform and rulers' long-term self-interests are much easier to grasp for everyone, such as in the process of institutionalizing secure property rights. For instance, the "control of coercive power by the state for social ends" in England's Glorious Revolution "did not arise naturally," of course, but was the (contingent) outcome of bitter, bloody struggles.[10] Again, good reasons for governmental self-restraint do not translate mechanically into good agencies of restraint. In sum, imposing institutional restraints on the state represents in most cases a "power game" rather than a "coordination game"; it is a conflict-ridden enterprise rather than some smooth and voluntary affair. Public officials are likely to resent the (immediate and enduring) costs and restrictions that effective accountability implies. And in the absence of salient public controversies, they are unlikely to anticipate significant electoral benefits from subjecting themselves to regular accountability; or the other way round, they are unlikely to fear the electoral costs of unaccountable decisionmaking.

The Binary Structure of Conflict

As a rule, agencies of accountability are not the product of lone institutional designers. Quite to the contrary, constructing them tends to involve a plethora of actors: governments, state officials, legislators, judges, journalists, citizens, interest groups, public interest organizations, international financial organizations, and so forth. For analytical as well as empirical reasons, however, it makes sense to simplify the picture and describe processes of accountability building as "two-person games"—as strategic interactions between two sets of antagonistic actors, who we may term "conservatives," on the one hand, and "agents of change," on the other.[11]

As conventional wisdom tells us, the study of institutional change represents an underexplored field of the "new institutionalism" in political science. According to a recurrent complaint in the literature, the new institutionalism in social sciences has provided us with rich accounts and understandings of institutional consequences, of institutions as independent variables. Neoinstitutional scholars have developed fairly reasonable understandings of the effects different institutional arrangements show. However, by comparison, they have apparently neglected the study of institutional creation and change.[12] This affirmation is true and is not true. It gives a fair portrait of the neoinstitutional literature in the narrow sense of "self-conscious" neoinstitutionalism.[13] But it overlooks that in many fields of research, political scientists have studied processes of institutional foundation and reform, and extensively so, even if they have not necessarily attached the fashionable label of "institutionalism" to their work.

If we draw on this wider literature, we can see that, in fact, reconstructing conflicts between reformers and their opponents represents a common procedure in empirical analyses of institutional reform. In numerous fields of research, students of politics have been describing the struggles that bring about (or block) institutional transformations in precisely these binary terms, as conflicts between the promoters of change and the defenders of the status quo. We might even say that the simple guiding distinction between pros and cons constitutes something like the hidden foundations of any "political economy" of institutional reform in the realm of politics. Many strands of inquiry that have been developing with little communication and exchange across their narrow boundaries of subdisciplinary specialization base their analytic narratives of institutional change, at least in an implicit way, on a homologous logic of bipolar conflict.

For instance, the whole literature on democratic transitions, starting from Guillermo O'Donnell and Philippe Schmitter's seminal "Uncertain Conclusions,"[14] can be read as a variation on this theme: the confrontation between democratic opposition versus representatives of the authoritarian ancien régime.[15] Also, recent studies on the political economy of economic reform have focused their attention on the conflict between two groups: liberal reformers on the one side (however termed—orthodox, promarket, free-market, neoliberal, liberalizing, Westernizing, or antistatist) versus opposing groups on the other side (however identified—statist, protectionist, neostructuralist, heterodox, gradualist, conservative, populist, or popular).[16] We can trace the same idea of dichotomous conflict, for example, in studies of judicial reform, electoral reform, state reform, civil service reform, the combat against corruption and clientelism, and the establishment of common property institutions. Everywhere, scholars paint pictures of conflictive interactions between institutional entrepreneurs who promote structural change and vested interests that form (tacit or open) coalitions of resistance.[17]

Most of the contributions to this book bear out the expectation of antagonistic institutional conflict as well. Mexico's long way to democratic elections was paved by repeated rounds of conflict and negotiation between regime and opposition (see Eisenstadt).[18] Ghana's "big leap" from unclean and unfair elections to a working infrastructure of electoral administration was possible only after the bloody postelectoral conflicts in 1992 and the subsequent opposition boycott of legislative activity (see Gyimah-Boadi). The protagonism of international election observers in the management of critical elections derives from their capacity to arbitrate between two antagonistic and distrustful parties (see Pastor). Antagonistic conflict seems to be widespread and frequent, even in the development of independent constitutional courts and in the operation of independent central banks. Today, the former appear as uncontroversial standard components of a "normal" democracy and the latter as necessary ingredients of "sound" economic policies. Nevertheless, the new constitutional courts of East Central Europe have had to assert their independence in open confrontations with recalcitrant governments (see Schwartz). And in Russia, both the presidency and the Duma wanted to see the central bank independent only from the other branch of government, while actually trying to subject it to its own wishes; and the bank could maintain its (injurious) autonomy only as long as the balance of power between the two contending forces allowed it (see Johnson). All this testifies to the general rule, the commonsense assumption: political institutions do not fall from heaven; they have to be conquered against the express will of those who defend the status quo (more often than not, because they benefit from it while they expect to lose in alternative futures).[19]

The Complex Structure of Conflict

If we accept the simple binary structure of conflict as an analytical starting point for the study of institutional change, nothing, of course, obliges us to stay there. We may immediately proceed to complicate the picture as empirical realities demand it. I think, above all, of three necessary complications. First, one may introduce further, internal distinctions into the two groups of actors. For example, the basic conflict between authoritarians and democrats usually forms just a part of the analytic stories students of democratic transitions tell us. More often than not, the "regime bloc" is divided into hard-liners (*duros*) and soft-liners (*blandos*), while the "opposition bloc" is not homogeneous either but contains "moderates" as well as "maximalists."[20] In addition, one may recognize that middle categories may exist in the institutional conflict being played out: the undecided, the indifferent, and the neutral.

Second, one may concede that the boundaries between the two groups are not always clear-cut. It may not always be easy to decide who belongs to which group and this uncertainty of identities is an important part of the game. In principle, it is difficult to discern sincere declarations from lip service, and more often than not actors reveal their "true identities" only ex post, through their actual conduct in office. For instance, the self-confident independence of the new constitutional courts in East Central Europe came as a surprise. At the outset, it was not clear at all whether these fledgling judicial institutions would act as pliant servants of their masters, the national governments, or indeed as impartial interpreters of constitutional norms (see Schwartz).

Third, one may also take into account that actors' membership in the two categories (and any subcategories) is not fixed. Where institutions are fluid, identities are in flux as well. People learn. They may change sides as their convictions change or as their calculus of self-interest makes them jump the bandwagon of anticipated winners. Who would have predicted, for example, that long-serving Chief Justice Francis Nyalali of Tanzania would develop into an active promoter of judicial independence and multiparty democracy? And who would have thought that he would be able to persuade President Julius Nyerere to take the lead in the demise of the one-party state (see Widner)?

Now, where do initiatives to enhance public accountability concretely come from? Where do they originate? Who generates the requisite pressure to institutionalize accountability? Who are, in concrete terms, the political carriers, the reformatory subjects, the agents of change, the heroes of accountability? I briefly review four possible sources of institutional creation and reform: governments (reform from above), civil society (reform from below), staff members (reform from within), and international actors (reform from the outside).

Reform from Above

To begin with, any state organization entitled and empowered to hold other state agencies accountable must be created according to established formal procedures; and it is invariably either the government or the parliament that holds the authority to do that. In games of horizontal accountability, top executives and legislators therefore appear as veto players who have the final say over the establishment, the formal structure, and the resource endowment of accounting agencies. By legal necessity, all paths of institutional creation pass through the offices of top state officials and, in this sense, accountability-promoting reforms cannot come from anywhere else than "from above." There is no way to ignore or bypass the centers of state power. Unless they consent to institutionalize "self-restraint," the road to horizontal accountability is blocked.

The contributions to this book fully reflect this simple fact of political life. In democratic settings, it is the national legislatures (though sometimes dominated by sitting presidents) who either deny or lay the legal foundations for clean and fair elections, independent and impartial courts, effective anticorruption agencies, and autonomous central banks. Yet, in accordance with much of the literature on institutional reform, authors tend to pay scant attention to legislators but rather focus on the role of heads of governments, whose "leadership" and "political will" they deem necessary for public accountability to take hold in effective institutions. Not surprising, the chapters on anticorruption measures contain the most explicit statements in this vein (see Heilbrunn, Quah, and Galtung and Pope).[21]

But why should state officials take the lead and devise mechanisms that constrain their future freedom of action? As argued above, it seems reasonable to expect that state officials will be hesitant at best to lobby actively for the noble cause of horizontal accountability.[22] Nevertheless, several counterweights to the maximization of short-term self-interests exist, several good reasons that may lower policymakers' inclination to either avert or subvert self-binding institutions (and which thus make these institutions "self-enforcing"): electoral accountability (the fear of electoral defeat), the calculus of macroeconomic benefit (the expectation that markets reward the rule of law), a calm consciousness (the conviction that public accountability will just affect the bad guys while revealing one's own goodness), the cross-cutting nature of institutions (the expectation that mechanisms of accountability will hurt political adversaries as well), the intertemporal nature of institutions (the expectation that agencies of accountability will restrain successor governments), the uncertain consequences of institutions (behind a Rawlsian "veil of ignorance" one's own future position in the system may be uncertain),[23] normative arguments (the valuation of public accountability on its own), miscalculation and human error (illusions of domination, false expectations about the subservience of new institutions), or historic accountability (the desire to retain a high personal reputation before history and historical textbooks).

In sum, there are various possible solutions to the puzzle of why decisionmakers should ever agree to tie their hands and subject themselves to annoying procedures of accountability. The book, however, seems to confirm the hypothesis formulated above: if the "electoral nexus" does not work properly and decisionmakers do not develop a tangible self-interest in the institutionalization of accountability, any progress on this front is likely to be fragile and vulnerable to contingent political junctures and political personalities. In this book, Schwartz is most explicit in stating this causal hypothesis: the new constitutional courts in Eastern Europe work as effective checks on power where democratic transitions are complete. In contexts that are still semiauthoritarian, personalist leaders tend to respond to the eventual insubordination of constitutional courts by either repressing or circumventing them, which condemns these institutions to keep a low and nonconfrontational profile.

Reform from Below

The often decisive role of civil society (a term used here to describe a broad ensemble of nonstate actors—citizens, social movements, voluntary associations, and independent media) in triggering, advancing, and completing processes of democratization—that is, their role in the conflictual establishment of vertical (electoral) accountability—has been widely acknowledged in the contemporary literature on democratic transitions.[24] By comparison, the contribution of civil society actors to the conquest of horizontal mechanisms of accountability is less well understood.

As noted above, citizens do not have the capacity (the formal authority) to design and establish agencies of horizontal accountability. As O'Donnell puts it, their "actions have limited effects if properly authorized state agencies do not take them up." Yet scholars as well as policymakers tend to share the assumption that not just leaders matter but people do as well. They tend to assume that popular support for institutional accountability, as well as popular protest against improper behavior in office, represent necessary (even if insufficient) conditions for agencies of horizontal accountability to be both effective and sustainable.

Rational choice institutionalists, for example, part from the idea that in democracies politicians are the driving forces of state reform, while public demands are the driving forces of politicians (who are concerned about reelection and thus about public support).[25] International financial institutions tend to put special emphasis on the need for crafting a comprehensive "national consensus" for state reform to be successful.[26] And the glamorous rediscovery of "civil society" in scholarly debate as well as in "enlightened" political circles expresses, among many other hopes, the expectation that nonstate actors may serve as "a vital instrument for containing the power of democratic governments, checking their potential abuses and violations of the law, and subjecting them to public scrutiny."[27] It expresses, in more general terms, the conviction that "the effectiveness of horizontal accountability is to a significant extent contingent on [democratic forms of] vertical accountability."[28]

Actually, much of the episodic empirical evidence we have at hand tends to support the idea that accountability-enhancing reforms do not come forward without a clear public "demand for reform." Swings in "public opinion" and popular protest campaigns are not always effective, and even if they reach their immediate goals, they often do not leave enduring institutional traces. For example, in the few contemporary instances where Latin American presidents fell victim to impeachment processes— Fernando Collor of Brazil, Carlos Andrés Pérez of Venezuela, and Abdalá Bucaram of Ecuador—(perceived) popular indignation about presidential misbehavior in office was a driving force behind these spectacular moves. Yet, for all their dramatic qualities, these movement-like instances of vertical accountability possibly do not represent more than ephemeral "episodes of accountability," whose institutional consequences are highly indeterminate. However, less visible and dramatic, but instead more modest, patient, and sustained, organizational efforts by civic associations often bear quite reasonable chances of achieving significant long-term institutional change. For example, in the "field reports" published regularly in the *Journal of Democracy,* civil society actors recount their experiences in constructing and sustaining civic associations whose central purpose lies in making the state observe basic rights, such as free and clean elections, the freedom of opinion, women rights, and human rights. As these reports underscore, at least active participants are (and obviously have to be) convinced that their sustained efforts will have over time some discernible positive effects on how states operate.[29]

Of course, the intuition that "civil society matters" cannot be but a starting point for exploring which part of it matters—and when and how.[30] Much of the analysis in this book revolves around elite dynamics. Nevertheless, the book does contain some tentative and somewhat indirect evidence (or at least grounded judgments) about the role of various nonstate actors. All contributions in the field of electoral administration acknowledge the importance of nongovernmental election monitors. O'Donnell and Domingo hint at the weighty presence of nongovernmental organizations that specialize in the defense of human rights. All chapters on judicial systems emphasize the critical role public opinion plays in safeguarding judicial independence, with Widner, reporting on judges' judgments, being the most emphatic about it. All the chapters on combating corruption also make at least passing reference to the importance of political culture at mass level. And both Domingo and Maxfield draw attention to the centrality of business representatives in judicial reform and central bank reform, respectively. This does not exhaust the list of relevant actors, nor can it substitute for further systematic comparative research. Yet it does add some small but valuable pieces to the overall mosaic, to the general picture of the potentialities and limitations that acts and attitudes "below" possess—in support of or in opposition or indifference to reform initiatives "above."

Reform from Within

Sometimes, institutionalizing horizontal accountability implies the creation of new agencies. But more often than not, it involves the reform of existing agencies.[31] In both cases, the internal staff of the agency in question plays a critical role in determining its performance. When organizations are already in place, however, the protagonism of the staff becomes more obvious (and often more deleterious). Top reformers usually cannot effect wholesale exchanges of personnel but must work with whoever may happen to sit in the agencies they target; and those people often do not embrace reform initiatives with much enthusiasm. The literature on structural reform accordingly tends to emphasize the resistance to change on behalf of "rent-seeking and vested interests"[32] within the targeted organizations. It also tends to stress the corresponding necessity of bringing these potential agents of resistance into the reform process. It is widely perceived that, minimally, reformers must have at least the passive assent of staff members, but ideally they should succeed in inciting their active involvement and thus make them feel (in fashionable economic terminology) like responsible "stakeholders" in the reform process.[33] In sum, scholars as well as policymakers tend to look at the "administrators of accountability" primarily as potential obstacles, as counterreformatory "conservative agents" who have to be convinced, converted, or coerced into accepting structural reforms. Accordingly, they tend to overlook their potential role as "agents of change," as promoters of institutional transformation. The theoretical justification for this "conservative bias" derives from key premises of rational choice theory.

On the one hand, the theory does not invariably neglect the role of norms. But *if* it takes norms and ideas into account, it still tends to give the calculus of self-interest a clear primacy, while conceding to norms and ideas a subsidiary place only. In essence, rational choice theory assumes that social norms regulate behavior only when it does not cost very much. As Jon Elster puts it, "ideas matter when . . . interest yields no clear answers."[34] Rational choice theory therefore is ill-equipped to explain the emergence of "moral actors" who struggle for public accountability, even if this endeavor runs against their manifest self-interest (and sometimes even includes direct threats to their lives). The theory is ill-equipped to account for choices made "when the payoffs to honesty, integrity, working hard, or voting are negative"[35]—and, as we may add here, when the payoffs to independent and impartial decisionmaking are negative.[36] But as Sklar reminds us (in this volume), "martyrs and prisoners of conscience" have made their imprint throughout the history of mankind, even if their occurrence may remain much of a dark and awe-inspiring "mystery" (see O'Donnell) to us, something we admire although we may not have a sound explanatory theory at hand. In contemporary politics, for instance, the painful statistics of international human rights organizations testify to the "irrational" courage of so many "heroes of accountability"—party leaders, grassroots activists, journalists, and judges—who have been sacrificing their careers, their health, their freedom, and their lives, in the struggle for democratic constitutionalism—for free, limited, and accountable government.

On the other hand, rational choice theory not only downplays the role of norms but also tends to underrate the weight of personal characteristics. The theory's microeconomic psychology assumes a uniform structure of motivation across all individuals. In its perspective, actors are fungible, interchangeable. They all follow uniform patterns of (unidimensional) rationality. What counts, therefore, is not human agency but the design of incentives. The job is getting the rules right, and that's it.[37] As a consequence, rational choice theory is ill-equipped to explain (other than by reference to differential degrees of information and risk aversion) why some people sometimes decide to alter established patterns of interaction (i.e., institutions) without preceding changes in their structure of incentives having taken place. The theory is ill-equipped to account for any institutional discontinuities that are not incentive-driven. It is ill-equipped to tell us, for instance, when and why "agents of accountability" stop acting as timid puppets tied to the strings of anticipatory obedience; when and why these actors start taking both their official mission and existing formal rules seriously; or when and why they start pushing biased and subservient organizations toward greater autonomy, impartiality, integrity, and professionalism.[38]

So, "moral actors" is just one theoretical puzzle. The other one is "agents of change" who emerge within existing institutions without preceding reforms from above, without any prior changes in formal rules and incentive structures. The Italian "clean hands" (*mani pulite*) campaign of the early 1990s can be regarded as *the* paradigmatic case of such large-scale institutional self-reform through practical changes rather than formal rule changes. Within a few months, a small group of young and telegenic judges, acting on their own and aggressively exploiting both their large formal powers and their secure institutional independence, set up the prevailing "culture of corruption" by putting a significant part of the ruling "political class" into jail (and in the course of that, bringing half of the party system to collapse).[39] After *mani pulite,* I would claim, we cannot think any more about processes of institutional change without seriously considering the possibility of such (seemingly) "spontaneous" reforms "from within," the possibility of internal staff members transforming subservient and corrupt institutions into self-confident, autonomous "agencies of restraint" (see Paul Collier, this volume).

In this book, several contributors stress the importance of taking the "administrators of accountability" seriously, be it as blockers or as promoters of change: Gyimah-Boadi describes the ambivalent role of Ghana's national election commissioners, who have orchestrated significant electoral reforms but still represent salient targets of distrust. Eisenstadt reports on opposition party views in Mexico that personnel holdovers from the authoritarian past are still able to subvert the formal autonomy that state-level electoral tribunals enjoy. Schwartz, in his recount of institutional success and failure of Eastern Europe's new constitutional courts, attributes considerable explanatory weight to variables such as fear versus courage on behalf of constitutional court members. Domingo warns about the potential resistance to judicial reform by sitting judges, but she also points to the increasingly active role judges are assuming in asserting judicial independence against executive encroachment. Widner argues that, in the African context, it is not outside pressure that explains judicial reform initiatives. It is neither presidents, nor legislators, nor businesspeople, nor international donors who account for judicial reforms. Rather, it is the judges themselves who "often play central roles in initiating bids for greater independence." Then, while the authors of the chapters on corruption control and on central banks tend to emphasize the need for "political will" at the commanding heights of the state, Johnson, for example, highlights the crucial role of the Bank of Russia's internal personnel: its ideological outlook, its (lack of) technical expertise, but also the personal aversions and ambitions of its chairpersons.

Reform from Outside

This book examines four institutional fields: electoral administration and dispute adjudication; judicial systems and constitutional courts; anticorruption agencies; and central banks. In all these fields, national advocates of public accountability are not "alone" anymore. Over the last decade or so, a myriad of international actors have arisen, some of them governmental but many not, who add pressure to national concerns about limited as well as accountable government. In all four fields, national sovereignty has been redefined, and the traditional *omertà*—the law of silence, of noninterference into internal affairs—does not hold anymore (see also Pastor).[40]

In the realm of electoral administration, it has become difficult to keep track of a dense scene populated by governmental as well as nongovernmental actors—some of them permanent, others fleeting, some of them professional, others improvising—who are dedicated to promoting democracy, among other things, by providing services of electoral assistance and monitoring.[41] With regard to the rule of law, international human rights associations and international financial agencies have discovered overlapping (though not converging) preoccupations. The former are primarily concerned with social and political rights (penal law), while the latter first worry about property rights (civil law). But even if their emphases differ, both groups of actors share a strong general interest in promoting judicial reform in new democracies.[42]

In the combat against corruption, too, the emergence of national actors has been paralleled by growing concerns about "good government" on behalf of international organizations as well as by the appearance of new international NGOs—above all, the Berlin-based nongovernmental Transparency International (reviewed by Galtung and Pope). In the field of central banking, several international factors intensify the worldwide push toward independent central banks: for instance, the global neoliberal zeitgeist in favor of central bank independence; the transnationalization of capital markets, which sets national governments under pressure to emulate the one and only organizational model that inspires investor confidence; the aggressive policies the World Bank and the International Monetary Fund pursue in favor of autonomous central banks; and new demanding standards for central bank autonomy set by the European Union for its member states as it moved toward the common European Central Bank (and which serve as institutional yardsticks for Eastern European countries).[43]

A whole new set of international push factors (or should we better say, push actors?) are thus in place and ready to move. But do they actually move anything? And, if yes, what do they move and under what conditions? The three chapters in this book that focus on international forces provide substantial insights into this. Pastor describes the multiple challenges international election monitors confront: becoming familiar with national conditions; getting admitted to observing and mediating critical elections; building trust and a reputation for impartiality among all parties; meeting the technical and financial requirements of professional election monitoring; and delivering comprehensive and unbiased reports about the quality of the electoral process in question.

Galtung and Pope analyze the nonpartisan and nonconfrontational strategy Transparency International (TI) pursues in order to make an impact on national corruption. Rather than a powerful pressure group, this transnational NGO projects itself as a self-restrained forum for communication and coalition building. Most of its basic instruments—the national chapters, the national integrity workshops, the integrity surveys, the integrity pacts, and the administrative waste indices—give evidence for the importance the organization attributes to its national counterparts and their creative capacity to identify problems and devise solutions. As the authors suggest, the key to the success story TI represents lies in its premise that anticorruption initiatives cannot be imposed from outside and in its ability to bring people together—across national boundaries, across party lines, and across the state-society divide.

Collier, finally, draws attention to counterintentional as well as counterproductive effects of international intervention. He draws a sober (and somber) balance of the macroeconomic conditionalities imposed, first of all, by the World Bank on African governments. Collier's basic message is that when external agents are seen as prime movers of economic reforms, those reforms will appear fragile and reversible, dependent on continuing international pressure. Put under salient international pressure, even committed reform governments will look like marionettes dancing to the baton of external conductors.

In sum, all three international chapters seem to be consistent with the basic conviction, widespread in contemporary political texts and in the scholarly literature, that external actors "must support domestically rooted processes of change, not attempt to artificially reproduce pre-selected results."[44] Under this condition, "external action is not often decisive," but "wisely conceived and sensitively executed [it] can do much to advance the democratic agenda."[45]

Conclusion

Domesticating the state, subjecting it to effective institutions of "self-restraint," runs against the entrenched interests of powerful actors and thus sparks conflict and provokes resistance. In most cases, it is not realistic to expect public officials to exercise voluntary self-restraint. As I have argued, we may search for possible reform constituencies at more then one place—in our spatial metaphorical terms, not just above but also below, within, and outside—though, of course, the mere analytical distinction of different categories of actors does not add up to a case for hope. Side by side with agents of change we are likely to encounter forceful foci of resistance at exactly the same places we have analyzed: the commanding heights of the state civil society, institutions of horizontal accountability, and the international community.

The preceding pages have treated these four groups of actors largely in isolation. But naturally the "bread and butter" of the political economy of accountability building lies in the interactive dynamics that unfold between them. The four "modes of change" I have outlined rarely occur in the purity their simple labels suggest. The trigger of reform or the major impulse may come from one side. But episodes of significant reform usually flow out of the convergence of various motors and promoters of change. Politicians, public officials, citizens, and international actors depend on each other. Both their chances of success and their willingness to expose themselves as advocates of institutional reform depend on the (expected as well as actual) support they receive from the other parts. They need each other to be successful; but they also need each other to become active in the first place. The former idea conveys common sense: agencies of accountability do not develop as the result of brilliant solo performances on behalf of sovereign institutional designers but need requisite coalitions to come together (whose size and composition vary depending on the concrete challenge at hand). The latter idea conveys complexity: the presence of powerful advocates of accountability at one place is neither a given nor is it exogenous to the emergence of like-minded agents at other places.

To exaggerate the point a bit: public opinion calls for institutional mechanisms of accountability, party politicians present themselves as champions of self-restraint, accounting agencies start taking their mission seriously and ruling against the rich and powerful, and international actors step in to aid the state in exercising the bourgeois virtue of self-control— when and only when all others do the same and join the bandwagon of accountability. It is a big opportunistic game of preference forming through preference revealing. Of course, if this circle of interdependence were to be fully closed, reform initiatives would never come from anywhere. Somebody has to kick the status quo from its point of equilibrium.

The literature on institutional reform places great emphasis on the necessity for "leadership" and "political will." It is right in doing so. To get reforms started, we do indeed need credible, courageous, and imaginative individuals who take the risk of breaking established routines and expectations. We need the "mystery" of human agency, which we cannot engineer or create by administrative decree. But we should not be mistaken. We need political entrepreneurs not just at the top of the state apparatus but everywhere—in civil society, within public institutions of accountability, and in the international community. Without their mysterious emergence, it is difficult to see how the modern Leviathan would ever accede to make itself at home in the golden cage of institutional self-restraint.

Notes

1. See, for example, Bates, "Contra Contractarianism," Knight, *Institutions,* Knight, "Models," and Moe, "Political Institutions."

2. The underlying premise is that we should not consider the emphasis on either collective benefits or distributive consequences to be simply a matter of theoretical predilections. It is first of all an empirical matter. It is not just authors adopting different perspectives. It is empirical institutions that vary greatly in the extent to which they distribute benefits and burdens evenly or unevenly within the "relevant community."

3. I owe this observation to Moe, "Political Institutions," p. 220.

4. See Greif et al., "Coordination." The quote is from p. 30.

5. See North and Weingast, "Constitutions and Commitment." The quotes are from pp. 139, 165.

6. Elster, "Introduction," p. 4.

7. In other words, for electoral accountability to translate into horizontal accountability (rather than legitimizing unrestrained rule in what Guillermo O'Donnell has termed "delegative democracies"), democracies must display a degree of interparty competition that exceeds the minimum levels that are indispensable for elections to qualify as democratic. Clearly, all other conditions for

elections to qualify as democratic—their free, fair, inclusive, and clean character—must be fulfilled as well.

8. In a recent essay, Barry Weingast elaborates a simple model to explain what makes constitutional restraints on political power both effective and sustainable. His explanation rests precisely on the causal link between vertical and horizontal accountability. Taking for granted that rulers act on their long-term interests, he identifies the first of the three conditions listed above—citizens' willingness to punish rulers (which he comprehends as a coordination problem)—as the key to constitutional democracy. In his model, constitutional restraints appear as "self-enforcing" (which means that rulers do not have an interest any more to transgress them) if, and only if, citizens are willing to defend them (see Weingast, "The Political Foundations").

9. On five Latin American cases of postelectoral policy switches that betray prior campaign commitments, see Stokes, "Democracy and the Limits of Popular Sovereignty." On the "normative force" of electoral promises (in the absence of any binding legal or contractual force), see Schedler, "The Normative Force."

10. See North and Weingast, "Constitutions and Commitment." The quotes are from pp. 136, 161.

11. The term *conservatives* is not meant here to have any ideological connotations. Often it is the advocates of change who are the right-wing conservatives, while the defenders of the institutional status quo place themselves to the left or "progressive" side on the political left-right axis.

12. For such statements, see Knight and Sened, "Introduction," pp. 1–2; Thelen and Steinmo, "Historical Institutionalism," pp. 13, 15–18. For overviews of the new institutionalism in the field (and elsewhere), see DiMaggio and Powell, "Introduction," Goodin, "Institutions," Koelble, "The New Institutionalism," and Schedler, "Neo-Institucionalismo."

13. At the same time, it is fair to say that to a certain extent the diagnoses that drew attention to the lack of attention to processes of institutional change have also had a (purposefully) self-defeating character. They have identified a lacuna of research more and more scholars have been willing to step into. For a balance of the advances both rational choice and historical institutionalists have made in the study of institutional change during the last five years or so, see Thelen, "Historical Institutionalism."

14. O'Donnell and Schmitter, *Transitions*.

15. The "transitological" literature has grown beyond the reading capacity of any individual. A good collection of some basic essays is Pridham, *Transitions to Democracy*.

16. This literature is quite extensive as well. An instructive collection of essays is Diamond and Plattner, *Economic Reform*.

17. For studies that (at least implicitly) adopt this perspective, describing institutional change as the result of conflictive interactions between agents of change and conservative agents, see, for example, on judicial reform, Buscaglia and Domingo, "Impediments," pp. 14–16; on civil service reform, Chaudry et al., *Civil Service Reform*, passim; on electoral reform, Dunleavy and Margetts, "Understanding the Dynamics"; on state reform, Grindle and Thomas, *Public Choices;* on the redefinition of civil-military relations, Hunter, *Eroding Military Influence;* on the combat against corruption, Johnston, "What Can Be Done"; on the erosion of clientelism, Fox, "The Difficult Transition"; on the negotiation of institutions that regulate common-pool resources, Ostrom, *Governing the Commons*.

18. As in Chapters 1 and 2, all references to chapters in this volume mention

authors only. References to Pastor and Schwartz refer to Chapters 8 and 12, respectively.

19. It is important to stress that I do not want to collapse the two things conceptually: if we part the world into reformists and counter-reformists we do not have to make any assumptions about motivations. Above all, we do not have to assume that people act solely on their material self-interests. As I note below (especially in the section on reform from within), actors may have strong normative motivations to join the ranks of one or the other group.

20. O'Donnell and Schmitter, *Transitions,* introduced this double distinction under the label of "hard-liners" versus "soft-liners."

21. See also O'Donnell's emphatic "individuals do matter" (in this volume).

22. Neoliberal policies of economic restructuring have faced a similar ("neoliberal" or "orthodox") paradox in their "attempt to use the agencies and personnel of the state to diminish or dismantle their own power" (Nelson, "The Politics of Long-Haul Economic Reform," p. 10).

23. See Rawls, *A Theory of Justice,* pp. 136–142. Constitution-making processes at an early stage of democratization, before the dust of the democratic transition has settled, revealing the new democratic landscape of political actors, identities, and resources, approximate Rawls's counterfactual idea.

24. As criticized by many, O'Donnell and Schmitter's classic text tended to treat civil society as a dependent variable of transition processes, rather than as an active protagonist. Later processes of transition, especially in Eastern Europe, revealed (to a certain extent) the empirical boundedness of their "elite-centered" approach (see, e.g., Bunce, "Comparing East and South," p. 90).

25. See, e.g., Geddes, *Politician's Dilemma,* and Hunter, *Eroding Military Influence.* As Robert Kaufman, "Approaches" (p. 23), observes, the tendency "[t]o treat such demands as givens . . . may leave crucial questions outside the theoretical framework: how preferences for reform emerge, how collective action problems are overcome, and the extent to which societal groups might bypass legislative institutions."

26. See, e.g., Dakolias, *The Judicial Sector,* pp. 65–67.

27. Diamond, "Rethinking Civil Society," p. 7. Diamond even describes the task to "monitor and restrain" the exercise of state power as "the first and most basic democratic function of civil society," side by side with its potential contribution "to democratize authoritarian states" (p. 7). Robert Putnam's *Making Democracy Work,* the single most influential work for the reintroduction of culture and civil society into studies of state reform, was mainly concerned about two specific dimensions of democratic institutional performance: responsiveness and efficiency. Whatever its attributed function, civil society is typically "the major victim" of unrestrained, abusive, wasteful, and predatory state power, which gives it a strong "vested interest" in limiting the state and making it accountable (the quotes are from Pope, *National Integrity Systems,* p. 36).

28. O'Donnell (this volume). For a theoretical statement of this causal relation between vertical and horizontal accountability, see Weingast, "The Political Foundations." We may add that accounting institutions of an ombudsman type blur the distinction between vertical and horizontal accountability insofar as they are state agencies that for their daily operation and effectiveness entirely depend on citizens filing complaints. Without citizens exercising vertical accountability, such agencies of horizontal accountability are simply condemned to idleness (since they usually do not have a mandate to open investigations on their own).

29. See, e.g., Aguayo, "A Mexican Milestone," on Mexico's electoral monitor-

ing group, Civic Alliance; Simonov, "Defending Glasnost," on the Moscow-based Glasnost Defense Foundation; Coronel, "Curbing Corruption," on the Venezuelan civic education association, Agrupación Pro Calidad de Vida; Afkhami, "Promoting Women's Rights," on the transnational Sisterhood Is Global Institute; and Neou, "Teaching Human Rights," on the Cambodian Institute of Human Rights.

30. As Kaufman, "Approaches" (pp. 38–41), speculates, the major and distinctive impact of civil society may well lay in transforming informal practices (while international trends set the agenda and politicians decide formal rule changes).

31. From a theoretical point of view, we may treat institutional creation and institutional change as equivalent problems. In essence, both involve a change in social expectations (see Schedler, "Credibility"). For a similar point, see Ostrom, *Governing the Commons,* pp. 139–142.

32. Dakolias, *The Judicial Sector,* p. 66.

33. See, e.g., Rowat et al., *Judicial Reform,* passim.

34. Elster, "Equal or Proportional?" p. 151. Yet Elster does allow for exceptions: ideas (and norms) matter "not necessarily *only* when" interests do not show us unequivocal pathways (p. 151, emphasis added). The critical question is, however, what accounts for these exceptions? For some remarks on the role of institutions in lowering the costs of acting on one's normative convictions, see North, *Institutions,* pp. 43–44.

35. North, *Institutions,* p. 42.

36. However, to the extent that some rational choice theorists give up the orthodox assumption of utility maximization, the divide between "materialists" and "idealists" develops into a cleavage that cuts across different theoretical schools (see Thelen, "Historical Institutionalism").

37. For a rational choice critique of an exclusive reliance on incentives (sanctions and rewards) to the detriment of attention to personnel selection, see Brennan, "Selection."

38. For an influential account from a rational choice perspective of how to change the relations between "principals" and "agents" within organizations through changes in incentives, information, and resources, see Klitgaard, *Controlling Corruption,* especially chapter 5, pp. 122–133.

39. For an effort to explain *mani pulite,* see Pizzorno, "Representation." For some contextual analysis, see Pasquino, "Italy."

40. The term *omertà* "traditionally refers to the silence a large sector of the Sicilian population is capable of maintaining in the face of public inquiries into crime" committed by the mafia (Gambetta, "The Sicilian Mafia," p. 35).

41. For a general overview, see Diamond, "Promoting Democracy." For a critical review of international election observations, see Carothers, "The Observers Observed."

42. For a skeptical note on the new international consensus about "the rule of law as a solution to the world's troubles" (p. 95), see Carothers, "The Rule of Law Revival."

43. See also Maxfield, this volume, and Maxfield, "International Sources of Central Bank Convergence."

44. Carothers, "The Rule of Law Revival," p. 104.

45. Farer, "Collectively Defending Democracy," pp. 4–5.

Bibliography

Afari-Gyan, Kwadwo, "Towards the Delivery of Fair Elections in Ghana," paper prepared for presentation at the Third Vienna Dialogue on Democracy, "Institutionalizing Horizontal Accountability," International Forum for Democratic Studies and the Institute for Advanced Studies, Vienna, 26–29 June 1997.

Afkhami, Mahnaz, "Promoting Women's Rights in the Muslim World," *Journal of Democracy* 8/1 (January 1998): 157–166.

Afriyie Badu, Kwasi, and John Larvie (eds.), *Elections in Ghana, 1996*, vol. 1 (Accra: Electoral Commission of Ghana and Friedrich Ebert Foundation, 1996).

Aguayo Quezada, Sergio, "A Mexican Milestone," *Journal of Democracy* 6/2 (April 1995): 156–167.

Alcántara, Juan Miguel, PAN federal congressional member and former national coordinator of state legislators, PAN Executive Committee, interview with Todd A. Eisenstadt, 17 June 1996, Guanajuato.

Alesina, Alberto, and Lawrence Summers, "Central Bank Independence and Macroeconomic Performance: Some Comparative Evidence," *Journal of Money, Credit, and Banking* 25/2 (May 1993): 151–173.

Alston, Lee J., Thráinn Eggertsson, and Douglass C. North, "The Evolution of Modern Institutions of Growth," in *Empirical Studies in Institutional Change*, eds. Lee J. Alston, Thráinn Eggertsson, and Douglass C. North (Cambridge: Cambridge University Press, 1996), pp. 129–133.

Alvaro, Arturo (ed.), *Electoral Patterns and Perspectives in Mexico* (La Jolla: Center for U.S.-Mexican Studies, University of California, San Diego, 1987).

Amara, Raksasataya, "Bureaucracy vs. Bureaucracy: Anti–Corrupt Practices Measures in Thailand," in *Politics and Administration in Changing Societies*, ed. Ramesh K. Arora (New Delhi: Associated Publishing House, 1992), pp. 220–244.

Anechiarico, Frank, and James B. Jacobs, *The Pursuit of Absolute Integrity: How Corruption Control Makes Government Ineffective* (Chicago: University of Chicago Press, 1996).

351

Appleby, Joyce, *Liberalism and Republicanism in the Historical Imagination* (Cambridge: Harvard University Press, 1992).

Arato, Andrew, "Constitution and Continuity in the Eastern European Transitions," in *Constitutionalism and Politics,* ed. Irena Grudzinska-Gross (Amsterdam: Slovak Committee of the European Cultural Foundation, 1994), pp. 155–171.

Asia Yearbook 1990, "Korea—South" (Hong Kong: Far Eastern Economic Review, 1990), pp. 155–158.

Asia Yearbook 1992, "Korea—South" (Hong Kong: Far Eastern Economic Review, 1992), pp. 137–140.

Aslund, Anders, *How Russia Became a Market Economy* (Washington, D.C.: Brookings Institution, 1995).

Association of Russian Banks, *Informatsionnyi bulletin* 6 (1994).

Austin, Dennis, *Politics in Ghana, 1946–60* (London: Oxford University Press, 1970).

Backman, Michael, "The Economics of Corruption," *Asian Wall Street Journal* (3 September 1996).

Banégas, Richard, and Patrick Quantin, "Orientations et limites de l'aide française au développement démocratique: Bénin, Congo et République centrafricaine," *Canadian Journal of Development Studies,* special issue (1996): 113–133.

Banerjee, Biswajit, Vincent Koen, Thomas Krueger, Mark S. Lutz, Michael Marrese, and Tapio O. Saavalainen, *Road Maps of the Transition* (Washington, D.C.: International Monetary Fund, 1995).

Bates, Robert H., "Contra Contractarianism: Some Reflections on the New Institutionalism," *Politics and Society* 16/2–3 (September 1988): 387–401.

———, "The Impulse to Reform," in *Economic Change and Political Liberalization in Sub-Saharan Africa,* ed. Jennifer A. Widner (Baltimore: Johns Hopkins University Press, 1994), pp. 13–28.

Bayart, Jean-François, "Le 'capital social' de l'État malfaiteur, ou les ruses de l'intelligence politique," in *La criminalisation de l'État en Afrique,* eds. Jean-François Bayart, Stephen Ellis, and Béatrice Hibou (Paris: Éditions Complexe, 1997), pp. 55–75.

Bayart, Jean-François, Stephen Ellis, and Béatrice Hibou, "De l'État kleptocrate à l'État malfaiteur," in *La criminalisation de l'État en Afrique,* eds. Jean-François Bayart, Stephen Ellis, and Béatrice Hibou (Paris: Éditions Complexe, 1997), pp. 17–54.

Becker, Gary S., "To Root Out Corruption, Boot Out Big Government," *Businessweek* (31 January 1994).

Bedeski, Robert E., *The Transformation of South Korea: Reform and Reconstruction in the Sixth Republic Under Roh Tae Woo, 1987–1992* (London: Routledge, 1994).

Bennett, W. Lance, "The Paradox of Public Discourse: A Framework for the Analysis of Political Accounts," *Journal of Politics* 42 (1980): 792–817.

Berezina, M. P., and Yu S. Krupnov, *Mezhbankovskie raschety* (Moscow: Finstatinform, 1994).

Bernhard, William T., "Legislatures, Governments, and Bureaucratic Structure: Explaining Central Bank Independence," (Durham, N.C.: Duke University, 1995), Ph.D. dissertation.

Bhalla, R. P., "Election Commission of India," *Journal of Constitutional and Parliamentary Studies* 18/1 (1984): 12–37.

Bhattacharya, Amar, Peter J. Montiel, and Sunil Sharma, "Private Capital Flows to Sub-Saharan Africa: An Overview of Trends and Determinants" (Washington,

D.C.: International Monetary Fund, Research Department, 1996), unpublished manuscript.

Biggs, Stephen, and Arthur Neame, "Negotiating Room for Manoeuvre: Reflections Concerning NGO Autonomy and Accountability Within the New Policy Agenda," in *Non-Governmental Organisations: Performance and Accountability—Beyond the Magic Bullet*, eds. Michael Edwards and David Hulme (London: Earthscan, 1995).

Biles, Robert E., "The Position of the Judiciary in the Political Systems of Argentina and Mexico," *Lawyer of the Americas* 8 (1976): 287–318.

Boahen, A. Adu, "Conflict Reoriented," in *Governance as Conflict Management: Politics and Violence in West Africa*, ed. I. William Zartman (Washington, D.C.: Brookings Institution, 1997), pp. 95–148.

Bowles, Paul, and Gordon White, "Central Bank Independence: A Political Economy Approach," *Journal of Development Studies* 31/2 (December 1994): 235–265.

Bratton, Michael, "Deciphering Africa's Divergent Transitions," *Political Science Quarterly* 112/1 (1997): 67–94.

Brennan, Geoffrey, "Selection and the Currency of Reward," in *The Theory of Institutional Design*, ed. Robert E. Goodin (Cambridge: Cambridge University Press, 1996), pp. 256–275.

Brewer-Carías, Allan R., *Judicial Review in Comparative Law* (Cambridge: Cambridge University Press, 1989).

Bruhn, Kathleen, *Taking on Goliath: The Emergence of a New Left Party and the Struggle for Democracy in Mexico* (University Park: Pennsylvania State University, 1997).

Brunner, Georg, "Preface," in *The Constitutional Judiciary in Hungary: Analysis and Collected Decisions 1990–1993*, ed. Georg Brunner (Ann Arbor: University of Michigan Press, forthcoming).

Brzezinski, Mark, "The Emergence of Judicial Review in Eastern Europe: The Case of Poland," *American Journal of Comparative Law* 41/2 (1993): 153–200.

Brzezinski, Mark, and Lech Garlicki, "Judicial Powers in Post-Communist Poland: The Emergence of a *Rechtsstaat?*" *Journal of International Law* 31/1 (1995): 13–59.

Bunce, Valerie, "Comparing East and South," *Journal of Democracy* 6/3 (July 1995): 87–100.

Burnside, Craig, and David Dollar, "Aid, Policies and Growth," Policy Research Working Paper 1777 (Washington, D.C.: World Bank, Policy Research Department, 1997).

Buscaglia, Edgardo, Jr., and Pilar Domingo, "The Impediments to Judicial Reform in Latin America," paper prepared for presentation at the Nineteenth International Congress of the Latin American Studies Association (LASA), Washington, D.C., 28–30 September 1995.

CADR, *Le livre rouge du pillage des banques* (Cotonou: Rapport Integral de la Commission Spéciale, 1990).

Caiden, Gerald E., and Jung H. Kim, "A New Anti-Corruption Strategy for Korea," *Asian Journal of Political Science* 1/1 (June 1993): 133–151.

Carothers, Thomas, *In the Name of Democracy: US Policy Toward Latin America in the Reagan Years* (Berkeley: University of California Press, 1991).

———, "The Observers Observed," *Journal of Democracy* 8/3 (July 1997): 17–31.

———, "The Rule of Law Revival," *Foreign Affairs* 77/2 (March/April 1998): 95–106.

Carroll, David, and Robert Pastor, "Moderating Ethnic Tensions by Electoral Mediation: The Case of Guyana," *Security Dialogue* (June 1993): 163–173.

Carter Center, "The Carter Center Delegation to Observe the July 6, 1997 Elections in Mexico" (Atlanta: Carter Center, 1997).

Casaus, Jesse, "Court Organisation and Court Reform Experience in Latin America," in *Judicial Reform in Latin America and the Caribbean: Proceedings of a World Bank Conference,* eds. Malcolm Rowat, Waleed H. Malik, and Maria Dakolias (Washington D.C.: World Bank, 1995), pp. 59–62.

Castillo Peraza, Carlos, former national PAN president, interview with Todd A. Eisenstadt, 16 August 1996, Mexico City.

Castro Rodríguez, C., *Historia judicial de Bolivia* (La Paz: Los Amigos del Libro, 1987).

Cavarozzi, Marcelo, "La transición y el Estado," *Nexos* 21/244 (April 1998): 47–50.

Centeno, Miguel, *Democracy Within Reason: Technocratic Revolution in Mexico* (University Park: Pennsylvania State University, 1994).

Central Bank of Russia, *Tekushie tendentsii v denezhno-kreditnoi sfere* 3 (1994).

Chadajo, Joshua, "The Independence of the Central Bank of Russia," *RFE/RL Research Report* 3/27 (8 July 1994): 26–32.

Chai-Anan, Samudavanija, "Problems of Bureaucratic Corruption in Thailand: A Study of Legal Codes, Administrative and Institutional Arrangements," paper prepared for presentation at the Bureaucratic Behaviour in Asia Project, Pattaya, Thailand, 18–23 January 1977.

Chai-Anan, Samudavanija, and Sukhumbhand Paribatra, "Thailand: Liberalization Without Democracy," in *Driven by Growth: Political Change in the Asia-Pacific Region,* ed. James W. Morley (Armonk, N.Y.: M.E. Sharpe, 1993), pp. 119–141.

Chand, Vikram, "Democratization from the Outside-In: NGO and International Efforts to Promote Open Elections," *Third World Quarterly* 18/3 (1997): 543–561.

Chang Ha-Joong, "Reform for the Long Term in South Korea," *International Herald Tribune* (17 February 1998).

Chaudry, Shahid Amjad, Gary James Reid, and Waleed Haider Malik (eds.), "Civil Service Reform in Latin America and the Carribbean," Technical Paper 259 (Washington, D.C.: World Bank, 1994).

Chazan, Naomi, "The Anomalies of Continuity: Perspectives on Ghanaian Elections Since Independence," in *Elections in Independent Africa,* ed. Fred Hayward (Boulder, Colo.: Westview Press, 1987), pp. 61–86.

Chiapas Electoral Tribunal, *Memoria del processo electoral 1995 en Chiapas* (Tuxtla Gutiérrez: Tribunal Estatal Electoral de Chiapas, 1996).

Chugaev, Sergei, "Central Bank Scored for Arbitrary Actions," *Izvestiia* (15 May 1992), translated in *Current Digest of the Post-Soviet Press* 44/20 (1992).

Clark, David, *"Dirigisme* in an Asian City-State: Hong Kong's ICAC," paper prepared for presentation at the Thirteenth World Congress of the International Political Science Association (IPSA), Paris, 10–13 July 1985.

Clark, William, and Usha Nair Reichert, with Sandra Lynn Thomas and Kevin L. Parker, "Constraints on Political Business Cycles in OECD Economies," *International Organization* 52/1 (Winter 1998): 87–120.

Clark, William, et al., "Central Rates and Central Banks: International and Domestic Constraints on the Political Control of OECD Economies" (Atlanta: Georgia Institute of Technology, 1994), unpublished manuscript.

Collier, David, and Steven Levitsky, "Democracy with Adjectives: Conceptual

Innovation in Comparative Research," *World Politics* 49 (April 1997): 430–451.

Collier, David, and James E. Mahon, "Conceptual 'Stretching' Revisited: Adapting Categories in Comparative Analysis," *American Political Science Review* 87/4 (December 1993): 845–855.

Collier, Paul, "Africa's External Relations: 1960–90," *African Affairs* 90/360 (1991): 339–356.

Collier, Paul, Patrick Guillaumont, Sylviane Guillaumont, and Jan Willem Gunning, "The Future of Lomé: Europe's Role in Africa's Growth," *The World Economy* 20/3 (1997): 285–306.

———, "Redesigning Conditionality," *World Development* 25/3 (1997).

Collier, Paul, and Jan Willem Gunning, "Explaining African Economic Performance," Working Paper WPS97-2 (Oxford: Centre for the Study of African Economies, 1997).

Collier, Paul, and Cathy Pattillo (eds.), *Risk and Agencies of Restraint: Reducing the Risks of African Investment* (London: Macmillan, 1997).

Collier, Ruth, and David Collier, *Shaping the Political Arena: Critical Junctures, the Labor Movement, and Regime Dynamics in Latin America* (Princeton: Princeton University Press, 1991).

Constant, Benjamin, *Political Writings,* ed. Biancamaria Fontana (Cambridge: Cambridge University Press, 1988).

Constitution of the Republic of Ghana, 1992 (Tema: Ghana Publishing Corporation, 1992).

"Constitution Watch," *East European Constitutional Review* 5/4 (1996): 2–30.

Cornelius, Wayne A., Todd A. Eisenstadt, and Jane Hindley (eds.), *Subnational Politics and Democratization in Mexico* (La Jolla: Center for U.S.-Mexican Studies, University of California, San Diego, 1998).

Coronel, Gustavo, "Curbing Corruption in Venezuela," *Journal of Democracy* 7/3 (July 1996): 157–165.

Correa Sutil, Jorge, "Capacitación y carrera judicial en Hispano América," in *Justicia y sociedad,* ed. Universidad Nacional Autónoma de México (Mexico City: UNAM, 1994), pp. 165–182.

———, "The Judiciary and the Political System in Chile: The Dilemmas of Judicial Independence During the Transition to Democracy," in *Transition to Democracy in Latin America: The Role of the Judiciary,* ed. Irwin Stotzky (Boulder, Colo.: Westview Press, 1993), pp. 89–106.

Cukierman, Alex, *Central Bank Strategy, Credibility, and Independence* (Cambridge: MIT Press, 1992).

Cukierman, Alex, Pantelis Kalaitzidakis, Lawrence Summers, and Steven B. Webb, "Central Bank Independence, Growth, Investment and Real Rates," *Carnegie-Rochester Conference on Public Policy* 39 (Autumn 1993): 541–569.

Cukierman, Alex, Steven Webb, and Bilin Neyapti, "Measuring the Independence of Central Banks and Its Effect on Policy Outcomes," *World Bank Economic Review* 6/3 (1992): 353–398.

Dahl, Robert A., *Democracy and Its Critics* (New Haven: Yale University Press, 1989).

———, *Polyarchy: Participation and Opposition* (New Haven: Yale University Press, 1971).

Dakolias, Maria, *The Judicial Sector in Latin America and the Caribbean: Elements of Reform,* Technical Paper 319 (Washington, D.C.: World Bank, 1996).

Dalpino, Catherin E., "Thailand's Search for Accountability," *Journal of Democracy* 2/4 (1991): 61–71.

Davies, S. Gethyn (ed.), *Central Banking in South and East Asia* (Hong Kong: Hong Kong University Press, 1960).

DeBusk, Susanna (ed.), *1996 International Directory of Election Offices* (Washington, D.C.: International Foundation for Election Systems, 1996).

de la Peza Muñoz Cano, José Luis, president of the Electoral Tribunal of the Judicial Power of the Federation, interview with Todd A. Eisenstadt, 14 December 1995, Mexico City.

del Villar, Samuel, PRD Secretariat of Judicial Affairs, interview with Todd A. Eisenstadt, 18 April 1996, Mexico City.

Demchenko, Irina, "Central Bank Chairman Accuses Russian Government of Distorting Facts," *Izvestiia* (10 February 1993), translated in the *Current Digest of the Post-Soviet Press* 45/6 (1993).

de Speville, Bertrand, "Hong Kong's War on Corruption," paper prepared for presentation at the seminar "Corruption and Integrity Improvement," OECD/UNDP, Paris, 24–25 October 1997.

Dezalay, Yves, and Bryant Garth, "Building the Law and Putting the State into Play: International Strategies Among Mexico's Divided Elite," Working Paper 9509 (Chicago: American Bar Foundation, 1996).

Di Tella, Rafael, "Volver a Sarmiento: Una propuesta para mejorar la eficiencia del gasto social basada en la competencia" (Cambridge: Harvard University, 1997), unpublished manuscript.

Diamond, Larry, "Democracy in Latin America: Degrees, Illusions, and Directions for Consolidation," in *Beyond Sovereignty: Collectively Defending Democracy in the Americas,* ed. Tom Farer (Baltimore: Johns Hopkins University Press, 1996), pp. 52–104.

———, *Developing Democracy: Toward Consolidation* (Baltimore: Johns Hopkins University Press, 1999).

———, "The End of the Third Wave and the Global Future of Democracy," Political Science Series 45 (Vienna: Institute for Advanced Studies, 1997).

———, "How Well Is Taiwan's Democracy Doing?" paper prepared for presentation at the Lincoln Society of Taipei, 17 June 1998.

———, "Political Corruption: Nigeria's Perennial Struggle," *Journal of Democracy* 2/1 (Autumn 1991): 73–85.

———, "Promoting Democracy in the 1990s: Actors and Instruments, Issues and Imperatives" (New York: Carnegie Corporation, 1995).

———, "Rethinking Civil Society: Toward Democratic Consolidation," *Journal of Democracy* 5/3 (July 1994): 4–17.

Diamond, Larry, and Marc F. Plattner (eds.), *Economic Reform and Democracy* (Baltimore: Johns Hopkins University Press, 1995).

Díaz, Luis Miguel, and Ben Lenhart (eds.), *Diccionario de términos jurídicos* (Mexico City: Editorial Themis, 1992).

DiMaggio, Paul J., and Walter W. Powell, "Introduction," in *The New Institutionalism in Organizational Life,* eds. Walter W. Powell and Paul J. DiMaggio (Chicago: University of Chicago Press, 1991), pp. 1–38.

Dobbs, Michael, "Russian Banker Urges Renegotiation of Economic Reform Plan," *Washington Post* (21 August 1992).

Domínguez, Jorge I., and James A. McCann, *Democratizing Mexico: Public Opinion and Electoral Choices* (Baltimore: Johns Hopkins University Press, 1995).

Drake, Paul, "From Good Men to Good Neighbors," in *Exporting Democracy: The United States and Latin America,* vol. 1, ed. Abraham F. Lowenthal (Baltimore: Johns Hopkins University Press, 1991).

Dubinin, Sergei, chairman of the Central Bank of Russia, interview with Juliet Johnson, Washington, D.C., 23 April 1996.

Dunleavy, Patrick, and Helen Margetts, "Understanding the Dynamics of Electoral Reform," *International Political Science Review* 16/1 (1995): 9–29.

Edwards, Michael, "Organizational Learning in Non-Governmental Organizations: What Have We Learned?" *Public Administration and Development* 17 (1997): 235–250.

Eigen, Peter, "Combating Corruption Around the World," *Journal of Democracy* 7/1 (January 1996): 158–168.

Eisenmann, Charles (ed.), *La justice constitutionnelle et la haute cour constitutionnelle d'Autriche* (Paris: Economica, 1986).

Eisenstadt, Todd A., "Electoral Federalism or Abdication of Presidential Authority in Tabasco?" in *Subnational Politics and Demcratization in Mexico*, ed. Wayne Cornelius (La Jolla, Calif.: Center for U.S.-Mexican Studies, 1998), see p. 355.

———, "Courting Democracy: Party Strategies, Electoral Institution-Building, and Political Opening—Mexico in Comparative Perspective" (La Jolla: University of California, San Diego, 1998), Ph.D. dissertation.

———, "Electoral Justice in Mexico: From Oxymoron to Legal Norm in Less Than a Decade," Working Paper (Atlanta: Carter Center, 1998).

Ekeh, Peter, "Colonialism and the Two Publics in Africa: A Theoretical Statement," *Comparative Studies of Society and History* 17/1 (1975): 91–112.

Elkit, Jorgen, and Palle Svenson, "What Makes Elections Free and Fair?" *Journal of Democracy* 8/3 (1997): 32–46.

Elliott, Kimberly Ann (ed.), *Corruption and the Global Economy* (Washington, D.C.: Institute for International Economics, 1997).

Elster, Jon, "Equal or Proportional? Arguing and Bargaining Over the Senate at the Federal Convention," in *Explaining Social Institutions*, eds. Jack Knight and Itai Sened (Ann Arbor: University of Michigan Press, 1995), pp. 145–160.

———, "The Impact of Constitutions on Economic Performance," paper prepared for presentation at the World Bank Annual Conference on Development Economics, Washington, D.C., 1994.

———, "Social Norms and Economic Theory," *Journal of Economic Perspectives* 3/4 (Fall 1989): 99–117.

———, "Introduction," in *Constitutionalism and Democracy*, eds. Jon Elster and Rune Slagstad (Cambridge: Cambridge University Press, 1988), pp. 1–17.

Esman, Milton J., and Norman T. Uphoff, *Local Organizations: Intermediaries in Rural Development* (Ithaca, N.Y.: Cornell University Press, 1984).

Espinosa, Simón, "Corrupción: Una agenda necesaria," in *Corrupción: Epidemia de fin de siglo*, ed. Simón Espinosa (Quito: ILDIS, Cedep, and Fundación J. Peralta, 1996), pp. 77–93.

Euromoney, "Russia Comes In from the Cold" (September 1995).

Euromonitor, *The World Economic Factbook 1996/97*, 4th ed. (London: Euromonitor, 1996).

Evans, Peter, *Embedded Autonomy: States and Industrial Transformation* (Princeton: Princeton University Press, 1995).

———, "Predatory, Developmental, and Other Apparatuses: A Comparative Political Economy Perspective on the Third World State," in *Comparative National Development: Society and Economy in the New Global Order*, eds. A. Douglas Kincaid and Alejandro Portes (Chapel Hill: University of North Carolina Press, 1994), pp. 84–111.

———, "State Structures, Government-Business Relations, and Economic Transformation," in *Business and the State in Developing Countries*, eds.

Sylvia Maxfield and Ben Ross Schneider (Ithaca, N.Y.: Cornell University Press, 1997), pp. 63–87.

Fadia, B. L., "Reforming the Election Commission," *Indian Journal of Political Science* 53/1 (January–March 1992): 78–88.

Farer, Tom, "Collectively Defending Democracy in the Western Hemisphere: Introduction and Overview," in *Beyond Sovereignty: Collectively Defending Democracy in the Americas,* ed. Tom Farer (Baltimore: Johns Hopkins University Press, 1996), pp. 1–25.

Favoreu, Louis, "American and European Models of Constitutional Justice," in *Comparative and Private International Law,* ed. David S. Clark (Berlin: Decker and Humboldt, 1990), pp. 38–62.

———, "La modernité des vues de Charles Eisenmann sur la justice constitutionelle," in *La justice constitutionelle et la haute cour constitutionelle d'Autriche* (Paris: Economica, 1986), pp. 105–120.

Federal Reserve Bank of Kansas City, *Central Banking Issues in Emerging Market-Oriented Economies* (Kansas City: Federal Reserve Bank of Missouri, 1990).

Fedorov, Boris, "Fedorov Confronts Gerashchenko on Credits," *Segodnia* (16 March 1993), translated in *Current Digest of the Post-Soviet Press* 45/13 (1993).

Feyzioglu, Tarhan, Vinaya Swaroop, and Min Zhu, "Foreign Aid's Impact on Public Spending" (Washington, D.C.: World Bank, Policy Research Department, 1996), unpublished manuscript.

Fidler, Stephen, "The IMF in Washington: Argentina Expected to Sign Agreement Soon," *Financial Times* (27 September 1989).

Finley, Moses, *Democracy, Ancient and Modern* (New Brunswick, N.J.: Rutgers University Press, 1973).

———, *Politics in the Ancient World* (Cambridge: Cambridge University Press, 1984).

Fishkin, James, *Democracy and Deliberation: New Directions for Democratic Reform* (New Haven: Yale University Press, 1991).

Fiss, Owen M., "The Right Degree of Independence," in *Transition to Democracy in Latin America: The Role of the Judiciary,* ed. Irwin Stotzky (Boulder, Colo.: Westview Press, 1993), pp. 55–72.

Fix-Zamudio, Hector, and Hector Fix-Fierro, "El consejo de la judicatura," *Cuadernos para la reforma de la justicia* (Mexico City: UNAM, Instituto de Investigaciones Jurídicas, 1996).

Fontana, Biancamaria, "The Roots of a Long Tradition," *UNESCO Courier* 49 (June 1996): 10–14.

Fossedal, Gregory, *The Democratic Imperative: Exporting the American Revolution* (New York: Basic Books, 1989).

Fox, Jonathan, "The Difficult Transition from Clientelism to Citizenship," *World Politics* 46/2 (1994): 151–184.

Franco, Andrés, "Independencia judicial y política en Colombia," paper prepared for presentation at the Twentieth International Congress of the Latin American Studies Association (LASA), Guadalajara, Mexico, 17–19 April 1997.

Frankel, Marvin E., "Concerning the Role the Judiciary May Serve in the Proper Functioning of a Democracy," in *Transition to Democracy in Latin America: The Role of the Judiciary,* ed. Irwin Stotzky (Boulder, Colo.: Westview Press, 1993), pp. 23–34.

Franzese, Robert J. "Central Bank Independence, Sectoral Interests, and the Wage Bargain," Working Paper Series 56 (Cambridge: Harvard University, Center for European Studies, 1995).

Freeman, John R., "Banking on Democracy: International Finance and the Possibilities for Popular Sovereignty," paper prepared for presentation at the annual meeting of the American Political Science Association (APSA), San Francisco, 29 August–2 September 1990.

French, Howard W., "Outcomes of the Cameroon Vote: Fear of the Future," *New York Times* (14 October 1997).

Frimpong, Kwame, "An Analysis of Corruption in Botswana," paper prepared for presentation at the seminar "Corruption and Integrity Improvement," OECD/UNDP, Paris, 24–25 October 1997.

Frisch, Dieter, "Les effets de la corruption sur le développement," Working Paper 7 (Berlin: Transparency International, 1995).

Gaidar, Yegor, remarks, Southern Economics Association Conference, 25 November 1996.

Gaidar, Yegor, and Georgii Matiukhin, "Memorandum ob ekonomicheskoi politike Rossiiskoi Federatsii," *Ekonomika i zhizn'* (10 March 1992).

Gaillard, Philippe, *Foccart parle: Entretiens avec Philippe Gaillard* (Paris: Fayard, 1997).

Galleguillos, Nibaldo, H., "Checks and Balances in New Democracies: The Role of the Judiciary in the Chilean and Mexican Transitions: A Comparative Analysis," paper prepared for presentation at the Twentieth International Congress of the Latin American Studies Association (LASA), Guadalajara, Mexico, 17–19 April 1997.

Galtung, Fredrik, "Criteria for Sustainable Development," *European Journal for Development Research* 10/1 (1998).

———, "Developing Agencies of Restraint in a Climate of Systematic Corruption: The National Integrity System at Work," paper prepared for presentation at the Third Vienna Dialogue on Democracy, "Institutionalizing Horizontal Accountability," International Forum for Democratic Studies and Institute for Advanced Studies, Vienna, 26–29 June 1997.

Gamarra, Eduardo, "The System of Justice in Bolivia: An Institutional Analysis" (Miami: Center of the Administration of Justice, Florida International University, 1991), unpublished manuscript.

Gambetta, Diego, *The Sicilian Mafia: The Business of Private Protection* (Cambridge: Harvard University Press, 1993).

Ganev, Venelin, "Interview with Todor Todorov and Tsanko Hadjistoichev, Justices of the Bulgarian Constitutional Court," *East European Constitutional Court* 6/1 (1997): 65–71.

Geddes, Barbara, "A Game-Theoretical Model of Reform in Latin American Democracies," in *Politics and Rationality*, eds. William James Booth, Patrick James, and Hudson Meadwell (Cambridge: Cambridge University Press, 1993).

———, *Politician's Dilemma: Building State Capacity in Latin America* (Berkeley: University of California Press, 1994).

Gellner, Ernest, *Conditions of Liberty: Civil Society and Its Rivals* (London: Penguin, 1994).

Genzberger, Christine A., et al., *Korea Business: The Portable Encyclopedia for Doing Business with Korea* (San Rafael, Calif.: World Trade Press, 1994).

Gerashchenko, Viktor, "Address to the Fourth Annual Congress of the Association of Russian Banks," 29 April 1994, printed in *Biznes i banki* (May 1994).

———, "Denezhno-kreditnaia sistema v Rossii v perekhodny period," *Biznes i banki* (September 1994).

Ghosh, Aparisim, et al., "Corruption: Reform's Dark Side," *Far Eastern Economic Review* (20 March 1997): 18–20.

Gibson, Edward, "The Populist Road to Market Reform: Policy and Electoral Coalitions in Mexico and Argentina," *World Politics* 49/3 (1997): 339–370.

Gill, M. S., "India: Running the World's Biggest Elections," *Journal of Democracy* 9/1 (January 1998): 165–168.

Gletton-Quenum, Michel, "Bénin: Nouvelle chasse aux fonctionnaires fictifs," *Jeune afrique économie* 241 (19 May 1997): 18–19.

———, "Bénin: Secousses au sein de la coalition au pouvoir," *Jeune afrique économie* 238 (April 1997): 32–33.

Gómez Tagle, Silvia, *De la alquimia al fraude en las elecciones mexicanas* (Mexico City: GV Editores, 1994).

González, Felipe, "Tribunales constitucionales y derechos humanos en América Latina," in *Justicia constitutional comparada* (Mexico City: UNAM, Instituto de Investigaciones Jurídicas, Centro de Estudios Constitucionales, 1993), pp. 31–41.

González Casanova, Pablo, *La democracia en México* (Mexico City: Serie Popular Era, 1965).

González Oropeza, Manuel, *La intervención federal en la desaparación de poderes* (Mexico City: Universidad Nacional Autónoma de México, 1987).

Goodhart, C. A. E., *The Central Bank and the Financial System* (Cambridge: MIT Press, 1995).

Goodin, Robert E., "Institutions and Their Design," in *The Theory of Institutional Design,* ed. Robert Goodin (Cambridge: Cambridge University Press, 1996), pp. 1–53.

———, "Keeping Political Time: The Rhythms of Democracy," *International Political Science Review* 19/1 (1998): 39–54.

Goodman, John, *Monetary Sovereignty: The Politics of Central Banking in Western Europe* (Ithaca, N.Y.: Cornell University Press, 1992).

Goodwin-Gill, Guy S., *Free and Fair Elections: International Law and Practice* (Geneva: Interparliamentary Union, 1994).

Gordenker, Leon, and Thomas Weiss, "NGO Participation in the International Policy Process," *Third World Quarterly* 16/3 (1995): 543–555.

Gorta, Angela, "Strategies for Preventing Corruption: The NSW Independent Commission Against Corruption Experience," paper prepared for presentation at the conference "Business Ethics," Philippine Business Ethics Network and University of Asia and the Pacific, Pasig City, Manila, 9–11 March 1997.

Gould, Ron, and Christine Jackson, *A Guide for Election Observers* (London: Dartmouth Publishing, 1995).

Gourevitch, Peter, *Politics in Hard Times* (Ithaca, N.Y.: Cornell University Press, 1986).

Greif, Avner, Paul Milgrom, and Barry R. Weingast, "Coordination, Commitment, and Enforcement: The Case of the Merchant Guild," in *Explaining Social Institutions,* eds. Jack Knight and Itai Sened (Ann Arbor: University of Michigan Press, 1995), pp. 27–56.

Grieder, William, *Secrets of the Temple* (New York: Simon and Schuster, 1987).

Grindle, Merilee S., and John W. Thomas, *Public Choices and Policy Change: The Political Economy of Reform in Developing Countries* (Baltimore: Johns Hopkins University Press, 1991).

Gurushina, Natalia, "Company Arrears Increase in the First Half of 1996," OMRI *Daily Digest* (10 September 1996).

———, "Economic Decline Continues," OMRI *Daily Digest* (21 October 1996).

Guttsman, Janet, "New Data Gives Scant Hope for Russian Economy," Reuters (3 June 1997).

Gyimah-Boadi, E., "Ghana's Encouraging Elections: The Challenges Ahead," *Journal of Democracy* 8/2 (April 1997): 78–91.

———, "Ghana's Uncertain Political Opening," *Journal of Democracy* 5/2 (April 1994): 75–86.

———, "Notes on Ghana's Current Transition to Constitutional Rule," *Africa Today* 38/4 (1991): 5–19.

Habermas, Jürgen, *Theorie des kommunikativen Handelns,* Volume 1 (Frankfurt/Main: Suhrkamp, 1981), p. 47.

Hadenius, Axel, *Democracy and Development* (London: Cambridge University Press, 1992).

Haggard, Stephan, and Robert R. Kaufman, *The Political Economy of Democratic Transitions* (Princeton: Princeton University Press, 1995).

Halisi, C. R. D., "From Liberation to Citizenship: Identity and Innovation in Black South African Political Thought," *Comparative Studies in Society and History* 39 (January 1997): 61–85.

Hall, Peter A., *The Political Power of Economic Ideas* (Princeton: Princeton University Press, 1989).

Han, Sung Joo, "South Korea: Politics in Transition," in *Democracy in Developing Countries: Asia,* eds. Larry Diamond, Juan J. Linz, and Seymour Martin Lipset (Boulder, Colo.: Lynne Rienner Publishers, 1989), pp. 267–303.

Hansen, Mogens Herman, *The Athenian Democracy in the Age of Demosthenes* (Oxford: Oxford University Press, 1991).

Haque, Nadeem U., Mark Nelson, and Donald T. Mathieson, "Creditworthiness Ratings: Their Political and Economic Content," in *Risk and Agencies of Restraint: Reducing the Risks of African Investment,* eds. Paul Collier and Cathy Pattillo (London: Macmillan, 1997).

Harris, Peter, "An Electoral Administration: Who, What, and Where?" summary paper prepared by IDEA for the South Pacific Electoral Administrators' Conference, Fiji, 8–10 October 1997.

Hart-Landsberg, Martin, *The Rush to Development: Economic Change and Political Struggle in South Korea* (New York: Monthly Review Press, 1993).

Hartlyn, Jonathan, *The Struggle for Democratic Politics in the Dominican Republic* (Chapel Hill: University of North Carolina Press, 1998).

Harvey, William Burnett, "The Rule of Law in Historical Perspective," *Michigan Law Review* 59/487 (1961).

Hausmaninger, Herbert, "From the Soviet Committee of Constitutional Supervision to the Russian Constitutional Court," *Cornell Law International Law Journal* 25/2 (1992): 305–337.

Havel, Vaclav, "NATO's Quality of Life," *New York Times* (16 May 1997).

Heilbrunn, John R., "Authority, Property, and Politics in Benin and Togo" (Los Angeles: UCLA, 1994), Ph.D. dissertation.

———, "Commerce, Politics, and Business Associations in Benin and Togo," *Comparative Politics* 29/4 (July 1997): 473–492.

———, "The Flea on Nigeria's Back: Benin's Foreign Policy 1975–1995," in *Africa's Foreign Policy,* ed. Steven Wright (Boulder, Colo.: Westview Press, 1998).

———, "Social Origins of National Conferences in Benin and Togo," *Journal of Modern African Studies* 31/2 (1993): 277–299.

Henning, C. Randall, "Finance, Industry and External Monetary Policy" (Washington, D.C.: Institute for International Economics, 1991), unpublished manuscript.

Hernández-Cata, Ernesto, "Russia and the IMF: The Political Economy of Macro-Stabilization," *Problems of Post-Communism* (May/June 1995): 19–26.

Hiatt, Fred, "Pro-Reform Russian Quits Top Bank Post," *Washington Post* (17 July 1992).

Hickok, Eugene W., "Accountability of Public Officials," in *The Encyclopedia of Democracy*, ed. Seymour Martin Lipset (London: Routlege, 1995), pp. 9–11.

Highton, Elena, and Elías Jassan, "Judicial Reform in Argentina," in *Judicial Reform in Latin America and the Caribbean: Proceedings of a World Bank Conference*, eds. Malcolm Rowat, Waleed H. Malik, and Maria Dakolias, (Washington, D.C.: World Bank, 1995), pp. 176–183.

HMSO, "Standards in Public Life: First Report of the Committee on Standards in Public Life" (Cmd. 2850-I) (London: HMSO, 1995).

Holmes, Stephen, "Constitutionalism," in *The Encyclopedia of Democracy*, ed. Seymour Martin Lipset (London: Routledge, 1995), pp. 299–305.

———, *Passions and Constraint: On the Theory of Liberal Democracy* (Chicago: University of Chicago Press, 1995).

———, "Precommitment and the Paradox of Democracy," in *Constitutionalism and Democracy*, eds. Jon Elster and Rune Slagstad (Cambridge: Cambridge University Press, 1988), pp. 195–240.

Hong Kong ICAC, "ICAC Operations Department Review 1996–97" (Hong Kong: Independent Commission Against Corruption, 1997).

———, website, http://www.icac.org.hk.

Horowitz, Morton, "Republicanism and Liberalism in American Constitutional Thought," *William and Mary Law Review* 29 (1987/1988): 55–74.

Hunter, Wendy, *Eroding Military Influence in Brazil: Politicians Against Soldiers* (Chapel Hill: University of North Carolina Press, 1997).

Huntington, Samuel P., "After Twenty Years: The Future of the Third Wave," *Journal of Democracy* 8/4 (1997): 3–12.

———, *Political Order in Changing Societies* (New Haven: Yale University Press, 1968).

Hwang, Kee Chul, "Administrative Corruption in the Republic of Korea" (Los Angeles: University of Southern California, 1996), Ph.D. dissertation.

Hydén, Göran, "Democracy and Administration," in *Democracy's Victory and Crisis*, ed. Axel Hadenius (Cambridge: Cambridge University Press, 1997), pp. 242–259.

ICAC (New South Wales), *Community Attitudes to Corruption and the ICAC 1995* (Sydney: Independent Commission Against Corruption, 1995).

Illarionov, Andrei, "What Is the Price of Friendship?" *Izvestiia* (16 September 1993), translated in the *Current Digest of the Post-Soviet Press* 45/37 (1993).

Information Services Department, *The Search for True Democracy in Ghana* (Accra: Information Services Department, n.d.).

Institute for the Comparative Study of Political Systems, *Costa Rican Election Factbook* (Washington, D.C.: Institute for the Comparative Study of Political Systems, 1966).

"Inter-American Affairs: Mercosur to Adopt Democracy Clause," reprinted in *FBIS* 26 (1996): 3.

International Chamber of Commerce, *Extortion and Bribery in Business Transactions*, Publication 315 (Paris: ICC, 1977, reprinted 1993).

International Commission of Jurists, "Draft Principles on the Independence of the Judiciary (Siracusa Principles)," *CIJL Bulletin* 25/26 (April–October 1990).

International Foundation for Electoral Systems, *Mexico's Mid-Term Elections July 6: 1997 International Visitors' Report* (Washington, D.C.: International Foundation for Electoral Systems, 1997).

Itar-TASS, "Yeltsin Orders Special Tax on Bank of Russia Profits" (28 February 1997).

Izvestiia, "Decree of the President of the USSR: On Cooperation Between Union and Republican Agencies in Financial and Credit Matters During the Period of Preparation of the Union Treaty" (30 July 1990), translated in *Current Digest of the Soviet Press* 42/30 (1990).

Jaeger, Werner, *Paideia: The Ideal of Greek Culture* (Oxford: Basil Blackwell, 1946).

Jaspersen, Frederick Z., Anthony H. Aylward, and A. David Knox, "The Effects of Risk on Private Investment: Africa Compared with other Developing Areas," in *Risk and Agencies of Restraint: Reducing the Risks of African Investment,* eds. Paul Collier and Cathy Pattillo (London: Macmillan, 1997).

Johnston, Michael, "What Can Be Done About Entrenched Corruption," paper prepared for presentation at the annual World Bank Conference on Development Economics, Washington D.C., 30 April–1 May 1997.

Jun, Jong Sup, "The Paradoxes of Development: Problems of Korea's Transformation," in *Administrative Dynamics and Development: The Korean Experience,* eds. Bun Woong Kim, David S. Bell, Jr., and Chong Bum Lee (Seoul: Kyobo Publishing, 1985), pp. 56–75.

Jun, Jong Sup, and Jae Poong Yoon, "Korean Public Administration at a Crossroads: Culture, Development and Change," in *Public Administration in the NICs: Challenges and Accomplishments,* eds. Ahmed S. Huque, Jermain T. M. Lam, and Jane C. Y. Lee (Basingstoke, England: Macmillan, 1996), pp. 90–113.

Kahn, Paul W. "Independence and Responsibility in the Judicial Role," in *Transition to Democracy in Latin America: The Role of the Judiciary,* ed. Irwin Stotzky (Boulder, Colo.: Westview Press, 1993), pp. 73–88.

Karl, Terry, "The Hybrid Regimes of Central America," *Journal of Democracy* 6/3 (July 1995): 72–86.

———, "Imposing Consent? Electoralism vs. Democratization in El Salvador," in *Elections and Democratization in Latin America, 1980–85,* eds. Paul Drake and Eduardo Silva (San Diego: Center for Iberian and Latin American Studies, 1986), pp. 9–36.

Kasem, Suwanagul, "The Civil Service of Thailand" (New York: New York University, 1962), Ph.D. dissertation.

Kaufman, Robert R., "Approaches to the Study of State Reform in Latin America and Post-Socialist Countries" (New Brunswick, N.J.: Rutgers University, Department of Political Science, 1998), unpublished manuscript.

Kaufmann, Daniel, "Corruption: The Facts," *Foreign Policy* (Summer 1997): 114–127.

———, "On the Transparency International Corruption Index: Some Methodological Suggestions for Discussion" (Washington, D.C.: World Bank, 1998), unpublished manuscript.

Keeler, John, "Opening the Window for Reform: Mandates, Crises, and Extraordinary Decision-Making," *Comparative Political Studies* 25/4 (1993): 433–486.

Kelley, Donald, *Historians and the Law in Post-Revolutionary France* (Princeton: Princeton University Press, 1984).

Kelly, Janet, "Democracy Redux: How Real Is Democracy in Latin America?" *Latin American Research Review* 33/1 (1998): 212–225.

Kelsen, Hans, "Judicial Review of Legislation: A Comparative Study of the Austrian and the American Constitution," *Journal of Politics* 4/2 (1942): 183–200.

Kessides, Christine, Timothy King, Mario Nuti, and Catherine Sokil, *Financial Reform in Socialist Economies* (Washington, D.C.: World Bank, 1989).

Khandruev, Aleksandr, "Statement of the Central Bank of the Russian Federation," in *Central Banking Technical Assistance to Countries in Transition*, eds. J. B. Zulu et al. (Washington, D.C.: International Monetary Fund, 1994), pp. 59–61.

Kiewiet, D. Roderick, and Mathew D. McCubbins, *The Logic of Delegation: Congressional Parties and the Appropriations Process* (Chicago: University of Chicago Press, 1991).

Kim, Bun Woong, David S. Bell, Jr., and Chong Bum Lee (eds.), *Administrative Dynamics and Development: The Korean Experience* (Seoul: Kyobo Publishing, 1985).

Kim, Young Jong, *Bureaucratic Corruption: The Case of Korea*, 4th ed. (Seoul: Chomyung Press, 1994).

Klingemann, Hans-Dieter, Richard I. Hofferbert, and Ian Budge, *Parties, Policies and Democracy* (Boulder, Colo.: Westview Press, 1994).

Klitgaard, Robert, *Controlling Corruption* (Berkeley: University of California Press, 1988).

Knight, Jack, *Institutions and Social Conflict* (Cambridge: Cambridge University Press, 1992).

———, "Models, Interpretations, and Theories: Constructing Explanations of Institutional Emergence and Change," in *Explaining Social Institutions*, eds. Jack Knight and Itai Sened (Ann Arbor: University of Michigan Press, 1995), pp. 95–119.

Knight, Jack, and Itai Sened, "Introduction," in *Explaining Social Institutions*, eds. Jack Knight and Itai Sened (Ann Arbor: University of Michigan Press, 1995), pp. 1–13.

Koelble, Thomas A., "The New Institutionalism in Political Science and Sociology," *Comparative Politics* 27/1 (1995): 231–243.

Kommersant-Daily, Financial Department, "Duma reshila otbirat' u TsB polovinu pribyli" (20 February 1997).

Kramnick, Isaac, "The 'Great National Discussion': The Discourse of Politics in 1787," *William and Mary Quarterly* 45 (1988): 3–32.

———, *Republicanism and Bourgeois Radicalism: Political Ideology in Late Eighteenth-Century England and America* (Ithaca, N.Y.: Cornell University Press, 1990).

Krasner, Stephen, "Approaches to the State: Alternative Conceptions and Historical Dynamics," *Comparative Politics* 16/2 (1984): 223–246.

Krueger, Anne O., "The Political Economy of the Rent-Seeking Society," *American Economic Review* 64 (1974): 291–303.

Krug, Peter, "Departure from the Centralized Model: The Russian Supreme Court and Constitutional Control of Legislation," *Virginia Journal of International Law* 37/3 (1997): 725–786.

Kulick, Elliott, and Dick Wilson, *Thailand's Turn: Profile of a New Dragon* (New York: St. Martin's Press, 1992).

Lamadrid, José Luis, PRI Jalisco senator, former party secretary-general, electoral affairs director, interview with Todd A. Eisenstadt, 2 September 1996, Mexico City.

Lancaster, Thomas D., and Gabriella R. Montinola, "Toward a Methodology for the Comparative Study of Political Corruption," *Crime, Law and Social Change* 27 (1997): 185–206.

Landes, William M., and Richard A. Posner, "The Independent Judiciary in an

Interest Group Perspective," *Journal of Law and Economics* 18/3 (December 1975): 875–901.

Langan, Patricia, and Brian Cooksey, *The National Integrity System in Tanzania: Proceedings from the Workshop Convened by the Prevention of Corruption Bureau, Tanzania* (Washington, D.C.: Economic Development Institute, 1995).

Langseth, Peter, Rick Stapenhurst, and Jeremy Pope, "The Role of a National Integrity System in Fighting Corruption," Working Paper 400/142 (Washington, D.C.: World Bank, Economic Development Institute, 1997).

Lavrushkin, O., and B. Mirkin, "Russia's Central Bank Continues to Follow a Policy of Supporting the State, Not Entrepreneurs," *Izvestiia* (20 May 1992), translated in the *Current Digest of the Post-Soviet Press* 46/20 (1992).

Lavrushkin, O., and Y. M. Mirkin, "Dolgosrochnaia konseptsiia razvitiia denezhno-kreditnoi sistema Rossii," *Den'gi i kredit* 1 (1993): 3–18.

Lay, Rupert, "Einem Stern folgen: Welche Ethik brauchen Manager? Der Jesuit, Professor und Managementtrainer Rupert Lay gibt Auskunft," *Das Sonntagsblatt* (17 February 1995).

Learned Hand, *The Spirit of Liberty* (New York: A.A. Knopf, 1952).

LeDuc, Lawrence, Richard G. Niemi, and Pippa Norris (eds.), *Comparing Democracies: Elections and Voting in Global Perspective* (London: Sage Publications, 1996).

Leff, Nathaniel, "Economic Development Through Bureaucratic Corruption," *American Behavioral Scientist* 8/3 (1964): 8–14.

Leiken, Robert S. "Controlling the Global Corruption Epidemic," *Foreign Policy* 105 (Winter 1996/1997): 55–73.

Lewarne, Stephen, "Legal Aspects of Monetary Policy in the Former Soviet Union," *Europe-Asia Studies* 45/2 (1993): 193–210.

———, "The Russian Central Bank and the Conduct of Monetary Policy," in *Establishing Monetary Stability in Emerging Market Economies,* eds. Thomas Willett, Richard C. K. Burdekin, Richard J. Sweeney, and Clas Wihlborg (eds.) (Boulder, Colo.: Westview Press, 1995), pp. 167–192.

Lijphart, Arend, *Democracies: Patterns of Majoritarian and Consensus Government in Twenty-One Countries* (New Haven: Yale University Press, 1984).

———, *Electoral Systems and Party Systems: A Study of Twenty-Seven Democacies, 1945–90* (Oxford: Oxford University Press, 1994).

Lijphart, Arend, and Carlos H. Waisman, "Institutional Design and Democratization," in *Institutional Design in New Democracies,* eds. Arend Lijphart and Carlos H. Waisman (Boulder, Colo.: Westview Press, 1996), pp. 1–11.

Lindberg, Mark, *The Human Development Race: Improving the Quality of Life in Developing Countries* (San Francisco: International Center for Economic Growth, 1993).

Linz, Juan J., "Totalitarian and Authoritarian Regimes," in *Handbook of Political Science,* eds. Fred Greenstein and Nelson Polsby (Reading, Mass.: Addison-Wesley, 1984), pp. 175–411.

Linz, Juan J., and Alfred Stepan, *Problems of Democratic Transition and Consolidation: Southern Europe, South America, and Post-Communist Europe* (Baltimore: Johns Hopkins University Press, 1996).

López Obrador, Andrés Manuel, national PRD president and former Tabasco gubernatorial candidate, interview with Todd A. Eisenstadt, 14 January 1996, Villahermosa.

Lowenthal, Abraham, and Jorge I. Domínguez, "Introduction," in *Constructing*

Democratic Governance: Latin America and the Carribean in the 1990s—Themes and Issues, eds. Jorge I. Domínguez and Abraham Lowenthal (Baltimore: Johns Hopkins University Press, 1996), pp. 3–8.

Lujambio, Alonso, *Federalismo y congreso en el cambio político de México* (Mexico City: Universidad Nacional Autónoma de México, 1995).

Lynch, Dennis O., "Legal Roles in Colombia: Some Social, Economic and Political Perspectives," in *Lawyers in the Third World: Comparative and Developmental Perspectives,* eds. Clarence J. Dias, Robin Luckham, and James C. N. Paul, (New York: Africana Publishing, 1981), pp. 26–75.

Lyons, Terence, "Ghana's Encouraging Elections: A Major Step Forward," *Journal of Democracy* 8/2 (April 1997): 65–77.

Macdonald, Donald Stone, and Donald N. Clark, *The Koreans: Contemporary Politics and Society,* 3d ed. (Boulder, Colo.: Westview Press, 1996).

Macedo, Stephen, *Liberal Virtues: Citizenship, Virtue, and Community in Liberal Constitutionalism* (Oxford: Clarendon Press, 1992).

Madison, James, Alexander Hamilton, and John Jay, *The Federalist Papers,* ed. Clinton Rossiter (New York: New American Library, 1961).

Magnusson, Bruce, "Benin: Legitimating Democracy, New Institutions, and the Historical Problems of Economic Crisis," in *L'Afrique politique: Démocratisation, arrêts sur images,* ed. Véronique Faure (Paris: Éditions Karthala, 1996), pp. 33–54.

Mainwaring, Scott, and David Samuels, "Robust Federalism and Democracy in Contemporary Brazil," paper presented at the Seventeenth World Congress of the International Political Science Association (IPSA), Seoul, 17–21 August 1997.

Mainwaring, Scott, and Timothy Scully, *Building Democratic Institutions: Party Systems in Latin America* (Stanford: Stanford University Press, 1995).

Mainwaring, Scott, and Matthew Soberg Shugart (eds.), *Presidentialism and Democracy in Latin America* (Cambridge: Cambridge University Press, 1997).

Makhdoom, Ahmed H., "The Government of Singapore," website, http://sunflower.singnet.com.sg/~makhdoom/singa8.html.

Manin, Bernard, "Checks, Balances and Boundaries: The Separation of Powers in the Constitutional Debate of 1787," in *The Invention of the Modern Republic,* ed. Biancamaria Fontana (Cambridge: Cambridge University Press, 1994), pp. 27–62.

———, *Metamorphoses du gouvernement représentatif* (Paris: Éditions du Seuil, 1996).

Manin, Bernard, Adam Przeworski, and Susan Stokes (eds.), *Democracy, Accountability, and Representation* (New York: Cambridge University Press, 1999).

Manion, Melanie, "Policy Instruments and Political Context: Transforming a Culture of Corruption in Hong Kong," paper prepared for presentation at the annual meeting of the Association for Asian Studies, Honolulu, 20–24 April 1996.

Manne, Robert, "Poland: The Cow Is Being Saddled Slowly," *The Age* (Melbourne, 5 January 1994), LEXIS-NEXIS, NEWS Library, Reuter File.

Maravall, José María: "Accountability and Manipulation," Working Paper 92 (Madrid: Instituto Juan March de Estudios e Investigaciones, 1996).

Margalit, Avishai, *The Decent Society* (Cambridge: Harvard University Press, 1996).

Martínez, Germán, former judicial affairs director, PAN National Executive Committee, interview with Todd A. Eisenstadt, 8 December 1995, Mexico City.

Martínez, Valero, José, judicial affairs subdirector, PAN National Executive Committee, interview with Todd A. Eisenstadt, 17 January 1998, Mexico City.

Matiukhin, Georgii, *Ya byl glavnim bankirom Rossii* (Moscow: Vyshaia Shkola, 1993).

Mauro, Paolo, "Corruption and Growth," *Quarterly Journal of Economics* 60/3 (August 1995): 681–712.

———, *Why Worry About Corruption?* (Washington, D.C.: International Monetary Fund, 1997).

Maxfield, Sylvia, "Financial Incentives and Central Bank Authority in Industrializing Nations," *World Politics* 46/4 (July 1994): 556–589.

———, *Gatekeepers of Growth: The International Political Economy of Central Banking in Developing Countries* (Princeton: Princeton University Press, 1997).

———, "International Sources of Central Bank Convergence in the 1990s," paper prepared for presentation at the Eighteenth International Congress of the Latin American Studies Association (LASA), Atlanta, 10–12 March 1994.

Maxfield, Sylvia, and Ben Ross Schneider, "Business, the State, and Economic Performance in Developing Countries," in *Business and the State in Developing Countries,* eds. Sylvia Maxfield and Benn Ross Schneider (Ithaca, N.Y.: Cornell University Press, 1997), pp. 3–35.

McCoy, Jennifer "Mediating Democracy: A New Role for International Actors," in *Security in a New World Order,* ed. David Bruce (Atlanta: Georgia State University Press, 1992), pp. 129–140.

———, "Monitoring and Mediating Elections During Latin American Democratization," in *Electoral Observation and Democratic Transition in Latin America,* ed. Kevin Middlebrook (La Jolla, Calif.: Center for U.S.-Mexican Studies, 1998), pp. 53–90.

McCoy, Jennifer, Larry Garber, and Robert Pastor, "Pollwatching and Peacemaking," *Journal of Democracy* 2 (Fall 1991): 102–114.

McCubbins, Mathew D., Roger G. Noll, and Barry R. Weingast, "Administrative Procedures as Instruments of Political Control," *Journal of Law, Economics and Organization* 3/2 (1987): 243–277.

McCubbins, Mathew D., and Thomas Schwartz, "Congressional Oversight Overlooked: Police Patrols Versus Fire Alarms," *American Journal of Political Science* 28/1 (1984): 165–179.

McIlwain, Charles Howard, *Constitutionalism: Ancient and Modern,* rev. ed. (Ithaca, N.Y.: Cornell University Press, 1947).

McIntyre, Richard, and Joseph Medley, "Democratic Reform of the Fed: The Impact of Class Relations on Policy Formation," *Review of Radical Political Economics* 20/2–3 (1988): 156–162.

Médard, Jean-François, "Corruption in Africa: A Comparative Perspective," *Corruption and Reform* 1 (1986): 115–131.

Méndez, Juan, Guillermo O'Donnell, and Paulo Sérgio Pinheiro (eds.), *The Rule of Law and the Underprivileged in Latin America* (Notre Dame, Ind.: University of Notre Dame Press, forthcoming).

Mény, Yves, *La corruption de la République* (Paris: Fayard, 1992).

Merkel, Wolfgang, "Institutions and Democratic Consolidation in East Central Europe," Working Paper 86 (Madrid: Instituto Juan March de Estudios e Investigaciones, 1996).

Merritt, Martha, "Review Essay: Contemplating Democracy in Russia," *Review of Politics* 59/2 (1997): 351–363.

Migdal, Joel S., *Strong Societies, Weak States: State-Society Relations and State Capabilities in the Third World* (Princeton: Princeton University Press, 1988).

Miller, Geoffrey P., "Constitutional Moments, Precommitment, and Fundamental Reform: The Case of Argentina," *Washington University Law Quarterly* 71/4 (1993): 1073–1074.

Mizrahi, Yemile, "Democracia, eficiencia y participación: Los dilemas de los gobiernos de oposición en México," *Política y gobiernos* 2 (1995): 177–205.

Moe, Terry M., "Political Institutions: The Neglected Side of the Story," *Journal of Law, Economics, and Organization* 6 (1990): 213–253.

Molinar Horcasitas, Juan, "Changing the Balance of Power in a Hegemonic Party System: The Case of Mexico," in *Institutional Design in New Democracies: Eastern Europe and Latin America*, eds. Arend Lijphart and Carlos Waisman (Boulder, Colo.: Westview Press, 1996), pp. 137–158.

———, *El tiempo de la legitimidad: Elecciones, autoritarismo y democracia en México* (Mexico City: Cal y Arena, 1991).

Montesquieu, Baron de, *The Spirit of the Laws*, trans. Thomas Nugent (New York: Hafner, 1949).

Moody-Stuart, George, *Grand Corruption: How Business Bribes Damage Developing Countries* (Oxford: World View Publishing, 1997).

———, "Grand Corruption in Third World Development" (Berlin: Transparency International, 1993), unpublished manuscript.

Moreno Ocampo, Luis, *En denfensa propia: Como salir de la corrupción* (Buenos Aires: Editorial Sudamericana, 1993).

Moreno Uriegas, María de los Angeles, senator and former PRI national president, interview with Todd A. Eisenstadt, 19 February 1996, Mexico City.

Morozova, Elena, head economist, Department of Analysis and Regulation of the Activities of Commercial Banks, CBR Riazan, interview with Juliet Johnson, 2 September 1994.

Morrisson, Christian, Jean-Dominique Lafay, and Sebastien Dessus, "Adjustment Programs and Politico-Economic Interactions in Developing Countries: Lessons from an Empirical Analysis of Africa in the 1980s," in *From Adjustment to Development in Africa*, eds. Giovani A. Cornia and Gerald K. Helleiner (London: Macmillan, 1994), pp. 174–193.

Moscow News, "Roundtable Discussion on the State of Russian Banking" (7–14 June 1992).

Moskovskaia pravda, "Payments Crisis Tied to Central Bank," 8 May 1992, translated in *FBIS Central Eurasia* (5 June 1992).

Mulder, Niels, *Inside Thai Society: Interpretations of Everyday Life* (Amsterdam: Pepin Press, 1996).

Murphy, Kevin M., Andrei Shleifer, and Robert Vishny, "Why Is Rent-Seeking So Costly to Growth," *American Economic Review* 83/2 (May 1993): 409–414.

National Democratic Institute, "Preliminary Statement by the National Democratic Institute (NDI) International Observer Delegation to the December 7 Elections in Ghana," press release, Accra, 10 December 1996.

Naylor, R. T., *Hot Money and the Politics of Debt* (Montreal: Black Rose Books, 1994).

Ndegwa, Stephen N., "Citizenship and Ethnicity: An Examination of Two Transition Movements in Kenyan Politics," *American Political Science Review* 91 (September 1997): 599–616.

Neher, Clark D., and Ross Marlay, *Democracy and Development in Southeast Asia: The Winds of Change* (Boulder, Colo.: Westview Press, 1996).

Nelson, Joan M., "The Politics of Economic Transformation: Is Third World Experience Relevant in Eastern Europe?" *World Politics* 45/3 (1993): 434–465.

———, "The Politics of Long-Term Economic Reform," in *Fragile Coalitions: The Politics of Economic Adjustment,* ed. Joan M. Nelson (Washington, D.C.: Overseas Development Council, 1989), pp. 3–36.

Nelson, Lynn, and Irina Kuzes, *Radical Reform in Yeltsin's Russia* (Armonk, N.Y.: M.E. Sharpe, 1995).

Neou, Kassie, "Teaching Human Rights in Cambodia," *Journal of Democracy* 8/4 (October 1997): 154–164.

Network of Domestic Election Observers, "Statement on the December 6 Elections," press release, Accra, International Press Center, 12 December 1996.

New Patriotic Party, *The Stolen Verdict: Ghana's November 1992 Presidential Elections* (Accra: New Patriotic Party, 1992).

Nezavisimaia gazeta, "Explanatory Memorandum on the Agenda Item of the Meeting of the Presidium of the Russian Federation Supreme Soviet 'On the Chairman of the Russian Federation Central Bank,'" (19 May 1992), translated in *FBIS Central Eurasia* (5 June 1992).

———, "Former Finance Minister on Central Bank's Role" (25 April 1992), translated in *FBIS Central Eurasia* (9 May 1992).

Nino, Carlos S., "On the Exercise of Judicial Review in Argentina," in *Transition to Democracy in Latin America: The Role of the Judiciary,* ed. Irwin Stotzky (Boulder, Colo.: Westview Press, 1993), pp. 309–336.

Nohlen, Dieter, "Electoral Systems and Electoral Reform in Latin America," in *Institutional Design in New Democracies,* eds. Arend Lijphart and Carlos H. Waisman (Boulder, Colo.: Westview Press, 1996), pp. 43–57.

Nordhaus, William, "The Political Business Cycle," *Review of Economic Studies* 42 (April 1975): 169–190.

Noriega, Manuel, and Peter Eisner, *The Memoirs of Manuel Noriega* (New York: Random House, 1997).

North, Douglass C., *Institutions, Institutional Change, and Economic Performance* (Cambridge: Cambridge University Press, 1990).

North, Douglass C., and Barry R. Weingast, "Constitutions and Commitment: The Evolution of Institutions Governing Public Choice in Seventeenth Century England," in *Empirical Studies in Institutional Change,* eds. Lee J. Alston, Thráinn Eggertsson, and Douglass C. North (Cambridge: Cambridge University Press, 1996), pp. 134–165.

Nuñez Jiménez, Arturo, federal deputy, former director of the Federal Electoral Institute (IFE) and subsecretary of the Interior Ministry, interview with Todd A. Eisenstadt, 18 August 1996, Mexico City.

O'Donnell, Guillermo, *Bureaucratic-Authoritarianism: Argentina 1966–1973 in Comparative Perspective* (Berkeley: University of California Press, 1988).

———, "Delegative Democracy," *Journal of Democracy* 5/1 (January 1994): 55–69.

———, "Illusions About Consolidation," *Journal of Democracy* 7/2 (April 1996): 34–51.

———, "On the State, Democratization and Some Conceptual Problems: A Latin American View with Glances at Some Postcommunist Countries," *World Development* 21/8 (August 1993): 1355–1370.

———, "The (Un)Rule of Law and Polyarchies in Latin America," in *The Rule of Law and the Underprivileged in Latin America,* eds. Juan Méndez, Guillermo O'Donnell, and Paulo Sérgio Pinheiro (Notre Dame, Ind.: University of Notre Dame Press, forthcoming).

O'Donnell, Guillermo, and Philippe C. Schmitter, *Transitions from Authoritarian*

Rule: Tentative Conclusions About Uncertain Democracies (Baltimore: Johns Hopkins University Press, 1986).

Ockey, James, "Political Parties, Factions, and Corruption in Thailand," *Modern Asian Studies* 28/2 (May 1994): 251–277.

Offe, Claus, and Ulrich K. Preuss, "Democratic Institutions and Moral Resources," in *Political Theory Today,* ed. David Held (Stanford: Stanford University Press, 1991), pp. 143–171.

Oh, Suek-Hong, "The Counter-Corruption Campaign of the Korean Government (1975–1977): Administrative Anti-Corruption Measures of the Seojungshaeshin," in *Korean Public Bureaucracy,* eds. Bun Woong Kim and Wha Joon Rho (Seoul: Kyobo Publishing, 1982), pp. 322–344.

Ojesto Martínez Porcayo, Fernando, president of the Appeals Circuit of the Electoral Tribunal of the Judicial Power of the Federation, interviews with Todd A. Eisenstadt, 14 November 1995 and 6 September 1996, Mexico City.

Olascoaga Valdés, Francisco, president of the Mexico State Electoral Tribunal, interview with Todd A. Eisenstadt, 19 March 1997, Toluca.

Olson, Mancur, *The Rise and Decline of Nations: Economic Growth, Stagflation, and Social Rigidities* (New Haven: Yale University Press, 1982).

Ostrom, Elinor, *Governing the Commons: The Evolution of Institutions of Collective Action* (Cambridge: Cambridge University Press, 1990).

Palermo, Vicente, and Marcos Novaro, *Política y poder en el gobierno de Menem* (Buenos Aires: Grupo Editorial Norma, 1996).

Panizza, Francisco, "Human Rights in the Processes of Transition and Consolidation in Latin America," *Political Studies* (special issue, "Politics and Human Rights") 43 (1995): 168–188.

Paramonova, Tatiana, Remarks, plenary session of the Russian-American Bankers' Forum, St. Petersburg, Russia (30 June 1995).

Parra Quijano, Jairo, "La administración de justicia en Colombia," in *Administración de justicia en Iberoamérica,* ed. José Ovalle Favela (Mexico City: UNAM, 1993), pp. 133–160.

Pasquino, Gianfranco, "Italy: The Twilight of the Parties," *Journal of Democracy* 5/1 (January 1994): 18–29.

Pastor, Robert A., *Condemned to Repetition: The United States and Nicaragua* (Princeton: Princeton University Press, 1987).

———, "How to Reinforce Democracy in the Americas: Seven Proposals," in *Democracy in the Americas: Stopping the Pendulum,* ed. Robert A. Pastor (New York: Holmes and Meier, 1989), pp. 139–155.

———, "Mediating Elections," *Journal of Democracy* 9/1 (January 1998): 154–163.

———, "Mission to Haiti 3: Elections for Parliament and Municipalities, June 23–26, 1995," Working Paper (Atlanta: Carter Center, 1995).

———, *Whirlpool: U.S. Foreign Policy Toward Latin America and the Caribbean* (Princeton: Princeton University Press, 1992).

———, "With Carter in Haiti," *Worldview* 8/2 (1995): 5–10.

Pasuk, Phongpaichit, and Sungsidh Piriyarangsan, *Corruption and Democracy in Thailand,* 2d ed. (Chiang Mai: Silkworm Books, 1996).

Peled, Yoav, "Ethnic Democracy and the Legal Construction of Citizenship: Arab Citizens of the Jewish State," *American Political Science Review* 86 (June 1992): 532–543.

Pérez Noriega, Fernando, former PAN federal deputy and president, Justice Commission of the Chamber of Deputies, interview with Todd A. Eisenstadt, 21 August 1996, Mexico City.

Peschard-Sverdrup, Armand B., *The 1997 Mexican Midterm Elections Post-Election Report* (Washington, D.C.: Center for Strategic and International Studies, 1997).

Pinheiro, Paulo Sérgio, "Democracies Without Citizenship," *NACLA Report on the Americas* 30/2 (1996): 17–23.

———, "The Legacy of Authoritarianism in Democratic Brazil," in *Latin American Development and Public Policy*, ed. Stuart S. Nagel (New York: St. Martin's Press, 1991), pp. 237–253.

———, "Popular Responses to State-Sponsored Violence in Brazil," in *The New Politics of Inequality in Latin America: Rethinking Participation and Representation*, eds. Douglas Chalmers, Carlos M. Vilas, and Scott B. Martin (New York: Columbia Press, 1997), pp. 261–280.

Pizzorno, Alessandro, "Representation, Corruption, and Circles of Control: The Case of 'Mani Pulite' in Italy," paper prepared for presentation at the Third Vienna Dialogue on Democracy, "Institutionalizing Horizontal Accountability," International Forum for Democratic Studies and Institute for Advanced Studies, Vienna, 26–29 June 1997.

Plato, *The Republic*, trans. Allan Bloom (New York: Basic Books, 1968).

Plattner, Marc F., "Comments on Fontana," paper prepared for presentation at the Third Vienna Dialogue on Democracy, "Institutionalizing Horizontal Accountability," International Forum for Democratic Studies and Institute for Advanced Studies, Vienna, 26–29 June 1997.

———, "Liberalism and Democracy: Can't Have One Without the Other," *Foreign Affairs* 77/2 (March/April 1998): 171–180.

Pognon, Alfred, "Communication du batonnier de l'Ordre des avocats du Bénin aux États Généraux," paper delivered at the États Généraux de la Justice, Cotonou, 4–7 November 1996.

Political Parties Law (PNDC Law 284), 1992.

Pope, Jeremy, "Strengthening the Role of Civil Society and the Private Sector in Fighting Corruption" (Berlin: Transparency International, 1998), unpublished manuscript.

——— (ed.), *National Integrity Systems: The TI Source Book* (Berlin: Transparency International, 1996).

Posen, Adam, "Why Central Bank Independence Does Not Cause Low Inflation: There Is No Institutional Fix for Politics," *The AMEX Bank Review* (thematic issue, "Finance and the International Economy") 7 (1994): 41–58.

Press reports and final communiqué from the Fifth Summit of the Group of Rio at Cartagena, reprinted in *Foreign Broadcasting Information Service*, Latin America, 3–4 December 1991, pp. 1–5.

Pridham, Geoffrey (ed.), *Transitions to Democracy* (Aldershot, England: Dartmouth, 1995).

Przeworski, Adam, *Democracy and the Market: Political and Economic Reforms in Eastern Europe and Latin America* (New York: Cambridge University Press, 1991).

Przeworski, Adam, and Susan Stokes, "Citizen Information and Government Accountability: What Must Citizens Know to Control Government" (New York: New York University; Chicago: University of Chicago, 1995), unpublished manuscript.

Putnam, Robert D., *Making Democracy Work: Civic Traditions in Modern Italy* (Princeton: Princeton University Press, 1993).

Pye, Lucien W., "Money Politics and Transitions to Democracy in East Asia," *Asian Survey* 37/3 (March 1997): 213–228.

Quah, Jon S. T., "Bureaucratic Corruption in the ASEAN Countries: A Comparative Analysis of Their Anti-Corruption Strategies," *Journal of Southeast Asian Studies* 13/1 (March 1982): 153–177.

———, "Controlling Corruption in City-States: A Comparative Study of Hong Kong and Singapore," *Crime, Law, and Social Change* 22/4 (1995): 391–414.

———, "Singapore's Experience in Curbing Corruption," in *Political Corruption: A Handbook*, eds. Arnold J. Heidenheimer, Michael Johnston, and Victor T. LeVine (New Brunswick, N.J.: Transaction Publishers, 1989), pp. 841–853.

Rahman, A. T. R., "Legal and Administrative Measures Against Bureaucratic Corruption in Asia," in *Bureaucratic Corruption in Asia: Causes, Consequences and Control,* ed. Ledivina V. Carino (Quezon City: JMC Press and College of Public Administration, University of the Philippines, 1986), pp. 109–162.

Ramseyer, J. Mark, "The Puzzling (In)Dependence of Courts: A Comparative Approach," *Journal of Legal Studies* 23 (1994): 721–747.

Rawls, John, "Justice as Fairness: Political Not Methaphysical," *Philosophy and Public Affairs* 14/3 (1985): 223–251.

———, *Political Liberalism* (New York: Columbia University Press, 1993).

———, *A Theory of Justice* (Cambridge: Harvard University Press, 1971).

Report of the Commonwealth Observer Group on Ghana's Elections (London: Commonwealth Secretariat, 1997).

Representation of the People (Parliamentary Constituencies) Instrument (LI 1538) 1992.

République de France, Ministère de la Coopération, *Réflexion sur les appuis en matière de la décentralisation,* Paris, 1994.

République du Bénin, Conférence économique nationale, "Atelier No. 9, Bonne gouvernance," *Les actes de la conférence,* Cotonou, 1997.

———, Ministère de l'Intérieur, de la Sécurité et de l'Administration Territoriale, *États Généraux de l'Administration Territoriale,* Cotonou, 7–10 January 1993 (Cotonou: Groupe Infres, 1993).

———, *États Généraux de la Justice,* Cotonou, 4–7 November 1996.

———, *Plan de réforme et de modernisation de l'Adminstration publique béninoise,* Cotonou, 1996.

———, "Portant création, organisation, attributions et fonctionnement de la Cellule de la moralisation de la vie publique," Décret No. 96–579 du 19 décembre 1996.

Reuters, "Russian Central Bank Faces First-Ever Loss" (25 July 1996).

———, "Russia Tightens Credit After Pre-Election Binge" (10 June 1996).

———, "Yeltsin Move on Central Bank Prompts Concern at IMF" (7 June 1996).

Reynolds, Andrew, and Ben Reilly, et al., *The International IDEA Handbook of Electoral System Design* (Stockholm: International Institute for Democracy and Electoral Assistance, 1997).

Rico, José María, and Luis Salas, *Independencia judicial en América Latina: Replanteamiento de un tema tradicional* (Miami: Center for the Administration of Justice, 1990).

Riggs, Fred W., *Thailand: The Modernization of a Bureaucratic Polity* (Honolulu: East-West Center Press, 1966).

Rodley, Nigel S., "Torture and Conditions of Detention in Latin America," paper prepared for presentation at the conference "The Rule of Law and the Underprivileged in Latin America," University of Notre Dame, 1996.

Rodríguez, Victoria, and Peter Ward (eds.), *Opposition Government in Mexico* (Albuquerque: University of New Mexico Press, 1995).

Rodrik, Dani, "Why Is There Multilateral Lending?" in *Annual Bank Conference on Development Economics, 1995,* eds. Michael Bruno and Boris Pleskovicz (Washington, D.C.: World Bank, 1996), pp. 167–193.

Roeder, Philip, *Real Sunset: The Failure of Soviet Politics* (Princeton: Princeton University Press, 1993).

Romero, Hector, legal adviser to the PRD representative to the Federal Electoral Commission (IFE), interview with Todd A. Eisenstadt, 17 January 1998, Mexico City.

Romero, Juan, associate director, PRD Secretariat of Judicial Affairs, interview with Todd A. Eisenstadt, 30 April 1996, Mexico City.

Rosanvallon, Pierre, "The Republic of Universal Suffrage," in *The Invention of the Modern Republic,* ed. Biancamaria Fontana (Cambridge: Cambridge University Press, 1994), pp. 27–62.

Rosberg, James, "The Rise of an Independent Judiciary in Egypt" (Boston: Department of Political Science, Massachusetts Institute of Technology, 1995), Ph.D. dissertation.

Rose-Ackerman, Susan, "Democracy and 'Grand' Corruption," *International Social Science Journal* 149 (September 1996): 365–380.

———, "The Political Economy of Corruption: Causes and Consequences," *Viewpoint* 74 (1996).

Rosenn, Keith S., "Judicial Review in Latin America," *Ohio State Law Journal* 35 (1974): 785–819.

Rosett, Claudia, "Obstacle to Reform: Rooted in Soviet Past, Russia's Central Bank Lacks Grasp of Basics," *Wall Street Journal* (23 September 1993).

Rossant, John, "Dirty Money," *Business Week* (18 December 1995).

Rossiiskaia gazeta, "Russian Congress Opens on Note of Discord" (8 April 1992), translated in *Current Digest of the Post-Soviet Press* 44/14 (1992).

Roth, Terence, "Fedorov Aims for Top Post at Russia's Bank," *Wall Street Journal* (1 November 1993).

Rousseau, Jean-Jacques, *The First and Second Discourses,* ed. Roger Masters (New York: St. Martin's Press, 1964).

Rowat, Malcolm, Waleed H. Malik, and Maria Dakolias (eds.), *Judicial Reform in Latin America and the Caribbean: Proceedings of a World Bank Conference,* Technical Paper 280 (Washington, D.C.: World Bank, 1995).

Rueschemeyer, Dieter, Evelyne Huber Stephens, and John D. Stephens, *Capitalist Development and Democracy* (Cambridge: Polity Press, 1992).

Russian Economic Trends 4/1 (1995).

Sachs, Jeffrey, and David Lipton, "Remaining Steps to a Market-Based Monetary System in Russia," in *Changing the Economic System in Russia,* ed. Anders Aslund (London: Pinter Publishers, 1992).

Sadek, María Tereza, "Perspectivas de reforma do judiciario no Brasil," paper prepared for presentation at the Twentieth International Congress of the Latin American Studies Association (LASA), Guadalajara, Mexico, 17–19 April 1997.

Sajo, Andras, "How the Rule of Law Killed Hungarian Welfare Reform," *East European Constitutional Review* 5/1 (1996): 31–56.

Salasy, Federico, minister for Congressional Relations, Mexican Embassy, interview with Todd A. Eisenstadt, 3 September 1997, Washington, D.C.

Salzberger, E. M., "A Positive Analysis of the Doctrine of Separation of Powers, or: Why Do We Have an Independent Judiciary?" *International Review of Law and Economics* 13 (1993).

Sartori, Giovanni, "Guidelines for Concept Analysis," in *Social Science Concepts:*

A Systematic Analysis, ed. Giovanni Sartori (Beverly Hills: Sage Publications, 1984), pp. 15–85.

———, *The Theory of Democracy Revisited,* 2 vols. (Chatham, N.J.: Chatham House Publishers, 1987).

Scalia, Antonin, "Common Law Courts in a Civil-Law System: The Role of United States Federal Courts in Interpreting the Constitution and Law," in *A Matter of Interpretation,* ed. Amy Guttman (Princeton: Princeton University Press, 1997), pp. 3–47.

Schedler, Andreas, "Credibility: Exploring the Bases of Institutional Reform in New Democracies," paper prepared for presentation at the Nineteenth International Congress of the Latin American Studies Association (LASA), Washington, D.C., 28–30 September 1995.

———, "Dimensionen der Demokratiequalität: Keine abschließenden Bemerkungen," in *Die Qualität der österreichischen Demokratie: Versuche einer Annäherung,* eds. David F. J. Campbell, Karin Liebhart, Renate Martinsen, Christian Schaller, and Andreas Schedler (Vienna: Manz, 1996), pp. 165–180.

———, "Hard to Observe and Hard to Believe: Mexico's Veiled Transition to Democracy," paper prepared for presentation at the 1998 annual meeting of the American Political Science Association (APSA), Boston, 3–6 September 1998.

———, "Neo-Institucionalismo," in *Léxico de la Política,* eds. Laura Baca Olamendi, Fernando Castañeda, Isidro H. Cisneros, and Germán Pérez Fernández del Castillo (Mexico City: FLACSO-CONACYT, 1999).

———, "The Normative Force of Electoral Promises," *Journal of Theoretical Politics* 10/2 (April 1998): 191–214.

———, "What Is Democratic Consolidation?" *Journal of Democracy* 9/2 (April 1998): 91–107.

Schmidt, Vivian A., *Democratizing France: The Political and Administrative History of Decentralization* (New York: Cambridge University Press, 1990).

Schmitter, Philippe C., and Terry Lynn Karl, "What Democracy Is . . . and Is Not," *Journal of Democracy* 2/3 (Summer 1991): 75–88.

Schürz, Martin, "Independence Versus Accountability: The Emerging European Central Bank," paper prepared for presentation at the Third Vienna Dialogue on Democracy, "Institutionalizing Horizontal Accountability," International Forum for Democratic Studies and Institute for Advanced Studies, Vienna, 26–29 June 1997.

Schwartz, Carl, "Jueces en la penumbra: La independencia del poder judicial en Estados Unidos y en México," *Anuario jurídico* (Mexico City, UNAM) 2 (1977): 143–219.

Shapiro, Martin, *Courts: A Comparative and Political Analysis* (Chicago: University of Chicago Press, 1981).

Sheridan, Greg, *Tigers: Leaders of the New Asia-Pacific* (St. Leonards, England: Allen and Unwin, 1994).

Shleifer, Andrei, and Robert Vishny, "Corruption," *Quarterly Journal of Economics* 58/3 (August 1993): 599–617.

Shugart, Matthew Soberg, and John M. Carey, *Presidents and Assemblies: Constitutional Design and Electoral Dynamics* (Cambridge: Cambridge University Press, 1992).

"Sierra Leone Military Arrests Five Cabinet Officers After Coup," *New York Times* (27 May 1997).

Simonov, Aleksey, "Defending Glasnost," *Journal of Democracy* 7/2 (April 1996): 158–166.

Sklar, Richard L., "Developmental Democracy," *Comparative Studies in Society and History* 29/4 (1987): 686–714.

——, "Reds and Rights: Zimbabwe's Experiment," in *Democracy and Pluralism in Africa*, ed. Dov Ronen (Boulder, Colo.: Lynne Rienner Publishers, 1986), pp. 135–144.

Smith, Peter H., "Crisis and Democracy in Latin America," *World Politics* 43 (July 1991): 608–634.

Smith, Tony, *America's Mission: The United States and the Worldwide Struggle for Democracy in the 20th Century* (Princeton: Princeton University Press, 1994).

Smulovitz, C., "El poder judicial en la nueva democracia Argentina: El trabajoso parto de un actor," paper prepared for presentation at the Twentieth International Congress of the Latin American Studies Association (LASA), Guadalajara, Mexico, 17–19 April 1997.

Soglo, Rosine, "Pourquoi nous avons perdu," *Jeune afrique*, no. 1884 (12–18 February 1997): 18–20.

South Commission, *The Challenge to the South* (Oxford: Oxford University Press, 1990).

"South Korea Leader's Son Sentenced to 3 Years," *San Francisco Chronicle* (14 October 1997).

"Special Team to Root Out Graft Among Top South Korean Officials," *Straits Times* (Singapore) (12 March 1993).

Stansifer, Charles L., "Application of the Tobar Doctrine to Central America," *The Americas* 23 (1967): 251–272.

Stark, David, and László Bruszt, *Postsocialist Pathways: Transforming Politics and Property in East Central Europe* (Cambridge: Cambridge University Press, 1998).

Stein, Jeff, "In Pakistan, the Corruption Is Lethal," *International Herald Tribune* (12 September 1997).

Stinchcombe, Arthur, *Constructing Social Theories* (New York: Harcourt, Brace and World, 1968).

Stokes, Susan, "Democracy and the Limits of Popular Sovereignty in South America," in *The Consolidation of Democracy in Latin America*, eds. Joseph S. Tulchin and Bernice Romero (Boulder, Colo.: Lynne Rienner Publishers, 1995), pp. 59–81.

Stotzky, Irwin (ed.), *Transition to Democracy in Latin America: The Role of the Judiciary* (Boulder, Colo.: Westview Press, 1993).

Swinburne, Mark, and Marta Castello-Branco, "Central Bank Independence and Central Bank Functions," in *The Evolving Role of Central Banks*, eds. Patrick Downes and Reza Vaez-Zadeh (Washington, D.C.: International Monetary Fund, 1991), pp. 414–444.

Tarigo, Enrique, "Legal Reform in Uruguay: General Code of Procedure," in *Judicial Reform in Latin America and the Caribbean: Proceedings of a World Bank Conference*, eds. Malcolm Rowat, Waleed H. Malik, and Maria Dakolias (Washington D.C.: World Bank, 1995), pp. 48–51.

Tarrow, Sidney, "Making Social Science Work Across Space and Time: A Critical Reflection on Robert Putnam's *Making Democracy Work*," *American Political Science Review* 90/2 (1996): 389–397.

Taylor, Charles, "Modes of Civil Society," *Public Culture* 3/1 (1990): 95–118.

Teitel, Ruti, "Transitional Jurisprudence: The Role of Law in Political Transformation," *Yale Law Journal* 106/7 (May): 2009–2080.

The Economist, "The Rouble Zone: Behind the Facade" (10 April 1993).

——, "Ukraine: Tough Enough" (13 March 1993).

Thelen, Kathleen, "Historical Institutionalism in Comparative Politics," in *Annual Review of Political Science*, ed. Nelson W. Polsby (Palo Alto, Calif.: Annual Reviews, 1999).

Thelen, Kathleen, and Sven Steinmo, "Historical Institutionalism in Comparative Politics," in *Structuring Politics: Historical Institutionalism in Comparative Analysis*, eds. Sven Steinmo, Kathleen Thelen, and Frank Longstreth (Cambridge: Cambridge University Press, 1992), pp. 1–32.

Thinapan, Nakata, "Corruption in the Thai Bureaucracy: Who Gets What, How and Why in Its Public Expenditures," *Thai Journal of Development Administration* 18/1 (January 1978): 102–128.

Thomson, James T., et al., *Benin Macro-Governance Assessment and Recommendations for Action*, revised final report (Washington, D.C.: ARD, Inc., 1997).

Thornhill, John, "Central Bank Attacks Yeltsin 'Violation,'" *Financial Times* (11 June 1996).

———, Economy Gives Rise to Growing Optimism," *Financial Times* (3 June 1997).

Thucydides, *History of the Peloponnesian War,* 4 vols., trans. Charles Foster Smith (Cambridge: Harvard University Press, 1962).

TI-Bangladesh, *Survey on Corruption in Bangladesh* (Dhaka: Survey and Research System, 1997).

Tidjani Serpos, Ismaël, "Allocation du garde des Sceaux, Ministre de la Justice, de la Législation et des Droits de l'Homme à la Cérémonie d'ouverture des États Généraux de la Justice," speech delivered at the États Généraux de la Justice, Cotonou, 4–7 Novembre 1996.

Tirole, Jean, "Persistence of Corruption," Working Paper 55 (Washington, D.C.: Institute for Policy Reform, 1992).

———, "A Theory of Collective Reputations (With Applications to the Persistence of Corruption and Firm Quality)," *Review of Economic Studies* 63 (1996): 113–133.

Toma, Eugenia Froedge, and Mark Toma, *Central Bankers, Bureaucratic Incentives, and Monetary Policy* (Boston: Kluwer Academic Publishers, 1986).

Tortosa, José María, *Corrupción* (Barcelona: Icaria, 1995).

Touraine, Alain, *La parole et le sang: Politique et société en Amérique Latine* (Paris: Odile Jacob, 1988).

Transparency International, *The Fight Against Corruption: Is the Tide Now Turning? Transparency International Report 1997* (Berlin: Transparency International, 1997).

———, "Transparency International Publishes 1997 Corruption Perception Index," *National Chapter Bulletin* 26 (8 August 1997): 1–3.

Tribunal Electoral del Poder Judicial de la Federación, Constitutional Revision Electoral Complaint 1/1996 (complaint and resolution) (Mexico City: Tribunal Electoral del Poder Judicial de la Federación, 1997).

———, Constitutional Revision Electoral Complaint 68/1997 (complaint and resolution) (Mexico City: Tribunal Electoral del Poder Judicial de la Federación, 1997).

Tribunal Estatal Electoral de Chiapas, *Memoria: Proceso Electoral 1995* (Tuxtla Gutierrez: Tribunal Estatal Electoral de Chiapas, 1995), pp. 32–89.

Tribunal Estatal Electoral de Puebla, Complaint of Inconformity 9/1995 (complaint and resolution) (Puebla: Puebla Electoral Tribunal, 1995).

———, Complaint of Inconformity 10/1995 (complaint and resolution) (Puebla: Puebla Electoral Tribunal, 1995).

Tribunal Federal Electoral, Complaint of Appeal 400/1994 (resolution) (Mexico City: Tribunal Federal Electoral, 1994).

Tsebelis, George, "Monitoring in Networks and Hierarchies: Congress and Organizations," in *Games in Hierarchies and Networks: Analytical and Empirical Approaches to the Study of Governance Institutions,* ed. Fritz W. Scharpf (Boulder, Colo.: Westview Press, 1993), pp. 351–385.

Tufte, Edward, *The Political Control of the Economy* (Princeton: Princeton University Press, 1978).

Tuñon, José Luis, assistant director, PRD Secretariat of Judicial Affairs, interview with Todd A. Eisenstadt, 23 March 1996, Mexico City.

Ungar, Mark, "All Justice Is Local: Judicial Access and Democracy in Latin America," paper prepared for presentation at the Twentieth International Congress of the Latin American Studies Association (LASA), Guadalajara, Mexico, 17–19 April 1997.

United Nations Development Programme, *Análisis del sistema electoral Mexicano: Informe de un grupo de expertos* (New York: United Nations Development Programme, 1997).

———, *Human Development Report 1992* (Oxford: Oxford University Press, 1992).

Valenzuela, J. Samuel, "Democratic Consolidation in Post-Transitional Settings: Notion, Process, and Facilitating Conditions," in *Issues in Democratic Consolidation: The New South American Democracies in Comparative Perspective,* eds. Scott Mainwaring, Guillermo O'Donnell, and J. Samuel Valenzuela (Notre Dame, Ind.: University of Notre Dame Press, 1992), pp. 57–104.

Vargas Manríquez, Fernando, legal adviser to the PRD representative before the Federal Electoral Commission (IFE), interview with Todd A. Eisenstadt, 17 January 1998, Mexico City.

Vatikiotis, Michael, and Gordon Fairclough, "Thailand: Mission Impossible," *Far Eastern Economic Review* (28 November 1996): 16–17.

Verner, Joel, "The Independence of Supreme Courts in Latin America: A Review of the Literature," *Journal of Latin American Studies* 16 (1984): 463–506.

Villavicencio, Lorena, PRD representative before the Federal Electoral Institute (IFE), interview with Todd A. Eisenstadt, 17 January 1998, Mexico City.

Volcker, Paul A. "The Independence of Central Banks: Its Value and Its Limits," paper prepared for presentation at the Centenary of the Banca d'Italia, Rome, 11 December 1993.

Vysman, Inna, "The New Banking Legislation in Russia: Theoretical Adequacy, Practical Difficulties, and Potential Solutions," *Fordham Law Review* 62 (October 1993): 265–286.

Waley, Daniel, *The Italian City-Republics* (London: Longman, 1988).

Waltman, Jerold, L., "The Courts and Political Change in Post-Industrial Society," in *The Political Role of Law Courts in Modern Democracies,* ed. Jerold L. Waltman (New York: St. Martin's Press, 1988), pp. 216–234.

Walzer, Michael, "Citizenship," in *Political Innovation and Cultural Change,* eds. Terence and Hanson Bell Russel (Cambridge: Cambridge University Press, 1989), pp. 211–219.

Weber, Max, *Economy and Society: An Outline of Interpretative Sociology,* 2 vols. (Berkeley: University of California Press, 1978).

Wei, Shang-Jin, "How Taxing Is Corruption on International Investors?" Working Paper (Cambridge: Kennedy School of Government, Harvard University, 1997).

Weingast, Barry R., "The Political Foundations of Democracy and the Rule of Law," *American Political Science Review* 91/2 (June 1997): 245–263.

Weingast, Barry, and William Marshall, "The Industrial Organization of Congress or Why Legislatures, Like Firms, Are Not Organized as Markets," *Journal of Political Economy* 96/1 (1988): 132–163.

Weir, Stuart, "Primary Control and Auxiliary Precautions: A Comparative Study of Democratic Institutions in Six Nations," in *Measuring Democracy*, ed. David Beetham (London: Sage, 1994), pp. 112–154.

Westebbe, Richard, "Structural Adjustment, Rent Seeking, and Liberalization in Benin," in *Economic Change and Political Liberalization in Sub-Saharan Africa*, ed. Jennifer A. Widner (Baltimore: Johns Hopkins University Press, 1994), pp. 80–100.

Wheeler, Harvey, "Constitutionalism," in *Handbook of Political Science: Governmental Institutions and Processes*, eds. Fred I. Greenstein and Nelson Polsby (Reading, Mass.: Addison-Wesley, 1975), pp. 1–91.

Whitehead, Laurence, "Models of Central Banking: How Much Convergence in Neo-Democracies" (Oxford: Nuffield College, 1997), unpublished manuscript.

Willett, Thomas, Richard C. K. Burdekin, Richard J. Sweeney, and Clas Wihlborg (eds.), *Establishing Monetary Stability in Emerging Market Economies* (Boulder, Colo.: Westview Press, 1995).

Williams, John, "The Political Manipulation of Macroeconomic Policy," *American Political Science Review* 84 (September 1980): 767–795.

Woo-Cummings, Meredith, Hyung-Ki Kim, Michio Muramatsu, T. J. Pempel, and Kozo Yamamura, "Developmental Bureaucracy in Comparative Perspective: The Evolution of the Korean Civil Service," in *The Japanese Civil Service and Economic Development: Catalysts of Change*, eds. Hyung-Ki Kim et al. (Oxford: Clarendon Press, 1995), pp. 431–458.

Wood, Gordon S., *The Creation of the American Republic 1776–1787* (Chapel Hill: University of North Carolina Press, 1969).

———, "Democracy and the American Revolution," in *Democracy: The Unfinished Journey, 508 BC to AD 1993*, ed. John Dunn (Oxford: Oxford University Press, 1992), pp. 91–106.

———, *The Radicalism of the American Revolution* (New York: Alfred A. Knopf, 1991).

Woolley, John T., "Central Banks and Inflation," in *The Politics of Inflation and Economic Stagnation*, eds. Leon N. Lindberg and Charles S. Maier (Washington, D.C.: Brookings Institution, 1985), pp. 319–348.

World Bank, *Adjustment in Africa: Reform, Results and the Road Ahead* (New York: Oxford University Press, 1994).

———, *Governance: The World Bank's Experience* (Washington, D.C.: World Bank, 1994).

———, *Helping Countries Combat Corruption: The Role of the World Bank* (Washington, D.C.: World Bank, 1997).

———, *Russia: The Banking System During the Transition* (Washington, D.C.: World Bank, 1993).

———, *Sub-Saharan Africa: From Crisis to Sustainable Growth—A Long Term Perspective Study* (Oxford: Oxford University Press, 1989).

———, *World Development Report 1990* (Washington, D.C.: World Bank, 1989).

———, *World Development Report 1997: The State in a Changing World* (New York: Oxford University Press, 1997).

Wormuth, Francis D., "Legislative Disqualifications as Bills of Attainder," *Vanderbilt Law Review* 4 (1951): 603–619; reprinted in Wormuth, *Essays in*

Law and Politics, eds. Dalmas H. Nelson and Richard L. Sklar (Port Washington, N.Y.: Kennikat Press, 1978), pp. 79–92.

————, *The Origins of Modern Constitutionalism* (New York: Harper and Brothers, 1949).

Zhagel, Ivan, "5,000 Ruble Notes Will Be Russian," *Izvestiia* (21 April 1992), translated in *Current Digest of the Post-Soviet Press* 44/16 (1992).

————, "We're Not Going to Rescind the Central Bank's Telegram," *Izvestiia* (4 August 1992), translated in *Current Digest of the Post-Soviet Press* 44/31 (1992).

Ziegler, Charles, "Transitional Paths of Delegative Democracies: Russia and South Korea" (Louisville: University of Louisville, 1998), unpublished manuscript.

The Contributors

Paul Collier is professor of economics at Oxford University, where he is director of the Centre for the Study of African Economies. From 1992 to 1995, he was visiting professor at the Kennedy School of Government at Harvard University. Since April 1998, he has been on leave as director of the Development Research Department of the World Bank.

Larry Diamond is senior research fellow at the Hoover Institution, coeditor of the *Journal of Democracy,* and codirector of the NED International Forum for Democratic Studies. His most recent book is *Developing Democracy: Toward Consolidation.*

Pilar Domingo lectures in the Department of Politics at Queen Mary and Westfield College, University of London. Previously she worked at the Centro de Investigación y Docencia Económicas (CIDE) in Mexico City. She has extensively published on questions of democracy, constitutionalism, and judicial reform in Mexico and Latin America.

Todd A. Eisenstadt is currently visiting professor at the Colegio de México. He is working on a book, based on extensive fieldwork in various Mexican federal states, on party strategies, electoral institution building, and political opening in Mexico.

Fredrik Galtung is a Ph.D. candidate in politics at the University of Cambridge. Since joining Transparency International (TI) as a founding staff member in 1993, he has worked on projects in Europe, Latin America, and West Africa. He continues to coordinate the TI Corruption Perception Index and the TI Council on Governance Research.

E. Gyimah-Boadi is director of the Governance Program at the Institute of Economic Affairs in Ghana. He is a former visiting fellow at the International Forum for Democratic Studies of the National Endowment for Democracy and the Woodrow Wilson International Center for Scholars in Washington, D.C. His research focuses on democratization, civil society development, and economic renewal in Africa.

John R. Heilbrunn is a research fellow at the Center for International Development and Conflict Management at the University of Maryland, College Park, and a consultant to the World Bank. His areas of research include Francophone Africa, social movements and democracy, and the political economy of development.

Juliet Johnson is assistant professor of political science at Loyola University, Chicago. Her research focuses on the political economy of post-communist financial systems. She is at present working on a book entitled *A Fistful of Rubles: The Evolution of the Russian Banking System, 1987–1997*, based on extensive fieldwork in the former Soviet Union and Eastern Europe in 1994–1995 and 1997.

Michael Johnston is professor of political science at Colgate University. He has studied political corruption for more than twenty years. In recent years he has served as a consultant on corruption and development issues for organizations such as the World Bank, the United States Agency for International Development, and the Asia Foundation.

Sylvia Maxfield is associate professor of political science at Yale University. Her most recent book, *Gatekeepers of Growth,* deals with the political economy of central banking in developing countries. She consults widely on policy aspects of political economy for public and private sector organizations.

Guillermo O'Donnell has published extensively on authoritarianism, democratization, and democratic theory. From 1982 to 1997, he served as academic director of the Kellogg Institute for International Studies, University of Notre Dame. He has been president of the International Political Science Association (1988–1991), and he is a fellow of the American Academy of Arts and Sciences.

Robert A. Pastor is professor of political science at Emory University and former director of the Latin American and Caribbean Program at the Carter Center. The author of ten books, he also has organized international missions to monitor and mediate elections in over fifteen countries in Latin America, the Caribbean, Africa, the Middle East, and China.

Marc F. Plattner is codirector of the NED International Forum for Democratic Studies, coeditor of the *Journal of Democracy,* and counselor of the National Endowment of Democracy, where he served as a program director from 1984 to 1989. He is author or editor of numerous books, and has published on a wide range of international and public policy issues.

Jeremy Pope joined Transparency International when it was launched in 1993 and served for four years as managing director. Previously (1980–1993), he was legal counsel to the Commonwealth Secretary General in London and director of the secretariat's Legal and Constitutional Affairs Division. He has been involved in monitoring elections in eight countries in Africa and Asia. His publications include *National Integrity Systems: The TI Source Book,* which has been published in nine languages.

Jon S. T. Quah is professor of political science and coordinator of the European Studies Programme at the National University of Singapore. He has published widely on public administration and policy in Singapore and the ASEAN countries, with an emphasis on administrative reform, anticorruption strategies, human resource development, and crime prevention strategies.

Andreas Schedler is professor of political science at the Facultad Latinoamericana de Ciencias Sociales (FLACSO) in Mexico City. Previously he was assistant professor of political science at the Austrian Institute for Advanced Studies. Currently he is carrying out a research project entitled "Institutional Change and Credibility: Building Democratic Electoral Institutions in Mexico."

Philippe C. Schmitter has been on the faculty of the European University Institute (EUI) since the fall of 1996, on leave from Stanford University. He has conducted research on comparative politics and regional integration in both Latin America and Western Europe, and in recent years, he has devoted increasing attention to the "emerging polity" of the European Community. He is currently completing a book, *Essaying the Consolidation of Democracy,* and a book manuscript tentatively entitled *Is It Possible to Democratize the EU and, If So, Why Bother?*

Herman Schwartz is professor at the Washington College of Law of the American University. A specialist in U.S. and European constitutional law and in the development and implementation of human rights, he has been advising numerous Central and Eastern European and former Soviet countries on constitutional and human rights reform. He has served on U.S. delegations to the UN Human Rights Commission and in 1993 was one of four public members of the U.S. delegation to the UN World Human Rights Conference in Vienna.

Richard L. Sklar is professor emeritus of political science at the University of California, Los Angeles. He is a past president of the African Studies Association (USA) and has written extensively about politics in Africa and theories of development. His publications include essays on the idea of developmental democracy.

Jennifer Widner is associate professor of political science at the University of Michigan. She has written on several aspects of African politics, including the changing character of authoritarian rule, patterns of participation, collective action, liberalization, and policy reform. She is currently completing a book on judges' efforts to build rule of law in common law eastern and southern Africa.

Index

Abiola, Moshood, 56
Accountability: abstract forms of, 28(n26); administrative, 22–23; agents of, 18–26, 335–337; celestial, 56–57; constitutional, 22–23; and democratic quality, 2–4; dimensions of, 14–15, 27(n7); dual aspects of, 4; electoral, 29–30, 334–335, 347(n7); enforcement of, 15–17, 22–23, 26–27, 28(n20); financial, 22–23, 28(n24); institutional creation and reform, 333–341; interdependence of agencies, 346–347; legal, 22–23, 151–152; moral, 22–23, 28(n24); oblique, 62(n4), 68; opacity of power and, 20–21; professional, 22–23; reform by "moral" actors, 342–344; second order, 25–26; in Soglo's Benin, 232–233. *See also* Answerability; Central Banks; Elections; Electoral process; Judicial independence; Judiciary; Horizontal accountability; Vertical accountability
Adams, John, 145
Adjai, Anne, 240
Afari Gyan, Kwadwo, 116
Africa, 6–8, 139, 149, 186; credibility of economic reform, 315–319; donor conditionality, 319–323; investment credibility, 313–315, 323, 328–330; judicial independence, 177–190. *See also individual countries*
Aid, financial, 187–188. *See also* Donor conditionality
Albania, 130, 131, 209
Alemán, Miguel, 111(n12)
Algeria, 137–138, 139
Alliance of Democratic Forces (ADF), 106
Alliances and coalitions: against corruption, 261–268; PAN-PRI (Mexico), 85–86

Amnesty International, 259
Amparo, 100(n25)
Annan, D. F., 117
Answerability, 14–18, 24, 26–27, 27(n6)
Antall, Joszef, 203–204
Anticorruption agencies and programs, 218; global coalitions, 261–268; increasing public awareness, 274–278; institutional reform, 272–274; national coalitions, 268–272. *See also* Independent Commission Against Corruption; Transparency International
Aquino, Corazón, 49(n37)
Argentina, 50(n40); central bank independence, 289; corruption study in, 277–278; defending democracy, 135–136; electoral commissions, 80; judicial independence, 156, 157, 159, 174(n23); judicial reform, 167, 169, 170
Aristide, Jean-Bertrand, 135, 140
Athens, ancient, 47(nn11, 12, 15), 63, 64
Australia, 222–223
Austria, 147–148, 149(n3), 213(n7)
Authoritarian rule, 37, 50(n40); effect on judicial independence, 157–158; obedience to law, 49(n33)
Authority, 38–42, 49(n39)
Autonomy, 17–18; of central banks, 294–299, 309(nn1, 6); of electoral institutions, 96–98; judicial, 44, 153–156; local, 200. *See also* Judicial independence

Babatounde, Berthaire, 240
BAI. *See* Board of Audit and Inspection
Bangladesh, 138, 263, 277
Banks, 5, 8–9, 17–18, 289, 301. *See also* Central bank independence; Central banks

385

About the Book

New democracies all over the world are finding themselves haunted by the old demons of clientelism, corruption, arbitrariness, and the abuse of power—leading to a growing awareness that, in addition to elections, democracy requires checks and balances. Democratic governments must be accountable to the electorate; but they must also be subject to restraint and oversight by other public agencies. It is not enough that citizens control the state. The state must control itself.

This collection explores how new democracies can achieve that goal. Focusing on electoral administration, judicial systems, corruption control, and central banks, the authors consider such issues as how governments can establish effective agencies of restraint, why they should accept them, and what those agencies can do to achieve credibility.

Andreas Schedler is professor of political science at the Facultad Latinoamericana de Ciencias Sociales (FLASCO) in Mexico City. **Larry Diamond,** senior research fellow at the Hoover Institution, and **Marc F. Plattner,** counselor at the National Endowment for Democracy (NED), are codirectors of NED's International Forum for Democratic Studies (IFDS) and coeditors of the *Journal of Democracy.*